WEBSTER'S
LEGAL SPELLER

Webster's

LEGAL
SPELLER

A Merriam-Webster ®

G. & C. MERRIAM COMPANY
Springfield, Massachusetts

Library of Congress Cataloging in Publication Data

Main entry under title:

Webster's legal speller.

  1. Law—United States—Terms and phrases.
  2. Legal secretaries—United States—Handbooks,
manuals, etc. 3. Spellers.
KF156.W4   340.1'4   78-9633

ISBN 0-87779-038-8

MADE IN THE U.S.A.

1 2 3 4 5 6 VHP 80 79 78

CONTENTS

INTRODUCTION

Scope *Webster's Legal Speller* is a pocket-sized guide to the spelling and division of about 28,000 legal words and words that occur frequently in legal contexts. The word divisions shown at each entry are based on the principles used for determining end-of-line division in *Webster's New Collegiate Dictionary,* the eighth in the Merriam-Webster series of Collegiate dictionaries.

This book is addressed primarily to the needs of American legal secretaries employed in offices concerned for the most part with the domestic practice of law but it is also adequate to confirm spellings and end-of-line divisions for most students of the law and legal writers. The American legal system is very complex in origin, having its roots not only in British common, equity, and statutory law but also in certain states having a strong infusion of continental law (as through the influence of the Code Napoleon in Louisiana or through Spanish influences in much of the southwestern United States). Its vocabulary is correspondingly complex. In compiling the corpus of *Webster's Legal Speller* a consistent effort has been made to cover this technical vocabulary as well as those general terms that occur frequently in legal contexts or that are often subject to judicial interpretation.

Special attention has been given to terms likely to cause confusion because of similarity in spelling (as in the trio *courtesy, curtesy,* and *curtsy* and in the pair *tort* and *torte*); only in such situations are terms (as *curtsy* and *torte*) that lack legal relevance entered in this book. Because of the increasing number of American law terms concerned with multinational aspects of the law, the more common British legal terms are included. Also entered are significant terms (as *gavelkind* and *habendum et tenendum*) that ical terms especially in conveyancely to occur in older reports, records, and

Another feature of the v uments.
is the inclusion of a generous that deserves special attention dical terms and terms

having medical senses which do or are likely to occur with considerable frequency in briefs, correspondence, and other documents relating to industrial compensation, accident, malpractice, and insurance cases.

Legal secretaries who transcribe, typewrite, or otherwise process written or dictated matter frequently need to know such things as whether a particular word is spelled with one *l* or two; whether a compound word is hyphened, solid, or open; which of several variant spellings is the one most widely used; and at what point a word may be divided at the end of a line. *Webster's Legal Speller* provides ready answers to these and similar questions.

Sources of vocabulary entries Although the corpus of approximately 28,000 terms is primarily based on the vocabulary of *Webster's Third New International Dictionary* (Merriam's unabridged book), additional vocabulary has been drawn from a variety of standard works in the fields of business and finance, criminology, economics, political science, and sociology. Furthermore, we would be less than fair if we did not mention our very real debt to *Words and Phrases* (St. Paul, MN: West Publishing Co., 1959). The editors of this series have produced a fine and consistent survey of the lexicon of law, especially with regard to general terms that have been the subject of judicial definition.

Inflected forms An especially helpful feature of this book is its inclusion of inflected forms. Entry of inflected forms has been decided according to the criteria used for their inclusion in *Webster's New Collegiate Dictionary,* except that all inflections are given in full without cutbacks. In general, inflected forms are entered

1. when they are irregular, as in the plural form of *decretum,* which is *decreta;*
2. when a letter is changed, as in the plural *bankruptcies;*
3. when a letter is doubled, as in *annul, annulled, annulling;*
4. when there are varying inflected forms, as with *abortus,* whose plural may be either *abortus* [zero plural] or *abortuses;* or

with *belibel,* whose inflected forms may be *belibeled* or *belibelled,* and *belibeling* or *belibelling;*

5. and when the user might have reasonable doubts or erroneous expectations as to the proper choice of suffixes: for example, with the plural form (*veniremen*), or the Latinized variant plurals (*dies nons* or *dies non juridici*).

The legal lexicon with its wealth of mass nouns and Latin words and phrases presents special pluralization problems. While it is theoretically possible to pluralize any normal term, it nevertheless seems more useful to show only *known* instances of plurals. Accordingly, the editors have avoided entry of hypothetical plurals for which there is no evidence of actual usage in the over 12 million citations in the Merriam-Webster files. Thus, no plural is shown for a term like *animus derelinquendi.* The indication of a plural at a basically mass noun means that the noun does have at least some count use. An example of this is the term *authority.* On the other hand, plurals are *not* shown for mass nouns such as *culpability* that have no count use. Plurals are also omitted from some highly specialized terms (such as the names of historically important writs) for which pluralization is very unlikely. Plurals are, however, shown

1. when the term is irregularly pluralized (i.e., when the plural is not formed by the addition of -*s* or -*es* to an unchanged base), as *availability* ⟶ *availabilities* and *encephalitis* ⟶ *encephalitides;*

2. when the plural is unchanged from the singular, as *undersigned* ⟶ *undersigned* and *habitus* ⟶ *habitus;*

3. when the terms have variant plurals, as *ultimatum* ⟶ *ultimatums* or *ultimata* and *attorney general* ⟶ *attorneys general* or *attorney generals;*

4. when the terms end in -*o,* because some such nouns pluralize with -*os,* -*oes,* or both, as *imbroglio* ⟶ *imbroglios* and *hobo* ⟶ *hoboes* or *hobos;*

5. when the plurals are formed in a way that the user might not expect, as *attorney-in-fact* $\longrightarrow$ *attorneys-in-fact;*

6. and when Latin plurals have been retained, as *testatrix* $\longrightarrow$ *testatrices* and *donatio* $\longrightarrow$ *donationes.*

The principal parts of verbs are shown

1. when the inflections are not formed by the addition of *-ed* and *-ing* to an unchanged base, as *authorize, authorized, authorizing;* and *reply, replied, replying;*

2. when it is felt that some ambiguity may exist in the user's mind as to the proper inflection of a particular verb, as *employ, employed, employing* where the *-y* is retained throughout inflection;

3. when the past tense and the past participle of a verb differ, in which case the past tense, the past participle, and the present participle are shown in that order, as with the verb *foresee, foresaw, foreseen, foreseeing;*

4. and when there are variant inflections, as *counsel, counseled* or *counselled, counseling* or *counselling.*

Adjectives and adverbs that are compared with some measure of frequency are entered in this book together with their comparative and superlative degrees. Such inflections are included because users are sometimes uncertain as to whether the words can be compared in the first place, and if so, how the comparisons should be styled. It ought to be remembered that *any* adjective or adverb capable of grammatical comparison may be compared by the addition of *more* and *most* to form the comparative and the superlative degrees, respectively. However, many adjectives and adverbs—through custom or for reason of euphony—are rarely or never compared by the addition of the comparative and the superlative suffixes *-er* and *-est.*

Variant spellings of main entries Entries having variant spellings show those variants. Variants that are used as often as the boldface main-entry styling are introduced by the italic word *or.*

Those that are less common spellings but are still acceptable are introduced by *also*. Examples:

aero-oti·tis med·ia
   also aero-oti·tis
   or aer·oti·tis

kat
   or khat
   or qat
   also quat

The *or* and the *also* variants are entered at their own alphabetical places in the vocabulary when they are not very near their main entries; thus, *khat* is entered as follows:

khat
   var of kat

Often-confused terms A few words that are similar enough in spelling to cause confusion have been entered in this book with very brief orienting definitions. Examples:

dis·creet·ly
   in a discreet manner
   (*see* discretely)

dis·crete·ly
   separately
   (*see* discreetly)

Limitations on homographs In order to avoid undesirable repetition and unnecessary bulk, homographs (i.e., words that are spelled *exactly* the same but are different parts of speech) are not repeated when the end-of-line division of one part of speech is identical with that of another. As an example, the word *hugger-mugger* (which can function as a noun, an adverb, an adjective, and a verb) appears in this book only as a verb. Its principal parts (*hugger-muggered, hugger-muggering*) are shown because there could be a question in the user's mind as to whether the final *r* doubles or not during inflection. The noun, on the other hand, is pluralized by the simple addition of *-s*. Hence, it is not entered. Neither the adverb nor the adjective undergo grammatical comparison, so they too have not been entered. Still another instance of homograph treatment in this book is the term *bill*—a word having some seven homographs, of which two are important in legal use. This word nevertheless appears in *Webster's Legal Speller* only once and without a part-of-speech label since there is no inflectional irregularity in any of the seven homographs.

Part-of-speech labels are not usually shown in *Webster's Legal Speller* since as indicated above, a particular spelling with end-of-line divisions shown therein is intended to cover all homographs identically spelled and divided. Part-of-speech labels are shown, however, when different parts of speech are styled differently (as **set off** *vb* and **set-off** *n;* **trusty** *adj* **-i·er, -i·est** and **trusty** *also* **trust·ee** *n, pl* **trust·ies** *also* **trust·ees;** and **ca·shier** *vb* and **cash·ier** *n*).

Derivative words Not only are base words like *toxicology* entered, but their derivatives such as *toxicological, toxicologic,* and *toxicologist* also appear in proper alphabetic sequence. If a verbal noun (as *decreeing*) does not appear at its own alphabetical place, the user should look for it at the parent verb (in this case at *decree*).

Entry of open compounds In general, the editors have omitted from the vocabulary open compounds (as *criminal law* and *gag order*) all of whose individual elements are already entered at their own alphabetical places in the word corpus, and open compounds (as *profit margin*) whose elements are very common general words that have not been entered in the book. Open compounds are, however, entered when there may be uncertainty in the user's mind as to their styling, and especially when a particular compounding element sometimes forms solid, open, or hyphened compounds, as: *heatstroke* but *heat exhaustion* and *heat prostration*.

Word division The vocabulary in this book was edited in accordance with the principles of end-of-line division used in *Webster's New Collegiate Dictionary* and as a result, the book provides a set of acceptable recommendations for word division which is consistent within itself. The word divisions indicated by centered dots (as in the terms *de·duct·ibil·i·ty, tax·a·tion·al,* and *ami·cus cu·ri·ae*) do not necessarily separate words into syllables. Rather, the centered dots are intended only to show the points at which words may be divided at the ends of lines. While considerable time and effort have been expended in achieving consistency in the end-of-line divisions shown in this book, it should also be pointed out that alternative divisions in some cases may be equally acceptable. The notion of "correctness" is, perhaps, too strong to be applied to end-of-line divisions in general, since reputable printers and publishers differ in theory and in practice. Common sense and the appearance of the typewritten or printed page are also important considerations in end-of-line division. It is better not to divide words at points where the divisions might intrude on the reader's attention or possibly cause misreading or misunderstanding. Compounds containing one or more hyphens will cause a reader less trouble if divided after the hyphen, though when space is tight, it may prove necessary to divide elsewhere. Thus, other possible divisions (as in *cross-ex·am·ine*) are shown. It is best not to divide a word so that a single letter begins a line, and no such divisions are shown in this book. The last word on a page is traditionally not divided by many typists; however, there is no ironclad rule forbidding the practice. It is wise not to divide abbreviations (as *LLB*), contractions (as *ass'n.*), personal names and eponyms (as *Franklin D. Mason, Esq.* and *Adam's apple*), dates (as *January 2, 19–*), and numbers (as *$2,500.00*).

Legal preferences   Since this book is addressed to people of the law, every effort has been made to conform to legal custom wherever any dichotomy of usage occurs with respect to spelling preference or the styling of compounds. For example, *Webster's Third New International Dictionary* shows **seisin** *or* **seizin** as equal variants, but a review of strictly legal usage makes apparent a decided modern preference for the spelling *seisin* in legal contexts. Thus, the entry appears in *Webster's Legal Speller* as **seisin** *also* **seizin.** Similarly, legal preference as to open, hyphened, or solid stylings of compounds is regularly followed (as at *per cent* which in legal use is usually an open compound though it is ordinarily solid [*percent*] in general use). Similarly, where legal preference with respect to hyphenation clearly differs from the general usage, the legal preference has been followed. Typical examples of this include the term *intransit* which is usually styled as a solid compound in legal writing but is ordinarily written with a hyphen (*in-transit*) in general contexts, and the term *pre-emptive* which is customarily hyphened in legal writing even though it is commonly solid (*preemptive*) in general sources. In this latter connection it must be kept in mind that many compound nouns normally styled open tend to be hyphened when used attributively (i.e., when used to modify another noun).

Back matter In addition to the vocabulary, this book contains back matter featuring a list of over 1600 legal and related abbreviations followed by their appropriate expansions. This material is followed by a section giving over 80 punctuation guidelines, each of which is exemplified by at least one verbal illustration. An Italicization section also appears in the back matter: it contains a number of rules for the italicizing or the underscoring of material especially in legal writing. Each rule is illustrated with an example of usage.

Editorial acknowledgments This book, like other Merriam-Webster publications, is the product of a collective editorial effort. The vocabulary was selected, compiled, and edited under a plan developed by Mairé Weir Kay, Joint Editorial Director and Francine A. Roberts, Editorial Assistant; the latter also maintained and correlated the editorial files, while Laverne W. King, Assistant Editor (retired), prepared the manuscript and assisted in proofreading. John K. Bollard, Assistant Editor, codified the principles of end-of-line division and made final word division decisions. Kathleen M. Doherty, Assistant Editor, prepared the section of abbreviations. Harold E. Niergarth, Assistant Editor copyedited the manuscript and assisted in proofreading. Cross-referencing was accomplished under the direction of Grace A. Kellogg, Associate Editor. The Editor accepts full responsibility for the Introduction and for the suggestions on punctuation in the back matter of the book which she hopes secretaries will find a handy guide to usage.

Anne H. Soukhanov
Editor

A

abac·te·ri·al
ab·alien·ate
  ab·alien·at·ed
  ab·alien·at·ing
ab·alien·ation
aban·don
aban·don·ee
aban·don·er
aban·don·ment
ab an·te
ab an·ti·quo
aba·sia
abat·able
abate
  abat·ed
  abat·ing
abate·ment
aba·tor
ab·ax·i·al
Ab·der·hal·den
  re·ac·tion
ab·di·cate
  ab·di·cat·ed
  ab·di·cat·ing
ab·di·ca·tion
ab·di·ca·tor
ab·do·men
ab·dom·i·nal
ab·dom·i·nal·ly
ab·dom·i·no·per·i·
  ne·al
ab·duce
  ab·duced
  ab·duc·ing

ab·du·cens
  pl ab·du·cen·tes
ab·duct
ab·duc·tion
ab·duc·tor
  pl ab·duc·to·res
  or ab·duc·tors
ab·er·ran·cy
  pl ab·er·ran·cies
ab·er·rant
ab·er·ra·tion
abet
  abet·ted
  abet·ting
abet·tor
  or abet·ter
abey·ance
abide
  abode
    or abid·ed
  abid·ing
ab in·i·tio
ab in·tes·ta·to
abio·tro·phic
abi·ot·ro·phy
  pl abi·ot·ro·phies
ab·judge
  ab·judged
  ab·judg·ing
ab·ju·di·cate
  ab·ju·di·cat·ed
  ab·ju·di·cat·ing
ab·ju·ra·tion
ab·jure
  ab·jured
  ab·jur·ing

ab·late
  ab·lat·ed
  ab·lat·ing
ab·la·tion
ab·la·tio
  pla·cen·tae
ab·nor·mal
ab·nor·mal·i·ty
  pl ab·nor·mal·i·ties
ab·nor·mal·ly
abol·ish
ab·o·li·tion
abort
abort·er
abor·ti·cide
abor·ti·fa·cient
abor·tion
abor·tion·ist
abor·tive
abor·to·gen·ic
abor·tus
  pl abor·tus
  or abor·tus·es
abou·lia
  var of abulia
abrade
  abrad·ed
  abrad·ing
abra·sion
abra·sive
ab·re·act
ab·re·ac·tion
abridge
  abridged
  abridg·ing

1

abridg·ment
  or abridge·ment

ab·ro·gate
  ab·ro·gat·ed
  ab·ro·gat·ing
ab·ro·ga·tion
ab·ro·ga·tive
ab·ro·ga·tor
ab·rup·tio
  pla·cen·tae
    pl ab·rup·tio
      pla·cen·ta·rum
    or ab·rup·ti·o·nes
      pla·cen·ta·rum

ab·scess
ab·scis·sion
  also ab·sci·sion

ab·scond
ab·scond·ence
ab·scond·er
ab·sent
ab·sen·tee
ab·sen·tee·ism
ab·sen·te reo
ab·sinthe
  or ab·sinth

ab·sin·thism
ab·so·lute
ab·so·lut·ism
ab·solve
  ab·solved
  ab·solv·ing
ab·sol·vi·tor
ab·sorb
ab·sorb·able

ab·sor·be·fa·cient
ab·sor·bent
ab·sorp·tion
abs·que hoc
ab·stain
ab·sten·tion
ab·sten·tion·ism
ab·sten·tion·ist
ab·sti·nence
ab·stract
ab·strac·tion
ab·strac·tor
  or ab·stract·er

abu·lia
  or abou·lia

abus·able
abus·age
abuse
  abused
  abus·ing
abus·er
abu·sive
abut
  abut·ted
  abut·ting
ab uti·li
abut·ment
abut·tals
abut·ter
ab·wab
acal·cu·lia
acan·thi·on
ac·an·tho·ma
  pl ac·an·tho·mas
  or ac·an·tho·ma·ta

ac·an·tho·sis
  pl ac·an·tho·ses

ac·an·thot·ic
ac·ce·das
  ad cu·ri·am
ac·cede
  ac·ced·ed
  ac·ced·ing
ac·cel·er·ant
ac·cel·er·ate
  ac·cel·er·at·ed
  ac·cel·er·at·ing
ac·cel·er·a·tion
ac·cel·er·a·tor
ac·cept
ac·cept·abil·i·ty
ac·cept·able
ac·cep·tance
ac·cep·ta·tion
ac·cept·er
ac·cep·ti·late
  ac·cep·ti·lat·ed
  ac·cep·ti·lat·ing
ac·cep·ti·la·tion
ac·cep·tor
  one that accepts an
    order or bill
  (*see* exceptor)

ac·cep·tor for
  hon·or
    or ac·cep·tor
      su·pra pro·test

ac·cess
  right to enter
  (*see* excess)

ac·ces·sa·ry
var of accessory

ac·ces·si·bil·i·ty
ac·ces·si·ble
ac·ces·si·ble·ness
ac·ces·si·bly
ac·ces·sion
ac·ces·so·ri·al
ac·ces·so·ry
  also ac·ces·sa·ry
  pl ac·ces·so·ries
  also ac·ces·sa·ries

ac·ci·dent
ac·ci·den·tal
ac·ci·den·tal·ly
ac·ci·dent-prone
ac·cla·ma·tion
ac·cli·mate
  ac·cli·mat·ed
  ac·cli·mat·ing
ac·cli·ma·tion
ac·cli·ma·ti·za·tion
ac·cli·ma·tize
  ac·cli·ma·tized
  ac·cli·ma·tiz·ing
ac·com·mo·date
  ac·com·mo·dat·
    ed
  ac·com·mo·dat·
    ing
ac·com·mo·da·tion
ac·com·mo·da·tive
ac·com·plice
ac·cord
ac·cor·dance

ac·cor·dant
ac·cost
ac·couche·ment
ac·couche·ment
  for·cé
  pl ac·couche·ments
    for·cés

ac·cou·cheur
ac·count
ac·count·abil·i·ty
ac·count·able
ac·count·ably
ac·coun·tan·cy
ac·coun·tant
ac·count·ing
ac·cred·it
  ac·cred·it·ed
  ac·cred·it·ing
ac·cred·i·ta·tion
ac·cred·it·ee
ac·cred·it·ment
ac·cre·tion
ac·cre·tion·ary
ac·croach
ac·cru·al
ac·crue
  ac·crued
  ac·cru·ing
ac·crue·ment
ac·cu·mu·la·ble
ac·cu·mu·late
  ac·cu·mu·lat·ed
  ac·cu·mu·lat·ing
ac·cu·mu·la·tion
ac·cus·able
ac·cus·al

ac·cus·ant
ac·cu·sa·tion
ac·cu·sa·tive
ac·cu·sa·tive·ly
ac·cu·sa·to·ri·al
ac·cu·sa·to·ri·al·ly
ac·cu·sa·to·ry
ac·cu·sa·trix
  pl ac·cu·sa·trix·es

ac·cuse
  ac·cused
  ac·cus·ing
ac·cus·er
ac·cus·ing·ly
ac·cus·ive
ace·dia
aceph·a·lus
  pl aceph·a·li

ac·er·o·la
ac·e·tab·u·lar
ac·e·tab·u·lum
  pl ac·e·tab·u·lums
  or ac·e·tab·u·la

ac·et·al·de·hyde
ac·et·amin·o·phen
ac·et·an·i·lide
  or ac·et·an·i·lid

ac·e·tate
ace·to·mor·phine
ac·e·tone
ace·to·ni·trile
ac·e·ton·uria
acet·y·lene
ace·tyl·sa·lic·y·late
ace·tyl·sal·i·cyl·ic

ache
  ached
  ach·ing
Achil·les' ten·don
achy
  ach·i·er
  ach·i·est
ac·i·do·sis
  pl ac·i·do·ses

ac·i·dot·ic
acid·u·lous
ac·knowl·edge
  ac·knowl·edged
  ac·knowl·edg·
    ing
ac·knowl·edge·
    able
ac·knowl·edg·
    ment
ac·ne
ac·ne·form
  or ac·ne·iform

ac·ne ro·sa·cea
  pl ac·nae ro·sa·ce·ae

ac·ne vul·gar·is
  pl ac·nae vul·gar·es

ac·o·nite
ac·o·nit·ic
acous·tic
acous·tics
ac·quest
ac·qui·esce
  ac·qui·esced
  ac·qui·esc·ing
ac·qui·es·cence

ac·quire
  ac·quired
  ac·quir·ing
ac·qui·si·tion
ac·quit
  ac·quit·ted
  ac·quit·ting
ac·quit·tal
ac·quit·tance
acre
acre·age
acre-foot
  pl acre-feet

acre-inch
ac·ro·me·gal·ic
ac·ro·meg·a·ly
  pl ac·ro·meg·a·lies

ac·ro·mi·al
ac·ro·mi·on
ac·ro·nar·cot·ic
ac·ro·pho·bia
across-the-board
ac·ry·late
acryl·ic
ac·ry·lo·ni·trile
act
ac·ta n pl
ac·tin·ic
ac·ti·no·my·co·sis
  pl ac·ti·no·my·co·ses

ac·ti·no·my·cot·ic
ac·ti·no·ther·a·py
  pl ac·ti·no·ther·a·pies

ac·tio
  pl ac·ti·o·nes

ac·tio bo·nae fi·dei
  pl ac·ti·o·nes bo·nae
    fi·dei

ac·tio ci·vi·lis
ac·tio in per·so·
    nam
ac·tio in rem
ac·tion
ac·tion·abil·i·ty
ac·tion·able
ac·tion ex de·lic·to
ac·tio non
ac·tio per·so·na·lis
ac·tive
ac·tiv·ism
ac·tiv·ist
ac·tiv·i·ty
  pl ac·tiv·i·ties

act of God
ac·tu·al
ac·tu·ar·i·al
ac·tu·ary
  pl ac·tu·ar·ies

ac·tus
  pl ac·tus

ac·tus Dei
ac·tus re·us
acu·ity
  pl acu·ities

acu·punc·ture
acute
ad ab·sur·dum
Ad·am's ap·ple
a da·tu
ad cap·tan·dum
  or ad cap·tan·dum
    vul·gus

ad·cu·ri·am
ad·dam·num
ad·den·dum
   pl ad·den·da

ad·dict
ad·dic·tion
ad·dic·tive
ad·dit·a·ment
ad·di·tion·al
ad·di·tive
ad·di·tur
ad·dress
ad·dress·ee
ad·dress·er
ad·dres·sor
ad·duce
   ad·duced
   ad·duc·ing
   ad·duc·ible
     also ad·duce·able

ad·duc·tion
ad·duc·tor
adeem
ademp·tion
ad·e·ni·tis
   pl ad·e·nit·i·des
   or ad·e·ni·tis·es

ad·e·no·car·ci·no·ma
   pl ad·e·no·car·ci·no·mas
   or ad·e·no·car·ci·no·ma·ta

ad·e·noid
ad·e·noi·dal
ad·e·noid·ec·to·my
   pl ad·e·noid·ec·to·mies

ad·e·noid·ism
ad·e·no·ma
   pl ad·e·no·mas
   or ad·e·no·ma·ta

ad·e·nop·a·thy
   pl ad·e·nop·a·thies

ad·e·no·sar·co·ma
   pl ad·e·no·sar·co·mas
   or ad·e·no·sar·co·ma·ta

ad·e·no·vi·rus
ad·e·qua·cy
   pl ad·e·qua·cies

ad·e·quate
ad·e·quate·ly
ad·e·quate·ness
ad·e·qua·tion
ad fi·lum aquae
ad gra·ve dam·num
ad·here
   ad·hered
   ad·her·ing
ad·her·ence
ad·he·sion
ad·he·sive
ad ho·mi·nem
ad idem
ad in·fi·ni·tum
ad in·ter·im
ad·i·po·cere
ad·i·poc·er·ous
ad·i·pose
ad·i·po·sis
   pl ad·i·po·ses
ad·i·pos·i·ty
   pl ad·i·pos·i·ties
adi·tio
   pl adi·ti·os

ad·i·tus
   pl ad·i·tus
   or ad·i·tus·es

ad·ja·cent
ad·jec·tive
ad·join
   to be next to
   (*see* adjourn)

ad·journ
   to suspend a session
   (*see* adjoin)

ad·jour·nal
ad·journ·ment
ad·judge
   ad·judged
   ad·judg·ing
ad·ju·di·ca·taire
ad·ju·di·cate
   ad·ju·di·cat·ed
   ad·ju·di·cat·ing
ad·ju·di·ca·tio
ad·ju·di·ca·tion
ad·ju·di·ca·tive
ad·ju·di·ca·tor
ad·ju·di·ca·to·ry
ad·ju·di·ca·ture
ad·junct
ad·junc·tion
ad·ju·ra·tion
ad·jure
   ad·jured
   ad·jur·ing
ad·jur·er
   also ad·ju·ror

ad·just
ad·just·able

ad·just·er
  also ad·jus·tor

ad·just·ment
ad·ju·vant
ad lib
ad li·bi·tum
ad li·tem
ad lo·cum
ad ma·num mor·
  tu·am
ad·mea·sure
  ad·mea·sured
  ad·mea·sur·ing
ad·mea·sure·ment
ad·min·i·cle
ad·mi·nic·u·lar
  also ad·mi·nic·u·lary

ad·min·is·ter
  ad·min·is·tered
  ad·min·is·ter·ing
ad·min·is·te·ri·al
ad·min·is·trant
ad·min·is·trate
  ad·min·is·trat·ed
  ad·min·is·trat·
    ing
ad·min·is·tra·tion
ad·min·is·tra·tive
ad·min·is·tra·tive·
  ly
ad·min·is·tra·tor
ad·min·is·tra·trix
  pl ad·min·is·tra·tri·ces

ad·mi·ral·ty
  pl ad·mi·ral·ties

ad mi·se·ri·cor·di·
  am
ad·mis·si·bil·i·ty
  also ad·mis·sa·bil·i·ty

ad·mis·si·ble
  also ad·mis·sa·ble

ad·mis·sion
ad·mit
  ad·mit·ted
  ad·mit·ting
ad·mit·tance
ad·mo·ni·tion
ad·nexa *n pl*
ad·nex·al
ad non ex·e·cu·ta
ad·o·les·cence
ad·o·les·cent
adopt
adopt·abil·i·ty
  pl adopt·a·bil·i·ties

adopt·able
adopt·ee
adopt·er
adop·tion
adop·tive
ad·pro·mis·sion
ad·pro·mis·sor
  pl ad·pro·mis·sors
  also ad·prom·is·so·res

ad quod dam·num
ad re·di·men·dam
  vex·a·tio·nem
ad rem
ad·re·nal
ad·re·nal·cor·ti·cal

adren·a·line
ad·ren·er·gic
ad·re·no·cor·ti·cal
ad·re·no·cor·ti·co·
  mi·met·ic
ad·re·no·cor·ti·co·
  ste·roid
ad·re·no·cor·ti·co·
  tro·phic
  or ad·re·no·cor·ti·co·
    trop·ic

ad re·spon·den·
  dum
ad·ro·gate
  ad·ro·gat·ed
  ad·ro·gat·ing
ad·ro·ga·tion
ad sec·tam
ad·ses·sor
ad·stip·u·late
  ad·stip·u·lat·ed
  ad·stip·u·lat·ing
ad·stip·u·la·tion
ad·stip·u·la·tor
ad tes·ti·fi·can·
  dum
adult
adul·ter·ant
adul·ter·ate
  adul·ter·at·ed
  adul·ter·at·ing
adul·ter·a·tion
adul·ter·a·tor
adul·ter·er
adul·ter·ess

adul·ter·ine
adul·ter·ous
adul·ter·ous·ly
adul·tery
  pl adul·ter·ies

adult·hood
ad va·lo·rem
ad·vance·ment
ad·van·tage
ad·ven·ture
ad·ven·tur·er
ad ver·bum
ad·ver·sary
  pl ad·ver·sar·ies

ad·ver·sa·tive
ad·verse
ad·verse·ly
ad·ver·si·ty
  pl ad·ver·si·ties

ad·ver·sus
ad·ver·tence
ad·ver·tent
ad·ver·tise
  also ad·ver·tize
  ad·ver·tised
  also ad·ver·tized
  ad·ver·tis·ing
  also ad·ver·tiz·ing

ad·ver·tise·ment
  also ad·ver·tize·ment

ad·ver·tis·er
  also ad·ver·tiz·er

ad·vice
  counsel or information
  (*see* advise)

ad·vis·a·to·ry
ad·vise
  ad·vised
  ad·vis·ing
  to give advice
  (*see* advice)

ad·vise·ment
ad·vis·er
  also ad·vi·sor

ad·vi·so·ry
ad vi·tam
ad vi·tam aut
  cul·pam
ad·vo·ca·cy
  pl ad·vo·ca·cies

ad·vo·cate
  ad·vo·cat·ed
  ad·vo·cat·ing
ad·vo·ca·tion
ad·vo·ca·tor
ad·vo·ca·to·ry
ad·vow·ee
ad·vow·son
ae·mu·la·tio vi·ci·ni
  pl ae·mu·la·ti·o·nes
  vi·ci·ni

aer·obe
aer·o·bic
aero·bul·lo·sis
aero·em·bo·lism
aero·med·i·cal
aero·med·i·cine
aero·neu·ro·sis
  pl aero·neuro·ses

aero·oti·tis med·ia
  also aero·oti·tis
  or aer·oti·tis

aero·pho·bia
aero·si·nus·itis
aero·sol
aero·sol·iza·tion
aero·sol·ize
  aero·sol·ized
  aero·sol·iz·ing
aer·oti·tis
  var of aero-otitis
  media

aes·the·sia
  var of esthesia

ae·ti·ol·o·gy
  var of etiology

afe·brile
af·fair
  or af·faire

af·fi·ance
  af·fi·anced
  af·fi·anc·ing
af·fi·ant
af·fi·da·vit
af·fil·i·ate
  af·fil·i·at·ed
  af·fil·i·at·ing
af·fil·i·a·tion
af·fi·nal
af·fine
af·fin·i·ty
  pl af·fin·i·ties

af·firm
af·fir·mance

af·fir·ma·tion
af·fir·ma·tive
af·fir·ma·tive
  preg·nant
af·fix
af·fix·a·tion
af·fix·ion
af·flict
af·flic·tion
af·flic·tive
af·force
  af·forced
  af·forc·ing
af·force·ment
af·for·est
af·for·es·ta·tion
af·fray
af·freight·er
af·freight·ment
af·fright
af·front
af·la·tox·in
afore·men·tioned
afore·said
afore·thought
a for·ti·o·ri
af·ter·birth
af·ter·care
af·ter·damp
af·ter·ef·fect
af·ter·mar·ket
af·ter·math
afunc·tion·al
agen·cy
  pl agen·cies

agen·da
  pl agen·das
agen·dum
  pl agen·da
  or agen·dums
agent
agent-gen·er·al
  pl agents-gen·er·al
agen·tial
agent pro·vo·ca·
  teur
    pl agents pro·vo·ca·
      teurs
agent·ry
  pl agent·ries
age of con·sent
age of dis·cre·tion
ag·glom·er·ate
  ag·glom·er·at·ed
  ag·glom·er·at·
    ing
ag·glom·er·a·tion
ag·glu·ti·nate
  ag·glu·ti·nat·ed
  ag·glu·ti·nat·ing
ag·glu·ti·na·tion
ag·gra·vate
  ag·gra·vat·ed
  ag·gra·vat·ing
ag·gra·va·tion
ag·gre·gate
  ag·gre·gat·ed
  ag·gre·gat·ing
ag·gre·ga·tion
ag·gres·sion

ag·gres·sive
ag·gres·sor
ag·grieve
  ag·grieved
  ag·griev·ing
agio·tage
agist
agist·er
  or agis·tor
agist·ment
ag·i·tate
  ag·i·tat·ed
  ag·i·tat·ing
ag·i·ta·tion
ag·i·ta·tor
ag·nate
ag·nat·ic
ag·na·tion
ag·no·gen·ic
ag·no·sia
ag·o·nal
ag·o·ny
  pl ag·o·nies
ag·o·ra·pho·bia
agram·ma·tism
agran·u·lo·cy·to·sis
  pl agran·u·lo·cy·to·ses
agraph·ia
agré·a·tion
agree
  agreed
  agree·ing
agree·able
agree·ment
agré·ment

aid·er
aid·man
   pl aid·men
ai·el
ail·ment
ai·lu·ro·phobe
ai·lu·ro·pho·bia
air·space
ai·ti·ol·o·gy
   var of etiology
aki·ne·sia
aki·net·ic
alarm
   also ala·rum
al·be·do
   pl al·be·dos
al·be·it
al·bu·men
al·bu·min
al·bu·min·uria
al·bu·min·uric
al·co·hol
al·co·hol·ate
al·co·hol·ic
al·co·hol·i·cal·ly
al·co·hol·ism
al·co·hol·ist
al·co·hol·ize
   al·co·hol·ized
   al·co·hol·iz·ing
al·co·hol·om·e·ter
al·co·hol·om·e·try
al·de·hyde
al·der·man
   pl al·der·men

al·der·man·ic
al·der·man·ry
   pl al·der·man·ries
al·der·wom·an
   pl al·der·wom·en
al·do·ste·rone
al·do·ste·ron·ism
al·drin
ale·a·to·ry
ale·con·ner
alex·ia
alex·ic
al·ga
   pl al·gae
   also al·gas
al·gal
al·ge·sia
al·ge·sic
al·go·gen·ic
al·go·lag·nia
al·go·pho·bia
alias
al·i·bi
   al·i·bied
   al·i·bi·ing
alien
alien·abil·i·ty
   pl alien·abil·i·ties
alien·able
alien·age
ali·e·na res
alien·ate
   alien·at·ed
   alien·at·ing
alien·ation

alien·ator
alien·ee
ali·e·ni ju·ris
alien·ism
alien·ist
alien·or
alii
al·i·ment
al·i·men·ta·tion
al·i·mo·ny
   pl al·i·mo·nies
al·i·mo·ny pen·
   den·te li·te
al·i·quot
ali·ter
al·i·un·de
al·ka·loid
al·lay·ment
al·le·ga·ta et pro·
   ba·ta
al·le·ga·tion
   a positive assertion
   (*see* alligation)
al·le·ga·tor
al·le·ga·tum
   pl al·le·ga·ta
al·lege
   al·leged
   al·leg·ing
al·lege·able
al·lege·ment
al·le·giance
al·le·giant
al·ler·gen
al·ler·gen·ic

al·ler·gic
al·ler·gist
al·ler·gy
  pl al·ler·gies

al·le·vi·ate
  al·le·vi·at·ed
  al·le·vi·at·ing
al·le·vi·a·tion
al·le·vi·a·tive
al·li·able
al·li·ance
al·li·ga·tion
  a binding together
  (*see* allegation)

al·lo·bar·bi·tal
al·lo·ca·bil·i·ty
al·lo·ca·ble
al·lo·cate
  al·lo·cat·ed
  al·lo·cat·ing
al·lo·cat·ee
al·lo·ca·tion
al·lo·ca·tor
  person who allocates
  (*see* allocatur)

al·lo·ca·tur
  kind of writ
  (*see* allocator)

al·lo·cu·tion
al·lo·di·al
  var of alodial

al·lo·di·al·ist
  var of alodialist

al·lo·di·al·i·ty
  var of alodiality

al·lo·di·um
  also alo·di·um

al·lo·erot·ic
al·lo·erot·i·cism
al·longe
al·lot
  al·lot·ted
  al·lot·ting
al·lot·ment
al·lot·ta·ble
al·lot·tee
al·low·able
al·low·ance
all risks
al·lu·vi·on
al·lu·vi·um
  pl al·lu·vi·ums
  or al·lu·via

al·lyl·nor·mor·
  phine
al·moign
  or al·moin

alo·di·al
  or al·lo·di·al

alo·di·al·ist
  or al·lo·di·al·ist

alo·di·al·i·ty
  or al·lo·di·al·i·ty

alo·di·um
  var of allodium

al·ter
  al·tered
  al·ter·ing
al·ter·abil·i·ty
al·ter·able
al·o·pe·cia
al·o·pe·cic
al·ter·ation

al·ter·ca·tion
al·ter·nate
al·ter·na·tive
al·ti·us non tol·
  len·di
alu·mi·na
alu·mi·no·sis
  pl alu·mi·no·ses

al·ve·o·lar
al·ve·o·lus
  pl al·ve·o·li

amal·gam·ate
  amal·gam·at·ed
  amal·gam·at·ing
amal·gam·ation
amal·gam·ative
amal·gam·ator
am·a·tho·pho·bia
am·au·ro·sis
  pl am·au·ro·ses

am·au·rot·ic
am·bas·sa·dor
  also em·bas·sa·dor

am·bas·sa·do·ri·al
am·bas·sa·dress
  also em·bas·sa·dress

am·bi·dex·ter
am·bi·dex·ter·i·ty
am·bi·dex·trous
am·bi·gu·ity
  pl am·bi·gu·ities

am·big·u·ous
am·biv·a·lence
am·biv·a·lent
am·bu·lance

am·bu·lance chas·
er
am·bu·lant
am·bu·la·to·ry
am·bush
am·bush·er
ame·lio·rate
 ame·lio·rat·ed
 ame·lio·rat·ing
ame·lio·ra·tion
ame·lio·ra·tive
ame·na·bil·i·ty
ame·na·ble
 accountable
 (*see* amendable)

amend
amend·able
 that can be amended
 (*see* amenable)

amen·da·to·ry
amende ho·no·ra·
ble
 pl amendes ho·no·
 ra·bles

amend·ment
amends *n pl*
a men·sa et tho·ro
amerce
 amerced
 amerc·ing
amerce·ment
amer·cia·ble
ameth·o·caine
am·i·ca·bil·i·ty
 pl am·i·ca·bil·i·ties

am·i·ca·ble

am·i·ca·bly
ami·cus cu·ri·ae
 pl ami·ci cu·ri·ae

am·ne·sia
am·ne·si·ac
am·nes·ty
 pl am·nes·ties

amok
 or amuck

amor·al
amor·phin·ism
amor·phous
am·or·tiz·able
am·or·ti·za·tion
 or am·or·ti·sa·tion

am·or·tize
 also am·or·tise
 am·or·tized
 also am·or·tised
 am·or·tiz·ing
 also am·or·tis·ing

am·or·tize·ment
amo·tion
amov·abil·i·ty
amov·able
amove
 amoved
 amov·ing
am·phet·amine
am·pho·ter·i·cin
am·pi·cil·lin
am·pli·a·tion
am·pul
 also am·pule
 or am·poule

am·pul·la
 pl am·pul·lae

am·pu·tate
 am·pu·tat·ed
 am·pu·tat·ing
am·pu·ta·tion
am·pu·tee
amuck
 var of amok

amyo·tro·phic
amy·ot·ro·phy
 pl amy·ot·ro·phies

ana·bo·lic
anab·o·lism
anae·mia
 var of anemia

an·aes·the·sia
 var of anesthesia

an·aes·thet·ic
 var of anesthetic

an·aes·the·tist
 var of anesthetist

an·aes·the·ti·za·
tion
 var of anesthetiza-
 tion

an·aes·the·tize
 var of anesthetize

an·al·ge·sia
an·al·ge·sic
anal·y·sis
 pl anal·y·ses

an·a·lyst
an·a·lyt·ic
 or an·a·lyt·i·cal

an·a·lyze
 an·a·lyzed
 an·a·lyz·ing

an·aph·ro·di·sia
an·aph·ro·dis·i·ac
ana·phy·lax·is
  pl ana·phy·lax·es

an·ar·chic
  also an·ar·chi·cal
  or an·ar·chi·al

an·ar·chism
an·ar·chist
an·ar·chy
  pl an·ar·chies

an·a·rith·mia
an·ar·thria
anas·to·mose
  anas·to·mosed
  anas·to·mos·ing
anas·to·mo·sis
  pl anas·to·mo·ses

anas·to·mot·ic
anat·o·cism
an·a·tom·ic
  or an·a·tom·i·cal·ly

anat·o·mist
anat·o·my
  pl anat·o·mies

an·ces·tor
an·ces·tral
an·ces·tress
an·ces·try
  pl an·ces·tries

an·chy·lo·sis
  var of ankylosis

an·chy·lot·ic
  var of ankylotic

an·cien ré·gime
  pl an·ciens ré·gimes

an·cient de·mesne
an·cient light
an·cil·lary
an·ci·pi·tis usus
an·cy·lo·sis
  var of ankylosis

an·cy·lot·ic
  var of ankylotic

an·dro·gyne
an·dro·gy·ne·i·ty
an·drog·y·nism
an·drog·y·nous
an·drog·y·ny
an·dro·pho·bia
ane·mia
  also anae·mia

ane·mic
  also anae·mic

anent
an·er·gic
an·er·gy
  pl an·er·gies

an·es·the·sia
  also an·aes·the·sia

an·es·thet·ic
  also an·aes·thet·ic

an·es·the·tist
  also an·aes·the·tist

an·es·the·ti·za·tion
  also an·aes·the·ti·za·
    tion

an·es·the·tize
  also an·aes·the·tize
  an·es·the·tized
  also an·aes·the·tized
  an·es·the·tiz·ing
  also an·aes·the·tiz·ing

an·eu·rysm
  also an·eu·rism

an·eu·rys·mal
  also an·eu·ris·mal

an·gar·ia
an·ga·ry
  pl an·ga·ries

an·ger
an·gi·itis
  pl an·gi·it·i·des

an·gi·na
an·gi·nal
an·gi·na pec·to·ris
an·gi·o·ma
  pl an·gi·o·mas
  or an·gi·o·ma·ta

an·gio·spasm
an·he·do·nia
ani
  pl of anus

anile
an·i·lide
an·i·line
ani·lin·gus
  or ani·linc·tus

an·i·lin·ism
an·i·mad·ver·sion
ani·mo
ani·mo et ac·to
ani·mo fu·ran·di
ani·mo re·ver·ten·
  di
ani·mo re·vo·can·di
ani·mo tes·tan·di
ani·mus
  pl ani·mus·es

ani·mus de·re·lin·
quen·di
ani·mus et fac·tum
ani·mus fu·ran·di
ani·mus ma·nen·di
ani·mus non re·
ver·ten·di
ani·mus re·ver·ten·
di
ani·mus sig·nan·di
ani·mus tes·tan·di
an·kle
an·kle·bone
an·ky·lo·sis
  also an·chy·lo·sis
  or an·cy·lo·sis
  pl an·ky·lo·ses
  also an·chy·lo·ses
  or an·cy·lo·ses

an·ky·lot·ic
  also an·chy·lot·ic
  or an·cy·lot·ic

ann
  or an·nat

an·nates n pl
an·nex
an·nex·ation
an·nex·ation·al
an·nex·ion
an·nex·ure
an·ni·hi·late
  an·ni·hi·lat·ed
  an·ni·hi·lat·ing
an·no·ta·tion
an·nounce
  an·nounced
  an·nounc·ing

an·nounce·ment
an·noy
an·noy·ance
an·nu·al
an·nu·al·ly
an·nu·itant
an·nu·ity
  pl an·nu·ities
an·nu·ity cer·tain
  pl an·nu·ities
  cer·tain
an·nu·ity due
  pl an·nu·ities due

an·nul
  an·nulled
  an·nul·ling
an·nul·er
an·nul·ment
an·o·dyne
anom·a·lous
anom·a·ly
  pl anom·a·lies

an·o·mie
  or an·o·my
  pl an·o·mies

an·o·nym·i·ty
  pl an·o·nym·i·ties

anon·y·mous
anon·y·mous·ly
anon·y·mous·ness
ano·rec·tal
an·o·rec·tic
  also an·o·ret·ic

an·orex·ia
an·ox·emia
  also an·ox·ae·mia

an·ox·emic
  also an·ox·ae·mic

an·ox·ia
an·swer
  an·swered
  an·swer·ing
an·swer·abil·i·ty
an·swer·able
an·te·ced·ent
an·te·ce·den·tal
an·te·ces·sor
an·te·date
  an·te·dat·ed
  an·te·dat·ing
an·te li·tem
an·te li·tem mo·
tam
an·te·mor·tem
an·te·na·tus
  pl an·te·na·ti

an·te·nup·tial
an·te·par·tum
an·te·ri·or
an·tero·lat·er·al
an·thra·cene
an·thra·co·sil·i·co·
sis
  pl an·thra·co·sil·i·co·
  ses

an·thra·co·sis
  pl an·thra·co·ses

an·thra·cot·ic
an·thrax
  pl an·thra·ces

an·ti·bac·te·ri·al
an·ti·bi·ot·ic

an·ti·chre·sis
pl an·ti·chre·ses

an·tic·i·pant
an·tic·i·pate
  an·tic·i·pat·ed
  an·tic·i·pat·ing
an·tic·i·pa·tion
an·tic·i·pa·tive
an·tic·i·pa·tor
an·tic·i·pa·to·ry
an·ti·co·ag·u·lant
an·ti·de·pres·sant
an·ti·dot·al
an·ti·dote
an·ti·emet·ic
an·ti·gen
an·ti·gen·ic
an·ti·hy·per·ten·
  sive
an·ti·lapse
an·ti·mo·ni·al
an·ti·mo·ny
pl an·ti·mo·nies
a chemical element
(*see* antinomy)

an·tin·o·my
pl an·tin·o·mies
contradiction between
laws
(*see* antimony)

an·ti·py·ret·ic
an·ti·quat·ed
an·ti·sep·sis
pl an·ti·sep·ses

an·ti·sep·tic
an·ti·ser·um
pl an·ti·ser·ums
or an·ti·sera

an·ti·so·cial
an·ti·syph·i·lit·ic
an·ti·trust
an·ti·tu·ber·cu·
  lous
also an·ti·tu·ber·cu·lar

an·ure·sis
pl an·ure·ses

an·uret·ic
anus
pl anus·es
or ani

aor·ta
pl aor·tas
or aor·tae

aor·tal
ap·a·nage
var of appanage

apex
pl apex·es
or api·ces

apha·sia
apha·sic
aphe·mia
aphe·mic
apho·nia
apho·nic
aph·o·rism
aphra·sia
aph·ro·di·sia
aph·ro·dis·i·ac
aph·ro·di·si·a·cal
api·cal
ap·o·graph
pl ap·og·ra·pha

apo·lit·i·cal

apo·mor·phine
ap·o·plec·tic
ap·o·plexy
pl ap·o·plex·ies

a pos·te·ri·o·ri
apoth·e·cary
pl apoth·e·car·ies

ap·o·thegm
or ap·o·phthegm

ap·pa·nage
also ap·a·nage

ap·pa·ra·tus
pl ap·pa·ra·tus
or ap·pa·ra·tus·es

ap·par·ent
ap·peal
ap·peal·abil·i·ty
ap·peal·able
ap·peal·er
ap·pear
ap·pear·ance
ap·pel·lant
ap·pel·late
ap·pel·la·tion
ap·pel·lee
ap·pel·lor
ap·pen·dec·to·my
pl ap·pen·dec·to·mies

ap·pen·di·ci·tis
ap·pen·dix
pl ap·pen·dix·es
or ap·pen·di·ces

ap·per·tain
ap·pli·ca·bil·i·ty
pl ap·pli·ca·bil·i·ties

ap·pli·ca·ble

argumentative

ap·pli·cant
ap·pli·ca·tion
ap·point
ap·poin·tee
ap·point·ive
ap·point·ment
ap·poin·tor
ap·por·tion
ap·por·tion·ment
ap·prais·al
  also ap·praise·ment

ap·praise
  ap·praised
  ap·prais·ing
  to set a value on
  (*see* apprise, apprize)

ap·prais·er
ap·pre·ci·ate
  ap·pre·ci·at·ed
  ap·pre·ci·at·ing
ap·pre·ci·a·tion
ap·pre·hend
ap·pre·hen·sion
ap·pren·tice
ap·pren·tice·ship
ap·prise
  also ap·prize
  ap·prised
  also ap·prized
  ap·pris·ing
  also ap·priz·ing
  to give notice of
  (*see* appraise, apprize)

ap·prize
  also ap·prise
  ap·prized
  also ap·prised

ap·priz·ing
  also ap·pris·ing
  to appreciate or value
  (*see* appraise, apprise)

ap·pro·bate
  ap·pro·bat·ed
  ap·pro·bat·ing
ap·pro·ba·tion
ap·pro·pri·a·ble
ap·pro·pri·ate
  ap·pro·pri·at·ed
  ap·pro·pri·at·ing
ap·pro·pri·a·tion
ap·pro·pri·a·tive
ap·pro·pri·a·tor
ap·prov·al
ap·prove
  ap·proved
  ap·prov·ing
ap·prove·ment
ap·pur·te·nance
ap·pur·te·nant
aprac·tic
  or aprax·ic

aprax·ia
a pri·o·ri
aq·uae·duc·tus
  pl aq·uae·duc·ti

aq·uae·haus·tus
  pl aq·uae·haus·ti

aq·uae im·mit·ten·
  dae *n pl*
aq·ue·duct
aq·ui·clude
aqui·fer
aqui·fuge

arach·nid·ism
ar·bi·ter
ar·bi·tra·ble
ar·bi·trage
ar·bi·trag·er
  also ar·bi·tra·guer

ar·bi·tral
ar·bit·ra·ment
  also ar·bit·re·ment

ar·bi·trari·ly
ar·bi·trari·ness
ar·bi·trary
ar·bi·trate
  ar·bi·trat·ed
  ar·bi·trat·ing
ar·bi·tra·tion
ar·bi·tra·tion·al
ar·bi·tra·tive
ar·bi·tra·tor
ar·bit·re·ment
  var of arbitrament

ar·ci·fin·i·ous
are·o·la
  pl are·o·lae
  or are·o·las

are·o·lar
ar·e·op·a·gus
ar·gu·able
ar·gu·ably
ar·gue
  ar·gued
  ar·gu·ing
ar·gu·en·do
ar·gu·ment
ar·gu·men·ta·tion
ar·gu·men·ta·tive
  or ar·gu·men·tive

aris·ings *n pl*

ar·ma·men·tar·i·um
  pl ar·ma·men·tar·ia
  or ar·ma·men·tar·i·ums

ar·mi·stice

arm's length

ar·o·mat·ic

ar·raign
  to bring before a court
  (*see* arrange)

ar·raign·er

ar·raign·ment

ar·rame
  ar·ramed
  ar·ram·ing

ar·range
  ar·ranged
  ar·rang·ing
  to come to an agreement
  (*see* arraign)

ar·range·ment

ar·ray

ar·ray·al

ar·rear·age

ar·rears *n pl*

ar·rent

ar·ren·ta·tion

ar·rest

ar·res·ta·tion

ar·rest·ee

ar·rest·er
  or ar·res·tor

ar·rest·ment

ar·ret

ar·rha
  pl ar·rhae

ar·ro·gate
  ar·ro·gat·ed
  ar·ro·gat·ing

ar·ro·ga·tion

ar·se·nic

ar·sen·i·cal

ar·sen·i·cal·ism

ar·son

ar·son·ist

art and part

ar·te·ri·al

ar·te·rio·cap·il·lary

ar·te·rio·scle·ro·sis
  pl ar·te·rio·scle·ro·ses

ar·te·rio·scle·rot·ic

ar·tery
  pl ar·ter·ies

ar·thral·gia

ar·thrit·ic

ar·thri·tis
  pl ar·thrit·i·des

ar·throp·a·thy
  pl ar·throp·a·thies

ar·ti·cle

ar·tic·u·lar

ar·tic·u·late
  ar·tic·u·lat·ed
  ar·tic·u·lat·ing

ar·tic·u·la·tion

ar·ti·cu·lo mor·tis

ar·ti·fice

ar·ti·fi·cial per·son

ar·y·te·noid

as·bes·to·sis
  pl as·bes·to·ses

as·cen·dant
  also as·cen·dent

as·cent

as·cer·tain

asep·sis
  pl asep·ses

asep·tic

asex·u·al·i·za·tion

ask·ing price

asper·ma·tism

asper·mia

as·perse
  as·persed
  as·pers·ing

as·per·sion

as·phyx·ia

as·phyx·i·ant

as·phyx·i·ate
  as·phyx·i·at·ed
  as·phyx·i·at·ing

as·phyx·i·a·tion

as·phyx·i·a·tor

as·pi·rate
  as·pi·rat·ed
  as·pi·rat·ing

as·pi·ra·tion

as·pi·ra·tor

as·pi·rin

as·por·ta·tion

as·sail

as·sail·ant
as·sail·ment
as·sart
as·sas·sin
as·sas·si·nate
  as·sas·si·nat·ed
  as·sas·si·nat·ing
as·sas·si·na·tion
as·sas·si·na·tor
as·sault
as·sault·able
as·saul·tive
as·say
  to test for valuable
    content
  (*see* essay)

as·sem·blage
as·sem·bly
  pl as·sem·blies

as·sem·bly·man
  pl as·sem·bly·men

as·sem·bly·wom·
an
  pl as·sem·bly·wom·
    en

as·sent
as·sent·ed
  or as·sent·ing

as·sen·tor
as·sess
as·sess·able
as·sess·ee
as·sess·ment
as·sess·ment work
as·ses·sor

as·ses·so·ri·al
as·ses·sor·ship
as·set
as·sets by de·scent
  or as·sets per
    de·scent

as·sets en·tre main
as·sets in hand
as·sid·u·ous
as·sign
as·sign·abil·i·ty
as·sign·able
as·sig·na·tion
as·sign·ee
as·sign·er
as·sign·ment
as·sign·or
as·size
as·siz·er
as·so·ci·ate
  as·so·ci·at·ed
  as·so·ci·at·ing
as·so·ci·a·tion
as·sume
  as·sumed
  as·sum·ing
as·sump·sit
as·sump·tion
as·sur·ance
as·sured
  pl as·sured
  or as·sureds

as·sur·er
  or as·sur·or

as·syth·ment

asta·sia
aste·re·og·no·sis
  pl aste·re·og·no·ses

as·the·nia
as·then·ic
asth·ma
asth·mat·ic
as·tig·mat·ic
astig·ma·tism
astray freight
as·trict
asyl·la·bia
asy·lum
  pl asy·lums

asym·bo·lia
asymp·tom·at·ic
atac·tic
atax·ia
  also ataxy
  pl atax·ias
  also atax·ies

at·el·ec·ta·sis
  pl at·el·ec·ta·ses

ath·ero·scle·ro·sis
  pl ath·ero·scle·ro·ses

ath·ero·scle·rot·ic
ath·e·toid
ath·e·to·sis
  pl ath·e·to·ses

ath·e·tot·ic
at·las
at·lo·ax·oid
atone
  atoned
  aton·ing

atone·ment
aton·ic
ato·nic·i·ty
  pl ato·nic·i·ties

at·o·ny
  pl at·o·nies

atox·ic
atri·al
atri·um
  pl atria

atroc·i·ty
  pl atroc·i·ties

atro·cious
atro·phic
at·ro·phy
  pl at·ro·phies

at·ro·phy
  at·ro·phied
  at·ro·phy·ing
at·ro·pine
at·ro·pin·ism
at·tach
at·tach·able
at·tach·ment
at·tack
at·tain·der
at·taint
at·taint·ment
at·tempt
at·ten·dant
at·ten·tat
at·ter·mine
  at·ter·mined
  at·ter·min·ing
at·ter·mine·ment
at·test

at·test·able
at·tes·tant
at·tes·ta·tion
at·tes·ta·tive
at·tes·ta·tor
at·test·er
  or at·tes·tor

at·torn
at·tor·ney
  pl at·tor·neys

at·tor·ney-at-law
  pl at·tor·neys-at-law

at·tor·ney gen·er·al
  pl at·tor·neys gen·er·al
  or at·tor·ney gen·er·als

at·tor·ney-in-fact
  pl at·tor·neys-in-fact

at·torn·ment
at·trac·tive
at·tri·tion
au·cep·tary
auc·tion
auc·tion·eer
auc·tor
  pl auc·tors
  also auc·to·res

au·dio·gram
au·di·ol·o·gist
au·di·ol·o·gy
au·di·om·e·ter
au·dio·met·ric
au·di·om·e·trist
au·di·om·e·try
au·dio·vi·su·al

au·dit
au·di·ta que·re·la
au·di·tor
au·di·tor-gen·er·al
  pl au·di·tors-gen·er·al

au·di·to·ri·al
au·di·to·ry
aug·men·ta·tion
aus·cul·ta·tion
aus·pic·es *n pl*
Aus·tra·lian bal·lot
au·then·tic
au·then·ti·cate
  au·then·ti·cat·ed
  au·then·ti·cat·ing
au·then·ti·ca·tion
au·then·ti·ca·tor
au·then·tic·i·ty
  pl au·then·tic·i·ties

au·thor·i·ty
  pl au·thor·i·ties

au·tho·ri·za·tion
au·tho·rize
  au·tho·rized
  au·tho·riz·ing
au·tho·riz·er
au·tism
au·tis·tic
au·tom·a·tism
au·ton·o·mous
au·ton·o·my
  pl au·ton·o·mies

au·top·sy
  pl au·top·sies

au·top·sy
  au·top·sied
  au·top·sy·ing
au·tre·fois ac·quit
au·tre·fois con·vict
aux·il·ia·ry goods
avail·abil·i·ty
  pl avail·abil·i·ties

avail·able
av·er·age
aver·ment
avert
  to anticipate and
  ward off
  (*see* overt)

a vin·cu·lo ma·tri·
  mo·nii
a vin·cu·lo mor·tis
avi·ta·min·osis
  pl avi·ta·min·oses

avoid
avoid·able
avoid·ance
avow
avow·al
avow·ant
avow·ry
  pl avow·ries

avulse
  avulsed
  avuls·ing
avul·sion
award
award·ee
award·er
away-go·ing

ax·il·la
  pl ax·il·lae
  or ax·il·las

ax·il·lary
ax·i·om
ax·is
  pl ax·es

aye
  also ay
  pl ayes

ayun·ta·mien·to
  pl ayun·ta·mien·tos

B

bach·e·lor
ba·cil·la·ry
ba·cil·lus
  pl ba·cil·li

bac·i·tra·cin
back·ache
back·a·da·tion
  var of backwardation
back·ber·end
  or back·ber·and
  or back·bear·ing

back bond
back·bone
back·date
  back·dat·ed
  back·dat·ing
back-door ref·er·
  en·dum
  pl back-door ref·er·
    en·da
  or back-door ref·er·
    en·dums

back·er
back·ing
back-time
back to back
back·ward·ation
  or back·a·da·tion

bac·te·re·mia
  or bac·te·ri·e·mia
  also bac·te·ri·ae·mia

bac·te·ri·al
bac·te·ri·o·log·ic
  or bac·te·ri·o·log·i·cal

bac·te·ri·ol·o·gist
bac·te·ri·ol·o·gy
  pl bac·te·ri·ol·o·gies

bac·te·ri·um
  pl bac·te·ria

bade
  past of bid

bad·ger *vb*
  bad·gered
  bad·ger·ing
badg·es of fraud
baf·fle
  baf·fled
  baf·fling
baf·fle·ment
baf·fling
bag·as·so·sis
  pl bag·as·so·ses

bag·gage
bail
  security given
  (*see* bale)

bail·able
bail·ee

bai·liff
bai·li·wick
bail·ment
bail·or
   or bail·er

bail·piece
bails·man
   pl bails·men

bait
bait and switch
bal·ance
   bal·anced
   bal·anc·ing
bale
   a bundle of goods
   (*see* bail)

ball-and-sock·et
bal·last
bal·last·age
bal·lis·tic
bal·lis·ti·cal·ly
bal·lis·ti·cian
bal·lis·tics
bal·loon mort·gage
bal·lot
   bal·lot·ed
   bal·lot·ing
bal·lo·tage
bal·lot box
bal·lot·a·ble
bal·lotte·ment
ban
   banned
   ban·ning
ban·co·gi·ro

ban·dage
   ban·daged
   ban·dag·ing
ban·dit
ban·dit·ry
   pl ban·dit·ries

bane
bang
   var of bhang

Bang's dis·ease
ban·ish
ban·ish·ment
bank
bank·able
bank·er
bank·ing
bank note
bank·roll
bank·rupt
bank·rupt·cy
   pl bank·rupt·cies

banns *n pl*
bar
   barred
   bar·ring
bar·ag·no·sis
   pl bar·ag·no·ses

bar·bar·i·an
bar·bar·i·an·ism
bar·bar·ic
bar·bar·i·cal·ly
bar·bar·i·ous
bar·ba·rism
bar·bar·i·ty
   pl bar·bar·i·ties

bar·ba·ri·za·tion
bar·ba·rize
   bar·ba·rized
   bar·ba·riz·ing
bar·ba·rous
bar·ba·rous·ly
bar·ba·rous·ness
bar·ber's itch
bar·bi·tal
bar·bi·tone
bar·bi·tu·rate
bar·bi·tu·ric
bare
   bar·er
   bar·est
bare·boat
bar·et
bar ex·am·i·na·
   tion
bar·gain
bar·gain·able
bar·gain·ee
bar·gain·or
bar·i·to·sis
bar·mote
bar·on bai·lie
baro·ti·tis
baro·trau·ma
   pl baro·trau·ma·ta
   or baro·trau·mas

bar·rage
bar·ra·tor
   also bar·ra·ter
   or bar·re·tor

bar·ra·trous

bar·ra·trous·ly
bar·ra·try
also bar·re·try
pl bar·ra·tries
also bar·re·tries

bar·ren
bar·ren·ness
bar·ri·cade
bar·ri·cad·ed
bar·ri·cad·ing
bar·ris·ter
bar·ris·te·ri·al
bar·tend
bar·tend·er
bar·ter
bar·ter·er
bary·glos·sia
bary·la·lia
base
based
bas·ing
base fee
or base fee sim·ple

ba·sic en·try
ba·si·cra·ni·al
ba·si·fa·cial
ba·si·hy·oid
ba·si·oc·cip·i·tal
ba·sis
pl ba·ses

ba·si·tem·po·ral
ba·si·ver·te·bral
bas·tard
bas·tard eigne
bas·tard·iza·tion

bas·tard·ize
bas·tard·ized
bas·tard·iz·ing
bas·tard·ly
bas·tardy
pl bas·tard·ies

bas·ti·na·do
or bas·ti·nade
pl bas·ti·na·does
or bas·ti·nades

bat
ba·thos
bat·ter
bat·tered
bat·ter·ing
bat·tery
pl bat·ter·ies

bat·tle
bat·tled
bat·tling
bat·ture
bawd
bawd·i·ly
bawd·i·ness
bawdy
bawd·i·er
bawd·i·est
bay·gall
bay·o·net
bay·o·net·ed
also bay·o·net·ted
bay·o·net·ing
also bay·o·net·ting

bay·ou
bea·con

beano
pl beanos

bear
bore
borne
bear·ing
bear·er
beast
beat
beat
beat·en
or beat
beat·ing
bed·lam
bed·rid·den
bed·rock
be·fall
be·fell
be·fall·en
be·fall·ing
be·fore
be·fore·hand
beg
begged
beg·ging
beg·gar
beg·gar·li·ness
beg·gar·ly
be·get
be·got
be·got·ten
or be·got
be·get·ting
be·half
pl be·halves

be·hav·ior
be·hav·ior·al
be·hoof
  pl be·hooves

be·hoove
  or be·hove
  be·hooved
  or be·hoved
  be·hoov·ing
  or be·hov·ing

be·la·bor
be·li·bel
  be·li·beled
  or be·li·belled
  be·li·bel·ing
  or be·li·bel·ling

be·lief
be·liev·abil·i·ty
be·liev·able
be·liev·ably
be·lieve
  be·lieved
  be·liev·ing
bel·la·don·na
bel·li·cist
bel·li·cose
bel·li·cose·ly
bel·li·cos·i·ty
  pl bel·li·cos·i·ties

bel·lig·er·ence
bel·lig·er·en·cy
  pl bel·lig·er·en·cies

bel·lig·er·ent
bel·lig·er·ent·ly
bel·ly·ache

be·long
be·long·ing
bench
bench·er
bench mark
bends *n pl*
be·neath
bene·fact
bene·fac·tion
bene·fac·tive
bene·fac·tor
bene·fac·tress
  or bene·fac·trix
  pl bene·fac·tress·es
  or bene·fac·trix·es
  or bene·fac·tri·ces

be·nef·ic
ben·e·fice
be·nef·i·cence
be·nef·i·cent
ben·e·fi·cial
ben·e·fi·cial·ly
ben·e·fi·cia·ry
  pl ben·e·fi·cia·ries

ben·e·fi·ci·ate
  ben·e·fi·ci·at·ed
  ben·e·fi·ci·at·ing
ben·e·fi·ci·um
  pl ben·e·fi·cia

ben·e·fi·ci·um
di·vi·si·o·nis
ben·e·fi·ci·um
ex·cur·si·o·nis
  or ben·e·fi·ci·um
  dis·cus·si·o·nis
  or ben·e·fi·ci·um
  or·di·nis

ben·e·fi·ci·um
in·ven·ta·rii
ben·e·fit
  ben·e·fit·ed
  or ben·e·fit·ted
  ben·e·fit·ing
  or ben·e·fit·ting

be·nev·o·lence
be·nev·o·lent
be·nign
be·nig·nan·cy
  pl be·nig·nan·cies

be·nig·nant
be·nig·nant·ly
be·nig·ni·ty
  pl be·nig·ni·ties

be·nign·ly
benz·an·thra·cene
Ben·ze·drine
ben·zene
ben·zi·dine
ben·zine
  also ben·zin
ben·zo·caine
ben·zo·lism
be·queath
be·queath·al
be·queath·ment
be·quest
be·reave
  be·reaved
  or be·reft
  be·reav·ing
be·reave·ment
beri·beri

berm
ber·serk
Ber·til·lon sys·tem
be·ryl·li·o·sis
    also ber·yl·lo·sis
    pl ber·yl·li·o·ses
    also ber·yl·lo·ses

be·ryl·li·um
be·seech
    be·sought
        or be·seeched
    be·seech·ing
be·set
    be·set
    be·set·ting
be·set·ment
be·sides
be·speak
    be·spoke
    be·spo·ken
    be·speak·ing
best
    superlative of good
    superlative of well

bes·tial
bes·ti·al·i·ty
    pl bes·ti·al·i·ties

bes·tial·ize
    bes·tial·ized
    bes·tial·iz·ing
bes·tial·ly
be·stow
be·stow·al
bet
    bet
        or bet·ted

bet·ting
be·tray
be·tray·al
be·tray·er
be·troth
be·troth·al
be·trothed
be·troth·ment
bet·ter
    comparative of good
    comparative of well

bet·ter·ment
bet·tor
    or bet·ter

be·wil·der
    be·wil·dered
    be·wil·der·ing
be·wil·der·ment
be·yond seas
bhang
    also bang

bib·lio·clast
bib·lio·klept
bib·li·ot·ic
bib·li·ot·ics
bib·u·los·i·ty
    pl bib·u·los·i·ties
bib·u·lous
bi·cam·er·al
bi·ceps
    pl bi·ceps·es

bi·chlo·ride
bick·er
bi·cus·pid
bid

bade
    or bid
bid·den
    or bid
bid·ding
bid·der
bi·en·ni·al
bi·en·ni·al·ly
bi·en·ni·um
    pl bi·en·ni·ums
    or bi·en·nia

biens
bi·fo·cal
bi·fur·cat·ed tri·al
big·a·mist
big·a·mis·tic
big·a·mize
    big·a·mized
    big·a·miz·ing
big·a·mous
big·a·mous·ly
big·a·my
    pl big·a·mies

big·ot
big·ot·ed
big·ot·ed·ly
big·ot·ry
    pl big·ot·ries

bi·lat·er·al
bi·lat·er·al·ism
bi·lat·er·al·is·tic
bi·lat·er·al·i·ty
    pl bi·lat·er·al·i·ties

bi·lat·er·al·ly
bilge

bilged
bilg·ing
bilk
bill
bill·head
bill·ing
bill quia ti·met
bi·na·ry
  pl bi·na·ries

bi·na·tion·al
bind
  bound
  bind·ing
bind·er
bind over
  bound over
  bind·ing over
Bi·net age
Bi·net-Si·mon test
bin·go
  pl bin·gos

bin·oc·u·lar
bio·as·say
bio·chem·i·cal
bio·chem·is·try
  pl bio·chem·is·tries

bio·cid·al
bio·cide
bio·de·grad·abil·i·ty
  pl bio·de·grad·abil·i·ties

bio·de·grad·able
bio·deg·ra·da·tion
bio·de·grade
  bio·de·grad·ed

bio·de·grad·ing
bio·en·vi·ron·men·tal
bio·haz·ard
bi·op·sy
  pl bi·op·sies

bi·or·bit·al
bio·rhythm
bio·ryth·mic
bio·sta·tis·tics
bio·trans·for·ma·tion
bi·pa·ren·tal
bi·par·ti·san
  also bi·par·ti·zan

bi·par·tite
birth
birth con·trol
birth·mark
birth·rate
bi·sect·ing meth·od
bi·sexed
bi·sex·u·al
bi·sex·u·al·i·ty
bi·sex·u·al·ly
bis·muth
bis·muth·ia
bis·muth·ism
bis·muth·osis
bitch
bit·ing rule
black-and-blue
black·damp
black eye
black·jack

black·leg
black·list
black lung
black·mail
black·mail·er
black·mail·ing
black·out n
black out vb
blad·der
blam·able
  also blame·able

blame
  blamed
  blam·ing
blame·ful
blame·less
blame·less·ly
blame·wor·thi·ness
blame·wor·thy
blanc seign
blank
blan·ket
blan·ket·ed
blan·ket·ing
blas·phe·mous
blas·phe·mous·ly
blas·phe·my
  pl blas·phe·mies

blast
blast·ing
blas·to·my·co·sis
  pl blas·to·my·co·ses

bla·tan·cy
  pl bla·tan·cies

bla·tant

bleed
  bled
  bleed·ing
blend
blend·ed
blend·ing
blen·nor·rhea
  also blen·nor·rhoea

blen·nor·rhe·al
  also blen·nor·rhoe·al

bleph·a·ri·tis
  pl bleph·a·rit·i·des

bleph·a·ro·con·
  junc·ti·vi·tis
bleph·a·ro·spasm
blight·ed
blind
blind·ness
blind spot
blind ti·ger
bloc
  a usually temporary
    combination
  (*see* block)

block
  a tract of land
  (*see* bloc)

block·ade
block·age
block-book·ing
block-hol·er
block·ing pat·ent
blood
blood broth·er
blood group
blood group·ing

blood·hound
blood·let·ting
blood poi·son·ing
blood·shed
blood·shed·der
blood·shed·ding
blood·stream
blood·test
blood-type
  blood-typed
  blood-typ·ing
bloody *adj*
  blood·i·er
  blood·i·est
bloody *vb*
  blood·ied
  bloody·ing
blot·ter
blow·out *n*
blow out *vb*
  blew out
  blown out
  blow·ing out
blow up *vb*
  blew up
  blown up
  blow·ing up
blow-up *n*
blud·geon
  blud·geoned
  blud·geon·ing
blue law
blue note
blue·print
blue-sky
  blue-skied
    or blue-skyed

blue-sky·ing
  blue-skies
blue sky law
bluff
blum·ba
blun·der
blunt in·stru·ment
board
board·er
boat·able
bob·tail cov·er·age
bodi·ly
body
  pl bod·ies

body pol·i·tic
bo·gus
boil·ary
  pl boil·ar·ies

bois·ter·ous
bo·li·ta
  also bo·li·to

bol·ster
  bol·stered
  bol·ster·ing
bomb
bo·na *n pl*

bo·na ad·ven·ti·tia
  or bo·na ad·ven·ti·cia

bo·na con·fis·ca·ta
bo·na fi·de
bo·na fi·dei
bo·na fi·des
bo·na ges·tu·ra
bo·na gra·tia

bo·na im·mo·bi·lia
bo·na me·mo·ria
bo·na mo·bi·lia
bo·na no·ta·bi·lia
bo·na par·a·pher·
na·lia
bo·na per·i·tu·ra
bo·na va·can·tia
bo·na wa·vi·a·ta
bond
bond·able
bond·age
bond·ag·er
bond·ed
bond·hold·er
bond·less
bonds·man
   pl bonds·men

bone·set·ter
bon·i·fi·ca·tion
bo·no·rum pos·ses·
sio
bo·num fac·tum
bo·num va·cans
   pl bo·na va·can·tia

bo·nus
bony
   pl bonyes
boo·dle
   boo·dled
   boo·dling
book
book·ing
book·keep·er
book·keep·ing
book·mak·er

book·mak·ing
boom
boom·age
boon·dog·gle
   boon·dog·gled
   boon·dog·gling
boose
   var of booze
boost·er
boot
boot·leg
   boot·legged
   boot·leg·ging
boot·leg·ger
boot·strap doc·
trine
boo·ty
   pl boo·ties

boo·ty·less
booze
   also boose
bor·del·lo
   pl bor·del·los
bor·der
bor·de·reau
   pl bor·de·reaux

bor·der·ing
bore
   past of bear

born
   produced by birth
   (see borne)

borne
   past participle of bear
   (see born)

bor·ough

bor·row
bor·row·er
botch
bot·ryo·my·co·sis
   pl bot·ryo·my·co·ses

bot·ryo·my·cot·ic
bot·tom
bot·tom·ry
   pl bot·tom·ries

bot·u·lin
bot·u·li·num
   also bot·u·li·nus

bot·u·lism
bought
   past and past partici·
   ple of buy

bou·gie
bou·le·vard
bounc·er
bound
bound·ary
   pl bound·aries

boun·ty
   pl boun·ties

bourse
bow·el
bow·legged
boy·cott
bra·dy·car·dia
bra·dy·es·the·sia
bra·dy·glos·sia
bra·dy·ki·ne·sia
brain·case
brain·pan
brain·sick
brain·wash

branch
brand
brand·ed
brand·ing
brass knuck·les
also brass knucks

brawl
brawl·er
brawl·ing·ly
brawly
breach
an infraction of law
(*see* breech)

break
broke
bro·ken
break·ing
break·able
break·age
break down *vb*
break·down *n*
break·through
breath
breathe
breathed
breath·ing
breech
the hind part of the body
(*see* breach)

breth·ren *n pl*
breve
pl breves
or bre·via

bre·ve de er·ro·re
cor·ri·gen·da
bre·vet

bre·vet·ted
or brev·et·ed
bre·vet·ting
or bre·vet·ing

bre·vi·ate
brib·able
or bribe·able
bribe
bribed
brib·ing
brib·ee
brib·er
brib·ery
pl brib·er·ies

bride·well
bridge·work
brief
brief·case
brief·ing
brief·less
brief·ly
bring
brought
bring·ing
broach
broad·side
Bro·ca's apha·sia
bro·chure
bro·kage
broke
past of break

bro·ken
past participle of break

bro·ker
bro·ker·age

bro·ker·ly
bro·mide
bro·mine
bro·min·ism
bro·mism
bron·chi·al
bron·chi·ec·ta·sis
pl bron·chi·ec·ta·ses

bron·chi·ec·tat·ic
bron·chit·ic
bron·chi·tis
pl bron·chit·i·des

bron·cho·pneu·mo·nia
bron·chus
pl bron·chi

broth·el
broth·er
broth·er·ger·man
broth·er·in·law
pl broth·ers·in·law

brought
past and past participle of bring

Brown de·cree
bru·cel·lo·sis
pl bru·cel·lo·ses

bruise
bruised
bruis·ing
bru·tal
bru·tal·i·ty
pl bru·tal·i·ties

bru·tal·ize
bru·tal·ized
bru·tal·iz·ing

bru·tal·ly
bru·tal·ness
brute
brut·ish
brut·ish·ly
bru·tum ful·men
bub·ble
  bub·bled
  bub·bling
buc·cal
buck·et
  buck·et·ed
  buck·et·ing
buck·et·er
buck·et shop
bud·get
  bud·get·ed
  bud·get·ing
bud·get·ary
Buer·ger's dis·ease
bug·ger
bug·gery
build·er
build·ing
bulk·head
bul·let
bul·le·tin
bul·lion
bump
bun·co
  or bun·ko

bun·ker·age
bunk·house rule
buoy
  pl buoys

bur·den

bu·reau
  pl bu·reaus
  also bu·reaux

bu·reau·cra·cy
  pl bu·reau·cra·cies

bu·reau·crat
bu·reau·crat·ic
bu·reau·crat·i·cal·
  ly
bu·reau·cra·tism
bu·reau·cra·ti·za·
  tion
bu·reau·cra·tize
  bu·reau·cra·tized
  bu·reau·cra·tiz·
    ing
bur·gess
bur·glar
bur·glar·i·ous
bur·glar·i·ous·ly
bur·glar·ize
  bur·glar·ized
  bur·glar·iz·ing
bur·glar·proof
bur·glary
  pl bur·glar·ies

buri·al

burn
  burned
    or burnt
  burn·ing

bur·sa
  pl bur·sas
  or bur·sae

bur·sal
bur·sar

bur·sar·i·al
bur·sar·ship
bur·si·tis
bury
  bur·ied
  bury·ing
bush·whack
  also bush·wack

bush·whack·er
  also bush·wack·er
  also bush·whack

busi·ness
busy·body
  pl busy·bod·ies

but for rule
but·ter·worth·ing
but·tock
buy
  bought
  buy·ing
buy·er
buy·ing club
by-bid·der
by law
  according to law
  (see by-law)

by-law
  or bye-law
  a local or corporate
    rule
  (see by law)

by-prod·uct
bys·si·no·sis
  pl bys·si·no·ses

by·stand·er
by way of

C

ca·bal
  ca·balled
  ca·bal·ling
cab·a·ret
cab·i·net
cab·o·tage
cache
  cached
  cach·ing
ca·chec·tic
cache-sexe
ca·chet
  ca·cheted
  ca·chet·ing
ca·chex·ia
  also ca·chexy
  pl ca·chex·ias
  also ca·chex·ies

caco·ë·thes
ca·cog·ra·phy
cad
ca·das·tral
ca·das·tral·ly
ca·das·tre
ca·dav·er
ca·dav·er·ic
ca·dav·er·ous
ca·dav·er·ous·ly
ca·den·cy
  pl ca·den·cies

ca·det
cadge
  cadged
  cadg·ing

ca·dit quae·stio
cad·mi·um
cad·re
ca·du·ca
ca·du·ca·ry
  or ca·du·ci·ary

ca·du·ci·ary
  pl ca·du·ci·ar·ies

ca·du·ci·ty
  pl ca·du·ci·ties

cae·cal
  var of cecal

cae·cum
  var of cecum

cae·sar·e·an,
  cae·sar·i·an
  vars of cesarean

cae·si·um
  var of cesium

caf·feine
caf·fein·ic
cage
  caged
  cag·ing
ca·gey
  also ca·gy
  ca·gi·er
  ca·gi·est
ca·gey·ness
  or ca·gi·ness

ca·gi·ly
ca·hoots *n pl*
cain
cais·son
cai·tiff
ca·jole

ca·joled
ca·jol·ing
ca·jole·ment
ca·jol·ery
  pl ca·jol·er·ies

ca·jol·ing·ly
cal·a·boose
ca·lam·i·tous
ca·lam·i·tous·ly
ca·lam·i·tous·ness
ca·lam·i·ty
  pl ca·lam·i·ties

cal·ca·ne·al
  also cal·ca·ne·an

cal·ca·ne·um
  pl cal·ca·nea

cal·ca·ne·us
  pl cal·ca·nei

cal·car·e·ous
  also cal·car·i·ous

cal·ci·co·sis
  pl cal·ci·co·ses

cal·cif·er·ol
cal·cif·er·ous
cal·cif·ic
cal·ci·fi·ca·tion
cal·ci·fy
  cal·ci·fied
  cal·ci·fy·ing
cal·ci·no·sis
  pl cal·ci·no·ses

cal·ci·um
cal·cu·la·bil·i·ty
  pl cal·cu·la·bil·i·ties

cal·cu·la·ble

cal·cu·la·ble·ness
cal·cu·la·bly
cal·cu·late
  cal·cu·lat·ed
  cal·cu·lat·ing
cal·cu·lat·ing·ly
cal·cu·la·tion
cal·cu·la·tion·al
cal·cu·la·tive
cal·cu·la·tor
cal·cu·la·to·ry
cal·cu·lo·sis
  pl cal·cu·lo·ses

cal·cu·lous
cal·en·dar
  cal·en·dared
  cal·en·dar·ing
cal·i·ber
  or cal·i·bre

cal·i·brate
  cal·i·brat·ed
  cal·i·brat·ing
call·back
call girl
call house
call·ing
cal·los·i·ty
  pl cal·los·i·ties

cal·lous
cal·loused
cal·lous·ly
cal·lous·ness
cal·low
cal·low·ness
call up *vb*
call-up *n*

cal·lus
  or cal·lous
  pl cal·lus·es
  or cal·lous·es
  also cal·li

calm·ant
calm·ative
cal·o·mel
cal·o·rie
  also cal·o·ry
  pl cal·o·ries

cal·um·ni·ate
  cal·um·ni·at·ed
  cal·um·ni·at·ing
cal·um·ni·a·tion
cal·um·ni·a·tor
cal·um·ni·ous
cal·um·ni·ous·ly
cal·um·ny
  pl cal·um·nies

cal·var·ia
  pl cal·var·ias

cal·var·i·al
cal·var·i·um
  pl cal·var·ia
cal·vi·ti·es
  pl cal·vi·ti·es

calx
  pl calx·es
  or cal·ces

cam·bist
cam·bist·ry
  pl cam·bist·ries

cam·era
  pl cam·er·as
  also cam·er·ae

cam·er·al

cam·er·a·lism
cam·er·a·list
cam·er·a·lis·tic
cam·er·a·lis·tics
cam·i·sole
cam·ou·flage
cam·paign
  cam·paigned
  cam·paign·ing
cam·paign·er
camp·er
camp fol·low·er
cam·pus
  pl cam·pus·es
  also cam·pi

ca·nal
  ca·nalled
  or ca·naled
  ca·nal·ling
  or ca·nal·ing

ca·nal·boat
can·a·li·za·tion
can·a·lize
  can·a·lized
  can·a·liz·ing
ca·nard
  pl ca·nards

can·cel
  can·celed
  or can·celled
  can·cel·ing
  or can·cel·ling

can·cel·able
  or can·cel·la·ble

can·cel·er
  or can·cel·ler

can·cel·la·tion
  also can·cel·ation

can·cer

can·cer·ate
  can·cer·at·ed
  can·cer·at·ing
can·cer·iza·tion
can·cer·o·gen·ic
  or can·cer·i·gen·ic

can·cer·ol·o·gist
can·cer·ol·o·gy
  pl can·cer·ol·o·gies

can·cer·ous
can·cer·pho·bia
  or can·cer·o·pho·bia
can·croid
can·crum oris
  pl can·cra oris

can·did
can·di·da
can·di·da·cy
  pl can·di·da·cies

can·di·date
can·di·da·ture
can·di·di·a·sis
  pl can·di·di·a·ses

can·did·ly
can·did·ness
  pl can·did·ness·es

can·dor
cane
  caned
  can·ing
can·ker
  can·kered
  can·ker·ing

can·ker·ous
can·na·bi·di·ol
can·na·bin
can·na·bi·nol
can·na·bis
can·na·bis in·di·ca
  pl can·na·bes in·di·cae

can·na·bism
can·na·bis sa·ti·va
  pl can·na·bes sa·ti·vae

can·ni·bal
can·ni·bal·ism
can·ni·bal·is·tic
can·ni·bal·is·ti·cal·ly

can·ni·bal·iza·tion
can·ni·bal·ize
  can·ni·bal·ized
  can·ni·bal·iz·ing
can·non·ism
can·nu·la
  also can·u·la
  pl can·nu·las
  or can·nu·lae
  also can·u·las
  or can·u·lae

can·nu·late
  can·nu·lat·ed
  can·nu·lat·ing
can·nu·la·tion
can·on
ca·non·i·cal
can·on·ist
can·on·is·tic
can·on·ry
  pl can·on·ries

can·thar·i·dal

can·thar·i·date
  can·thar·i·dat·ed
  can·thar·i·dat·ing
can·tha·rid·i·an
  or can·tha·rid·e·an

can·thar·i·din
can·thar·i·dism
can·thar·i·dize
  can·thar·i·dized
  can·thar·i·diz·ing
can·tha·ris
  pl can·thar·i·des

can·ton
can·u·la
  var of cannula

can·vass
  also can·vas
  can·vassed
  also can·vased
  can·vass·ing
  also can·vas·ing

can·vass·er

ca·pa·bil·i·ty
  pl ca·pa·bil·i·ties

ca·pa·ble
ca·pa·ble·ness
ca·pa·bly
ca·pac·i·ty
  pl ca·pac·i·ties

ca·per
ca·pi·as
  pl ca·pi·as·es

ca·pi·as ad
  fa·ci·en·dum
ca·pi·as ad
  re·spon·den·dum
ca·pi·as ad
  sa·tis·fa·ci·en·
    dum
ca·pi·as pro fine
cap·il·lary
  pl cap·il·lar·ies

ca·pi·ta
  pl of caput

cap·i·tal
cap·i·tal bud·get
cap·i·tal gain
cap·i·tal·ism
cap·i·tal·ist
cap·i·tal·is·tic
cap·i·tal·is·ti·cal·ly
cap·i·tal·iza·tion
cap·i·tal·ize
  also cap·i·tal·ise
  cap·i·tal·ized
  also cap·i·tal·ised
  cap·i·tal·iz·ing
  also cap·i·tal·is·ing

cap·i·tal loss
cap·i·tal·ly
ca·pi·ta·re
cap·i·ta·tim
cap·i·ta·tion
cap·i·tel·lum
  pl cap·i·tel·la

ca·pit·u·lar
ca·pit·u·lary
  pl ca·pit·u·lar·ies

ca·pit·u·late
ca·pit·u·lat·ed
ca·pit·u·lat·ing
ca·pit·u·la·tion
ca·pit·u·la·tor
ca·pit·u·la·to·ry
cap·per
ca·price
ca·pri·cious
ca·pri·cious·ly
cap·size
  cap·sized
  cap·siz·ing
cap·sule
cap·tain
cap·tain·cy
  pl cap·tain·cies

cap·ta·tion
cap·tion
cap·tious
cap·tive
cap·tiv·i·ty
  pl cap·tiv·i·ties

cap·tor
cap·tress
  pl cap·tress·es

cap·ture
  cap·tured
  cap·tur·ing
ca·put
  pl ca·pi·ta

ca·put
  suc·ce·da·ne·um
  pl ca·pi·ta suc·ce·da·nea

car·at
  weight
  (*see* caret)

car·a·van
car·bo·late
car·bo·lat·ed
car·bo·lat·ing
car·bol·ic
car·bon·iza·tion
car·bon·ize
car·bon·ized
car·bon·iz·ing
car·bun·cle
car·bun·cu·lar
car·bun·cu·lo·sis
  pl car·bun·cu·lo·ses

car·cass
  pl car·cass·es

car·cin·o·gen
car·ci·no·gen·e·sis
  pl car·ci·no·gen·e·ses

car·ci·no·gen·ic
car·ci·no·ge·nic·i·ty
car·ci·noid
car·ci·no·ma
  pl car·ci·no·mas
  or car·ci·no·ma·ta

car·ci·no·ma·toid
car·ci·no·ma·to·sis
  pl car·ci·no·ma·to·ses

car·ci·no·ma·tous
car·ci·no·sar·co·ma
  pl car·ci·no·sar·co·mas
  or car·ci·no·sar·co·
    ma·ta

car·ci·no·sis
  pl car·ci·no·ses

car·dia
  pl car·di·ae
  or car·di·as

car·di·ac
car·di·nal
car·di·o·log·ic
car·di·o·log·i·cal
car·di·ol·o·gist
car·di·ol·o·gy
  pl car·di·ol·o·gies
car·dio·path
car·di·op·a·thy
  pl car·di·op·a·thies
car·dio·re·spi·ra·to·ry
car·di·or·rha·phy
  pl car·di·or·rha·phies
car·dio·ther·a·py
  pl car·dio·ther·a·pies
car·dio·tox·ic
car·dio·vas·cu·lar
card·room
card·sharp·er
  or card·sharp

care
  cared
  car·ing
care·free
care·ful
care·ful·ly
care·ful·ness
care·less
care·less·ly
care·less·ness
car·et
  mark
  (*see* carat)
care·tak·er
care·tak·ing

car·go
  pl car·goes
  or car·gos
car·i·ca·ture
car·load
car·lot
car·nage
car·nal
car·nal·i·ty
  pl car·nal·i·ties
car·nal knowl·edge
car·ni·fi·ca·tion
car·ni·fi·cial
car·ni·val
ca·rot·id
ca·rous·al
  drunken party
  (*see* carrousel)
ca·rouse
  ca·roused
  ca·rous·ing
car·ou·sel
  var of carrousel
ca·rous·er
ca·rous·ing·ly
car·pal
car·pa·le
  pl car·pa·lia
car·pec·to·my
  pl car·pec·to·mies
car·po·car·pal
car·po·meta·car·pal
car·po·pha·lan·ge·al

car·pus
  pl car·pi
  wrist
  (*see* corpus)

car·riage
car·riage·able
car·riage·way
car·ri·er
car·rou·sel
  or car·ou·sel
  merry-go-round,
  conveyor
  (*see* carousal)

car·ry
  carried
  car·ry·ing
car·ry back *vb*
car·ry-back *n*
car·ry·ing-on
  pl car·ry·ings-on

car·ry on
  car·ried on
  car·ry·ing on
cart·age
cart-bote
carte blanche
  pl cartes blanches

car·tel
car·tel·ism
car·tel·ist
  or car·tel·is·tic
car·tel·iza·tion
  or car·tel·li·za·tion
car·ti·lage
car·ti·lag·i·noid

car·ti·lag·i·nous
  or car·ti·la·gin·e·ous

car·tog·ra·phy
  pl car·tog·ra·phies

car·to·man·cy
  pl car·to·man·cies

car·tridge
car·tu·lary
  pl car·tu·la·ries

cart·way
carve
  carved
  carv·ing
Ca·sa·no·va's
  char·ter
case
  cased
  cas·ing
ca·se·ate
  ca·se·at·ed
  ca·se·at·ing
ca·se·ation
case·book
case·made
ca·se·ous
cas for·tu·it
ca·shier·*vb*
cash·ier·*n*
cas·ing
cas·ing·head
ca·si·no
  pl ca·si·nos

cas·ket
cas·sa·tion
cast

cast
cast·ing
cast·away
caste
caste·less
cas·ti·gate
  cas·ti·gat·ed
  cas·ti·gat·ing
cas·ti·ga·tion
cas·ti·ga·tor
cas·ti·ga·to·ry
cas·tle
cast off *vb*
cast off
cast·ing off
cast·off *n*
cast-off *adj*
cas·trate
  cas·trat·ed
  cas·trat·ing
cas·tra·tion
ca·su·al
  not planned
  (see causal)

ca·su·al·ly
  by chance or accident
  (see casualty)

ca·su·al·ty
  pl ca·su·al·ties
  one injured or
  killed
  (see casually)

ca·su·ist
ca·su·is·tic
ca·su·is·ti·cal
ca·su·ist·ry
  pl ca·su·ist·ries

ca·sus bel·li
  pl ca·sus bel·li

ca·sus foe·de·ris
  pl ca·sus foe·de·ris

ca·sus for·tu·i·tus
  pl ca·sus for·tu·i·ti

ca·sus omis·sus
  pl ca·sus omis·si

cat
  cat·ted
  cat·ting
cat·a·bol·ic
ca·tab·o·lism
  also ka·tab·o·lism

ca·tab·o·lize
  ca·tab·o·lized
  ca·tab·o·liz·ing
cat·a·lep·sy
  pl cat·a·lep·sies

cat·a·lep·tic
cat·a·lep·ti·cal·ly
cat·a·log
  or cat·a·logue
cat·a·loged
  or cat·a·logued
cat·a·log·ing
  or cat·a·logu·ing

cat·a·lo·gia
cata·me·nia
cata·me·ni·al
cat·a·mite
cat·am·ne·sis
  pl cat·am·ne·ses

cat·am·nes·tic
cata·pha·sia
cat·a·plec·tic

cat·a·plexy
  pl cat·a·plex·ies

cat·a·ract

cat·a·rac·tous

ca·tarrh

ca·tarrh·al

ca·tarrh·al·ly

ca·tas·tro·phe

cat·a·stroph·ic
  or ca·tas·tro·phal
  also cat·a·stroph·i·cal

cat·a·stroph·i·cal·ly

cata·to·nia
  also cata·to·ny
  pl cata·to·nias
  also cata·to·nies

cata·ton·ic

catch
  caught
  catch·ing

catch·all

catch·ment

catch·pen·ny

catch·pole
  or catch·poll

cat·e·gor·i·cal
  also cat·e·gor·ic

ca·ter-cous·in

ca·thar·sis
  also ka·thar·sis
  pl ca·thar·ses
  also ka·thar·ses

ca·thar·tic
  also ka·thar·tic

ca·thar·ti·cal·ly

cath·e·ter

cath·e·ter·iza·tion

cath·e·ter·ize
  cath·e·ter·ized
  cath·e·ter·iz·ing

cat·house

cat-o'-nine tails
  pl cat-o'-nine tails

Cau·ca·sian

cau·cus
  cau·cused
  cau·cus·ing

cau·dal

cau·sa
  pl cau·sae

caus·al
  being a cause
  (*see* casual)

cau·sal·gia

cau·sal·gic

cau·sal·i·ty
  pl cau·sal·i·ties

caus·al·ly

cau·sa mor·tis

cau·sa pri·ma

cau·sa prox·i·ma

cau·sa qua su·pra

cau·sa re·mo·ta

cau·sa se·cun·da

cau·sa si·ne qua non

cau·sa·tion

cause
  caused
  caus·ing

cause cé·lè·bre
  pl causes cé·lè·bres

cause·less

cause·less·ly

caus·er

cause·way

caus·tic

cau·tio
  pl cau·ti·o·nes

cau·tion

cau·tion·ary

cau·tion·er

cau·tious

cau·tious·ly

cau·tious·ness

ca·va
  pl ca·vae

ca·val

ca·ve·at
  ca·ve·at·ed
  ca·ve·at·ing

ca·ve·at ac·tor

ca·ve·a·tee

ca·ve·at emp·tor

ca·ve·at·or

ca·ve·at ven·di·tor

cav·i·tate
  cav·i·tat·ed
  cav·i·tat·ing

cav·i·ta·tion

cav·i·ty
  pl cav·i·ties

cease
  ceased
  ceas·ing

cease-and-de·sist

ce·cal
  or cae·cal

ce·ci·tis

ce·cum
or cae·cum
pl ce·ca
or cae·ca

cede
ced·ed
ced·ing

ce·dent
also ce·dens
pl ce·dents
also ce·dens·es

ce·la·tion

cel·e·brate
cel·e·brat·ed
cel·e·brat·ing

ce·li·ac
or coe·li·ac

cel·i·ba·cy
pl cel·i·ba·cies

cel·i·bate

cell·block

cel·lu·li·tis

ce·lom
var of coelom

ce·lo·mic
var of coelomic

cem·e·tery
pl cem·e·ter·ies

cen·ser
vessel for incense
(see censor, censure*)*

cen·sor
cen·sored
cen·sor·ing
to examine writings
for improper con-
tent
(see censer, censure*)*

cen·sor·able

cen·sor·ate

cen·so·ri·al

cen·so·ri·ous

cen·so·ri·ous·ly

cen·so·ri·ous·ness

cen·sor·ship

cen·sure
cen·sured
cen·sur·ing
to express dis-
approval of
(see censer, censor*)*

cen·sure·less

cen·sur·er

cen·sus

cen·ter

cen·te·sis
pl cen·te·ses

cen·ti·grade

cen·ti·gram

cen·ti·li·ter

cen·ti·me·ter

cen·tral

cen·tral·i·ty

cen·tral·iza·tion

cen·tral·ize
cen·tral·ized
cen·tral·iz·ing
cen·tral·iz·er

cen·tral·ly

cen·trist

cen·trum
pl cen·trums
or cen·tra

cen·tu·ry doc·trine

ceph·a·lal·gia

ce·phal·ic

ceph·a·lop·a·thy
pl ceph·a·lop·a·thies

ceph·a·lo·pel·vic

ceph·a·lo·tho·rac·ic

ceph·a·lot·o·my
pl ceph·a·lot·o·mies

ce·ra im·pres·sa

cer·a·tin
var of keratin

cer·a·ti·tis
var of keratitis

cer·a·to·con·junc·ti·vi·tis
var of keratocon-
junctivitis

cer·car·ia
pl cer·car·i·ae

cer·e·bel·lar

cer·e·bel·lum
pl cer·e·bel·lums
or cer·e·bel·la

ce·re·bral

ce·re·bral-pal·sied

cer·e·brate
cer·e·brat·ed
cer·e·brat·ing

cer·e·bra·tion

ce·re·bro·scle·ro·sis
pl ce·re·bro·scle·ro·ses

ce·re·bro·spi·nal

ce·re·bro·vas·cu·lar

ce·re·brum
pl ce·re·brums
or ce·re·bra

cer·e·mo·ni·al
cer·e·mo·ni·al·ly
cer·e·mo·ni·ous
cer·e·mo·ni·ous·ly
cer·e·mo·ni·ous·
  ness
cer·e·mo·ny
  pl cer·e·mo·nies

cer·tain
cer·tain·ly
cer·tain·ness
cer·tain·ty
  pl cer·tain·ties

cer·ti·fi·able
cer·ti·fi·ably
cer·tif·i·cate
  cer·tif·i·cat·ed
  cer·tif·i·cat·ing
cer·ti·fi·ca·tion
cer·tif·i·ca·to·ry
cer·ti·fi·er
cer·ti·fy
  cer·ti·fied
  cer·ti·fy·ing
cer·tio·ra·ri
cer·ti·tude
cer·vi·cal
cer·vi·ci·tis
cer·vix
  pl cer·vi·ces
  or cer·vix·es

cer·vix ute·ri

ce·sar·e·an
  or ce·sar·i·an
  also cae·sar·e·an
  or cae·sar·i·an

ce·si·um
  also cae·si·um

cess
ces·sa·tion
ces·ser
ces·set pro·ces·sus
ces·sio bo·no·rum
ces·sion
ces·sio·naire
ces·sion·ary
ces·sion·ee
ces·tui
ces·tui que trust
  pl ces·tui que trust
  also ces·tuis que trust·
    ent

ces·tui que use
  pl ces·tuis que use

ces·tui que vie
  pl ces·tuis que vie

chace
  var of chase

chain
chain·man
  pl chain·men

chair
chair·la·dy
  pl chair·la·dies

chair·man n
  pl chair·men

chair·man vb
  chair·maned
    or chair·manned
  chair·man·ing
    or chair·man·ning

chair·man·ship

chair·per·son
chair·wom·an
  pl chair·wom·en

cha·la·zi·on
  pl cha·la·zia

chal·co·sis
  copper in body tissue
  (see chalicosis)

chal·i·co·sis
  pl chal·i·co·ses
  industrial lung disease
  (see chalcosis)

chal·lenge
  chal·lenged
  chal·leng·ing
chal·lenge·able
chal·leng·er
chal·leng·ing·ly
cham·ber
cham·ber·lain
cham·per·tor
cham·per·tous
cham·per·ty
  also cham·par·ty
  pl cham·per·ties
  also cham·par·ties

cham·pi·on
cham·pi·on·ship
chance
  chanced
  chanc·ing
chan·cel·lery
  or chan·cel·lory
  pl chan·cel·ler·ies
  or chan·cel·lor·ies

chan·cel·lor
chan·cel·lor·ate

chan·cel·lor·ship

chance·man
pl chance·men

chance-med·ley
pl chance-med·leys

chan·cer
chan·cered
chan·cer·ing
chan·cery
pl chan·cer·ies

chan·cre
chan·cri·form
chan·croid
chan·croi·dal
chan·crous
chan·nel
chan·neled
or chan·nelled
chan·nel·ing
or chan·nel·ling

cha·os
cha·ot·ic
cha·ot·i·cal·ly
cha·ot·ic·ness
chap·ter
chap·ter 10
chap·ter 11
chap·ter 12
char·ac·ter
char·ac·ter·iza·tion
char·ac·ter·ize
char·ac·ter·ized
char·ac·ter·iz·ing
char·ac·ter·olog·i·
cal

char·ac·ter·olog·i·
cal·ly
char·ac·ter·ol·o·
gist
char·ac·ter·ol·o·gy
pl char·ac·ter·ol·o·gies

cha·ras
or chur·rus
also chur·us

Char·cot joint
charge
charged
charg·ing
charge·able
charge-a-plate
char·gé d'af·faires
pl char·gés d'af·faires

charg·ee
charg·er
char·i·ta·ble
char·i·ty
pl char·i·ties

char·la·tan
char·la·tan·ic
or char·la·tan·i·cal

char·la·tan·ish
char·la·tan·ism
char·la·tan·ry
also char·la·tan·ery
or char·la·tan·erie
pl char·la·tan·ries
also char·la·tan·eries

char·ley horse
char·ter
char·tered
char·ter·ing

char·ter·er
char·ter par·ty
chase
also chace
chased
also chaced
chas·ing
also chac·ing

chaste
chast·er
chast·est
chaste·ly
chas·tise
chas·tised
chas·tis·ing
chas·tise·ment
chas·tis·er
chas·ti·ty
pl chas·ti·ties

chat·tel
chat·tel·ism
chat·tel·iza·tion
chat·tel·ize
chat·tel·ized
chat·tel·iz·ing
chauf·feur
chauf·feuse
cheap-jack
also cheap-john

cheat
cheat·er
cheat·ery
or cheat·ry
pl cheat·er·ies
or cheat·ries

cheat·ing·ly

check
check·book
check off *vb*
check·off *n*
check out *vb*
check·out *n*
check up *vb*
check·up *n*
chei·li·on
chei·li·ous
chei·li·tis
  or chi·li·tis
chei·lo·car·ci·no·
ma
  pl chei·lo·car·ci·no·
  mas
  or chei·lo·car·ci·no·
  ma·ta
chei·lo·plas·ty
  pl chei·lo·plas·ties
chei·ro·spasm
  or chi·ro·spasm
che·loid
  var of keloid
chem·i·cal
chem·i·cal·ly
che·min de fer
  pl che·mins de fer
chem·ist
chem·is·try
  pl chem·is·tries
che·mo·pro·phy·
lac·tic
che·mo·pro·phy·
lax·is
  pl che·mo·pro·phy·
  lax·es

che·mo·sen·si·tive
che·mo·sen·si·tiv·i·
ty
  pl che·mo·sen·si·tiv·
  i·ties
che·mo·sis
  pl che·mo·ses
che·mo·ster·il·ant
che·mo·ster·il·iza·
tion
che·mo·ster·il·ize
che·mo·ster·il·
ized
che·mo·ster·il·iz·
ing
che·mo·sur·gi·cal
che·mo·sur·gery
  pl che·mo·sur·ger·ies
che·mo·ther·a·peu·
tic
  or che·mo·ther·a·
  peu·ti·cal
che·mo·ther·a·peu·
ti·cal·ly
che·mo·ther·a·peu·
tics
che·mo·ther·a·pist
che·mo·ther·a·py
  pl che·mo·ther·a·pies
che·mot·ic
cheque
  British var of check
chev·i·sance
Cheyne-Stokes
res·pi·ra·tion
  or Cheyne-Stokes
  breath·ing

chi·cane
  chi·caned
  chi·can·ing
chi·can·er
chi·ca·nery
  pl chi·ca·ner·ies

chick·en pox
chief
chief·ly
child
  pl chil·dren

child·bear·ing
child·bed
child·birth
child·less
child·less·ness
chi·li·tis
  var of cheilitis

chill·ing the bid·
ding
  or chill·ing a sale

chin·a·crin,
  chin·a·crine
  vars of quinacrine

chin·bone
chin·cho·na,
  chin·co·na
  vars of cinchona

chin·o·line
  var of quinoline

chi·ro·meg·a·ly
  pl chi·ro·meg·a·lies
chi·rop·o·dist
chi·rop·o·dy
  pl chi·rop·o·dies

chi·ro·prac·tic
chi·ro·prac·tor
chi·ro·prax·is
chi·ro·spasm
   var of cheirospasm

chis·el
   chis·eled
     or chis·elled
   chis·el·ing
     or chis·el·ling

chis·el·er
   or chis·el·ler

chlor·ac·ne
chlo·ral
chlo·ral hy·drate
chlo·ral·ism
chlo·ra·lose
chlo·ra·mine
chlor·am·phen·i·col
chlor·dane
   or chlor·dan

chlo·rine
chlor·mez·a·none
chlo·ro·bu·ta·nol
   also chlor·bu·ta·nol

chlo·ro·form
chlo·ro·form·ism
chlo·rop·sia
chlor·prom·a·zine
chlor·tet·ra·cy·cline
choice
choke
   choked
   chok·ing

choke·damp
chok·er
cho·le·cyst
   also cho·le·cys·tis

cho·le·lith
cho·le·li·thi·a·sis
   pl cho·le·li·thi·a·ses

cho·les·ter·ic
cho·les·ter·ol
cho·les·ter·ol·emia
   also cho·les·ter·ol·ae·mia
   or cho·les·ter·emia
   or cho·les·ter·ae·mia

chon·dri·fi·ca·tion
chon·dri·fy
   chon·dri·fied
   chon·dri·fy·ing
chon·dro·cos·tal
chon·dro·dys·tro·phic
chon·dro·dys·tro·phy
   or chon·dro·dys·tro·phia
   pl chon·dro·dys·tro·phies
   or chon·dro·dys·tro·phi·as

chon·dro·ma
   pl chon·dro·mas
   also chon·dro·ma·ta

chon·drom·a·tous
chon·dro·sar·co·ma
   pl chon·dro·sar·co·mas
   also chon·dro·sar·co·ma·ta

chon·dro·sep·tum
   pl chon·dro·sep·ta
   or chon·dro·sep·tums

chon·dro·sis
   pl chon·dro·ses

chon·dro·ster·nal
chon·dro·xi·phoid
choose
   chose
   cho·sen
   choos·ing
Cho·part's joint
chor·dee
chor·di·tis
cho·rea
cho·re·al
cho·re·ic
cho·re·i·form
cho·reo·ath·e·toid
   or cho·reo·ath·e·tot·ic

cho·reo·ath·e·to·sis
   pl cho·reo·ath·e·to·ses

cho·ri·oid
cho·ri·on
cho·ri·on·ic
cho·ri·op·tic
chose
chose in ac·tion
chose in pos·ses·sion
chose ju·gée
chouse
   choused
   chous·ing
Chris·tian name
chron·ic

chron·i·cal·ly
chro·nic·i·ty
   pl chro·nic·i·ties

chuck-a-luck
   also chuck-luck

chur·rus,
   chur·us
   vars of charras

chy·lo·peri·to·ne·
   um
chy·lo·tho·rax
   pl chy·lo·tho·rax·es
   or chy·lo·tho·ra·ces

cic·a·tri·cial
ci·ca·trix
   pl ci·ca·tri·ces
   also ci·ca·trix·es

cic·a·tri·zant
cic·a·tri·za·tion
cic·a·trize
   cic·a·trized
   cic·a·triz·ing
cin·cho·na
   also chin·cho·na
   or chin·co·na

cin·cho·nism
cin·cho·nize
   cin·cho·nized
   cin·cho·niz·ing
cin·e·plas·tic
cin·e·plas·ty
   also kin·e·plas·ty
   pl cin·e·plas·ties
   also kin·e·plas·ties

ci·on
   var of scion

cir·ca
cir·cuit
cir·cuit·al
cir·cuit·er
   also cir·cui·teer

cir·cu·itous
cir·cu·itous·ly
cir·cu·ity
   pl cir·cu·ities

cir·cu·lar
cir·cu·lar·ize
   cir·cu·lar·ized
   cir·cu·lar·iz·ing
cir·cu·late
   cir·cu·lat·ed
   cir·cu·lat·ing
cir·cu·la·tion
cir·cum·am·bu·
   late
   cir·cum·am·
      bu·lat·ed
   cir·cum·am·
      bu·lat·ing
cir·cum·am·bu·la·
   tion
cir·cum·anal
cir·cum·cise
   cir·cum·cised
   cir·cum·cis·ing
cir·cum·ci·sion
cir·cum·stance
cir·cum·stan·tial
cir·cum·stan·tial·
   ly
cir·cum·stan·ti·ate

cir·cum·stan·ti·
   at·ed
cir·cum·stan·ti·
   at·ing
cir·cum·ven·tion
cir·rho·sis
   pl cir·rho·ses

cir·rhot·ic
ci·ta·tion
ci·ta·tor
ci·ta·to·ry
cite
   cit·ed
   cit·ing
   to summon; to quote
   (*see* sight, site)

cit·i·zen
cit·i·zen·ly
cit·i·zen·ry
   pl cit·i·zen·ries

cit·i·zen·ship
city
   pl cit·ies

civ·ic
civ·i·cal·ly
civ·il
ci·vil·ian
ci·vi·li·ter mor·tu·
   us
civ·i·li·za·tion
civ·i·lize
   civ·i·lized
   civ·i·liz·ing
civ·il·ly
ci·vi·tas
   pl ci·vi·ta·tes

claim
claim·ant
claim·er
claim·less
clan·des·tine
clan·des·tine·ly
clan·des·tin·i·ty
clar·i·fi·ca·tion
clar·i·fy
  clar·i·fied
  clar·i·fy·ing
clash
class
clas·si·fi·ca·tion
clas·si·fy
  clas·si·fied
  clas·si·fy·ing
clau·di·ca·tion
clause
claus·tro·phobe
claus·tro·pho·bia
claus·tro·pho·bic
  or claus·tro·pho·bi·ac
clav·i·cle
cla·vic·u·la
  pl cla·vic·u·lae
cla·vic·u·lar
claw back *vb*
claw-back *n*
clean
clean hands
clean up *vb*
clean·up *n*
clean-up *adj*

clear
  cleared
  clear·ing
clear·ance
clear·ing house
clear·ly
clear·ness
clei·do·cos·tal
clei·do·cra·ni·al
clem·en·cy
  pl clem·en·cies
clem·ent
clep·to·ma·nia
  var of kleptomania
clep·to·ma·ni·ac
  var of kleptomaniac
cler·i·cal
clerk
clerk·ly
clerk·ship
cli·ent
cli·en·tal
  relating to clients
  (*see* clientele)
cli·en·tele
  a body of clients
  (*see* cliental)
cli·ent·less
cli·mac·te·ri·al
cli·mac·ter·ic
cli·mac·te·ri·um
  pl cli·mac·te·ria
clin·ic
clin·i·cal
clin·i·cal·ly

cli·ni·cian
clin·i·co·path·o·
  log·ic
  also clin·i·co·path·o·
  log·i·cal
clip joint
cli·to·ral
  or cli·tor·ic
cli·to·ri·dec·to·my
  pl cli·to·ri·dec·to·mies
cli·to·ri·di·tis
cli·to·ris
  pl cli·to·ris·es
cli·to·ri·tis
cloak-and-dag·ger
clog
  clogged
  clog·ging
clo·mi·phene
clon·ic
clo·nic·i·ty
  pl clo·nic·i·ties
clo·nism
clo·nus
close
  closed
  clos·ing
closed-end
close·ly
clos·trid·i·al
  or clos·trid·i·an
clos·trid·i·um
  pl clos·trid·ia
clo·sure

clo·sured
clo·sur·ing
clot
  clot·ted
  clot·ting
clothe
  clothed
    or clad
  cloth·ing

clo·ture
  clo·tured
  clo·tur·ing
co·ac·cused
co·act
co·ac·tion
co·ad·ven·tur·er
co·ag·u·la·bil·i·ty
  pl co·ag·u·la·bil·i·ties

co·ag·u·la·ble
co·ag·u·lant
co·ag·u·late
  co·ag·u·lat·ed
  co·ag·u·lat·ing
co·ag·u·la·tion
co·ag·u·la·tive
co·ag·u·lum
  pl co·ag·u·la

co·alesce
  co·alesced
  co·alesc·ing
co·ali·tion
co·ali·tion·al
co·ali·tion·ist
  or co·ali·tion·er

co·ap·pel·lee
co·apt
co·ap·ta·tion
co·arct
co·arc·ta·tion
coast·er
coast·ing
coast·wise
co·au·thor
co·balt
co·balt 60
co·ben·e·fi·cia·ry
  pl co·ben·e·fi·cia·ries

co·ca
co·caine
co·cain·ism
co·cain·iza·tion
co·cain·ize
  co·cain·ized
  co·cain·iz·ing
coc·cal
coc·cus
  pl coc·ci

coc·cy·geal
coc·cy·go·dyn·ia
coc·cyx
  pl coc·cy·ges
  also coc·cyx·es

co·chlea
  pl co·chle·as
  or co·chle·ae

co·chle·ar
co·chleo·ves·tib·
  u·lar
co·con·spir·a·tor

co·con·trac·tor
co·cotte
cod·al
code
  cod·ed
  cod·ing
co·debt·or
co·de·fen·dant
co·deine
code·less
co·dex
  pl co·di·ces

cod·i·cil
cod·i·cil·la·ry
cod·i·fi·ca·tion
cod·i·fy
  cod·i·fied
  cod·i·fy·ing
coe·li·ac
  var of celiac

coe·lom
  also coe·lome
  or ce·lom
  pl coe·loms
  or coe·lo·ma·ta
  also coe·lomes
  or ce·loms

coe·lo·mic
  or ce·lo·mic

co·em·ployee
  or co·em·ploye

co·emp·tio
co·emp·tion
co·emp·tive
co·equal
co·equal·i·ty

co·equal·ly
co·erce
 co·erced
 co·erc·ing
co·erc·ible
co·er·cion
co·er·cive
co·er·cive·ly
co·ex·ist
co·ex·is·tent
co·ex·ten·sive
co·ex·ten·sive·ly
cof·fer
 cof·fered
 cof·fer·ing
co·gen·cy
 also co·gence
 pl co·gen·cies
 also co·genc·es

co·gent
cog·nate
cog·nat·ic
cog·na·tion
cog·na·tus
 pl cog·na·ti

cog·ni·za·ble
 or cog·ni·sa·ble

cog·ni·za·bly
cog·ni·zance
 or cog·ni·sance

cog·ni·zant
cog·no·men
 pl cog·no·mens
 or cog·no·mi·na

cog·nosce
 cog·nosced

cog·nosc·ing
cog·no·vit
cog·no·vit
 ac·tio·nem
co·hab·it
 co·hab·it·ed
 co·hab·it·ing
 co·hab·i·tant
 co·hab·i·ta·tion
co·heir
co·heir·ess
co·in·sur·ance
co·in·sure
 co·in·sured
 co·in·sur·ing
 co·in·sur·er
co·ital
co·ition
co·ition·al
co·ito·pho·bia
co·itus
 pl co·itus·es

co·itus in·ter·
 rup·tus
 also co·itus reser·
  va·tus
 pl co·itus in·ter·
  rup·ti
 also co·itus re·ser·va·ti

co·ju·ror
cold-blood·ed
cold tur·key
co·leg·a·tee
co·li·tis
 pl co·li·tis·es

col·lab·o·rate

col·lab·o·rat·ed
col·lab·o·rat·ing
 to work or act jointly
 (see corroborate*)*

col·lab·o·ra·tion
col·lab·o·ra·tor
col·lapse
 col·lapsed
 col·laps·ing
col·laps·ible
col·lar
 col·lared
 col·lar·ing
col·lar·bone
col·late
 col·lat·ed
 col·lat·ing
col·lat·er·al
col·lat·er·al·i·ty
col·lat·er·al·ize
 col·lat·er·al·ized
 col·lat·er·al·iz·
  ing
col·lat·er·al·ly
col·la·tio bo·no·
 rum
 pl col·la·tio·nes
  bo·no·rum
 or col·la·tio bo·no·
  rums

col·la·tion
col·la·tion·al
col·la·tion in·ter
 hae·re·des
col·la·tion in·ter
 li·be·ros
col·lect

col·lect·ible
  or col·lect·able

col·lec·tion
col·lec·tive
col·lec·tor
col·lide
  col·lid·ed
  col·lid·ing
col·li·qua·tion
col·li·qua·tive
col·li·sion
  action of colliding
  (*see* collusion)

col·lo·di·on
  also col·lo·di·um

col·lo·qui·um
  pl col·lo·qui·ums
  or col·lo·quia

col·lu·sion
  secret agreement
  (*see* collision)

col·lu·sive
col·lu·sive·ly
co·lon
  pl co·lons
  or co·la

col·on·ic
col·or
  col·ored
  col·or·ing
col·or·abil·i·ty
col·or·able
col·or·ably
col·or·blind
co·lo·re of·fi·ci
co·los·to·my
  pl co·los·to·mies

col·pi·tis
  pl col·pi·tis·es

col·por·tage
col·por·teur
  also col·por·ter

co·ma
  unconscious state
  (*see* comma)

co·mak·er
co·ma·tose
  also co·ma·tous

com·bat
  com·bat·ed
    or com·bat·ted
  com·bat·ing
    or com·bat·ting

com·bat·ant
  also com·bat·tant

com·bi·na·tion
com·bine
  com·bined
  com·bin·ing
com·bu·rent
  also com·bu·rant

com·bus·ti·bil·i·ty
  pl com·bus·ti·bil·i·ties

com·bus·ti·ble
com·bus·ti·bly
com·bus·tion
com·bus·tive
com·bus·tive·ly
come·back
come on *vb*
  came on
  com·ing on

come-on *n*
com·fort
com·fort·able
com·fort·ably
com·ing-of-age
  pl com·ings-of-age

co·mi·tas gen·ti·
  um
    also co·mi·tas in·ter·
    gen·tes

co·mi·ty
  pl co·mi·ties

com·ma
  punctuation mark
  (*see* coma)

com·mand
com·man·dite
com·mand·ment
com·mence
  com·menced
  com·menc·ing
com·mence·ment
com·men·su·rate
com·ment
com·merce
com·mer·cia bel·li
com·mer·cial
com·mer·cial·ly
com·min·gle
  com·min·gled
  com·min·gling
com·mi·nute
  com·mi·nut·ed
  com·mi·nut·ing
com·mi·nu·tion
com·mis·sion

com·mis·sioned
com·mis·sion·
  ing
com·mis·sion de
lu·na·ti·co in·
  qui·ren·do
com·mis·sion·er
com·mis·sive
com·mit
  com·mit·ted
  com·mit·ting
com·mit·ment
com·mit·ta·ble
com·mit·tal
com·mit·tee
com·mit·tee·man
  pl com·mit·tee·men

com·mit·tee·
  wom·an
  pl com·mit·tee·wom·en

com·mit·ti·tur
com·mix·tio
  pl com·mix·tio·nes

com·mix·tion
com·mix·ture
com·mo·da·ta·ry
  pl com·mo·da·ta·ries

com·mo·date
com·mo·da·tion
com·mo·da·tum
  pl com·mo·da·ta

com·mod·i·ty
  pl com·mod·i·ties

com·mon

com·mon·able
com·mon·age
com·mon·al·ty
  or com·mon·al·i·ty
  pl com·mon·al·ties
  or com·mon·al·i·ties

com·mon
  ap·pen·dant
com·mon ap·pur·
  te·nant
com·mon
  as·sump·sit
com·mon·er
com·mon-law
com·mon·ly
com·mon·ty
  pl com·mon·ties

com·mon·wealth
com·mo·ran·cy
  pl com·mo·ran·cies

com·mo·rant
com·mo·ri·ent
  pl com·mo·ri·ents
  or com·mo·ri·en·tes

com·mo·tio
  pl com·mo·tio·nes

com·mo·tion
com·mu·nal
com·mu·nal·ism
com·mu·nal·ist
com·mu·nal·i·ty
  pl com·mu·nal·i·ties

com·mu·nal·iza·
  tion
com·mu·nal·ize

com·mu·nal·ized
com·mu·nal·iz·
  ing
com·mu·nal·ly
com·mu·nard
com·mune
com·mu·ni·ca·bil·i·
  ty
com·mu·ni·ca·ble
com·mu·ni·cate
  com·mu·ni·cat·
    ed
  com·mu·ni·cat·
    ing
com·mu·ni·ca·tion
com·mu·nion
com·mu·ni·qué
com·mu·nism
com·mu·nist
com·mu·nis·tic
com·mu·nis·ti·cal·
  ly
com·mu·ni·ty
  pl com·mu·ni·ties

com·mut·able
com·mu·ta·tion
com·mu·ta·tive
com·mute
  com·mut·ed
  com·mut·ing
com·pact
com·pan·ion·ate
  mar·riage
com·pa·ny
  pl com·pa·nies

com·pa·ra·ble
com·par·a·tive
com·par·i·son
com·pass
com·pat·i·bil·i·ty
  pl com·pat·i·bil·i·ties

com·pat·i·ble
com·pel
  com·pelled
  com·pel·ling
com·pel·la·bil·i·ty
com·pel·la·ble
com·pen·sa·bil·i·ty
com·pen·sa·ble
com·pen·sate
  com·pen·sat·ed
  com·pen·sat·ing
com·pen·sa·tion
com·pen·sa·to·ry
com·pete
  com·pet·ed
  com·pet·ing
com·pe·tence
com·pe·ten·cy
  pl com·pe·ten·cies

com·pe·tent
com·pe·ti·tion
com·pet·i·tive
com·pet·i·tor
com·plain·ant
com·plain·er
com·plaint
com·plete
  com·plet·ed

com·plet·ing
com·plete·ly
com·pli·ance
com·pli·an·cy
  pl com·pli·an·cies

com·pli·ant
com·pli·ant·ly
com·pli·cate
  com·pli·cat·ed
  com·pli·cat·ing
com·pli·ca·tion
com·ply
  com·plied
  com·ply·ing
com·po·si·tion
com·pos men·tis
com·pound
com·pound·ing
com·pre·hend
com·pre·hen·sive
com·pro·mis·able
com·pro·mise
  com·pro·mised
  com·pro·mis·ing
com·pro·mis·sion
com·pro·mit
  com·pro·mit·ted
  com·pro·mit·
    ting
compte ar·rê·té
comp·trol·ler
com·pul·sion
com·pul·sive
com·pul·so·ri·ly
com·pul·so·ry

con
  conned
  con·ning
con·cav·i·ty
  pl con·cav·i·ties

con·ceal
con·ceal·ment
con·cede
  con·ced·ed
  con·ced·ing
con·ceive
  con·ceived
  con·ceiv·ing
con·cen·trate
  con·cen·trat·ed
  con·cen·trat·ing
con·cen·tra·tion
con·cept
con·cep·tion
con·cep·tive
con·cep·tus
  pl con·cep·tus·es
  also con·cep·ti

con·cern
con·cerned
con·cern·ing
con·cert
con·cert·ed
con·ces·si
con·ces·sion
con·cil·i·ate
  con·cil·i·at·ed
  con·cil·i·at·ing
con·cil·i·a·tion
con·clude

con·clud·ed
con·clud·ing
con·clu·sion
con·clu·sive
con·clu·sive·ly
con·com·i·tant
con·cor·dat
con·course
con·crete
con·cu·bi·nage
con·cu·bine
con·cur
  con·curred
  con·cur·ring
  con·cur·rence
con·cur·rent
con·cur·rent·ly
con·cur·so
  pl con·cur·sos
  a legal proceeding
  (*see* concursus)

con·cur·sus
  pl con·cur·sus
  a religious doctrine
  (*see* concurso)

con·cuss
con·cus·sion
con·cus·sive
con·cus·sive·ly
con·demn
  con·demned
  con·demn·ing
con·dem·na·ble
con·dem·na·tion
con·dem·na·tory

con·demn·er
  or con·dem·nor

con·de·scen·dence
con·di·tion
con·di·tion·al
con·di·tion·al·i·ty
  pl con·di·tion·al·i·ties

con·di·tion·al·ly
con·di·tion prec·
  e·dent
con·di·tion sub·
  se·quent
con·di·tio si·ne
  qua non
con·dom
con·do·min·i·um
  pl con·do·min·i·ums
  also con·do·min·ia

con·do·na·tion
con·done
  con·doned
  con·don·ing
con·duce
  con·duced
  con·duc·ing
con·duct
  con·duct·ed
  con·duct·ing
con·dy·lar
con·dy·lar·thro·sis
  pl con·dy·lar·thro·ses

con·dyle
con·dyl·i·on
con·dy·loid

con·fed·er·a·cy
  pl con·fed·er·a·cies

con·fed·er·ate
con·fer
  con·ferred
  con·fer·ring
con·fer·ence
con·fess
con·fes·sion
con·fide
  con·fid·ed
  con·fid·ing
con·fi·dence
con·fi·dence game
con·fi·dent
con·fi·den·tial
con·fi·den·ti·al·i·ty
  pl con·fi·den·ti·al·i·ties

con·fi·den·tial·ly
con·fi·den·tial·ness
con·fine
  con·fined
  con·fin·ing
con·fine·ment
con·firm
con·fir·ma·tion
con·fir·mor
con·fis·ca·ble
con·fis·cate
  con·fis·cat·ed
  con·fis·cat·ing
con·fis·ca·tion
con·fis·ca·tor
con·fis·ca·to·ry
con·fla·gra·tion

con·flict
con·form
con·form·able
con·form·ably
con·for·mi·ty
  pl con·for·mi·ties
con·front
con·fron·ta·tion
con·fuse
  con·fused
  con·fus·ing
con·fu·sio
  pl con·fu·sio·nes

con·fu·sio
  bo·no·rum
con·fu·sion
con·fut·able
con·fu·ta·tion
con·fu·ta·tive
con·fu·ta·tor
con·fute
  con·fut·ed
  con·fut·ing
con·gen·i·tal
con·gest
con·gest·ed
con·ges·tion
con·ges·tive
con·glom·er·ate
con·gre·gate
  con·gre·gat·ed
  con·gre·gat·ing
con·gre·ga·tion
con·gress
con·gres·sio·nal

con·gres·sio·nal·ly
con·gress·man
  pl con·gress·men
con·gress·man-at-
  large
  pl con·gress·men-at-
  large
con·gress·wom·an
  pl con·gress·wom·en
co·ni·ine
co·ni·ol·o·gy
  var of koniology
con·jec·tur·al
con·jec·ture
  con·jec·tured
  con·jec·tur·ing
con·joint adj
con·joint·ly
con·joints n pl
con·ju·gal
con·ju·gal·i·ty
  pl con·ju·gal·i·ties
con·ju·gal·ly
con·junct
con·junc·tion
con·junc·ti·va
  pl con·junc·ti·vas
  or con·junc·ti·vae
con·junc·ti·val
con·junc·ti·vi·tis
con·ju·ra·tion
con·niv·ance
con·nive
  con·nived
  con·niv·ing

con·niv·er
con·niv·ery
  pl con·niv·er·ies
con·san·guine
con·san·guin·e·ous
con·san·guin·e·
  ous·ly
con·san·guin·i·ty
  pl con·san·guin·i·ties
con·science
con·sci·en·tious
con·sci·en·tious·ly
con·scious
con·scious·ly
con·scious·ness
con·script
con·scrip·tion
con·sec·u·tive
con·sec·u·tive·ly
con·sen·su·al
con·sen·su·al·ly
con·sen·sus
con·sent
con·se·quence
con·se·quen·tial
con·ser·va·tor
con·ser·va·tor·ship
con·sid·er
  con·sid·ered
  con·sid·er·ing
con·sid·er·able
con·sid·er·ation
con·sign
con·sig·na·tary
  pl con·sig·na·ta·ries

con·sig·na·tion
con·sign·ee
con·sign·ment
con·sign·or
con·sis·tent
con·sol·i·date
  con·sol·i·dat·ed
  con·sol·i·dat·ing
con·sol·i·da·tion
con·so·nant
con·sor·tium
  pl con·sor·tiums
  also con·sor·tia

con·sort·ship
con·spir·a·cy
  pl con·spir·a·cies

con·spir·a·tor
con·spir·a·to·ri·al
con·spir·a·to·ri·al·
  ly
con·spire
  con·spired
  con·spir·ing
con·spir·ing·ly
con·sta·ble
con·stab·u·lary
  pl con·stab·u·lar·ies

con·stat
con·stit·u·en·cy
  pl con·stit·u·en·cies

con·stit·u·ent
con·stit·u·ent·ly
con·sti·tute
  con·sti·tut·ed
  con·sti·tut·ing

con·sti·tu·tion
con·sti·tu·tion·al
con·sti·tu·tion·al·
  i·ty
con·sti·tu·tion·al·
  ly
con·strain
con·strain·ment
con·straint
con·struc·tion
con·struc·tion·ism
con·struc·tion·ist
con·struc·tive
con·struc·tive·ly
con·struc·tive·ness
con·strue
  con·strued
  con·stru·ing
con·sue·tude
con·sue·tu·di·nal
con·sue·tu·di·nary
con·sue·tu·do
  pl con·sue·tu·di·nes

con·sul
con·sul·age
con·sul·ar
con·sul·ate
  con·sul·at·ed
  con·sul·at·ing
con·sul gen·er·al
  pl con·suls gen·er·al

con·sul·ship
con·sult
con·sul·tant
con·sul·ta·tion

con·sul·ta·tive
con·sul·ta·to·ry
con·sult·er
con·sul·tive
con·sum·able
con·sume
  con·sumed
  con·sum·ing
con·sum·er
con·sum·mate
  con·sum·mat·ed
  con·sum·mat·
  ing
con·sum·ma·tion
con·sum·ma·tor
con·sump·tion
con·sump·tive
con·sump·tive·ly
con·ta·gion
con·ta·gious
con·ta·gious·ly
con·ta·gious·ness
con·ta·gium
  pl con·ta·gia

con·tam·i·nant
con·tam·i·nate
  con·tam·i·nat·ed
  con·tam·i·nat·ing
con·tam·i·na·tion
con·tan·go *n*
  pl con·tan·gos
  or con·tan·goes

con·tan·go *vb*
  con·tan·goed
  con·tan·go·ing
con·temn

con·temned
con·temn·ing
scorn
(*see* condemn)

con·tem·ner
or con·tem·nor

con·tem·plate
con·tem·plat·ed
con·tem·plat·ing
con·tem·pla·tion
con·tem·po·ra·
ne·ous
con·tem·po·ra·ne·
ous·ly
con·tempt
con·tend
con·ten·tion
con·ten·tion·al
con·ten·tious
con·ten·tious·ly
con·ten·tious·ness
con·test
con·test·able
con·test·ably
con·tes·ta·tion
con·test·ee
con·ti·gu·ity
pl con·ti·gu·ities

con·tig·u·ous
con·tig·u·ous·ly
con·tig·u·ous·ness
con·ti·nence
con·ti·nent
con·tin·gen·cy
pl con·tin·gen·cies

con·tin·gent

con·tin·gent·ly
con·tin·u·ance
con·tin·u·an·do
con·tin·u·ant
con·tin·u·a·tion
con·tin·ue
con·tin·ued
con·tin·u·ing
con·ti·nu·ity
pl con·ti·nu·ities

con·tin·u·ous
con·tin·u·ous·ly
con·tra
con·tra·band
con·tra·band·age
con·tra·band·ist
con·tra bo·nos
mo·res
con·tra·cep·tion
con·tra·cep·tive
con·tract
con·trac·tion
con·trac·tor
con·trac·tu·al
con·trac·tu·al·ly
con·trac·ture
con·tra·dic·tion
con·tra·dic·tive
con·tra·dic·tive·ly
con·tra·dic·to·ri·ly
con·tra·dic·to·ri·
ness
con·tra·dic·to·ry
con·tra for·mam
sta·tui
con·tra·in·di·cate

con·tra·in·di·
cat·ed
con·tra·in·di·
cat·ing
con·tra·in·di·ca·
tion
con·tra·in·dic·a·
tive
con·tra pa·cem
con·tra pro·fe·
ren·tum
con·trary
con·tra·vene
con·tra·vened
con·tra·ven·ing
con·tra·ven·tion
con·tre·coup
con·trec·ta·tion
con·trib·ute
con·trib·ut·ed
con·trib·ut·ing
con·tri·bu·tion
con·trib·u·tor
con·trib·u·tor·i·ly
con·trib·u·to·ry
pl con·trib·u·to·ries

con·trive
con·trived
con·triv·ing
con·trol
con·trolled
con·trol·ling
con·trol·ler
con·tro·ver·sy
pl con·tro·ver·sies

con·tro·vert

con·tu·ma·cious
con·tu·ma·cious·ly
con·tu·ma·cy
  pl con·tu·ma·cies
con·tu·me·li·ous
con·tume·ly
  pl con·tume·lies
con·tuse
  con·tused
  con·tus·ing
con·tu·sion
con·va·lesce
  con·va·lesced
  con·va·lesc·ing
con·va·les·cence
con·va·les·cent
con·vene
  con·vened
  con·ven·ing
con·ve·nience
con·ve·nient
con·ve·nient·ly
con·ven·ti·cle
con·ven·tion
con·ven·tion·al
con·ven·tion·ary
con·ver·sa·tion
con·ver·sion
con·vert
con·vey
con·vey·ance
con·vey·anc·er
con·vey·anc·ing
con·vey·er
  or con·vey·or
con·vict

con·vic·tion
con·vince
  con·vinced
  con·vinc·ing
  con·vinc·ing·ly
con·vul·sant
con·vulse
  con·vulsed
  con·vuls·ing
con·vul·sion
con·vul·sive
con·vul·sive·ly
co-ob·li·gant
co-ob·li·gor
cool·ing-off
cool·ing time
cool-off
co·op·er·ate
  co·op·er·at·ed
  co·op·er·at·ing
co·op·er·a·tion
co·op·er·a·tive
co-opt
co-op·tate
  co-op·tat·ed
  co-op·tat·ing
co-op·ta·tion
co-op·ta·tive
co-op·tion
co-op·tive
co·or·di·nate
  co·or·di·nat·ed
  co·or·di·nat·ing
co·or·di·na·tion
co·os·si·fi·ca·tion
co·os·si·fy

co·os·si·fied
co·os·si·fy·ing
co-own·er
co-own·er·ship
co·par·ce·nary
  pl co·par·ce·nar·ies
co·par·ce·ner
co·part·ner
co·part·ner·ship
co·par·ty
  pl co·par·ties
cop·ro·lag·nia
cop·ro·lag·nist
cop·ro·la·lia
co·prol·o·gy
  pl co·prol·o·gies
cop·ro·phil·ia
cop·ro·phil·i·ac
cop·ro·phil·ic
cop·u·la
  pl cop·u·las
  also cop·u·lae
cop·u·late
  cop·u·lat·ed
  cop·u·lat·ing
cop·u·la·tion
cop·u·la·to·ry
copy
  cop·ied
  copy·ing
copy·hold
copy·hold·er
copy·right
copy·right·able
cor·a·co·cla·vic·u·
lar

cor·a·co·hu·mer·al

cor·a·coid

co·ram

co·ram ju·di·ce

co·ram no·bis

co·ram non ju·di·ce

co·ram pa·ri·bus

co·ram po·pu·lo
  or co·ram pu·bli·co

co·ram vo·bis

co·re·spon·dent
  joint respondent
  (*see* correspondent)

cor·nea

cor·ne·al

cor·ne·itis

cor·ni·fi·ca·tion

cor·ni·fy
  cor·ni·fied
  cor·ni·fy·ing

cor·o·nary
  pl cor·o·nar·ies

cor·o·ner

co·ro·ni·on
  pl co·ro·nia

cor·po·ral

cor·po·rate

cor·po·ra·tion

cor·po·ra·tive

cor·po·ra·tor

cor·po·re·al

corps di·plo·
  ma·tique
  pl corps diplomatique

corpse

corps·man
  pl corps·men

cor·pu·len·cy
  or cor·pu·lence

cor·pu·lent

cor pul·mo·na·le
  pl cor·dia pul·mo·na·lia

cor·pus
  pl cor·po·ra
  body
  (*see* carpus)

cor·pus·cle

cor·pus de·lic·ti
  pl cor·po·ra de·lic·ti

cor·pus ju·ris
  pl cor·po·ra ju·ris

cor·re·al

cor·re·al·i·ty
  pl cor·re·al·i·ties

cor·rect

cor·rec·tion

cor·rec·tion·al

cor·rec·tive

cor·re·spon·dence

cor·re·spon·dent
  one who communicates
  (*see* corespondent)

cor·ri·gi·ble

cor·ri·gi·bly

cor·rob·o·rate
  cor·rob·o·rat·ed
  cor·rob·o·rat·ing

cor·rob·o·ra·tion

cor·rob·o·ra·tive

cor·rob·o·ra·tive·ly

cor·rob·o·ra·tor

cor·rob·o·ra·to·ry

cor·rode

cor·rod·ed

cor·rod·ing

cor·ro·sion

cor·ro·sive

cor·ro·sive·ly

cor·ro·sive·ness

cor·rupt

cor·rupt·er
  or cor·rup·tor

cor·rupt·ibil·i·ty
  pl cor·rupt·ibil·i·ties

cor·rupt·ible

cor·rupt·ible·ness

cor·rup·tion

cor·rup·tion·ist

cor·rup·tive

cor·rupt·ly

cor·rupt·ness

cor·rup·tor
  var of corrupter

cor·tex
  pl cor·ti·ces
  or cor·tex·es

cor·ti·cal

cor·ti·cal·ly

cor·ti·sol

cor·ti·sone

co·ser·vant

cos·met·ic

cos·me·ti·cian

cost

cos·ta
  pl cos·tae

cos·tal

cos·tal·gia

cos·to·chon·dral

cos·to·cla·vic·u·lar
cos·to·cor·a·coid
cos·to·scap·u·lar
cos·to·ver·te·bral
cos·to·xi·phoid
cost-plus
co·sure·ty
co·sure·ty·ship
co·swear·er
co·ten·an·cy
  pl co·ten·an·cies

co·ten·ant
co·ter·mi·nous
co·tres·pass·er
co-trust·ee
couch·ant and
  lev·ant
coun·cil
  an administrative body
  (see counsel)

coun·cil·lor
  also coun·cil·or

coun·cil·lor·ship
coun·cil·man
  pl coun·cil·men

coun·cil·man·ic
coun·cil·wom·an
  pl coun·cil·wom·en

coun·sel
  coun·seled
    or coun·selled

  coun·sel·ing
    or coun·sel·ling
  n a legal representative
  (see council)
  vb to give advice

coun·sel·able
  or coun·sel·lable

coun·sel·ee
coun·sel·or
  or coun·sel·lor

coun·sel·or-at-law
  pl coun·sel·ors-at-law

count
coun·te·nance
  coun·te·nanced
  coun·te·nanc·ing
coun·ter·claim
coun·ter·es·pi·o·
  nage
coun·ter·feit
coun·ter·feit·er
coun·ter·feit·ing
coun·ter·feit·ly
coun·ter·feit·ness
coun·ter·mand
coun·ter·mea·sure
coun·ter·of·fer
coun·ter·part
coun·ter·plea
coun·ter·plot
  coun·ter·plot·
    ted
  coun·ter·plot·
    ting
coun·ter·shock
coun·ter·sign
coun·ter·sig·na·
  ture
coun·ter·vail

coun·try
  pl coun·tries

coun·ty
  pl coun·ties

cou·ple
  cou·pled
  cou·pling
cou·pon
cou·ri·er
course
court
cour·te·sy
  pl cour·te·sies
  something allowed or
  accepted
  (see curtesy, curtsy)

court·house
court-mar·tial *n*
  pl courts-mar·tial
  also court-mar·tials

court-mar·tial *vb*
  court-mar·tialed
    also court mar-
    tialled
  court-mar·tial·
    ing
    also court-mar-
    tial·ling

cous·in
cous·in·age
cous·in-ger·man
  pl cous·ins-ger·man

cov·e·nant *n and vb*
cov·e·nan·tee
cov·e·nan·tor
cov·er
cov·er·age

co·vert
cov·er·ture
co·vin
   also co·vine

co·vi·nous
cow·ard·ice
cox·a
   pl cox·ae

cox·al
cox·al·gia
   also cox·al·gy
   pl cox·al·gias
   also cox·al·gies

cox·i·tis
   pl cox·it·i·des

cox·o·fem·o·ral
crack-up
craft
crafts·man
   pl crafts·men

cra·ni·al
cra·ni·al·ly
cra·ni·op·a·thy
   pl cra·ni·op·a·thies

cra·nio·plas·ty
cra·nio·sa·cral
cra·nio·spi·nal
cra·ni·um
   pl cra·ni·ums
   or cra·nia

crap·u·lence
crap·u·lous
cre·ate
   cre·at·ed
   cre·at·ing

cre·ation
cre·ative
crèche
cre·den·tial
cre·den·tialed
cred·i·bil·i·ty
   pl cred·i·bil·i·ties

cred·i·ble
cred·i·ble·ness
cred·it
cred·it·abil·i·ty
   pl cred·it·abil·i·ties

cred·it·able
cred·it·able·ness
cred·it·ably
cred·i·tor
cre·mains
cre·mate
   cre·mat·ed
   cre·mat·ing
cre·ma·tion
cre·ma·to·ri·um
   pl cre·ma·to·ria
   or cre·ma·to·ri·ums

crep·i·tant
crep·i·ta·tion
crep·i·tus
   pl crep·i·tus

cre·tin
cre·tin·ism
cre·tin·ize
   cre·tin·ized
   cre·tin·iz·ing
cre·tin·oid
cre·tin·ous

cri·co·ar·y·te·noid
cri·coid
cri·co·thy·roid
crime
crime·less
cri·men
   pl crim·i·na

crime pas·si·o·nel
   also crime pas·si·on·nel
   pl crimes pas·si·o·nels

crim·i·nal
crim·i·nal·ism
crim·i·nal·ist
crim·i·nal·is·tic
crim·i·nal·i·ty
   pl crim·i·nal·i·ties

crim·i·nal·ly
crim·i·nal·ness
crim·i·nal·oid
crim·i·nate
   crim·i·nat·ed
   crim·i·nat·ing
crim·i·na·tion
crim·i·na·tive
crim·i·na·tor
crim·i·na·to·ry
crim·i·no·gen·e·sis
   or cri·mo·gen·e·sis

crim·i·no·gen·ic
   or cri·mo·gen·ic

crim·i·no·log·i·cal
   also crim·i·no·log·ic

crim·i·no·log·i·cal·ly
crim·i·nol·o·gist

crim·i·nol·o·gy
   pl crim·i·nol·o·gies

crip·ple
  crip·pled
  crip·pling
cri·sis
  pl cri·ses

cri·te·ri·on
  pl cri·te·ria
  or cri·te·ri·ons

cri·te·ri·um
  pl cri·te·ria

crit·ic
crit·i·cal
crit·i·cal·i·ty
crit·i·cal·ly
crit·i·cism
crit·i·cize
  crit·i·cized
  crit·i·ciz·ing
  crit·i·ciz·er
crook·ed
crook·ed·ness
crook·ery
  pl crook·er·ies

cross-ac·tion
cross-bill
cross-com·plaint
cross-ex·am·i·na·
  tion
cross-ex·am·ine
  cross-ex·am·ined
  cross-ex·am·in·
   ing
cross-ex·am·in·er
cross-eye

cross-eyed
cross·ing
cross match·ing
cross re·ac·tion
cross-re·ac·tive
crotch
cru·el
  cru·el·er
   or cru·el·ler
  cru·el·est
   or cru·el·lest

cru·el·ly
cru·el·ness
cru·el·ty
  pl cru·el·ties

cryp·tic
cuck·old
cui bo·no
cul·do·scop·ic
cul·dos·co·py
  pl cul·dos·co·pies

cul·pa
  pl cul·pae

cul·pa·bil·i·ty
cul·pa·ble
cul·pa·ble·ness
cul·pa·bly
cul·pa la·ta
  or cul·pa mag·na

cul·pa le·vis
cul·pa le·vis in
  ab·strac·to
cul·pa le·vis in
  con·cre·to
cul·pa le·vis·si·ma
cul·prit

cum da·tu
cum one·re
cum tes·ta·men·to
  an·nexo
cu·mu·late
  cu·mu·lat·ed
  cu·mu·lat·ing
cu·mu·la·tive
cun·ni·lin·gu·ism
cun·ni·lin·gus
  or cun·ni·linc·tus

cun·nus
  pl cun·ni

cur·abil·i·ty
cur·able
cur·able·ness
cur·ably
cur·ra·re
  or cu·ra·ri

cu·ra·ri·form
cu·ra·rine
cu·ra·ri·za·tion
cu·ra·rize
  cu·ra·rized
  cu·ra·riz·ing
cu·ra·tive
cu·ra·tor
cu·ra·tor bo·nis
  pl cu·ra·tors bo·nis

cu·ra·to·ri·al
cu·ra·tor·ship
cu·ra·trix
  pl cu·ra·tri·ces

cure
  cured

cur·ing
cu·ret·tage
cu·rette
   or cu·ret
  cu·ret·ted
  cu·ret·ting
cu·rette·ment
  or cu·ret·ment

cur·few
  cur·fewed
  cur·few·ing
cu·ria
cur·rant
  fruit
  (*see* current)

cur·ren·cy
  pl cur·ren·cies

cur·rent
  n stream
  adj belonging to the
    present
  (*see* currant)

cur·so·ry
cur·tail
cur·tail·ment
cur·te·sy
  pl cur·te·sies
  husband's right in
    dead wife's land
  (*see* courtesy, curtsy)

curt·sy
  or curt·sey
  pl curt·sies
  or curt·seys
  a slight bow
  (*see* courtesy, curtesy)

cur·ti·lage
cus·pid
cus·pi·date
  or cus·pi·dat·ed

cus·to·dee
cus·to·di·al
cus·to·dia le·gis
cus·to·di·am
cus·to·di·an
cus·to·di·er
cus·to·dy
  pl cus·to·dies

cus·tom
cus·tom·ari·ly
cus·tom·ary
cus·tom·er
cus·tom·house
  also cus·toms·house

cus·tos
  pl cus·to·des

cus·tos ro·tu·lo·rum
  pl cus·to·des
    ro·tu·lo·rum

cu·ta·ne·ous
cut·purse
cut·throat
cy·a·nide
cy·ano·gen
cy·a·no·gen·e·sis
  pl cy·a·no·gen·e·ses

cy·a·no·ge·net·ic
cy·a·nosed
cy·a·no·sis
  pl cy·a·no·ses

cy·a·not·ic
cy·cli·tis
cy·clo·thyme
cy·clo·thy·mia
cy·clo·thy·mic

cy·e·sis
  pl cy·e·ses

cy·no·sure
  one that attracts
  (*see* sinecure)

cy pres
cys·ti·tis
  pl cys·tit·i·des

D

dac·ty·li·tis
dac·tyl·o·gram
dac·tyl·og·ra·pher
dac·tyl·o·graph·ic
dac·tyl·og·ra·phy
  pl dac·ty·log·ra·phies

dac·tyl·o·scop·ic
dac·tyl·os·co·pist
dac·tyl·os·co·py
  pl dac·ty·los·co·pies

dai·ly
  pl dai·lies

Dal·ton·ism
dam
  dammed
  dam·ming
dam·age
  dam·aged
  dam·ag·ing
dam·age·able
dam·age fea·sant
dam·ag·es
dam·ag·ing·ly
damn
  damned
  damn·ing

dam·na·bil·i·ty
  pl dam·na·bil·i·ties

dam·na·ble
dam·na·ble·ness
dam·ni·fi·ca·tion
dam·ni·fy
  dam·ni·fied
  dam·ni·fy·ing
dam·no·sa he·re·
  di·tas
  or dam·no·sa hae·
    re·di·tas

dam·num
  pl dam·na

dam·num abs·que
  in·ju·ria
dam·num et
  in·ju·ria
dam·num fa·ta·le
dam·num in·fec·
  tum
dam·num rei amis·
  sae
dan·ger
dan·ger·ous
dan·ger·ous·ly
dan·ger·ous·ness
dar·rein
dat·able
  or date·able

dat·al
date
  dat·ed
  dat·ing
date·line

da·tion
da·tion in pay·
  ment
  or da·tion en paie·
    ment

da·ti·val
da·tive
da·tive·ly
da·tum
  pl da·ta
  or da·tums

da·tu·ra
da·tu·ric
daugh·ter
daugh·ter-in-law
  pl daugh·ters-in-law

day·book
day in court
day·light
day·time
de·acid·i·fi·ca·tion
de·acid·i·fy
  de·acid·i·fied
  de·acid·i·fy·ing
dead
dead·beat
dead·en
dead hand
dead·head
dead·line
dead·li·ness
dead·lock
dead·locked
dead·ly
  dead·li·er

dead·li·est
dead·ly night·
  shade
dead·man
  or dead·man con·trol

dead·man brake
dead·weight
de ae·qui·ta·te
deaf
  deaf·er
  deaf·est
deaf·en
deaf-mute
deaf-mut·ism
deaf·ness
deal
  dealt
  deal·ing
deal·er
deal·er·ship
death
death·bed
death·blow
death rat·tle
death·trap
death·watch
de·bar
  de·barred
  de·bar·ring
de·bar·ment
de·base
  de·based
  de·bas·ing
de·based·ness
de·base·ment

de·bas·er
de·bat·able
   also de·bate·able

de·bate
  de·bat·ed
  de·bat·ing
de·bat·er
de·bauch
de·bauched
de·bauched·ly
de·bauched·ness
de·bauch·ee
de·bauch·er
de·bauch·ery
  pl de·bauch·er·ies

de·bel·la·tio
de be·ne es·se
de·ben·ture
de·ben·ture·hold·er
de·bet si·ne breve
de·bil·i·tant
de·bil·i·tate
  de·bil·i·tat·ed
  de·bil·i·tat·ing
de·bil·i·ta·tion
de·bil·i·ty
  de·bil·i·ties
deb·it
  deb·it·ed
  deb·it·ing
deb·it·able
deb·i·tum fun·di
  pl deb·i·ta fun·di

deb·i·tum in prae·
  sen·ti

deb·i·tum si·ne
  brevi
de bo·nis
  as·por·ta·tis
de bo·nis non
de bo·nis non ad·
  min·i·stra·tis
de bo·nis pro·pri·
  is
de bo·nis tes·ta·
  to·ris
de·bride
  de·brid·ed
  de·brid·ing
de·bride·ment
de·brief
de·bris
  pl de·bris

debt
debt·ee
debt·or
de·cal·ci·fi·ca·tion
de·cal·ci·fy
  de·cal·ci·fied
  de·cal·ci·fy·ing
de·camp
de·camp·ment
de·cap·i·tate
  de·cap·i·tat·ed
  de·cap·i·tat·ing
de·cap·i·ta·tion
de·cap·i·ta·tor
dec·ar·chy
  also dek·ar·chy
  pl dec·ar·chies
  also dek·ar·chies

de·car·tel·iza·tion
de·car·tel·ize
  de·car·tel·ized
  de·car·tel·iz·ing
de·cay
  de·cayed
  de·cay·ing
de·cay·able
de·cayed·ness
de·cease
  de·ceased
  de·ceas·ing
de·ce·dent
  a deceased person
  (*see* dissident)

de·ceit
de·ceit·ful
de·ceit·ful·ly
de·ceit·ful·ness
de·ceiv·able
de·ceive
  de·ceived
  de·ceiv·ing
de·ceiv·er
de·ceiv·ing·ly
de·cem ta·les
de·cen·cy
  pl de·cen·cies

de·cen·na·ry
de·cen·ni·al
de·cen·ni·al·ly
de·cen·ni·um
  pl de·cen·ni·ums
  or de·cen·nia

de·cent
*conforming to a stan-
    dard*
(*see* descent)

de·cen·tral·ism
de·cen·tral·ist
de·cen·tral·iza·tion
de·cen·tral·ize
  de·cen·tral·ized
  de·cen·tral·iz·ing
de·cep·tion
de·cep·tive
de·cep·tive·ly
de·cep·tive·ness
de cer·ti·fi·can·do
de·cer·ti·fi·ca·tion
de·cer·ti·fy
  de·cer·ti·fied
  de·cer·ti·fy·ing
de cer·tio·ran·do
de·ces·sit si·ne
  pro·le
deci·bel
de·cide
  de·cid·ed
  de·cid·ing
de·cid·ed·ly
de·cid·ua
  pl de·cid·u·ae

de·cid·u·al
de·cid·u·ate
de·cid·u·itis
de·cid·u·ous
dec·i·mate
  dec·i·mat·ed

dec·i·mat·ing
dec·i·ma·tion
de·ci·sion
de·ci·sive
de·ci·sive·ly
de·ci·sive·ness
de·clar·able
de·clar·ant
dec·la·ra·tion
de·clar·a·tive
de·clar·a·tor
de·clar·a·to·ry
de·clare
  de·clared
  de·clar·ing
de·clas·si·fi·ca·tion
de·clas·si·fy
  de·clas·si·fied
  de·clas·si·fy·ing
dec·li·na·tion
dec·li·na·tion·al
de·clin·a·to·ry
de·clin·a·ture
de·cline
  de·clined
  de·clin·ing
de·coc·tion
de·code
  de·cod·ed
  de·cod·ing
de·cod·er
de·col·late
  de·col·lat·ed
  de·col·lat·ing
de·col·la·tion

de com·mu·ni di·
  vi·den·do
de·com·pen·sate
  de·com·pen·sat·
    ed
  de·com·pen·sat·
    ing
de·com·pen·sa·tion
de·com·pose
  de·com·posed
  de·com·pos·ing
de·com·po·si·tion
de·com·press
de·com·pres·sion
de·com·pres·sive
de·con·di·tion
de·con·tam·i·nate
  de·con·tam·i·
    nat·ed
  de·con·tam·i·
    nat·ing
de·con·tam·i·na·
  tion
de·con·trol
  de·con·trolled
  de·con·trol·ling
de cor·po·re co·mi·
  ta·tus
de·co·rum
de·coy
  de·coyed
  de·coy·ing
de·crease
  de·creased
  de·creas·ing

de·cree
  de·creed
  de·cree·ing
de·cree ar·bi·tral
de·cree da·tive
de·cree in in·vi·
  tum
de·cree in rem
de·cree-law
de·cree ni·si
de·cree pro
  con·fes·so
de·cre·er
de·creet
de·crep·it
  also de·crep·id
de·crep·i·tude
de·cre·tal
de·cre·to·ri·al
de·cre·to·ry
de·cre·tum
  pl de·cre·ta
de·cry
  de·cried
  de·cry·ing
de·cu·ba·tion
de cur·su
de·den·ti·tion
de·di
ded·i·cate
  ded·i·cat·ed
  ded·i·cat·ing
ded·i·ca·tee
ded·i·ca·tion
ded·i·ca·tion·al

ded·i·ca·tor
de die in di·em
de·di·mus
  or de·di·mus
  po·tes·ta·tem
de·dit
de·di·tion
de do·lo ma·lo
de·duce
  de·duced
  de·duc·ing
de·duc·ibil·i·ty
  pl de·duc·ibil·i·ties
de·duc·ible
de·duct
de·duct·ibil·i·ty
de·duct·ible
de·duc·tion
de·duc·tive
de·duc·tive·ly
deed
deed·box
deed poll
  pl deeds poll
deem
deem·ster
deem·ster·ship
de·face
  de·faced
  de·fac·ing
de·face·ment
de·fac·er
de fac·to
de·fal·cate
  de·fal·cat·ed

de·fal·cat·ing
de·fal·ca·tion
de·fal·ca·tor
de·falk
de·fam·a·cast
def·a·ma·tion
de·fam·a·to·ry
de·fame
  de·famed
  de·fam·ing
de·fam·er
de·fam·ing·ly
de·fault
de·fault·er
de·fea·sance
de·fea·si·ble
de·fea·sive
de·feat
def·e·cate
  def·e·cat·ed
  def·e·cat·ing
def·e·ca·tion
de·fect
de·fec·tion
de·fec·tive
de·fec·tive·ly
de·fec·tive·ness
de·fec·tor
de·fem·i·na·tion
de·fem·i·nize
  de·fem·i·nized
  de·fem·i·niz·ing
de·fend
de·fen·dant
de·fend·er

de·fense
de·fense·less
de·fense·less·ly
de·fense·less·ness
de·fen·si·bil·i·ty
de·fen·si·ble
de·fen·si·bly
de·fen·sive
de·fen·sive·ly
de·fen·sive·ness
de·fen·sor
de·fer
  de·ferred
  de·fer·ring
de·fer·ment
de·fer·ra·ble
  also de·fer·able

de·fer·ral
de·fer·rer
de·fer·ves·cence
de·fi·ance
de·fi·ant
de·fi·ant·ly
de·fi·bril·late
  de·fi·bril·lat·ed
  de·fi·bril·lat·ing
de·fi·bril·la·tion
de·fi·bril·la·tor
de·fi·bril·la·to·ry
de·fi·cien·cy
  pl de·fi·cien·cies

de·fi·cient
de·fi·cient·ly
def·i·cit
de·file
  de·filed

de·fil·ing
de·file·ment
de·fil·er
de·fil·ing·ly
de·fine
de·fined
de·fin·ing
def·i·nite
def·i·nite·ly
def·i·ni·tion
de·fin·i·tive
de·fin·i·tive·ly
de·fin·i·tive·ness
de·flect
de·flo·ra·tion
de·flo·res·cence
de·flow·er
de·flux·ion
de·force
de·forced
de·forc·ing
de·force·ment
de·force·or
de·for·ciant
de·form
de·form·able
de·for·ma·tion
de·for·ma·tive
de·formed
de·for·mi·ty
  pl de·for·mi·ties

de·fraud
de·frau·da·tion
de·fraud·er
de·fray
  de·frayed

de·fray·ing
de·fray·al
de·fray·ment
de·funct
de·func·tus si·ne
  pro·le
de·fuse
  also de·fuze
de·fused
  also de·fuzed
de·fus·ing
  also de·fuz·ing

de·fy
de·fied
de·fy·ing
de·gen·er·a·cy
  pl de·gen·er·a·cies

de·gen·er·ate
de·gen·er·at·ed
de·gen·er·at·ing
de·gen·er·ate·ly
de·gen·er·ate·ness
de·gen·er·a·tion
de·gen·er·a·tive
de·glu·ti·tion
deg·ra·da·tion
de·grade
de·grad·ed
de·grad·ing
de·grad·ed·ly
de·grad·ed·ness
de·grad·er
de gra·tia
de·gree
de·hors
de·hy·drate

de·hy·drat·ed
de·hy·drat·ing
de·hy·dra·tion
de·hyp·no·tize
  de·hyp·no·tized
  de·hyp·no·tiz·ing
Dei gra·tia
de in·cre·men·to
de in·ju·ria
de in·te·gro
dé·jà vu
  or dé·jà vue

de·jec·ta
de·jec·tion
de ju·re
dek·ar·chy
  var of decarchy

de·lac·ta·tion
de·late
  de·lat·ed
  de·lat·ing
de·la·tion
de·la·tor
de·lay
  de·layed
  de·lay·ing
de·lay·er
del cre·de·re
de·le
  de·led
  de·le·ing
de·lec·tus per·so·
  nae
de·lec·tus per·so·
  na·rum
del·e·ga·ble

del·e·ga·cy
  del·e·ga·cies
de·le·gal·ize
  de·le·gal·ized
  de·le·gal·iz·ing
del·e·gant
del·e·gate
  del·e·gat·ed
  del·e·gat·ing
del·e·ga·tee
del·e·ga·tio
del·e·ga·tion
del·e·ga·tor
del·e·ga·to·ry
de le·ge fe·ren·da
del·e·te·ri·ous
del·e·te·ri·ous·ly
del·e·te·ri·ous·ness
de·lib·er·ant
de·lib·er·ate
  de·lib·er·at·ed
  de·lib·er·at·ing
de·lib·er·ate·ly
de·lib·er·a·tion
de·lib·er·a·tive
de·lib·er·a·tive·ly
de·lib·er·a·tive·ness
de·lib·er·a·tor
de·lict
de·lic·tu·al
de·lic·tum
  pl de·lic·ta
de·lim·it
de·lim·i·tate
  de·lim·i·tat·ed
  de·lim·i·tat·ing

de·lim·i·ta·tion
de·lim·i·ta·tive
de·lim·it·er
de·lin·quen·cy
  pl de·lin·quen·cies

de·lin·quent
de·lin·quent·ly
de·lir·i·ant
de·lir·i·fa·cient
de·lir·i·ous
de·lir·i·um
  pl de·lir·i·ums
  also de·lir·ia

de·lir·i·um fe·brile
de·lir·i·um tre·
  mens
de·liv·er
  de·liv·ered
  de·liv·er·ing
de·liv·er·able
de·liv·er·ance
de·liv·ery
  pl de·liv·er·ies

de·lude
  de·lud·ed
  de·lud·ing
de·lud·er
de·lud·ing·ly
de lu·na·ti·co
  in·qui·ren·do
de·lu·sion
de·lu·sion·al
de·lu·sion·ary
de·lu·sion·ist
de·lu·sive
de·lu·sive·ly

de·lu·sive·ness
de·lu·so·ry
de·mand
de·mand·able
de·man·dant
de·mar·cate
  de·mar·cat·ed
  de·mar·cat·ing
  de·mar·ca·tion
    also de·mar·ka·tion

de·mar·ca·tor
de·mar·ca·ture
de·mas·cu·lin·iza·
  tion
de·mas·cu·lin·ize
  de·mas·cu·lin·
    ized
  de·mas·cu·lin·iz·
    ing
de·mean
  to behave
  (*see* demesne, domain)

de·mean·or
de me·di·e·ta·te
  lin·guae
de·mem·bra·tion
de·ment·ed
dé·men·ti
de·men·tia
de·men·tia af·fec·
  ta·ta
de·men·tial
de·men·tia par·a·
  lyt·i·ca
    pl de·men·ti·ae
    par·a·lyt·i·cae

de·men·tia prae·
  cox
    also de·men·tia pre·
    cox
    pl de·men·ti·ae
    prae·co·ces
    also de·men·ti·ae
    pre·co·ces

de·mesne
  landed property
  (*see* demean, domain)

de·mesn·i·al
demi·mon·dain *adj*
demi·mon·daine *n*
demi·monde
de mi·ni·mis
demi·sang
  also demi·sangue

de·mise
  de·mised
  de·mis·ing
de·mi·si
de·mit
  de·mit·ted
  de·mit·ting
de·mo·bi·li·za·tion
de·mo·bi·lize
  de·mo·bi·lized
  de·mo·bi·liz·ing
de·moc·ra·cy
  pl de·moc·ra·cies

dem·o·crat
dem·o·crat·ic
  also dem·o·crat·i·cal

dem·o·crat·i·cal·ly
de·moc·ra·tism

de·moc·ra·ti·za·
  tion
de·moc·ra·tize
  de·moc·ra·tized
  de·moc·ra·tiz·
    ing
de·mog·ra·phy
  pl de·mog·ra·phies

de·mol·ish
de·mo·li·tion
de·mon·e·ti·za·tion
de·mon·e·tize
  de·mon·e·tized
  de·mon·e·tiz·ing
de·mon·stra·ble
dem·on·strate
  dem·on·strat·ed
  dem·on·strat·
    ing
dem·on·stra·tion
dem·on·stra·tion·
  al
dem·on·stra·tive
dem·on·stra·tor
de·mor·al·iza·tion
de·mor·al·ize
  de·mor·al·ized
  de·mor·al·iz·ing
de·mor·phin·iza·
  tion
de·mote
  de·mot·ed
  de·mot·ing
de·mo·tion
de·mur

de·murred
de·mur·ring
to protest
(*see* demure)

de·mure
shy
(*see* demur)

de·mur·ra·ble
de·mur·rage
de·mur·ral
de·mur·rant
de·mur·rer
de·nar·co·tize
  de·nar·co·tized
  de·nar·co·tiz·ing
de·na·tion·al·iza·
  tion
de·na·tion·al·ize
  de·na·tion·al·
    ized
  de·na·tion·al·iz·
    ing
de·nat·u·ral·iza·
  tion
de·nat·u·ral·ize
  de·nat·u·ral·ized
  de·nat·u·ral·iz·
    ing
de·na·tur·ant
de·na·tur·a·tion
de·na·ture
  de·na·tured
  de·na·tur·ing
de·ni·a·ble

de·ni·al
den·i·grate
  den·i·grat·ed
  den·i·grat·ing
den·i·gra·tion
den·i·gra·tor
den·i·gra·to·ry
den·i·za·tion
den·i·zen
de·nom·i·na·tion
de·noue·ment
de·nounce
  de·nounced
  de·nounc·ing
de·nounce·ment
de·nounc·er
de no·vo
dens
  pl den·tes

den·tal
den·tist
den·tist·ry
  pl den·tist·ries

den·ti·tion
den·to·le·gal
den·tu·lous
den·ture
de·ny
  de·nied
  de·ny·ing
de·o·dand
de·os·si·fi·ca·tion
de·part
de·part·ment
de·part·men·tal

de·part·men·tal·
  ism
de·part·men·tal·
  iza·tion
de·part·men·tal·ize
de·part·men·tal·
  ized
de·part·men·tal·
  iz·ing
de·part·men·tal·ly
de·par·ture
de·pend·abil·i·ty
  pl de·pend·abil·i·ties

de·pend·able
de·pen·dence
  also de·pen·dance
de·pen·den·cy
  pl de·pen·den·cies

de·pen·dent
  also de·pen·dant

de·per·son·al·iza·
  tion
de·per·son·al·ize
  de·per·son·al·
    ized
  de·per·son·al·iz·
    ing
de·pig·men·ta·tion
dep·i·late
  dep·i·lat·ed
  dep·i·lat·ing
dep·i·la·tion
de·pil·a·to·ry
  pl de·pil·a·to·ries

de pla·ci·to

de·plet·able
de·plete
  de·plet·ed
  de·plet·ing
de·ple·tion
de·ple·tive
de·pone
  de·poned
  de·pon·ing
de·po·nent
de·pon·er
de·port
de·port·abil·i·ty
de·port·able
de·por·ta·tion
de·por·tee
de·pos·able
de·pos·al
de·pose
  de·posed
  de·pos·ing
de·pos·er
de·pos·it
de·pos·i·tary
  pl de·pos·i·tar·ies

de·po·si·tion
de·po·si·tion·al
de·po·si·tion de
  bene es·se
de·pos·i·tor
de·pos·i·to·ry
  pl de·pos·i·to·ries

de·pos·i·tum
  pl de·pos·i·ta
  or de·pos·i·tums

de·pos·i·tum mi·se·
  ra·bi·le
  or de·pos·i·tum ne·
    ces·sa·ri·um
  pl de·pos·i·tum mi·
    se·ra·bi·lia
  or de·pos·i·tum ne·
    ces·sa·ria

de·pot
de·pra·va·tion
de·prave
  de·praved
  de·prav·ing
de·prave·ment
de·prav·er
de·prav·i·ty
  pl de·prav·i·ties

dep·re·cate
  dep·re·cat·ed
  dep·re·cat·ing
  to disapprove of
  (see depreciate)

de·pre·cia·ble
de·pre·ci·ate
  de·pre·ci·at·ed
  de·pre·ci·at·ing
  to lower the worth of
  (see deprecate)

de·pre·ci·at·ing·ly
de·pre·ci·a·tion
de·pre·ci·a·tive
de·pre·ci·a·tive·ly
de·pre·ci·a·tor
dep·re·date
  dep·re·dat·ed
  dep·re·dat·ing

dep·re·da·tion
dep·re·da·tor
de·pre·da·to·ry
de·press
de·pres·sant
de·press·ibil·i·ty
  pl de·press·ibil·i·ties

de·press·ible
de·pres·sion
de·pres·sion·al
de·pres·sion·ary
de·pres·sive
de·pres·sive·ly
de·pres·sor
de·pri·va·tion
de·prive
  de·prived
  de·priv·ing
de·priv·er
de pro·prio mo·tu
de·purge
  de·purged
  de·purg·ing
dep·u·ta·tion
dep·u·ta·tion·al
dep·u·ta·tive
de·pute
  de·put·ed
  de·put·ing
dep·u·tize
  dep·u·tized
  dep·u·tiz·ing
dep·u·ty
  pl dep·u·ties

de·raign
to prove
(*see* derange)

de·raign·ment
de·range
    de·ranged
    de·rang·ing
    to disorder
    (*see* deraign)

de·range·ment
de·rate
    de·rat·ed
    de·rat·ing
de·ra·tion
de·re·al·iza·tion
de·re·ism
de·re·is·tic
der·e·lict
der·e·lic·tion
de·re·press
de·re·pres·sion
de·req·ui·si·tion
de·re·strict
de·ri·sion
de·ri·sive
de·ri·sive·ly
de·ri·sive·ness
de·ri·so·ry
der·i·va·tion
de·riv·a·tive
de·rive
    de·rived
    de·riv·ing
der·mal

der·ma·ti·tis
    pl der·ma·ti·tis·es
    or der·ma·tit·i·des

der·ma·tol·o·gist
der·ma·tol·o·gy
    pl der·ma·tol·o·gies

der·ma·to·plas·ty
    pl der·ma·to·plas·ties

der·mic
der·mis
der·mop·a·thy
    pl der·mop·a·thies

der·o·gate
    der·o·gat·ed
    der·o·gat·ing
der·o·ga·tion
de·rog·a·to·ri·ly
de·rog·a·to·ri·ness
de·rog·a·to·ry
de·scend
de·scen·dance
    also de·scen·dence

de·scen·dant
    also de·scen·dent

de·scend·ible
de·scent
    passing of an estate by
    inheritance
    (*see* decent)

de·scribe
    de·scribed
    de·scrib·ing
de·scrip·tion
de·scrip·tio per·so·
nae

de·scrip·tive
des·e·crate
    des·e·crat·ed
    des·e·crat·ing
des·e·crat·er
    or des·e·cra·tor

des·e·cra·tion
de·seg·re·gate
    de·seg·re·gat·ed
    de·seg·re·gat·ing
de·seg·re·ga·tion
de·sen·si·ti·za·tion
de·sen·si·tize
    de·sen·si·tized
    de·sen·si·tiz·ing
de·sert
de·sert·er
de·ser·tion
de·serve
    de·served
    de·serv·ing
de·sex
de·sex·u·al·iza·tion
de·sex·u·al·ize
    de·sex·u·al·ized
    de·sex·u·al·iz·ing
de·sign
    de·signed
    de·sign·ing
des·ig·nate
    des·ig·nat·ed
    des·ig·nat·ing
des·ig·na·tion
des·ig·na·tio
    per·so·nae

de·sign·ed·ly
de·sire
 de·sired
 de·sir·ing
de·sist
 de·sist·ed
 de·sist·ing
de·sis·tance
 also de·sis·tence
de·sis·te·ment
de son tort
des·patch
 var of dispatch
des·per·ate
des·per·ate·ly
des·per·ate·ness
des·per·a·tion
de·spoil
de·spoil·er
de·spoil·ment
de·spo·li·a·tion
de·spon·den·cy
 pl de·spon·den·cies
des·pot·ic
des·pot·i·cal·ly
des·po·tism
des·qua·mate
 des·qua·mat·ed
 des·qua·mat·ing
des·qua·ma·tion
des·qua·ma·tive
des·qua·ma·to·ry
des·ti·na·tion
des·ti·tute
des·ti·tute·ly
des·ti·tute·ness

des·ti·tu·tion
de·stroy
de·stroy·able
de·stroy·er
de·stroy·ing·ly
de·struct
de·struc·ti·ble
de·struc·tion
de·struc·tive
de·struc·tor
de·sue·tude
de·tached
de·tail
de·tailed
de·tain
de·tain·ee
de·tain·er
de·tain·ment
de·tect
de·tect·able
de·tec·tion
de·tec·tive
de·tec·tor
de·ten·tion
de·ter
 de·terred
 de·ter·ring
de·te·ri·o·rate
 de·te·ri·o·rat·ed
 de·te·ri·o·rat·ing
de·te·ri·o·ra·tion
de·te·ri·o·ra·tive
de·ter·min·abil·i·ty
de·ter·min·able
de·ter·min·able·
 ness

de·ter·min·ably
de·ter·mi·na·tion
de·ter·mi·na·tive
de·ter·mine
de·ter·mined
de·ter·min·ing
de·ter·rence
de·ter·rent
de·throne
de·throned
de·thron·ing
de·throne·ment
det·i·net
det·i·nue
de·tin·u·it
de·tour
dé·tour·ne·ment
de·tox·i·cant
de·tox·i·cate
 de·tox·i·cat·ed
 de·tox·i·cat·ing
de·tox·i·ca·tion
de·tox·i·fi·ca·tion
de·tox·i·fi·er
de·tox·i·fy
de·tox·i·fied
de·tox·i·fy·ing
de·trac·tion
de·trac·tive
det·ri·ment
det·ri·men·tal
det·ri·men·tal·ly
det·ri·men·tal·ness
de·tu·ba·tion
de·tu·mes·cence
de·tu·mes·cent

de·tur·ges·cence
deu·ter·an·ope
deu·ter·an·opia
deu·ter·an·opic
deu·te·ri·um
deu·ter·og·a·my
   pl deu·ter·og·a·mies

deu·ter·on
   also deu·ton

de·val·u·ate
   de·val·u·at·ed
   de·val·u·at·ing
de·val·u·a·tion
de·val·ue
   de·val·ued
   de·val·u·ing
dev·as·tate
   dev·as·tat·ed
   dev·as·tat·ing
dev·as·ta·tion
dev·as·tat·ive
dev·as·ta·tor
dev·as·ta·vit
de vas·to
de·vel·op
   also de·vel·ope
   de·vel·oped
   de·vel·op·ing
de·vel·op·er
de·vel·op·ment
de·vest
de·vi·ance
de·vi·an·cy
   pl de·vi·an·cies

de·vi·ant
de·vi·ate

de·vi·at·ed
de·vi·at·ing
de·vi·a·tion
de·vi·a·tion·al
de·vi·a·tor
de·vice
dev·il
   dev·iled
   or dev·illed
   dev·il·ing
   or dev·il·ling
de·vir·gin·ate
   also de·vir·gin·ize
   de·vir·gin·at·ed
   also de·vir·gin·ized
   de·vir·gin·at·ing
   also de·vir·gin·iz·ing

de·vis·abil·i·ty
de·vis·able
dev·i·sat yel non
de·vise
   de·vised
   de·vis·ing
de·vi·see
de·vise sim·pli·
   ci·ter
de·vi·sor
de·voir
de·vo·lu·tion
de·vo·lu·tion·ary
de·vo·lu·tive
de·volve
   de·volved
   de·volv·ing
de·vote
   de·vot·ed

de·vot·ing
dex·ter
dex·tral
dex·tral·i·ty
   pl dex·tral·i·ties
di·a·be·tes
   pl di·a·be·tes

di·a·be·tes
  in·sip·i·dus
di·a·be·tes mel·li·
  tus
di·a·bet·ic
di·ag·nos·able
   or di·ag·nose·able

di·ag·nose
   di·ag·nosed
   di·ag·nos·ing
di·ag·no·sis
   pl di·ag·no·ses

di·ag·nos·tic
di·ag·nos·ti·cal·ly
di·ag·nos·ti·cian
di·ag·o·nal
di·a·per
di·a·phragm
di·a·phrag·mat·ic
di·aph·y·se·al
   or di·a·phys·i·al
di·aph·y·sis
   pl di·aph·y·ses

di·a·plas·tic
di·apoph·y·sis
   pl di·apoph·y·ses

di·ar·rhea
   or di·ar·rhoea

di·ar·rhe·al
or di·ar·rhe·ic
also di·ar·rhoe·al
or di·ar·rhoe·ic

di·as·ta·sis
   pl di·as·ta·ses

di·as·to·le

di·a·stol·ic

dia·ther·my
   pl dia·ther·mies

di·a·the·sis
   pl di·a·the·ses

di·a·thet·ic

di·az·e·pam

di·bu·caine

dice

di·chlo·ro·di·flu·o·
  ro·meth·ane

di·chro·mat

di·chro·ma·top·sia

Dick test

dic·ta·men
   pl dic·tam·i·na

dic·tate
  dic·tat·ed
  dic·tat·ing

dic·ta·tor

dic·ta·to·ri·al

dic·ta·to·ri·al·ly

dic·ta·to·ri·al·ness

dic·ta·tor·ship

dic·ta·to·ry

dic·tum
   pl dic·ta
   also dic·tums

die

died

dy·ing

diel·drin

die·ner

di·es do·mi·ni·cus
   pl di·es do·mi·ni·ci

di·es ju·ri·di·cus
   pl di·es ju·ri·di·ci

di·es non
  or di·es non ju·ri·di·cus
   pl di·es nons
  or di·es non ju·ri·di·ci

di·et

di·etary
   pl di·etar·ies

di·et·er

di·etet·ic

di·etet·i·cal·ly

di·etet·ics

dif·fer·ence

dif·fer·ent

dif·fer·en·ti·ate

dif·fer·en·ti·a·tion

dif·fi·cult

dif·fi·cul·ty
   pl dif·fi·cul·ties

dig·a·my
   pl dig·a·mies

di·gest

di·ges·tant

di·ges·tion

dig·it

dig·i·tal

dig·i·tal·in

dig·i·tal·is

dig·i·ta·li·za·tion

dig·i·tal·ize

dig·i·tal·ized

dig·i·tal·iz·ing

digi·tox·in

dig·ni·ty
   pl dig·ni·ties

di·ju·di·cate

di·ju·di·cat·ed

di·ju·di·cat·ing

di·ju·di·ca·tion

di·lap·i·date

di·lap·i·dat·ed

di·lap·i·dat·ing

di·lap·i·da·tion

di·la·ta·tion

di·la·ta·tion·al

di·la·ta·tor

di·late
  di·lat·ed
  di·lat·ing

di·la·tion

di·la·tor

dil·a·to·ri·ly

dil·a·to·ri·ness

dil·a·to·ry

dil·i·gence

dil·i·gent

dil·i·gent·ly

di·lu·tion doc·trine

di·min·ish

dim·i·nu·tion

di·mi·si

di·ovu·lar

dip
  dipped
  dip·ping

diph·the·ria
diph·the·ri·al
  or diph·the·ri·an

diph·the·ric
diph·the·rin
diph·the·rit·ic
diph·the·roid
di·ple·gia
dip·lo·coc·cal
dip·lo·coc·cic
dip·lo·coc·cus
  pl dip·lo·coc·ci

di·plo·ma·cy
  pl di·plo·ma·cies

dip·lo·mat
  one employed in diplo-
  macy
  (see diplomate)

dip·lo·mate
  one certified as quali-
  fied
  (see diplomat)

dip·lo·mat·ic
dip·lo·mat·i·cal·ly
dip·so·ma·nia
dip·so·ma·ni·ac
dip·so·ma·ni·a·cal
di·rect
di·rec·tion
di·rec·tive
di·rect·ly
di·rec·tor
di·rec·to·ry
  pl di·rec·to·ries

di·remp·tion
dir·i·ment

dis·abil·i·ty
  pl dis·abil·i·ties
dis·able
dis·abled
dis·abling
dis·able·ment
dis·af·fec·tion
dis·af·fil·i·ate
dis·af·fil·i·at·ed
dis·af·fil·i·at·ing
dis·af·fil·i·a·tion
dis·af·fect·ed
dis·af·firm
dis·af·fir·mance
dis·af·fir·ma·tion
dis·agree
dis·agree·ment
dis·al·low
dis·al·low·ance
dis·an·nex
dis·an·nul
  dis·an·nulled
  dis·an·nul·ling
dis·ap·pear
dis·ap·pear·ance
dis·ap·prov·al
dis·ap·prove
  dis·ap·proved
  dis·ap·prov·ing
dis·ar·tic·u·late
  dis·ar·tic·u·lat·
  ed
  dis·ar·tic·u·lat·
  ing
dis·ar·tic·u·la·tion
dis·as·so·ci·ate

dis·as·so·ci·at·ed
dis·as·so·ci·at·
  ing
dis·as·so·ci·a·tion
di·sas·ter
di·sas·trous
di·sas·trous·ly
dis·avow
dis·avow·al
dis·band
dis·bar
  dis·barred
  dis·bar·ring
dis·bar·ment
dis·burs·al
dis·burse
  dis·bursed
  dis·burs·ing
dis·burse·ment
dis·burs·er
dis·charge
  dis·charged
  dis·charg·ing
dis·ci·plin·ary
dis·ci·pline
  dis·ci·plined
  dis·ci·plin·ing
dis·claim
dis·claim·ant
dis·claim·er
dis·cla·ma·tion
dis·clam·a·to·ry
dis·close
  dis·closed
  dis·clos·ing
dis·clo·sure

dis·con·firm
dis·con·tin·u·ance
dis·con·tin·u·a·tion
dis·con·tin·ue
  dis·con·tin·ued
  dis·con·tinu·ing
dis·con·tin·u·ous
dis·count
dis·count·able
dis·cov·er
dis·co·vert
dis·cov·er·ture
dis·cov·ery
  pl dis·cov·er·ies

dis·cred·it
dis·cred·it·able
dis·cred·it·ed
dis·creet·ly
  in a discreet manner
  (*see* discretely)

dis·crep·an·cy
  pl dis·crep·an·cies
dis·crete·ly
  separately
  (*see* discreetly)

dis·cre·tion
dis·cre·tion·al
dis·cre·tion·ary
dis·crim·i·nate
  dis·crim·i·nat·ed
  dis·crim·i·nat·
    ing
dis·crim·i·na·tion
dis·crim·i·na·tion·
  al
dis·crim·i·na·tor

dis·crim·i·na·to·ry
dis·cuss
  dis·cussed
  dis·cuss·ing
dis·cus·sion
dis·ease
  pl dis·eas·es

dis·eased
dis·en·fran·chise
  dis·en·fran·
    chised
  dis·en·fran·chis·
    ing
dis·en·fran·chise·
  ment
dis·en·able
  dis·en·abled
  dis·en·abling
dis·en·gage
  dis·en·gaged
  dis·en·gag·ing
dis·en·gage·ment
dis·en·tail
  or dis·en·tail·ment

dis·en·ti·tle
  dis·en·ti·tled
  dis·en·ti·tling
dis·equi·lib·ri·um
  pl dis·equi·lib·ri·ums
  or dis·equi·lib·ria

dis·es·tab·lish
dis·fig·ure
  dis·fig·ured
  dis·fig·ur·ing
dis·fig·ure·ment
dis·fig·ur·er

dis·fig·ur·ing·ly
dis·fran·chise
  dis·fran·chised
  dis·fran·chis·ing
dis·fran·chise·ment
dis·func·tion
  var of dysfunction

dis·grace
  dis·graced
  dis·grac·ing
dis·grace·ful
dis·guise
  dis·guised
  dis·guis·ing
dis·her·i·son
dis·hon·est
dis·hon·es·ty
  pl dis·hon·es·ties

dis·hon·or
dis·hon·or·able
dis·hon·or·able·
  ness
dis·hon·or·ably
dis·in·cor·po·rate
  dis·in·cor·po·rat·
    ed
  dis·in·cor·po·rat·
    ing
dis·in·cor·po·ra·
  tion
dis·in·fect
dis·in·fec·tant
dis·in·fec·tion
dis·in·fest
dis·in·fes·tant
dis·in·fes·ta·tion

dis·in·her·i·son
dis·in·her·it
dis·in·her·i·tance
   also dis·in·her·i·ta·tion
dis·in·ter
  dis·in·terred
  dis·in·ter·ring
dis·in·ter·est·ed
dis·in·ter·est·ed·ly
dis·in·vest
dis·in·vest·ment
dis·join
dis·joint·ed
dis·junc·tive
dis·lo·cate
  dis·lo·cat·ed
  dis·lo·cat·ing
dis·lo·ca·tion
dis·loy·al
dis·loy·al·ty
  pl dis·loy·al·ties
dis·man·tle
  dis·man·tled
  dis·man·tling
dis·mem·ber
dis·mem·ber·ment
dis·miss
dis·miss·al
dis·mort·gage
  dis·mort·gaged
  dis·mort·gag·ing
dis·obe·di·ence
dis·obe·di·ent
dis·obe·di·ent·ly
dis·obey
  dis·obeyed

dis·obey·ing
dis·or·der
dis·or·der·li·ness
dis·or·der·ly
dis·ori·ent
dis·ori·en·ta·tion
dis·par·age
  dis·par·aged
  dis·par·ag·ing
dis·par·age·ment
dis·patch
  or des·patch
dis·pen·sa·ry
  pl dis·pen·sa·ries
dis·pen·sa·tion
dis·pense
  dis·pensed
  dis·pens·ing
dis·place
  dis·placed
  dis·plac·ing
dis·place·ment
dis·pone
  dis·poned
  dis·pon·ing
dis·pon·ee
dis·pon·er
dis·po·net
dis·pos·able
dis·pos·al
dis·pose
  dis·posed
  dis·pos·ing
dis·po·si·tion
dis·pos·i·tive
dis·pos·sess

dis·pos·ses·sion
dis·pos·ses·sor
dis·pos·ses·so·ry
dis·proof
dis·prove
  dis·proved
  dis·prov·ing
dis·pu·ta·bil·i·ty
dis·pu·ta·ble
dis·pu·ta·bly
dis·pu·tant
dis·pute
  dis·put·ed
  dis·put·ing
dis·qual·i·fi·ca·tion
dis·qual·i·fy
  dis·qual·i·fied
  dis·qual·i·fy·ing
dis·re·gard
dis·rep·u·ta·bil·i·ty
dis·rep·u·ta·ble
dis·rep·u·ta·bly
dis·re·pute
dis·seise
  or dis·seize
dis·seised
  or dis·seized
dis·seis·ing
  or dis·seiz·ing
dis·seis·ee
  or dis·seiz·ee
dis·sei·sin
  or dis·sei·zin
dis·sei·sor
  or dis·sei·zor
dis·sem·blance

dis·sem·ble
  dis·sem·bled
  dis·sem·bling
dis·sem·bler
dis·sem·bling·ly
dis·sem·i·nate
  dis·sem·i·nat·ed
  dis·sem·i·nat·ing
dis·sem·i·na·tion
dis·sen·sion
  also dis·sen·tion

dis·sent
dis·sent·er
dis·si·dent
  one who disagrees
  (*see* decedent)

dis·si·pate
  dis·si·pat·ed
  dis·si·pat·ing
dis·so·ci·ate
  dis·so·ci·at·ed
  dis·so·ci·at·ing
dis·so·ci·a·tion
dis·so·lute
dis·so·lu·tion
dis·so·lu·tive
dis·solv·abil·i·ty
dis·solv·able
dis·solve
  dis·solved
  dis·solv·ing
dis·suad·able
dis·suade
  dis·suad·ed
  dis·suad·ing
dis·suad·er

dis·sua·sion
dis·sua·sive
dis·sua·sive·ly
dis·sua·sive·ness
dis·till
  also dis·til
dis·tilled
dis·till·ing
dis·till·able
dis·til·la·tion
dis·till·ery
  pl dis·till·er·ies

dis·tinct
dis·tinc·tion
dis·tinc·tive
dis·tinc·tive·ly
dis·tinct·ly
dis·tin·guish
dis·tin·guish·able
dis·tin·guished
dis·train
dis·train·able
dis·train·ee
dis·train·er
  or dis·train·or

dis·traint
dis·tress
dis·trib·ut·able
dis·trib·ute
  dis·trib·ut·ed
  dis·trib·ut·ing
dis·trib·u·tee
dis·tri·bu·tion
dis·trib·u·tive
dis·trib·u·tive·ly

dis·trib·u·tor
  also dis·trib·ut·er
dis·trib·u·tor·ship
dis·trict
di·strin·gas
dis·turb
dis·tur·bance
dis·turbed
dis·turb·ing
dit·tay
dit·to
  pl dit·tos
  also dit·toes
di·verge
  di·verged
  di·verg·ing
di·ver·gence
di·ver·gent
di·vers
di·verse
di·ver·sion
di·ver·si·ty
  pl di·ver·si·ties

di·vert
di·vest
di·ves·ti·tive
di·ves·ti·ture
di·vest·ment
di·ves·ture
di·vide
  di·vid·ed
  di·vid·ing
div·i·dend
di·vis·i·bil·i·ty
  pl di·vis·i·bil·i·ties

di·vis·i·ble

doomage

di·vis·i·ble·ness
di·vi·sion
di·vi·sion·al
di·vorce
  di·vorced
  di·vorc·ing
di·vorce·able
di·vor·cée
  also di·vor·cee

di·vorc·er
di·vulge
  di·vulged
  di·vulg·ing
di·vulge·ment
di·vul·gence
diz·zi·ness
diz·zy
  diz·zi·er
  diz·zi·est
dock
dock·age
dock·et
  dock·et·ed
  dock·et·ing
doc·trin·al
doc·trine
doc·u·ment
doc·u·ment·able
doc·u·men·tal
doc·u·men·ta·ry
doc·u·men·ta·tion
dog·ma
  pl dog·mas
  also dog·ma·ta

dog·mat·ic
  also dog·mat·i·cal

do·li ca·pax
do·li in·ca·pax
do·lus
do·lus bo·nus
do·lus ma·lus
do·main
  territory possessed and
  governed
  (*see* demean, demesne)

do·mes·tic
do·mes·ti·cate
  do·mes·ti·cat·ed
  do·mes·ti·cat·ing
do·mes·ti·ca·tion
do·mes·ti·ca·tor
do·mi·cile
  do·mi·ciled
  do·mi·cil·ing
do·mi·cile
  also dom·i·cil

do·mi·cil·i·ary
  also do·mi·cil·i·ar

do·mi·cil·i·ate
  do·mi·cil·i·at·ed
  do·mi·cil·i·at·ing
do·mi·cil·i·a·tion
do·mi·na li·tis
  pl do·mi·nae li·tis

dom·i·nant
dom·i·nate
  dom·i·nat·ed
  dom·i·nat·ing
dom·i·na·tion
dom·i·na·tor
do·min·ion

do·mi·ni·um
em·e·nens
do·mi·nus
  pl do·mi·ni

do·mi·nus li·tis
  pl do·mi·ni li·tis

do·mi·tae
na·tu·rae
do·nate
  do·nat·ed
  do·nat·ing
do·na·tee
do·na·tio
  pl do·na·tio·nes

do·na·tio in·ter
  vi·vos
do·na·tio mo·da·lis
do·na·tio mor·tis
  cau·sa
do·na·tion
do·na·tio
  om·ni·um
  bo·no·rum
do·na·tio re·la·ta
do·na·tio
  re·mu·no·ra·
  to·ria
do·na·tio sub mo·
  do
do·na·tive
do·na·tor
do·nee
do·nor
doom
doom·age

dope
  doped
  dop·ing
dope·sheet
dor·man·cy
  pl dor·man·cies
dor·mant
dor·sal
dor·sal·gia
dor·so·lat·er·al
dor·so·ven·tral
dor·so·ven·tral·ly
dos·age
dose
  dosed
  dos·ing
do·sim·e·ter
  also dose·me·ter
do·si·met·ric
do·sim·e·try
dos ra·ti·o·na·bi·lis
dos·sier
dot
dot·age
do·tal
dou·ble
dou·ble cross *n*
dou·ble-cross *vb*
doubt
doubt·able
doubt·er
doubt·ful
doubt·ful·ly
doubt·ful·ness
douche

douched
douch·ing
Do·ver's pow·der
dow·able
dow·a·ger
dow·er
  or dow·ry
  pl dow·ers
  or dow·ries
dow·er·less
  or dow·ry·less

dow·ment
dra·co·ni·an
dra·con·ic
draft
drafts·man
  pl drafts·men

drag·net
drain
drain·age
dras·tic
draw
  drew
  drawn
  draw·ing
draw·back *n*
draw back *vb*
  drew back
  drawn back
  draw·ing back
draw·ee
draw·er
dray·age
drift
drift·ing

drift·way
drink
  drank
  drunk
  drink·ing
drink·able
drink·om·e·ter
drip
drive
  drove
  driv·en
  driv·ing
driv·er
driv·er·less
droit
  ad·mi·nis·tra·tif
droit de
  de·trac·tion
droit-droit
droi·tu·ral
drop·si·cal
drop·sy
  pl drop·sies
drown
drug
  drugged
  drug·ging
drug·gist
drug·mak·er
drug·store
drum·mer
drunk
  drunk·er
  drunk·est
drunk·ard

drunk·en·ness
drunk·o·me·ter
dry
dry dock *n*
dry-dock *vb*
dry nurse *n*
dry-nurse *vb*
  dry-nursed
  dry-nurs·ing
du·al
du·bi·ous
du·bi·tan·te
du·bi·ta·tur
du·ces te·cum
duc·tile
duc·tus ar·te·ri·o·sus
duc·tus ve·no·sus
due
du·ly
dum be·ne se ges·se·rit
dum cas·ta
dum fer·vet opus
dum·my
  pl dum·mies
dump
dump·ing
dump·ing syn·drome
dum so·la
dun
  dunned
  dun·ning
Dun·ham rule

dun·nage
du·o·de·nal
du·o·de·num
  pl du·o·de·na
  or du·o·de·nums
du·pli·cate
du·pli·cat·ed
du·pli·cat·ing
du·pli·ca·tion
du·plic·i·tous
du·plic·i·ty
  pl du·plic·i·ties
Du·puy·tren's con·trac·ture
du·ra·ble
du·ral
du·ra ma·ter
du·ran·te
du·ran·te ab·sen·tia
du·ran·te vi·ta
du·ra·tion
du·ress
Dur·ham rule
dur·ing
du·ti·able
du·ti·ful
du·ti·ful·ly
du·ty
  pl du·ties
dwell
  dwelt
    also dwelled
  dwell·ing
dy·ing

dy·na·mite
dy·na·mit·ed
dy·na·mit·ing
dy·nas·ty
  pl dy·nas·ties
dys·acou·sia
  also dys·acou·sis
  pl dys·acou·sias
  also dys·acou·ses
dys·ad·ap·ta·tion
dys·ba·rism
dys·bu·lia
dys·cra·sia
dys·en·ter·ic
dys·en·tery
  pl dys·en·ter·ies
dys·er·gia
  also dys·er·gy
  pl dys·er·gias
  also dys·er·gies
dys·es·the·sia
dys·es·thet·ic
dys·func·tion
  also dis·func·tion
dys·func·tion·al
dys·gno·sia
dys·graph·ia
dys·ki·ne·sia
dys·ki·net·ic
dys·lec·tic
dys·lex·ia
dys·lo·gia
dys·mne·sia
dys·no·my
  pl dys·no·mies

dys·os·mia
dys·pa·reu·nia
dys·pep·sia
dys·pep·tic
  also dys·pep·ti·cal

dys·pep·ti·cal·ly
dys·pha·sia
dys·pha·sic
dys·phe·mia
dys·pnea
  also dys·pnoea

dys·pne·ic
  or dys·pnoe·ic

dys·sta·sia
dys·tro·phic
dys·tro·phy
  also dys·tro·phia
  pl dys·tro·phies
  also dys·tro·phi·as

dys·uria

E

ea in·ten·ti·o·ne
ear·ache
ear·drum
ear·lobe
ear·ly
  ear·li·er
  ear·li·est
ear·mark
earn
earn·able
earn·er

ear·nest
earn·ings *n pl*
earth
earth·quake
ear·wit·ness
ease·ment
ease·ment ap·pur·
  te·nant
ease·ment in gross
east·bound
east·er·ly
east·ern
east·ward
east·ward·ly
easy
  eas·i·er
  eas·i·est
eaves
eaves·drop
  eaves·dropped
  eaves·drop·ping
  eaves·drop·per
ebri·e·ty
  pl ebri·e·ties

ebri·os·i·ty
  pl ebri·os·i·ties

ec·cen·tric
ec·cen·tri·cal·ly
ec·cen·tric·i·ty
  pl ec·cen·tric·i·ties

ec·chy·mosed
ec·chy·mo·sis
  pl ec·chy·mo·ses

ec·chy·mot·ic

ec·cle·si·as·tic
ec·cle·si·as·ti·cal
ec·cle·si·as·ti·cal·ly
ec·cy·e·sis
  pl ec·cy·e·ses

echi·no·coc·co·sis
  pl echi·no·coc·co·ses

echi·no·coc·cus
  pl echi·no·coc·ci

echo·la·lia
eclamp·sia
eclamp·tic
eco·nom·ic
eco·nom·i·cal
eco·nom·i·cal·ly
econ·o·my
  pl econ·o·mies

e con·tra
e con·ver·so
ec·ta·sia
ec·ta·sis
  pl ec·ta·ses

ec·tat·ic
ect·eth·moid
  also ect·eth·moi·dal
  or ec·to·eth·moid

ec·to·cer·vix
  pl ec·to·cer·vi·ces
  or ec·to·cer·vix·es

ec·to·derm
ec·to·der·mal
  or ec·to·der·mic

ec·to·gen·ic
ec·tog·e·nous

ec·to·par·a·site
ect·os·te·al
ec·ze·ma
ec·ze·ma·tous
ede·ma
   also oe·de·ma
   pl ede·mas
   or ede·ma·ta
   also oe·de·mas
   or oe·de·ma·ta

edem·a·tous
eden·tu·lous
ed·i·bil·i·ty
ed·i·ble
edict
edic·tal
edic·tal·ly
ed·it
   ed·it·ed
   ed·it·ing
edi·tion
ed·i·tor
ed·i·to·ri·al
ed·u·cate
   ed·u·cat·ed
   ed·u·cat·ing
ed·u·ca·tion
ed·u·ca·tion·al
ed·u·ca·tion·al·ly
ed·u·ca·tive
ed·u·ca·tor
educe
   educed
   educ·ing
educ·ible
ef·fect

ef·fect·ed
ef·fec·tive
ef·fects
ef·fec·tu·al
ef·fec·tu·al·i·ty
ef·fec·tu·al·ly
ef·fec·tu·ate
   ef·fec·tu·at·ed
   ef·fec·tu·at·ing
ef·fem·i·na·cy
ef·fem·i·nate
ef·fi·cient
ef·frac·tion
ef·frac·tor
   pl ef·frac·to·res

egress
eigne
ejac·u·late
   ejac·u·lat·ed
   ejac·u·lat·ing
ejac·u·la·tion
ejac·u·la·to·ry
ejac·u·lum
   pl ejac·u·la
eject
ejec·tion
eject·ment
ejec·tor
ejec·tum
   pl ejec·ta

ejus·dem ge·ne·ris
elapse
   elapsed
   elaps·ing
el·bow

el·der
el·der·ly
el·dest
elect
elec·tion
elec·tion·eer
elec·tive
elec·tive·ly
elec·tor
elec·tor·al
elec·tor·ate
elec·to·ri·al
elec·tro·car·dio·
   gram
elec·tro·car·dio·
   graph
elec·tro·car·di·og·
   ra·phy
elec·tro·cau·ter·i·
   za·tion
elec·tro·cau·tery
   pl elec·tro·cau·ter·ies

elec·tro·co·ag·u·la·
   tion
elec·tro·con·vul·
   sive
elec·tro·cute
   elec·tro·cut·ed
   elec·tro·cut·ing
elec·tro·cu·tion
elec·tro·cu·tion·al
elec·tro·des·ic·ca·
   tion
elec·tro·en·ceph·a·
   lo·gram

elec·tro·en·ceph·a·
lo·graph
elec·tro·en·ceph·a·
lo·graph·ic
elec·tro·en·ceph·a·
log·ra·phy
elec·tro·plexy
pl elec·tro·plex·ies
elec·tro·shock
elec·tro·sleep
elec·tro·sur·gery
pl elec·tro·sur·ger·ies
el·ee·mos·y·nary
el·e·gan·ter
el·e·git
el·e·men·ta·ry
el·e·va·tion
el·e·va·tor
elic·it
elic·it·ed
elic·it·ing
to draw or bring out
(see illicit)
el·i·gi·bil·i·ty
el·i·gi·ble
qualified to have
(see illegible)
elim·i·nate
elim·i·nat·ed
elim·i·nat·ing
elim·i·na·tion
eli·sion
eli·sor
el·lip·sis
pl el·lip·ses
eloign
eloign·ment

elope
eloped
elop·ing
elope·ment
elop·er
else·where
elu·ci·date
elu·ci·dat·ed
elu·ci·dat·ing
elu·ci·da·tion
elude
elud·ed
elud·ing
to evade
(see illude)
elu·sion
elu·sive
ema·ci·ate
ema·ci·at·ed
ema·ci·at·ing
ema·ci·a·tion
eman·ci·pate
eman·ci·pa·ted
eman·ci·pat·ing
eman·ci·pa·tio
eman·ci·pa·tion
eman·ci·pa·tor
emas·cu·late
emas·cu·lat·ed
emas·cu·lat·ing
emas·cu·la·tion
em·bar·go *n*
also im·bar·go
pl em·bar·goes
also im·bar·goes

em·bar·go *vb*
also im·bar·go

em·bar·goed
also im·bar·goed
em·bar·go·ing
also im·bar·go·ing

em·bar·rass
em·bar·rass·ment
em·bas·sa·dor
var of ambassador
em·bas·sa·dress
var of ambassadress
em·bas·sy
pl em·bas·sies

em·bez·zle
em·bez·zled
em·bez·zling
em·bez·zle·ment
em·bez·zler
em·ble·ments *n pl*
em·bol·ic
em·bo·lism
em·bo·li·za·tion
em·bo·lo·la·lia
also em·bol·la·lia

em·brace
em·braced
em·brac·ing
em·bra·ceor
em·brac·er
em·brac·ery
pl em·brac·er·ies

em·bro·glio
var of imbroglio

em·bryo
pl em·bry·os

emend

emend·able
emen·da·tion
emer·gen·cy
   pl emer·gen·cies

emer·gent
eme·sis
   pl eme·ses

emet·ic
em·e·tine
em·i·grant
em·i·grate
   em·i·grat·ed
   em·i·grat·ing
em·i·gra·tion
em·i·gra·tion·al
émi·gré
   or emi·gré
   also emi·gre
   or emi·gree

emi·nence
   high position
   (*see* immanence, immi-
   nence)

émi·nence grise
   pl éminences grises

emi·nent
   of higher status
   (*see* immanent, immi-
   nent)

emi·nent do·main
em·is·sary
   pl em·is·sar·ies

emis·sion
emit
   emit·ted
   emit·ting
emol·u·ment

emo·tion
emo·tion·al
emo·tion·al·ly
em·pan·el
   var of impanel

em·parl
   var of imparl

em·phy·se·ma
em·phy·se·ma·tous
em·ploy
   em·ployed
   em·ploy·ing
em·ploy·abil·i·ty
em·ploy·able
em·ploy·ee
   or em·ploye

em·ploy·er
em·ploy·ment
em·po·ri·um
   pl em·po·ri·ums
   or em·po·ria

em·pow·er
em·pow·er·ment
emp·tion
emp·tio·ven·di·tio
   or emp·tio et ven·di·tio

emp·tor
emp·ty *adj*
   emp·ti·er
   emp·ti·est
emp·ty *vb*
   emp·tied
   emp·ty·ing
em·py·ema
   pl em·py·ema·ta
   or em·py·emas

em·py·emic
en·able
en·abled
en·abling
en·abler
en·act
en·act·ment
en·an·them
   or en·an·the·ma
   pl en·an·thems
   or en·an·the·ma·ta

en·an·them·a·tous
en·ar·thro·sis
   pl en·ar·thro·s2s

en·cap·su·late
   en·cap·su·lat·ed
   en·cap·su·lat·ing
en·cap·su·la·tion
en·ceinte
en·ceph·a·lal·gia
en·ceph·a·lit·ic
en·ceph·a·li·tis
   pl en·ceph·a·lit·i·des

en·ceph·a·li·to·
gen·ic
   also en·ceph·a·li·
   tog·e·nous

en·ceph·a·lo·gram
en·ceph·a·lo·graph
en·ceph·a·log·ra·
phy
   pl en·ceph·a·log·ra·
   phies

en·ceph·a·lo·men·
in·gi·tis
   pl en·ceph·a·lo·men·
   in·git·i·des

en·ceph·a·lo·my·
eli·tis
pl en·ceph·a·lo·my·
elit·i·des
en·ceph·a·lon
pl en·ceph·a·la
en·ceph·a·lop·a·thy
pl en·ceph·a·lop·a·thies
en clair
en·clave
en·close
or in·close
en·closed
or in·closed
en·clos·ing
or in·clos·ing
en·clo·sure
or in·clo·sure
en·coun·ter
en·coun·tered
en·coun·ter·ing
en·cour·age
en·cour·aged
en·cour·ag·ing
en·cour·age·ment
en·croach
en·croach·ment
en·cum·ber
or in·cum·ber
en·cum·bered
or in·cum·bered
en·cum·ber·ing
or in·cum·ber·ing
en·cum·brance
or in·cum·brance
en·cum·branc·er
or in·cum·branc·er

en·dam·age
en·dam·age·ment
en·dan·ger
en·dan·gered
en·dan·ger·ing
end·aor·ti·tis
end·ar·te·ri·tis
end·ar·te·ri·tis
ob·lit·er·ans
en·deav·or
also en·deav·our
en·deav·ored
also en·deav·oured
en·deav·or·ing
also en·deav·our·ing
en dec·la·ra·tion
de si·mu·la·tion
en de·meure
en·dem·ic
en·den·i·za·tion
en·den·i·zen
en·do·car·di·al
en·do·car·di·tis
en·do·car·di·um
pl en·do·car·dia
en·do·cer·vi·cal
en·do·cer·vi·ci·tis
en·do·crine
en·do·crin·ic
en·do·cri·no·log·ic
or en·do·cri·no·log·i·cal
en·do·cri·nol·o·gist
en·do·cri·nol·o·gy
pl en·do·cri·nol·o·gies
end·odon·tics
end·odon·tist

en·dog·a·mous
en·dog·a·my
en·do·me·tri·tis
en·do·phle·bi·tis
en·dors·able
en·dorse
en·dorsed
en·dors·ing
en·dors·ee
en·dorse·ment
en·dors·er
en·do·scope
en·do·scop·ic
en·dos·co·py
pl en·dos·co·pies
en·do·the·li·al
en·do·the·li·um
pl en·do·the·lia
en·do·tox·in
en·dow
en·dow·ment
en·dur·ance
en·dure
en·dured
en·dur·ing
en·e·ma
pl en·e·mas
also en·e·ma·ta
en·e·my
pl en·e·mies
en·er·vate
en·er·vat·ed
en·er·vat·ing
en·er·va·tion
en fait
en·feoff

en·feoff·ment
en·force
 en·forced
 en·forc·ing
en·force·abil·i·ty
en·force·able
en·force·ment
en·fran·chise
 en·fran·chised
 en·fran·chis·ing
en·fran·chise·ment
en·gage
 en·gaged
 en·gag·ing
en·gage·ment
en·gen·der
 en·gen·dered
 en·gen·der·ing
en·gorge
 en·gorged
 en·gorg·ing
en·gorge·ment
en·gross
 prepare a text; pur-
 chase in quantity
 (*see* in gross)

en·hance
 en·hanced
 en·hanc·ing
en·hance·ment
enig·ma
 pl enig·mas
 also enig·ma·ta

en·join
en·join·der
en·joy

en·joyed
en·joy·ing
en·joy·ment
en·large
 en·larged
 en·larg·ing
en·large·ment
en·list
en·list·ment
en·quire
 var of inquire

en·qui·ry
 var of inquiry

en·rich·ment
en·roll
 or en·rol
 en·rolled
 en·roll·ing
en·roll·ment
 or en·rol·ment

en route
ens le·gis
 pl en·tia le·gis

en·su·ant
en·sue
 en·sued
 en·su·ing
en·tail
 en·tailed
 en·tail·ing
en·tail·er
en·tail·ment
en·ter
 en·tered
 en·ter·ing
en·ter·al·gia

en·ter·i·tis
 pl en·ter·it·i·des
 or en·ter·i·tis·es

en·tero·co·li·tis
en·ter·op·a·thy
 pl en·ter·op·a·thies

en·ter·os·to·my
 pl en·ter·os·to·mies

en·ter·prise
 also en·ter·prize

en·ter·tain
 en·ter·tained
 en·ter·tain·ing
en·ter·tain·ment
en·tice
 en·ticed
 en·tic·ing
en·tice·ment
en·tire
en·tire·ly
en·tire·ty
 pl en·tire·ties

en·ti·tle
 en·ti·tled
 en·ti·tling
en·ti·tle·ment
en·ti·ty
 pl en·ti·ties

en·trance
en·trap
 en·trapped
 en·trap·ping
en·trap·ment
en·treat
en·treaty
 pl en·treat·ies

en·tre·pre·neur
en·tro·pi·on
en·trust
  or in·trust

en·trust·ment
en·try
  pl en·tries

en·try·man
  pl en·try·men

enu·cle·ate
  enu·cle·at·ed
  enu·cle·at·ing
enu·cle·ation
enu·mer·a·ble
  countable
  (*see* innumerable)

enu·mer·ate
  enu·mer·at·ed
  enu·mer·at·ing
enu·mer·a·tion
enu·mer·a·tor
en·ure
  var of inure

en·ure·sis
  pl en·ure·ses

en ven·tre sa mère
en·voy
eo ip·so
eon·ism
eo no·mi·ne
ep·ar·te·ri·al
ep·ax·i·al
  also ep·ax·on·ic

ephed·rine

epi·can·thic
epi·can·thus
epi·car·di·al
epi·car·di·um
  pl epi·car·dia

epi·cra·ni·al
epi·cra·ni·um
  pl epi·cra·ni·ums
  or epi·cra·nia

ep·i·dem·ic
epi·de·mi·o·log·ic
  or ep·i·de·mi·o·log·i·cal

ep·i·de·mi·o·log·i·cal·ly
ep·i·de·mi·ol·o·gist
ep·i·de·mi·ol·o·gy
  pl ep·i·de·mi·ol·o·gies

epi·der·mal
  also epi·der·mic

epi·der·mis
epi·der·mol·y·sis
  pl epi·der·mol·y·ses

ep·i·did·y·mal
ep·i·did·y·mis
  pl ep·i·did·y·mi·des

epi·glot·tal
  also epi·glot·tic

epi·glot·tis
  pl epi·glot·tis·es
  or epi·glot·tid·es

ep·i·lep·sy
  pl ep·i·lep·sies

ep·i·lep·tic
ep·i·lep·ti·form
ep·i·lep·to·gen·ic

ep·i·lep·toid
epiph·y·se·al
  or ep·i·phys·i·al

epiph·y·sis
  pl epiph·y·ses

ep·i·stax·is
  pl ep·i·stax·es

ep·i·the·li·al
ep·i·the·li·o·ma
  pl ep·i·the·li·o·mas
  or ep·i·the·li·o·ma·ta

ep·i·the·li·um
  pl ep·i·the·lia
  also ep·i·the·li·ums

ep·i·thet
equa·ble
  lacking variation
  (*see* equitable)

equal
  equaled
  or equalled
  equal·ing
  or equal·ling
equal·i·ty
  pl equal·i·ties

equal·iza·tion
equal·ize
  equal·ized
  equal·iz·ing
equal·ly
equi·dis·tant
equi·lib·ri·um
  pl equi·lib·ri·ums
  or equi·lib·ria

equip
  equipped

equip·ping
equip·ment
eq·ui·ta·ble
  involving equity
  (*see* equable)

eq·ui·ta·bly
eq·ui·ty
  pl eq·ui·ties

equiv·a·lence
  or equiv·a·len·cy
  pl equiv·a·lenc·es
  or equiv·a·len·cies

equiv·a·lent
equiv·o·ca·cy
  pl equiv·o·ca·cies

equiv·o·cal
equiv·o·cal·i·ty
  pl equiv·o·cal·i·ties

equiv·o·cal·ly
equiv·o·cate
  equiv·o·cat·ed
  equiv·o·cat·ing
equiv·o·ca·tion
equiv·o·ca·tor
erase
  erased
  eras·ing
era·sure
erec·tile
erec·tion
er·e·thism
er·e·this·mic
er·got
er·got·a·mine
er·got·ism
er·got·ized

Er·ic doc·trine
erode
  erod·ed
  erod·ing
erog·e·nous
  also er·o·gen·ic

ero·sion
erot·ic
  also erot·i·cal

erot·i·cal·ly
erot·i·cism
ero·to·gen·e·sis
  pl ero·to·gen·e·ses

ero·to·gen·ic
ero·to·path
er·o·top·a·thy
  pl er·o·top·a·thies

er·ran·cy
  pl er·ran·cies

er·rant
er·ra·tum
  pl er·ra·ta

er·ro·ne·ous
er·ro·ne·ous·ly
er·ror
eruc·tate
  eruc·tat·ed
  eruc·tat·ing
eruc·ta·tion
erupt
erup·tion
erup·tion·al
erup·tive
ery·sip·e·las

ery·si·pel·a·tous
ery·sip·e·loid
eryth·ro·cyte
eryth·ro·der·ma
  pl eryth·ro·der·mas
  or eryth·ro·der·ma·ta

eryth·ro·my·cin
eryth·ro·poi·e·sis
eryth·ro·poi·et·ic
es·ca·la·tor
es·cape
  es·caped
  es·cap·ing
es·cape·way
es·cap·ism
es·cap·ist
es·char
es·cha·rot·ic
es·cheat
es·cheat·able
es·chew
es·chew·al
es·crow
es·crow·ee
esoph·a·ge·al
  also esoph·a·gal
  or oe·soph·a·ge·al

esoph·a·gus
  also oe·soph·a·gus
  pl esoph·a·gi
  also oe·soph·a·gi

es·pi·o·nage
es·plees *n pl*
es·pous·al
es·pouse
  es·poused

es·pous·ing
es·quire
es·say
  to try tentatively
  (*see* assay)

es·sence
es·sen·tial
es·sen·tial·ly
es·soin
es·soin·ee
es·soin·er
es·tab·lish
es·tab·lish·able
es·tab·lish·er
es·tab·lish·ment
es·tate
es·tate tail
es·the·sia
  or aes·the·sia

es·ti·mate
  es·ti·mat·ed
  es·ti·mat·ing
es·ti·ma·tion
es·top
  es·topped
  es·top·ping
es·top·pel
es·top·pel in pais
es·to·vers *n pl*
es·trange
  es·tranged
  es·trang·ing
es·trange·ment
es·tray
es·treat

es·trepe
es·trepe·ment
es·tro·gen
  also oes·tro·gen
es·tro·gen·ic
  also oes·tro·gen·ic
es·tru·al
  or oes·tru·al
es·trus
  or es·trum
  or oes·trus
  or oes·trum
eth·a·nol
ether
ether·iza·tion
ether·ize
  ether·ized
  ether·iz·ing
eth·moid
eth·moid·al
eth·yl·mor·phine
eti·o·log·ic
  or eti·o·log·i·cal
eti·ol·o·gy
  or ae·ti·ol·o·gy
  also ai·ti·ol·o·gy
  pl eti·ol·o·gies
  or ae·ti·ol·o·gies
  also ai·ti·ol·o·gies
et se·quens
et sic
et ux·or
et vir
eu·caine
eu·nuch
eu·nuch·ism
eu·nuch·oid

eu·nuch·oi·dal
eu·pho·ria
eu·phor·ic
eu·sta·chian
eu·tha·na·sia
eu·tha·na·sic
evac·u·ate
  evac·u·at·ed
  evac·u·at·ing
evac·u·a·tion
evac·u·ee
evade
  evad·ed
  evad·ing
eval·u·ate
  eval·u·at·ed
  eval·u·at·ing
eval·u·a·tion
eva·sion
eva·sive
event
even·tu·al
even·tu·al·ly
ever·sion
evict
evict·ee
evic·tion
evic·tor
ev·i·dence
ev·i·dent
ev·i·den·tial
ev·i·den·tia·ry
ev·i·dent·ly
evince
  evinced

evinc·ing
ev·i·ra·tion
evis·cer·ate
  evis·cer·at·ed
  evis·cer·at·ing
evis·cer·a·tion
evo·lu·tion
evul·sion
ex abun·dan·ti
  cau·te·la
ex·act
ex·ac·tion
ex·act·ly
ex ad·ver·so
ex ae·qui·ta·te
ex ae·quo et bo·no
ex al·te·re par·te
ex·am·i·na·tion
ex·am·ine
  ex·am·ined
  ex·am·in·ing
ex·am·in·er
ex·an·them
  also ex·an·the·ma
  pl ex·an·thems
  also ex·an·the·ma·ta
  or ex·an·the·mas
ex·an·them·a·tous
ex·ap·pro·pri·a·tion
ex·camb
ex·cam·bi·on
ex·cam·bi·um
ex ca·the·dra
ex·ca·vate
  ex·ca·vat·ed
  ex·ca·vat·ing

ex·ca·va·tor
ex·ceed
ex·cept
  also ex·cept·ing
ex·cep·tio
  pl ex·cep·ti·o·nes
ex·cep·tion
ex·cep·tion·al
ex·cep·tio rei
  ju·di·ca·ta
ex·cep·tor
  one who objects
  (see acceptor)
ex·cess
  intemperance
  (see access)
ex·ces·sive
ex·ces·sive·ly
ex·change
ex·che·quer
ex·cise
  or ex·cise tax
ex·cise·man
  pl ex·cise·men
ex·clude
  ex·clud·ed
  ex·clud·ing
ex·clu·sion
ex·clu·sive
ex·clu·sive·ly
ex co·mi·ta·te
ex com·mo·da·tio
ex com·pa·ra·tio·
  ne scrip·to·rum
ex con·ces·sio·ne

ex·con·ces·sus
ex con·ti·nen·tia
ex con·trac·tu
ex·con·vict
ex·co·ri·ate
  ex·co·ri·at·ed
  ex·co·ri·at·ing
ex·co·ri·a·tion
ex·cre·ment
ex·crete
  ex·cret·ed
  ex·cret·ing
ex·cul·pate
  ex·cul·pat·ed
  ex·cul·pat·ing
ex·cul·pa·tion
ex·cul·pa·to·ry
ex cu·ria
ex·cus·able
ex·cuse
  ex·cused
  ex·cus·ing
ex de·bi·to
  jus·ti·ti·ae
ex de·lic·to
ex·div·i·dend
ex do·lo ma·lo
ex·e·cute
  ex·e·cut·ed
  ex·e·cut·ing
ex·e·cu·tion
ex·e·cu·tion·al
ex·e·cu·tio·ne ju·
  di·cii
ex·e·cu·tion·er

ex·ec·u·tive
ex·ec·u·tor
ex·ec·u·tor-da·tive
ex·ec·u·tor de son
  tort
ex·ec·u·to·ri·al
ex·ec·u·tor-nom·i·
  nate
ex·ec·u·tor·ship
ex·ec·u·to·ry
ex·ec·u·trix
ex·ec·u·trix de son
  tort
ex·ec·u·try
  pl ex·ec·u·tries

ex·em·pla·ry
ex·em·pli·fi·ca·tion
ex·em·pli gra·tia
ex·empt
ex·emp·tion
ex·emp·tive
ex·e·qua·tur
ex·er·cis·able
ex·er·cise
  ex·er·cised
  ex·er·cis·ing
ex fa·cie
ex fac·to
ex fic·tio·ne ju·ris
ex gra·tia
ex·haust
ex·hib·it
ex·hib·i·tant
ex·hi·bi·tion
ex·hi·bi·tion·ism
ex·hi·bi·tion·ist

ex·hu·ma·tion
ex·hume
  ex·humed
  ex·hum·ing
ex hy·po·the·si
ex·i·gen·cy
  pl ex·i·gen·cies
ex·i·gent
ex·i·gi·ble
ex·i·gi fa·ci·as
ex·ile
  ex·iled
  ex·il·ing
ex in·du·stria
ex in·teg·ro
ex·ist
ex·is·tence
ex·i·tus
  pl ex·i·tus

ex jus·ta cau·sa
ex le·ge
ex ma·le·fi·cio
ex ma·li·tia
ex mo·ra
  because of delay
  (see ex more)

ex mo·re
  according to custom
  (see ex mora)

ex na·tu·ra rei
ex ne·ces·si·ta·te
exo·crine
ex·o·cri·nol·o·gy
  pl ex·o·cri·nol·o·gies

ex·odon·tia
ex·odon·tist

ex-of·fi·cer
ex of·fi·cio
  also ex of·fi·ci·is

ex·og·a·mous
ex·og·a·my
ex·on·er·ate
  ex·on·er·at·ed
  ex·on·er·at·ing
ex·on·er·a·tion
ex·on·er·e·tur
exo·tox·in
ex par·te
ex par·te
  ma·ter·na
ex par·te pa·ter·na
ex·pa·tri·ate
  ex·pa·tri·at·ed
  ex·pa·tri·at·ing
ex·pa·tri·a·tion
ex·pect
ex·pect·able
ex·pec·tan·cy
  pl ex·pec·tan·cies

ex·pec·tant
ex·pec·ta·tion
ex·pec·ta·tive
ex·pec·to·rate
  ex·pec·to·rat·ed
  ex·pec·to·rat·ing
ex·pec·to·ra·tion
ex·pe·di·en·cy
  or ex·pe·di·ence
  pl ex·pe·di·en·cies
  or ex·pe·di·enc·es

ex·pe·di·ent
ex·pe·dite

ex·pe·dit·ed
ex·pe·dit·ing
ex·pe·dit·er
  or ex·pe·di·tor

ex·pe·di·tious
ex·pe·di·tious·ly
ex·pel
  ex·pelled
  ex·pel·ling
ex·pend
ex·pen·di·ture
ex·pense
ex·pe·ri·ence
ex·per·i·ment
ex·per·i·men·tal
ex·pert
ex·pi·ate
  ex·pi·at·ed
  ex·pi·at·ing
ex·pi·ra·tion
ex·pire
  ex·pired
  ex·pir·ing
ex·pi·ry
  pl ex·pi·ries

ex·plain
ex·pla·na·tion
ex·plic·it
ex·plode
  ex·plod·ed
  ex·plod·ing
ex·ploit
ex·ploit·able
ex·ploi·ta·tion
ex·ploit·ative

ex·ploit·ee
ex·ploit·er
ex·plor·ato·ry
ex·plore
  ex·plored
  ex·plor·ing
ex·plo·sion
ex·plo·sive
ex·port
ex·port·able
ex·por·ta·tion
ex·pose
  ex·posed
  ex·pos·ing
ex·posé
  or ex·pose

ex·po·si·tion
ex·pos·i·to·ry
ex post fac·to
ex·po·sure
ex·press
ex·pres·sion
ex·press·ly
ex pro·pria ju·ris·
  dic·tio·ne
ex·pro·pri·ate
  ex·pro·pri·at·ed
  ex·pro·pri·at·ing
ex·pro·pri·a·tion
ex·pro·pri·a·tor
ex pro·prio mo·tu
ex pro·prio vi·go·re
ex·pul·sion
ex·punge
  ex·punged

ex·pung·ing
ex re·la·ti·o·ne
ex rights
ex·san·gui·nate
  ex·san·gui·nat·ed
  ex·san·gui·nat·ing
ex·san·gui·na·tion
ex·san·guine
ex·scind
ex·sect
ex·sec·tion
ex ship
ex sta·tu·to
ex stric·to ju·re
ex sum·ma
  ne·ces·si·
  ta·te
ex tem·po·re
ex·tend
ex·ten·sion
ex·tent
ex·ten·u·ate
  ex·ten·u·at·ed
  ex·ten·u·at·ing
ex·ten·u·a·tion
ex·te·ri·or·ize
  ex·te·ri·or·ized
  ex·te·ri·or·iz·ing
ex·ter·ri·to·ri·al·i·ty
ex tes·ti·men·to
ex·tinc·tion
ex·tin·guish
ex·tin·guish·able
ex·tin·guish·ment
ex·tir·pate
  ex·tir·pat·ed

ex·tir·pat·ing
ex·tir·pa·tion
ex·tir·pa·tor
ex·tor·sive
ex·tor·sive·ly
ex·tort
ex·tor·tion
ex·tract
ex·trac·tion
ex·trac·tive
ex·tra·dit·able
ex·tra·dite
  ex·tra·dit·ed
  ex·tra·dit·ing
ex·tra·di·tion
ex·tra·do·tal
ex·tra·haz·ard·ous
ex·tra·ju·di·cial
ex·tra·ju·di·cial·ly
ex·tra ju·di·ci·um
ex·tra·le·gal
ex·tra le·gem
ex·tra·lim·i·nal
ex·tra·mar·i·tal
ex·tra·ne·ous
ex·tra·ne·us he·res
  pl ex·tra·nei he·re·des

ex·traor·di·nary
ex·tra
  pat·ri·mo·ni·um
ex·tra·sys·to·le
ex·tra·ter·ri·to·ri·al
ex·tra·ter·ri·to·ri·al·i·ty
ex·tra·uter·ine

ex·trav·a·sate
  ex·trav·a·sat·ed
  ex·trav·a·sat·ing
  ex·trav·a·sa·tion
ex·tra·ver·sion
  or ex·tro·ver·sion

ex·tra·vert
  or ex·tro·vert

ex·tra·vert·ed
  or ex·tro·vert·ed

ex·treme
ex·trem·i·ty
  pl ex·trem·i·ties

ex·trin·sic
ex·u·date
ex·u·da·tion
ex vis·cer·i·bus
ex vis·i·ta·ti·o·ne
  Dei
ex vi ter·mi·ni
eye·ball
eye·brow
eye·lid
eye·sight
eye·strain
eye·wit·ness

F

fab·ri·cate
  fab·ri·cat·ed
  fab·ri·cat·ing
  fab·ri·ca·tion
  fab·ri·ca·tor

fa·cade
  also fa·çade

face
face-to-face
fa·cia
  var of fascia

fa·cial
fa·cial·ly
fa·cias
fa·cies
  pl fa·cies

fac·ile
fac·ile·ly
fac·ile·ness
fa·cil·i·tate
  fa·cil·i·tat·ed
  fa·cil·i·tat·ing
fa·cil·i·ta·tion
fa·cil·i·ty
  pl fa·cil·i·ties

fa·cio ut des
fa·cio ut fa·ci·as
fac·sim·i·le
fact
fact find·er
fact-find·ing
fact in
  con·tro·ver·sy
fact in is·sue
fac·tion
fac·ti·tious
fac·to
fac·to et ani·mo
fac·tor

fac·tor·age

fac·tor·ing

fac·tor·ize
  fac·tor·ized
  fac·tor·iz·ing

fac·tor·ship

fac·to·ry
  pl fac·to·ries

fac·tu·al

fac·tu·al·ism

fac·tum
  pl fac·ta
  also fac·tums

fac·tum ju·ri·di·
ci·um

fac·tum
pro·ban·dum

fac·tum pro·bans

fac·ul·ta·tive

fac·ul·ty
  pl fac·ul·ties

fae·cal
  var of fecal

fae·ces
  var of feces

fago·py·rism

fail

failed

fail·ure

faint plead·er

fair
  fair·er
  fair·est

fair·ly

fair·ness

fair trade *n*

fair-trade *vb*
  fair-trad·ed
  fair-trad·ing

fair-trade *adj*

fair·way

fait

fait ac·com·pli
  pl faits ac·com·plis

fait en·rol·le
  pl faits en·rol·les

faith

faith·ful

faith·ful·ly

faith·ful·ness

faith·less

faith·less·ly

faith·less·ness

fake
  faked
  fak·ing

fak·er

fald·age
  var of foldage

fall
  fell
  fall·en
  fall·ing

fal·la·cious

fal·la·cy
  pl fal·la·cies

Fal·lo·pi·an

fall·out

fal·low

false

false·hood

false·ly

false·ness

fal·si cri·men

fal·si·fi·abil·i·ty

fal·si·fi·able

fal·si·fi·ca·tion

fal·si·fi·er

fal·si·fy
  fal·si·fied
  fal·si·fy·ing

fal·si·ty
  pl fal·si·ties

fa·mil·ia
  pl fa·mil·i·ae

fa·mil·ial

fa·mil·iar

fa·mil·iar·i·ty
  pl fa·mil·iar·i·ties

fam·i·ly
  pl fam·i·lies

fa·nat·ic
  or fa·nat·i·cal

fa·nat·i·cal·ly

fa·nat·i·ca ma·nia

fa·nat·i·cism

fa·nat·i·cize
  fa·nat·i·cized
  fa·nat·i·ciz·ing

fare

farm out *vb*

farm·out *n*

faro

far·ra·go
  pl far·ra·goes

far-sight
far-sight·ed
far-sight·ed·ness
fas·cia
  or fa·cia
  pl fas·ci·ae
  or fas·cias
  or fa·cias

fas·cial
fast
  fast·er
  fast·est
fa·tal
fa·tal·i·ty
  pl fa·tal·i·ties

fa·tal·ly
fa·tal vari·ance
fa·ther
fa·ther·hood
fa·ther-in-law
  pl fa·thers-in-law

fa·ther·less
fath·om
fa·ti·ga·bil·i·ty
  also fa·tigu·abil·i·ty
  pl fa·ti·ga·bil·i·ties
  also fa·tigu·abil·i·ties

fa·ti·ga·ble
  also fa·tigu·able

fa·tigue
  fa·tigued
  fa·tigu·ing
fau·ces
fau·ces ter·rae
fau·cial

fault
fault·i·ly
fault·i·ness
fault·ing
fault·less
faulty
  fault·i·er
  fault·i·est
fau·vism
fa·vor
fa·vor·able
fa·vus
fe·al·ty
  pl fe·al·ties

fear
fear·ful
fear·ful·ly
fear·ful·ness
fea·sance
fea·sant
fea·si·bil·i·ty
fea·si·ble
fea·si·ble·ness
fea·si·bly
fea·sor
feath·er·bed
  feath·er·bed·ded
  feath·er·bed·ding
fe·brile
fe·cal
  also fae·cal

fe·ces
  also fae·ces

fe·cun·date
  fe·cun·dat·ed

fe·cun·dat·ing
fe·cun·da·tion
fed·er·al
fed·er·al·ism
fed·er·al·ist
fed·er·al·ly
fed·er·ate
  fed·er·at·ed
  fed·er·at·ing
fed·er·a·tion
fed·er·a·tion·al
fed·er·a·tive
fed·er·a·tive·ly
fed·er·a·tor
fee
  feed
  fee·ing
fee·ble
  fee·bler
  fee·blest
fee·ble-mind·ed
fee·ble-mind·ed·ness
feed
  fed
  feed·ing
feed·back
feed·er
fee farm
feel
  felt
  feel·ing
fee sim·ple
fee tail
  pl fees tail

feign
feigned

feigned·ly
fel·late
  fel·lat·ed
  fel·lat·ing
fel·la·tee
fel·la·tio
  also fel·la·tion
  pl fel·la·tios
  also fel·la·tions
fel·la·to·ry
fel·la·trice
  or fel·la·trix
  pl fel·la·tri·ces
  or fel·la·trix·es
fel·low
felo-de-se
  pl fe·lo·nes-de-se
  or felos-de-se
fel·on
fe·lo·ni·ous
fe·lo·ni·ous·ly
fe·lo·ni·ous·ness
fel·on·ry
  pl fel·on·ries
fel·o·ny
  pl fel·o·nies
fe·male
feme co·vert
  also femme cou·vert
  pl femes co·vert
  also femmes cou·vertes
feme sole
  pl femes sole
fem·i·cide
fem·i·nine
fem·i·nism
fem·i·nist
femme de fait

fem·o·ral
fe·mur
  pl fe·murs
  or fem·o·ra
fe·na·gle
  var of finagle
fence
  fenced
  fenc·ing
fence view·er
fend·er
feo·dal
feoff·ee
feoff·ment
feof·for
  or feoff·er
fe·rae na·tu·rae
fer·ment
fer·men·ta·tion
fer·men·ta·tive
fer·ment·ed
fer·mer
fer·ret
  fer·ret·ed
  fer·ret·ing
fer·ri·age
  or fer·ry·age
fer·ry
  fer·ried
  fer·ry·ing
fer·ry
  pl fer·ries
fer·ry·boat
fer·ry·man
  pl fer·ry·men
fer·tile

fer·til·i·ty
  pl fer·til·i·ties
fer·til·iza·tion
fer·til·ize
  fer·til·ized
  fer·til·iz·ing
fes·ter
fes·ti·nate
  fes·ti·nat·ed
  fes·ti·nat·ing
fes·ti·na·tion
fes·ti·num re·me·di·um
fe·tal
  also foe·tal
fe·ta·tion
fe·ti·ci·dal
  also foe·ti·ci·dal
fe·ti·cide
  also foe·ti·cide
fe·tish
  also fe·tich
fe·tish·ism
  also fe·tich·ism
fe·tus
  also foe·tus
  pl fe·tus·es
  also foe·tus·es
  or foe·ti
fe·ver
fe·ver·ous
fi·an·cé
fi·an·cée
fi·at
fi·at jus·ti·tia
fi·at ut pe·ti·tur

fi·bril·late
  fi·bril·lat·ed
  fi·bril·lat·ing
fi·bril·la·tion
fi·bro·ad·e·no·ma
  pl fi·bro·ad·e·no·mas
  or fi·bro·ad·e·no·ma·ta

fi·bro·car·ti·lage
fi·bro·car·ti·lag·i·
  nous
fi·bro·elas·tic
fi·broid
fi·bro·ma
  pl fi·bro·mas
  also fi·bro·ma·ta

fi·bro·ma·tous
fi·bro·mus·cu·lar
fi·bro·pla·sia
fi·bro·plas·tic
fi·brose
fi·bro·sis
  pl fi·bro·ses

fi·bro·si·tis
fib·u·la
  pl fib·u·lae
  or fib·u·las

fib·u·lar
fic·tion
fic·ti·tious
fic·ti·tious·ly
fi·dei·com·mis·sary
  pl fi·dei·com·mis·sar·ies

fi·dei com·mis·sum
  pl fi·dei com·mis·sa

fi·de·jus·sio
  pl fi·de·jus·si·o·nes

fi·de·jus·sion
fi·de·jus·sion·ary
fi·de·jus·sor
  pl fi·de·jus·so·res

fi·del·i·ty
  pl fi·del·i·ties

fi·du·cial
fi·du·cial·ly
fi·du·ci·ar·i·ly
fi·du·cia·ry
  pl fi·du·cia·ries

field book
fi·eri fa·cias
fi·eri fe·ci
fif·ty-fif·ty
fig·ure
filch
filch·ing
file
  filed
  fil·ing
file wrap·per
fil·ial
fil·i·ate
  fil·i·at·ed
  fil·i·at·ing
fil·i·a·tion
fil·i·bus·ter
fil·i·bus·ter·er
fi·li·us
  adul·te·ri·nus
fi·li·us mu·
  li·e·ra·tus
fi·li·us nul·li·us
fi·li·us po·pu·li
  pl fi·lii po·pu·li

filth
filth·i·ness
filthy
  filth·i·er
  filth·i·est
fi·lum aquae
fin·able
  or fine·able

fi·na·gle
  also fe·na·gle
fi·na·gled
  also fe·na·gled
fi·na·gling
  also fe·na·gling

fi·nal
fi·nal·i·ty
  pl fi·nal·i·ties

fi·nal·iza·tion
fi·nal·ize
  fi·nal·ized
  fi·nal·iz·ing
fi·nal·ly
fi·nance
  fi·nanced
  fi·nanc·ing
fi·nan·cial
fi·nan·cial·ly
fi·nan·cier
find
  found
  find·ing
find·er
find·ing
fine n
fine vb
  fined

fin·ing
fine *adj*
 fin·er
 fin·est
fine·able
 var of finable

fines *n pl*
fin·ger
fin·ger·nail
fin·ger·print
fi·nis
fin·ish
fire·arm
fire·bote
fire·bug
fire·damp
fire door
fire es·cape
fire·man
 pl fire·men

fire·proof
fire·re·sis·tant
fire·re·sis·tive
 or fire·re·sist·ing

fire·re·tar·dant
fire·wood
fire·works
firm *n*
firm *adj*
 firm·er
 firm·est
firm·ly
first
first·born
first class *n*
first-class *adj*

first-de·gree
first in, first out
fisc
 or fisk
fis·cal
fis·cal·ly
fish·er·man
 pl fish·er·men

fish·ery
 pl fish·er·ies

fis·sion
fis·sion·able
fis·sur·al
fis·sure
 fis·sured
 fis·sur·ing
fis·tu·la
 pl fis·tu·las
 or fis·tu·lae

fis·tu·lous
fit·ful
fit·ness
fit·ting
five-per·cent·er
fix·a·tion
fixed
fix·er
fix·ture
flac·cid
flac·cid·i·ty
flag
 flagged
 flag·ging
flag·man
 pl flag·men

fla·grant

fla·gran·te bel·lo
fla·gran·te de·lic·to
fla·grant·ly
flat·foot
flat-foot·ed
flat·u·lence
 or flat·u·len·cy
 pl flat·u·lenc·es
 or flat·u·len·cies

flat·u·lent
fla·tus
 pl fla·tus·es
 or fla·tus

flea·bite
flea·bit·ten
flee
 fled
 flee·ing
flex·i·bil·i·ty
flex·i·ble
flight
flim·flam
flim·flam·mer
float
float·abil·i·ty
float·able
float·age
 var of flotage

floa·ta·tion
 var of flotation

float·er
float·ing
flog
 flogged
 flog·ging
flood

floor brok·er
floor plan·ning
flo·tage
    also float·age

flo·ta·tion
    or floa·ta·tion

flot·sam
flow·age
fluc·tu·ate
    fluc·tu·at·ed
    fluc·tu·at·ing
fluc·tu·a·tion
fluc·tu·a·tion·al
flu·o·ri·date
    flu·o·ri·dat·ed
    flu·o·ri·dat·ing
flu·o·ri·da·tion
flu·o·ride
flu·o·ri·di·za·tion
flu·o·ri·dize
    flu·o·ri·dized
    flu·o·ri·diz·ing
flu·o·ri·nate
    flu·o·ri·nat·ed
    flu·o·ri·nat·ing
flu·o·ri·na·tion
flu·o·rine
flu·o·ro·scope
flu·o·ro·scop·ic
flu·o·ro·scop·i·cal·
    ly
flu·o·ros·co·pist
flu·o·ros·co·py
    pl flu·o·ros·co·pies

flu·o·ro·sis

fly
    flew
    flown
    fly·ing
fly-by-night
    also fly-by-night·er

fo·cal
fo·cal·ize
    fo·cal·ized
    fo·cal·iz·ing
fo·cus
    pl fo·cus·es
    or fo·ci

foe·tal
    var of fetal

foe·ti·ci·dal
    var of feticidal

foe·ti·cide
    var of feticide

foe·tus
    var of fetus

fold·age
    or fald·age

fold·er
fo·lie à deux
    pl fo·lies à deux

fo·lio
    pl fo·lios

fol·li·cle
fol·lic·u·lar
fol·lic·u·li·tis
fol·low up *vb*
fol·low-up *n*
fo·ment
fo·men·ta·tion

fo·men·ter
fonds
fon·ta·nel
    also fon·ta·nelle

foot·age
foot-front·age rule
foot·ing
foot·path
foot·print
foot·way
for·age
fo·ra·men
    pl fo·ram·i·na
    or fo·ra·mens

for·as·much as
for·bear
    for·bore
    for·borne
    for·bear·ing
for·bear
    var of forebear

for·bear·ance
for·bear·ing·ly
for·bid
    for·bade
    or for·bad
    for·bid·den
    for·bid·ding
force
    forced
    forc·ing
force and ef·fect
force-feed
    force-fed
    or forced-fed
    force-feed·ing
    or forced-feed·ing

force·ful
force·ful·ly
force·less
force ma·jeure
forc·ible
forc·ibly
fore·arm
fore·bear
   or for·bear

fore·cast
fore·cast·er
fore·close
   fore·closed
   fore·clos·ing
fore·clo·sure
fore·fa·ther
fore·fin·ger
fore·gift
fore·go
   fore·went
   fore·gone
   fore·go·ing
   precede
   (see forgo)

fore·go
   var of forgo

fore·go·er
fore·hand rent
fore·head
for·eign
for·eign·er
fore·judge
   or for·judge

fore·judg·er
   or for·judg·er

fore·judg·ment

fore·man
   pl fore·men

fore·most
fore·named
fore·no·tice
fo·ren·sic
fo·ren·si·cal·ly
fore·or·dain
fore·or·di·na·tion
fore·see
   fore·saw
   fore·seen
   fore·see·ing
fore·see·abil·i·ty
fore·see·able
fore·shore
fore·sight
fore·sight·ed
fore·sight·ed·ly
fore·sight·ed·ness
fore·skin
for·est
fore·stall
fore·stall·er
fore·swear
   var of forswear

fore·thought
for·ev·er
fore·warn
fore·wa·ters
for·feit
for·feit·able
for·feit·able·ness
for·fei·ture
forge

forged
forg·ing
forg·er
forg·ery
   pl forg·er·ies

for·give
   for·gave
   for·giv·en
   for·giv·ing
for·give·ness
for·go
   also fore·go
   for·went
   also fore·went
   for·gone
   also fore·gone
   for·go·ing
   also fore·go·ing
   to give up
   (see forego)

for·judge
   var of forejudge

for·judg·er
   var of forejudger

form
for·mal
for·mal·de·hyde
for·mal·i·ty
   pl for·mal·i·ties

for·mal·ize
   for·mal·ized
   for·mal·iz·ing
for·mal·ly
for·ma·tion
forme fruste
   pl formes frustes

for·mer

for·mer·ly
for·mi·ca·tion
for·mu·la
  pl for·mu·las
  also for·mu·lae

for·mu·lary
  pl for·mu·lar·ies

for·mu·late
  for·mu·lat·ed
  for·mu·lat·ing
for·mu·la·tion
for·ni·cate
  for·ni·cat·ed
  for·ni·cat·ing
for·ni·ca·tion
for·ni·ca·tor
for·ni·ca·to·ry
for·ni·ca·trix
  pl for·ni·ca·tri·ces

for·nix
  pl for·ni·ces

for·prise
for·sake
  for·sook
  for·sak·en
  for·sak·ing
for·swear
  or fore·swear
  for·swore
  or fore·swore
  for·sworn
  or fore·sworn
  for·swear·ing
  or fore·swear·ing

forth·com·ing
forth·right
forth·with

for·ti·fy
  for·ti·fied
  for·ti·fy·ing
for·ti·or
for·tu·itous
for·tune
fo·rum
  pl fo·rums
  or fo·ra

fo·rum do·mi·ci·lii
fo·rum non
  con·ve·ni·ens
for·ward
for·ward·er
for·ward·ing
fos·ter
fos·ter·age
fos·ter·ling
found
foun·da·tion
foun·da·tion·al
found·er
found·ling
found·ress
fo·vea
  pl fo·ve·ae

fra·cas
  pl fra·cas·es

frac·tion
frac·tion·al
frac·tion·al·ize
  frac·tion·al·ized
  frac·tion·al·iz·ing
frac·tion·ate
  frac·tion·at·ed
  frac·tion·at·ing

frac·tion·ation
frac·ture
  frac·tured
  frac·tur·ing
fra·gil·i·tas os·si·
  um
frame
  framed
  fram·ing
frame of
  ref·er·ence
frame-up
frame·work
fran·chise
  fran·chised
  fran·chis·ing
fran·chis·er
frank
frank·al·moign
  or frank·al·moin
  also frank·al·moigne

frank-mar·riage
fra·ter·nal
fra·ter·nal·ism
fra·ter·nal·ly
fra·ter·ni·ty
  pl fra·ter·ni·ties

frat·er·ni·za·tion
frat·er·nize
  frat·er·nized
  frat·er·niz·ing
frat·er·niz·er
frat·ri·age
frat·ri·cide
fraud
fraud·u·lence

fraud·u·lent
fraud·u·lent·ly
fraud·u·lent·ness
free *vb*
  freed
  free·ing
free *adj*
  fre·er
  fre·est
free·dom
free·hold
free·hold·er
free·ly
free·man
  pl free·men

freeze
  froze
  fro·zen
  freez·ing
freeze out *vb*
freeze-out *n*
freight
freight·er
freight·ing
freight·yard
frem·i·tus
fren·zied
fren·zy
  pl fren·zies

fre·quen·cy
  pl fre·quen·cies

fre·quent
fre·quen·ta·tion
fre·quent·er
fre·quent·ly

fre·quent·ness
Freud·ian
fric·tion
Fried·länd·er's ba·
cil·lus
    also Fried·länd·er
    ba·cil·lus

Fried·man test
    also Fried·man's test

friend
friend·less
friend·ly
fright·en
  fright·ened
  fright·en·ing
frig·id
fri·gid·i·ty
  pl fri·gid·i·ties

frisk
friv·o·lous
friv·o·lous·ly
frons
  pl fron·tes

front·age
front·ag·er
fron·tal
fron·tal·ly
front-foot rule
fron·to-oc·cip·i·tal
fron·to-pa·ri·e·tal
fron·to-tem·po·ral
frost·bite
frost·bit
frost·bit·ten
    also frost·bit
frost·bit·ing

fruc·tu·ary
  pl fruc·tu·ar·ies

fruc·tus
fruc·tus ci·vi·les
fruc·tus in·dus·
tri·a·les
fruc·tus na·tu·ra·
les
fru·gal
fru·gal·i·ty
  pl fru·gal·i·ties

fruit
fruit·less
frus·trate
  frus·trat·ed
  frus·trat·ing
frus·tra·tion
fu·gi·tive
ful·fill
  or full·fil
  ful·filled
  ful·fill·ing
ful·fill·ment
ful·gu·rant
ful·gu·rate
  ful·gu·rat·ed
  ful·gu·rat·ing
full·term
full time *n*
full-time *adj*
ful·ly
ful·mi·nant
ful·mi·nate
  ful·mi·nat·ed
  ful·mi·nat·ing
func·tion

func·tion·al
func·tion·al·ly
func·tion·ary
  also func·tion·aire
  or func·tion·naire
  pl func·tion·ar·ies
  also func·tion·aires
  or func·tion·naires

func·tus of·fi·cio
fund
fun·da·men·tal
fun·da·men·tal·ly
fund·ed
fund·ing
fun·dus
  pl fun·di

fu·ner·al
fu·ne·re·al
fun·gal
fun·gi·bil·i·ty
fun·gi·ble
fun·gi·cid·al
fun·gi·cide
fun·gi·stat·ic
fun·gi·tox·ic
fun·gus
  pl fun·gi
  also fun·gus·es

fu·ri·ous
fur·long
  one eighth of a mile
  (*see* furlough)

fur·lough
  leave of absence
  (*see* furlong)

fur·nish
fur·nished

fur·nish·er
fur·nish·ings *n pl*
fur·ni·ture
fu·ror bre·vis
fur·ther
fur·ther·ance
fur·ther·more
fur·ther·most
fur·tive
fur·tive·ly
fur·tive·ness
fur·tum
  pl fur·ta

fur·tum usus
  pl fur·ta us·us

fu·run·cle
fu·run·cu·lar
fu·run·cu·lo·sis
  pl fu·run·cu·lo·ses

fu·sil·lade
fu·tile
fu·tile·ly
fu·tile·ness
fu·til·i·ty
  pl fu·til·i·ties

fu·ture

G

gag
  gagged
  gag·ging
gage
  security
  (*see* gauge)

gage
  var of gauge

gag·er
  giving of a gage
  (*see* gauger)

gager
  var of gauger

gain
gain·ful
gain·ful·ly
gain·ful·ness
gain·less
gain·say
  gain·said
  gain·say·ing
ga·lac·ta·gogue
  or ga·lac·to·gogue

ga·lac·to·poi·e·sis
  pl ga·lac·to·poi·e·ses

ga·lac·to·poi·et·ic
gal·ac·to·sis
  pl gal·ac·to·ses

gale
ga·lea
ga·lea apo·neu·ro·ti·ca
gale·age
gale day
gal·ee
ga·len·i·cal
gall·blad·der
gal·lery
  pl gal·ler·ies

gal·lows
  pl gal·lows

gall·stone

gam·ble
  gam·bled
  gam·bling
gam·bler
game
  gamed
  gam·ing
game bird
game·cock
game fish
game fowl
game·keep·er
game·ster
ga·mete
ga·met·ic
ga·me·to·cide
ga·me·to·gen·e·sis
  pl ga·me·to·gen·e·ses
game war·den
gam·ma-ben·zene
  hexa·chlo·ride
gamy
    also gam·ey
  gam·i·er
  gam·i·est
ga·nan·cial
gang·land
gan·gli·al
gan·gli·on
  pl gan·glia
  also gan·gli·ons
gan·gli·on·at·ed
  also gan·gli·on·ate
gan·gli·on·ic
gan·gli·on·itis
gan·grene
gan·gre·nous

gang·ster
gang·ster·ism
Gan·ser syn·drome
gaol
gar·ble
  gar·bled
  gar·bling
gar·den
gar·nish
gar·nish·able
gar·nish·ee
  gar·nish·eed
  gar·nish·ee·ing
  gar·nish·ment
gar·rote
  or gar·rotte
  also ga·rotte
  gar·rot·ed
  or gar·rot·ted
  also ga·rot·ted
  gar·rot·ing
  or gar·rot·ting
  also ga·rot·ting
gar·rot·er
  or gar·rot·ter
gar·ru·li·ty
  pl gar·ru·li·ties
gas·tral·gia
gas·tral·gic
gas·trec·to·my
  pl gas·trec·to·mies
gas·tri·tis
  pl gas·trit·i·des
gas·tro·en·ter·ic
gas·tro·en·ter·i·tis
  pl gas·tro·ent·er·
    it·i·des
  or gas·tro·en·ter·
    i·tis·es

gas·tro·en·ter·ol·
  o·gist
gas·tro·en·ter·ol·
  o·gy
gas·tro·ga·vage
gas·tro·lav·age
gas·trol·o·gist
gas·trol·o·gy
gas·tro·phren·ic
gas·tro·splen·ic
gate·way
gath·er·ing charge
gauge
    or gage
  gauged
    or gaged
  gaug·ing
    or gag·ing
    measure
    (*see* gage)
gauge·able
gaug·er
    or gag·er
    one that gauges
    (*see* gager)

Gault de·ci·sion
ga·vage
gave
  past of give

gav·el
  gav·eled
  or gav·elled
  gav·el·ing
  or gav·el·ling
gav·el·kind
gav·el·ler
  also gav·el·er

ga·zette
  ga·zett·ed
  ga·zett·ing
gear·ing
Gei·ger count·er
  or Gei·ger-Mül·ler
    count·er
gel·ig·nite
gen·darme
gen·der
gen·e·al·o·gy
  pl gen·e·al·o·gies
gen·er·al
gen·er·al·i·ty
  pl gen·er·al·i·ties
gen·er·al·iz·able
gen·er·al·iza·tion
gen·er·al·ize
  gen·er·al·ized
  gen·er·al·iz·ing
gen·er·al·ly
gen·er·a·tion
gen·er·a·tive
ge·ner·ic
ge·net·ic
ge·net·i·cist
ge·net·ics
Ge·ne·va con·ven·
  tion
gen·i·tal
gen·i·ta·lia *n pl*
gen·i·tals *n pl*
gen·i·tor
gen·i·to·uri·nary
geno·cid·al
geno·cide

genu
  pl gen·ua
gen·u·ine
gen·u·ine·ly
geo·graph·i·cal
ge·og·ra·phy
  pl ge·og·ra·phies
ge·rat·ic
ger·a·to·log·ic
  or ger·a·tol·o·gous
ger·a·tol·o·gy
ge·ri·at·ric
ge·ri·a·tri·cian
ge·ri·at·rics
ge·ri·a·trist
ger·mane
germ-free
ger·mi·cid·al
ger·mi·cide
ger·mi·nate
  ger·mi·nat·ed
  ger·mi·nat·ing
germ-proof
germy
  germ·i·er
  germ·i·est
ge·ron·tal
ge·ron·tic
ger·on·tol·o·gy
ges·tate
  ges·tat·ed
  ges·tat·ing
ges·ta·tion
ges·ta·tion·al
get

got
  got·ten
  get·ting
get away *vb*
get·away *n*
get-rich-quick
get-tough
ghet·to
  ghet·tos
  also ghet·toes
ghost·write
  ghost·wrote
  ghost·writ·ten
  ghost·writ·ing
ghost-writ·er
gib·ber·ish
gift
gift in prae·sen·ti
gift over
  pl gifts over
gig·o·lo
  pl gig·o·los
gim·crack·ery
gim·mick
gin·gi·va
  pl gin·gi·vae
gin·gi·val
gist
gi·tal·in
give
  gave
  giv·en
  giv·ing
give up *vb*
give-up *n*

gla·bel·la
  pl gla·bel·lae

glairy
  glair·i·er
  glair·i·est
glans
  glan·des
glans cli·to·ri·dis
glans pe·nis
glare
  glared
  glar·ing
glau·co·ma
glau·co·ma·tous
gle·no·hu·mer·al
gle·noid
  also gle·noi·dal

gle·noid cav·i·ty
gle·noid fos·sa
gli·o·sis
  pl gli·o·ses

glob·al·iza·tion
glob·al·ize
  glob·al·ized
  glob·al·iz·ing
Globe doc·trine
glob·u·lin
glo·bus hys·ter·i·cus
glo·mer·u·lar
glo·mer·u·li·tis
glo·mer·u·lo·ne·phri·tis
  pl glo·mer·u·lo·ne·phrit·i·des

glo·mer·u·lo·scle·ro·sis
  pl glo·mer·u·lo·scle·ro·ses

glo·mer·u·lus
  pl glo·mer·u·li
glos·sa
  pl glos·sae
  also glos·sas

glos·si·tis
glos·so·pha·ryn·geal
glot·tal
glot·tis
  pl glot·tis·es
  or glot·tid·es

glu·cos·uria
glu·ta·mate
glu·tam·ic
glu·te·al
glu·te·us
  pl glu·tei

glyc·er·in
  or glyc·er·ine

glyc·er·ol
gly·co·side
gly·co·sid·ic
G-man
  pl G-men

gnath·al·gia
gnath·ic
  or gna·thal

go
  went
  gone
  go·ing

gob·ble·dy·gook
  or gob·ble·de·gook

go·ing and com·ing rule
go·ing-con·cern val·ue
goi·ter
  also goi·tre

gold·brick
go·nad
go·nad·al
go·nal·gia
go·ni·tis
gono·coc·cal
  or gono·coc·cic

gono·coc·cus
  pl gono·coc·ci

gon·or·rhea
  also gon·or·rhoea

gon·or·rhe·al
good
  bet·ter
  best
good faith
good·ly
goods *n pl*
good will
gory
  gor·i·er
  gor·i·est
gos·sy·pol
gouge
  gouged
  goug·ing
goug·er

gov·ern
gov·ern·able
gov·er·nance
gov·ern·ment
gov·ern·men·tal
Gov·ern·ment-
Gen·er·al
  pl Gov·ern·ments-
  Gen·er·al

gov·ern·ment-in-
ex·ile
  pl gov·ern·ments-
  in·ex·ile

gov·er·nor
gov·er·nor·ate
gov·er·nor-gen·
er·al
  pl gov·er·nors-gen·
  er·al
  or gov·er·nor-gen·
  er·als

gov·er·nor-gen·
er·al-in-coun·cil
  pl gov·er·nors-
  gen·er·al-in-
  coun·cil
  or gov·er·nor-
  gen·er·als-
  in·coun·cil

gov·er·nor-gen·
er·al·ship
gov·er·nor-in-
coun·cil
  pl gov·er·nors-in-
  coun·cil

gov·er·nor·ship
grab
  grabbed

grab·bing
grace
grade
  grad·ed
  grad·ing
grade cross·ing
grad·u·ate
  grad·u·at·ed
  grad·u·at·ing
graft
graft·er
graft·ing
gram·i·ci·din
grand
grand·child
  pl grand·chil·dren

grand·daugh·ter
grand·fa·ther
gran·di·ose
grand mal
grand·ma·ter·nal
grand·moth·er
grand·par·ent
grand·son
grant
grant·able
grant·ee
grant-in-aid
  pl grants-in-aid

grant·or
gran·u·la·tion tis·
sue
gran·u·lo·ma
  pl gran·u·lo·mas
  or gran·u·lo·ma·ta

gran·u·lo·ma in·
gui·na·le
  or gran·u·lo·ma
  ve·ne·re·um

gran·u·lo·ma·tous
graph·o·log·i·cal
gra·phol·o·gist
gra·phol·o·gy
  pl gra·phol·o·gies

gra·phom·e·try
grapho·mo·tor
grap·ple
  grap·pled
  grap·pling
grap·pling iron
grasp·ing
gra·tia cu·ri·ae
gra·tis
gra·tis dic·tum
gra·tu·itous
gra·tu·itous·ly
gra·tu·ity
  pl gra·tu·ities

gra·va·men
  pl gra·va·mens
  or gra·vam·i·na

gra·va·tus
grave
grav·id
grav·i·da
  pl grav·i·das
  or grav·i·dae

gra·vid·ic
gra·vid·i·ty
  pl gra·vid·i·ties

grav·id·ness

grav·i·ty
pl grav·i·ties

gray mar·ket
gray mar·ke·teer
gray-mar·ket·ing
gray out *vb*
gray·out *n*
graz·ing
grease
  greased
  greas·ing
great
  great·er
  great·est
great·ly
green·back
green goods
green·sick·ness
green·stick frac·
  ture
gref·fi·er
gre·nade
grew·some
  var of gruesome

griev·ance
griev·ant
grieve
  grieved
  griev·ing
griev·er
griev·ous
griev·ous·ly
griffe
  also griff

grif·fonne

grift
grift·er
gro·cer's itch
grog·shop
gross
gross·ly
ground
ground·age
ground·less
ground rent
ground·wa·ter
group prac·tice
group ther·a·py
  or group psy·cho·ther·
  a·py

grow
  grew
  grown
  grow·ing
grow·er
grow·ing crop
grown-up
  pl grown-ups

grow up
  grew up
  grown up
  grow·ing up
grub·stake
  grub·staked
  grub·stak·ing
grudge
  grudged
  grudg·ing
grue·some
  also grew·some

grue·some·ly

guar·an·tee
  guar·an·teed
  guar·an·tee·ing
guar·an·tor
guar·an·ty
  pl guar·an·ties

guard
guard·er
guard·house
guard·ian
guard·ian ad li·
  tem
guard·ian de son
  tort
guard·ian·ship
gu·ber·na·tive
gu·ber·na·to·ri·al
guest
guild
guild·ry
  pl guild·ries

Guil·lain-Bar·ré
  syn·drome
guil·lo·tine
guilt·i·ly
guilt·i·ness
guilt·less
guilt·less·ly
guilty
  guilt·i·er
  guilt·i·est
guin·ea pig
gul·let
gull·ibil·i·ty
gull·ible

gull·ibly
gum·boil
gum·ma
  pl gum·mas
  also gum·ma·ta

gum·ma·tous
gun
  gunned
  gun·ning
gun·fight
gun·fire
gun·man
  pl gun·men

gun·point
gun·run·ner
gun·run·ning
gun·shot
gur·ges
  pl gur·gi·tes

gus·ta·tion
gus·ta·tive
gus·ta·to·ry
gut
  gut·ted
  gut·ting
gut·ter
gyn·atre·sia
gy·ne·co·log·ic
  or gy·ne·co·log·i·cal

gy·ne·col·o·gist
gy·ne·col·o·gy
gyp
  gypped
  gyp·ping
gy·ro·spasm

H

ha·be·as cor·pus
ha·be·as cor·pus ad
  de·li·be·ren·dum
  et re·ci·pi·en·
  dum
ha·be·as cor·pus ad
  fa·ci·en·dum et
  re·ci·pi·en·dum
ha·be·as cor·pus ad
  pro·se·quen·dum
ha·be·as cor·pus ad
  re·spon·den·dum
ha·be·as cor·pus ad
  sa·tis·fa·ci·en·
  dum
ha·be·as cor·pus ad
  sub·ji·ci·en·dum
ha·be·as cor·pus ad
  sub·ji·ci·en·dum
  et re·ci·pi·en·
  dum
ha·be·as cor·pus ad
  tes·ti·fi·can·dum
ha·be·as cor·pus
  cum cau·sa
ha·ben·dum
ha·ben·dum et te·
  nen·dum
ha·be·re
ha·be·re fa·ci·as
  pos·ses·sio·nem
ha·be·re fa·ci·as
  sei·si·nam

ha·be·re fa·ci·as
  vi·sum
hab·it
hab·it·abil·i·ty
hab·it·able
hab·it·able·ness
hab·it·ably
hab·i·tan·cy
  pl hab·i·tan·cies

ha·bi·tant
hab·i·ta·tion
hab·it-form·ing
ha·bit·u·al
ha·bit·u·al·i·ty
ha·bit·u·al·ly
ha·bit·u·al·ness
ha·bit·u·ate
  ha·bit·u·at·ed
  ha·bit·u·at·ing
ha·bit·u·a·tion
hab·i·tude
ha·bi·tué
hab·i·tus
  pl hab·i·tus

hack
hade
  had·ed
  had·ing
haec ver·ba
hae·mo·glo·bin
  var of hemoglobin

hae·re·di·tas
  var of hereditas

hae·res
  var of heres

hae·res fac·tus
  pl hae·re·des fac·ti

hag·gle
  hag·gled
  hag·gling
hag·gler
hail
  to greet
  (see hale)

haim·suck·en
  var of hamesucken

hair·split·ter
hair·split·ting
hale *vb*
  haled
  hal·ing
  to compel to go
  (see hail)

hale *adj*
  also hail
  healthy
  (see hail, hale *vb*)

half
  pl halves

half blood
half-blood·ed
half-bred
half-breed
half broth·er
half-caste
half cous·in
half-hol·i·day
half-life
half neph·ew
half-or·phan

half-proof
half run
half-sib
  also half-sib·ling

half sis·ter
half-tim·er
half-tongue
half-truth
half·way house
hal·i·ste·re·sis
  pl hal·is·ste·re·ses

hal·i·ste·ret·ic
hall·mark
hal·lu·ci·nate
  hal·lu·ci·nat·ed
  hal·lu·ci·nat·ing
hal·lu·ci·na·tion
hal·lu·ci·na·tion·al
hal·lu·ci·na·tive
hal·lu·ci·na·to·ry
hal·lu·ci·no·gen
hal·lu·ci·no·gen·ic
hal·lu·ci·no·sis
  pl hal·lu·ci·no·ses

hal·lux
  pl hal·lu·ces

halo·gen
ha·lo·ge·nate
  ha·lo·ge·nat·ed
  ha·lo·ge·nat·ing
hal·o·per·i·dol
hal·o·thane
hal·ter
  hal·tered

hal·ter·ing
halv·ers *n pl*
hame·suck·en
  also haim·suck·en

Ham·il·to·ni·an
ham·let
ham·mer·toe
ham·per *vb*
ham·string
  ham·strung
  ham·string·ing
han·a·per
hand
hand·bill
hand·book
hand·cuff
hand down
hand·i·cap
  hand·i·capped
  hand·i·cap·ping
hand·i·craft
hand·i·work
han·dle
  han·dled
  han·dling
han·dler
hand·made
hand mon·ey
hand out *vb*
hand·out *n*
hand·pick
hand·sale
hand·sel
  also han·sel

hand·write

hand·wrote
hand·writ·ten
hand·writ·ing

hang
   hung
      also hanged
   hang·ing

hang·able
han·gar
   shelter for aircraft
   (*see* hanger)

hang·er
   one that hangs
   (*see* hangar)

hang·er-on
   pl hang·ers-on
   or hang·er-ons

hang·man
   pl hang·men

hang·over
han·sel
   var of handsel

han·sen·osis
han·sen·ot·ic
Han·sen's ba·cil·
   lus
      pl Han·sen's ba·cil·
      li

Han·sen's dis·ease
ha·pax le·go·me·
   non
      pl ha·pax le·go·me·
      na

hap·pen
   hap·pened
   hap·pen·ing

ha·rangue
ha·rangued
ha·rangu·ing
ha·rangu·er
ha·rass
ha·rass·ing
ha·rass·ing·ly
ha·rass·ment
har·bin·ger
har·bor
har·bor·age
har·bor·er
har·bor·ing
hard-and-fast
hard-bit·ten
hard·bought
hard-core
hard·en·ing
hard-of-hear·ing
hard·pan
hard·ship
har·lot
har·lot·ry
   pl har·lot·ries

harm·ful
harm·ful·ly
harm·ful·ness
harm·less
harm·less·ly
harm·less·ness
har·mo·ni·ous
har·mo·ni·ous·ly
har·mo·ni·ous·ness
har·mo·nize
   har·mo·nized

har·mo·niz·ing
har·mo·ny
   pl har·mo·nies

harsh
harsh·er
harsh·est
harsh·ly
hash·ish
hatch
hatch·et job
hatch·way
hate·mon·ger
hate·mon·ger·ing
ha·tred
haul·age
haul·er
haul·ing
ha·ven
ha·ver
have up
   had up
   hav·ing up

hawk
hawk·er
hawk·ing
hay·bote
hay·ward
haz·ard
haz·ard·less
haz·ard·ous
haz·ard·ous·ly
haz·ard·ous·ness
haze
   hazed
   haz·ing

hematopoiesis

head·ache
head·achy
head·line
head·long
head·man
   pl head·men

head·note
head·quar·ters
head·right
head·stone
head·strong
heal
heal·able
heal·er
heal·ing
health
health·ful
healthy
   health·i·er
   health·i·est
hear
   heard
   hear·ing
hear·ing de no·vo
hear·say
heart·beat
heart·break
   heart·broke
   heart·brok·en
   heart·break·ing
heat ex·haus·tion
heat pros·tra·tion
heat·stroke
heb·do·mad
heb·dom·a·dal

he·be·phre·nia
he·be·phre·nic
hec·tic
hec·ti·cal·ly
hedge
   hedged
   hedg·ing
hedge·bote
hedg·er
heed·ful
heed·ful·ly
heed·ful·ness
heed·less
heed·less·ly
heed·less·ness
he·ge·mon
he·ge·mon·ic
   also he·ge·mon·i·cal

he·ge·mo·ny
   pl he·ge·mo·nies

heif·er
hei·nous
hei·nous·ly
hei·nous·ness
heir
heir·ess
heir·less
heir·loom
heir por·tion·er
   pl heirs por·tion·ers

heir·ship
he·li·um
he·lix
   pl he·li·ces
   also he·lix·es

hel·le·bore
hel·le·bo·rine
help·er
help·ful
help·ful·ly
help·ful·ness
help·less
help·less·ly
help·less·ness
he·ma·cy·tom·e·ter
   or he·mo·cy·tom·e·ter

hem·ag·glu·ti·nate
   hem·ag·glu·ti·
     nat·ed
   hem·ag·glu·ti·
     nat·ing
hem·ag·glu·ti·na·
   tion
hem·ag·glu·ti·nin
   or he·mo·ag·glu·ti·nin

he·ma·poi·e·sis
   or he·mo·poi·e·sis
   pl he·ma·poi·e·ses
   or he·mo·poi·e·ses

hem·ar·thro·sis
   pl hem·ar·thro·ses

he·ma·to·log·ic
   or he·ma·to·log·i·cal

he·ma·tol·o·gist
he·ma·tol·o·gy
   pl he·ma·tol·o·gies

he·ma·to·ma
   pl he·ma·to·mas
   also he·ma·to·ma·ta

he·ma·to·poi·e·sis
   pl he·ma·to·poi·e·ses

he·ma·to·poi·et·ic
he·ma·tu·ria
hem·er·a·lo·pia
hem·er·a·lo·pic
hemi·an·al·ge·sia
hemi·an·es·the·sia
hemi·anop·sia
hemi·anop·tic
hemi·at·ro·phy
  pl hemi·at·ro·phies

hemi·bal·lism
  also hemi·bal·lis·mus

hemi·cra·nia
hemi·fa·cial
hemi·hy·per·es·the·
  sia
hemi·hyp·es·the·sia
hemi·o·pia
  or hemi·op·sia

hemi·op·ic
hemi·pa·re·sis
  pl hemi·pa·re·ses

hemi·ple·gia
hemi·ple·gic
hemi·sphere
hemi·spher·ic
  or hemi·spher·i·cal

he·mo·ag·glu·ti·nin
  var of hemagglutinin

he·mo·clas·tic
he·mo·cy·tom·e·ter
  var of hemacytometer

he·mo·glo·bin
  also hae·mo·glo·bin

he·mo·glo·bi·ne·
  mia
he·mo·glo·bin·ic
he·mo·glo·bi·nom·
  e·ter
he·mo·glo·bi·nom·
  e·try
  pl he·mo·glo·bi·
  nom·e·tries

he·mo·glo·bin·uria
he·mo·glo·bin·uric
he·mo·ly·sis
  pl he·mo·ly·ses

he·mo·lyt·ic
he·mo·lyze
  he·mo·lyzed
  he·mo·lyz·ing
he·mo·peri·car·di·
  um
  pl he·mo·peri·car·
  dia

he·mo·peri·to·ne·
  um
he·mo·phil·ia
he·mo·phil·i·ac
he·mo·phil·ic
he·mo·pneu·mo·
  tho·rax
  pl he·mo·pneu·mo·
  tho·rax·es
  or he·mo·pneu·mo·
  tho·ra·ces

he·mo·poi·e·sis
  var of hemapoiesis

he·mo·poi·et·ic

he·mop·ty·sis
  pl he·mop·ty·ses

hem·or·rhage
  hem·or·rhaged
  hem·or·rhag·ing
hem·or·rhag·ic
hem·or·rhoid
hem·or·rhoid·al
he·mo·sta·sis
  pl he·mo·sta·ses

he·mo·stat·ic
he·mo·tho·rax
  pl he·mo·tho·rax·es
  or he·mo·tho·ra·ces

hence
hence·forth
  or hence·for·ward

hench·man
  pl hench·men

he·par
he·pat·ic
hep·a·ti·tis
  pl hep·a·tit·i·des

hep·a·to·por·tal
hep·a·to·spleno·
  meg·a·ly
  pl hep·a·to·spleno·
  meg·a·lies

hep·a·to·tox·ic
hep·a·to·tox·ic·i·ty
  pl hep·a·to·tox·ic·i·ties

hep·ta·chlor
herb·age
herd
herd·er

here·af·ter
here·by
he·red·i·ta·ble
her·e·dit·a·ment
he·red·i·tar·i·ly
he·red·i·tar·i·ness
he·red·i·tary
he·re·di·tas
 also hae·re·di·tas
 pl he·re·di·ta·tes
 also hae·re·di·ta·tes

he·re·di·tas ja·cens
he·red·i·ty
 pl he·red·i·ties

here·in
here·in·above
here·in·af·ter
here·in·be·fore
here·in·be·low
here·of
here·on
he·res
 or hae·res
 pl he·re·des
 or hae·re·des

here·to
here·to·fore
her·e·trix
 var of heritrix

here·un·der
here·un·to
here·up·on
here·with
her·i·ot
her·i·ot·able

her·i·ta·bil·i·ty
her·i·ta·ble
her·i·ta·bly
her·i·tage
her·i·tor
her·i·trix
 or her·e·trix
 pl her·i·trix·es
 or her·i·tri·ces
 or her·e·trix·es
 or her·e·tri·ces

her·maph·ro·dite
her·maph·ro·dit·ic
her·maph·ro·dit·ism
her·me·neu·tic
 or her·me·neu·ti·cal
her·me·neu·ti·cal·ly
her·me·neu·tics
her·nia
 pl her·ni·as
 or her·ni·ae

her·ni·al
her·ni·ate
 her·ni·at·ed
 her·ni·at·ing
her·ni·a·tion
her·ni·or·rha·phy
 pl her·ni·or·rha·phies

her·o·in
 also her·o·ine

her·o·in·ism
her·o·ism
her·pes
her·pes sim·plex

her·pes·vi·rus
her·pes zos·ter
her·pet·ic
hes·i·tant
hes·i·tant·ly
hes·i·tate
 hes·i·tat·ed
 hes·i·tat·ing
 hes·i·tat·er
 also hes·i·ta·tor

hes·i·tat·ing·ly
hes·i·ta·tion
he·tae·ra
 or he·tai·ra
 pl he·tae·rae
 or he·tae·ras
 or he·tai·ras
 or he·tai·rai

het·ero·dox
het·ero·doxy
het·er·ol·o·gous
het·er·on·o·mous
het·er·on·o·mous·ly
het·er·on·o·my
het·ero·sex·u·al
het·ero·sex·u·al·i·ty
het·ero·sex·u·al·ly
hi·a·tal
hi·a·tus
hic·cup
 also hic·cough

hide
 hid

hid·den
or hid

hid·ing

hide·away

hid·eous

hide out *vb*

hide·out *n*

hi·er·arch

hi·er·ar·chal
or hi·er·ar·chi·al

hi·er·ar·chi·cal
or hi·er·ar·chic

hi·er·ar·chi·cal·ly

hi·er·ar·chism

hi·er·ar·chy
pl hi·er·ar·chies

high

high·er

high·est

high·bind·er

high-du·ty

high·er-up

high grade *n*

high-grade *adj*

high-grade *vb*

high-grad·ed

high-grad·ing

high-grad·er

high-hand·ed

high·jack
var of hijack

high·jack·er
var of hijacker

high·ly

high-rise

high-ten·sion

high·way

high·way·man
pl high·way·men

hi·jack
or high-jack

hi·jack·er
or high-jack·er

hi·jack·ing
or high-jack·ing

Hil·a·ry rules

hin·der

hin·dered

hin·der·ing

hind·er·most

hind·most

hin·drance
also hin·der·ance

Hip·po·crat·ic

hire

hired

hir·ing

hire·ling

hire pur·chase

hir·er

his·to·chem·i·cal

his·to·chem·i·cal·ly

his·to·chem·is·try
pl his·to·chem·is·tries

his·to·com·pat·i·bil·i·ty
pl his·to·com·pat·i·bil·i·ties

his·to·com·pat·i·ble

his·to·log·i·cal
or his·to·log·ic

his·to·log·i·cal·ly

his·tol·o·gist

his·tol·o·gy
pl his·tol·o·gies

his·tol·y·sis
pl his·tol·y·ses

his·tor·i·cal

his·tor·i·cal·ly

his·to·ry
pl his·to·ries

hit-and-run

hit-and-run·ner

hitch

hitch·hike

hitch·hiked

hitch·hik·ing

hith·er·to

hit-run

hoard

hoard·ing

hoax

Hobbes·ian

Hob·bism

hob·ble

hob·bled

hob·bling

ho·bo
pl ho·boes
or ho·bos

Hob·son's choice

hoc

hoc lo·co

hoc no·mi·ne

hoc ti·tu·lo
hodge·podge
Hodg·kin's
 dis·ease
hog-tight
hold
 held
 held
  also hold·en
 hold·ing
hold back *vb*
hold·back *n*
hold·er
hold·er-in-due-
 course doc·trine
hold out *vb*
hold·out *n*
hold over *vb*
hold·over *n*
hold up *vb*
hold·up *n*
hole-and-cor·ner
 also hole-in-cor·ner
hole·proof
hol·i·day
Holmes note
ho·lo·graph
ho·lo·graph·ic
hom·age
hom·at·ro·pine
home brew
home·grown
home·less
home·made
ho·meo·path

ho·meo·path·ic
ho·me·op·a·thy
home·own·er
home rule
homes·fall
home·site
home·stead
home·stead·er
home·work
home·work·er
ho·mi·cid·al
ho·mi·cid·al·ly
ho·mi·cide
ho·mi·cide per in·
 for·tu·ni·um
ho·mo
 pl ho·mi·nes
ho·mo ali·e·ni
 ju·ris
ho·mo·erot·ic
ho·mo·erot·i·cism
ho·mo le·ga·lis
ho·mol·o·gate
ho·mol·o·gat·ed
ho·mol·o·gat·ing
ho·mol·o·ga·tion
ho·mo sa·pi·ens
ho·mo·sex·u·al
ho·mo·sex·u·al·i·ty
ho·mo·sex·u·al·ly
hon·est
hon·est·ly
hon·est·ness
hon·es·ty
hon·ky-tonk

hon·or·able
hon·or·able·ness
hon·or·ably
hon·o·rar·i·um
 pl hon·o·rar·ia
 also hon·o·rar·i·ums
hon·or·ary
hon·or·er
ho·no·ris cau·sa
hon·or·less
hood·lum
hood·wink
hoo·li·gan
hoo·li·gan·ism
hootch
hope
 hoped
 hop·ing
hope·less
hope·less·ly
ho·rae ju·di·ci·ae
 or ho·rae ju·ri·di·cae
hor·i·zon·tal
hor·i·zon·tal·ly
hor·mon·al
hor·mon·al·ly
hor·mone
horn·book
horn·swog·gle
 horn·swog·gled
 horn·swog·gling
hor·ta·to·ry
hor·ti·cul·tur·al
hor·ti·cul·ture
hor·ti·cul·tur·ist

Hos·kold for·mu·la

hos·pi·ta·ble

hos·pi·ta·bly

hos·pi·tal

hos·pi·tal·iza·tion

hos·pi·tal·ize

  hos·pi·tal·ized

  hos·pi·tal·iz·ing

hos·pi·ti·cide

host

hos·tage

hos·ti·cide

hos·tile

hos·tile·ly

hos·til·i·ty

  pl hos·til·i·ties

hot

  hot·ter

  hot·test

hotch·pot

hotch·potch

ho·tel

ho·tel·keep·er

house

house·age

house·bote

house·break·er

house·break·ing

house·hold

house·hold·er

house·keep·er

house·wife

hous·ing

how·be·it

how·ev·er

how·so·ev·er

huck·ster

huck·ster·ing

hug·ger-mug·ger

  hug·ger-
    mug·gered

  hug·ger-
    mug·ger·ing

hu·man

hu·mane

hu·man·i·tar·i·an

hu·man·i·tar·i·an·ism

hu·man·i·ty

  pl hu·man·i·ties

hu·man·iza·tion

hu·man·ize

  hu·man·ized

  hu·man·iz·ing

hu·man·kind

hu·man·ly

hum·bug

  hum·bugged

  hum·bug·ging

hu·mer·al

hu·mer·us

  pl hu·meri

hu·mil·i·ate

  hu·mil·i·at·ed

  hu·mil·i·at·ing

hu·mil·i·a·tion

hun·dred

hun·dred-proof

hun·ger

hunt·er

hunt·ing

Hunt·ley hear·ing

hur·ri·cane

hur·ry

  hur·ried

  hur·ry·ing

hurt

  hurt

  hurt·ing

hurt·ful

hus·band

hus·band·like

hus·band·ly

hus·band·man

  pl hus·band·men

hus·band·ry

hush-hush

hush mon·ey

hus·tings

hy·a·line

  also hy·a·lin

hy·a·lin·iza·tion

hy·a·li·no·sis

  pl hy·a·li·no·ses

hybrid

hy·da·tid

hy·da·tid·o·sis

  pl hy·da·tid·o·ses

hy·dra·gogue

  also hy·dra·gog

hy·drar·gyr·ia

  also hy·drar·gy·ri·a·sis

hy·drar·gy·rism
hy·drate
hy·drat·ed
hy·drat·ing
hy·dra·tion
hy·drau·lic
hy·dro·car·bon
hy·dro·chlo·ric
hy·dro·chlo·ride
hy·dro·cor·ti·sone
hy·dro·gen
hy·dro·peri·car·di·um
   pl hy·dro·peri·car·dia

hy·dro·peri·to·ne·um
   pl hy·dro·peri·to·ne·ums
   or hy·dro·peri·to·nea

hy·dro·pho·bia
hy·dro·pho·bic
hy·dro·pneu·mo·tho·rax
   pl hy·dro·pneu·mo·tho·rax·es
   or hy·dro·pneu·mo·tho·ra·ces

hy·dro·ther·a·peu·tic
   or hy·dro·ther·a·peu·ti·cal

hy·dro·ther·a·peu·tics
hy·dro·ther·a·pist

hy·dro·ther·a·py
   pl hy·dro·ther·a·pies

hy·giene
   also hy·gien·i·cal

hy·gien·ic
hy·gien·i·cal·ly
hy·gien·ics
hy·gien·ist
hy·men
hy·men·al
hy·oid
   also hy·oi·dal
   or hy·oi·de·an

hy·o·scine
hy·o·scy·a·mine
hy·o·scy·a·mus
hyp·acu·sic
   or hyp·acou·sic

hyp·al·ge·sia
   also hyp·al·gia

hy·per·ac·tive
hy·per·ac·tiv·i·ty
hy·per·al·ge·sia
hy·per·al·ge·sic
hy·per·em·ploy·ment
hy·per·ex·cit·abil·i·ty
hy·per·ex·cit·able
hy·per·ex·ten·sion
hy·per·gly·ce·mia
hy·per·in·fla·tion
hy·perm·ne·sia
hy·perm·ne·sic
hy·per·ope

hy·per·opia
hy·per·opic
hy·per·os·mia
hy·per·os·mic
hy·per·sen·si·tive
hy·per·sen·si·tiv·i·ty
   pl hy·per·sen·si·tiv·i·ties

hy·per·sen·si·ti·za·tion
hy·per·sen·si·tize
hy·per·sen·si·tized
hy·per·sen·si·tiz·ing
hy·per·ten·sion
hy·per·ten·sive
hy·per·thy·roid
hy·per·thy·roid·ism
hy·per·to·nia
   or hy·per·to·ny
   pl hy·per·to·ni·as
   or hy·per·to·nies

hy·per·ton·ic
hy·per·to·nic·i·ty
hy·per·ven·ti·la·tion
hyp·es·the·sia
hyp·na·go·gic
   or hyp·no·go·gic

hyp·no·anal·y·sis
   pl hyp·no·anal·y·ses

hyp·no·ther·a·py
   pl hyp·no·ther·a·pies

hyp·not·ic

hyp·no·tism
hyp·no·tist
hyp·no·tize
  or hyp·no·tise
  hyp·no·tized
    or hyp·no·tised
  hyp·no·tiz·ing
    or hyp·no·tis·ing

hy·po·chon·dria
hy·po·chon·dri·a·
  cal
hy·po·chon·dri·a·
  cal·ly
hy·po·chon·dri·a·
  sis
hy·poc·ri·sy
  pl hy·poc·ri·sies

hypo·o·crite
hypo·o·crit·i·cal
  or hypo·o·crit·ic

hypo·o·crit·i·cal·ly
hy·po·der·mic
hy·po·der·mi·cal·ly
hy·po·gly·ce·mia
hy·poph·y·se·al
  also hy·poph·y·si·al

hy·poph·y·sis
  pl hy·poph·y·ses

hy·po·po·tas·se·mia
hy·po·po·tas·se·mic
hy·po·sen·si·tive
hy·po·sen·si·tiv·i·ty
  pl hy·po·sen·si·tiv·i·ties

hy·po·sen·si·ti·za·
  tion
hy·po·sen·si·tize

hy·po·sen·si·tized
hy·po·sen·si·tiz·
  ing
hy·pos·ta·sis
  pl hy·pos·ta·ses

hy·pos·ta·tize
  or hy·pos·ta·tise
  hy·pos·ta·tized
    or hy·pos·ta·tised
  hy·pos·ta·tiz·ing
    or hy·pos·ta·tis·ing

hy·po·ten·sion
hy·po·ten·sive
hy·po·tha·lam·ic
hy·po·thal·a·mus
  pl hy·po·thal·a·mi

hy·poth·ec
hy·poth·e·cary
hy·poth·e·cate
  hy·poth·e·cat·ed
  hy·poth·e·cat·ing
hy·poth·e·ca·tion
hy·poth·e·ca·tor
hy·poth·e·sis
  pl hy·poth·e·ses

hy·poth·e·size
  hy·poth·e·sized
  hy·poth·e·siz·ing
hy·po·thet·i·cal
hy·po·thet·i·cal·ly
hy·po·thy·roid
hy·po·thy·roid·ism
hy·po·to·nia
  or hy·pot·o·ny
  pl hy·po·to·nias
    or hy·pot·o·nies

hy·po·ton·ic
hy·po·ton·i·cal·ly
hy·po·to·nic·i·ty
  pl hy·po·to·nic·i·ties

hy·po·tri·cho·sis
  pl hy·po·tri·cho·ses
    or hy·po·tri·cho·sis·es

hy·po·vi·ta·min·o·
  sis
  pl hy·po·vi·ta·min·o·
    ses
    or hy·po·vi·ta·min·o·
      sis·es

hys·ter·ec·to·mize
hys·ter·ec·to·
  mized
hys·ter·ec·to·
  miz·ing
hys·ter·ec·to·my
  pl hys·ter·ec·to·mies

hys·te·ria
hys·ter·ic
  or hys·ter·i·cal

hys·ter·i·cal·ly
hys·ter·ics
hys·tero·trau·ma·
  tism

I

iat·ric
  also iat·ri·cal

iat·ro·gen·ic
iat·ro·gen·i·cal·ly
iat·ro·ge·nic·i·ty
  pl iat·ro·ge·nic·i·ties

ibi·dem

ibo·ga·ine

ich·no·graph·ic
  or ich·no·graph·i·cal

ich·nog·ra·phy
  pl ich·nog·ra·phies

ich·thy·ism
  or ich·thy·is·mus
  pl ich·thy·isms
  or ich·thy·is·mus·es

ich·thy·ol·o·gist

ich·thy·ol·o·gy

ich·thyo·tox·ism

ic·ter·ic

ic·tero·gen·ic
  also ic·ter·og·e·nous

ic·ter·us

ic·ter·us gra·vis

ic·tus

idea

idea·logue
  var of ideologue

ide·al·o·gy
  var of ideology

idée fixe
  pl idées fixes

idem

idem per·so·na

idem so·nans

iden·ta·code

iden·tate no·mi·nis

iden·tate per·so·
  nae

iden·tic

iden·ti·cal

iden·ti·cal·ly

iden·ti·fi·abil·i·ty

iden·ti·fi·able

iden·ti·fi·ably

iden·ti·fi·ca·tion

iden·ti·fi·er

iden·ti·fy

iden·ti·fied

iden·ti·fy·ing

iden·ti·ty
  pl iden·ti·ties

ideo con·si·de·ra·
  tum est

ideo·log·i·cal
  or ideo·log·ic

ideo·log·i·cal·ly

ide·ol·o·gist

ide·ol·o·gize

ide·ol·o·gized

ide·ol·o·giz·ing

ideo·logue
  also idea·logue

ide·ol·o·gy
  also ide·al·o·gy
  pl ide·ol·o·gies
  also ide·al·o·gies

id est

id·i·oc·ra·sy
  pl id·i·oc·ra·sies

idio·crat·ic
  or idio·crat·i·cal

id·i·o·cy
  pl id·i·o·cies

id·io·path·ic

id·io·path·i·cal·ly

id·i·op·a·thy
  pl id·i·op·a·thies

id·io·syn·cra·sy
  also id·io·syn·cra·cy
  pl id·io·syn·cra·sies
  also id·io·syn·cra·cies

id·io·syn·crat·ic

id·io·syn·crat·i·
  cal·ly

id·i·ot

id·i·ot·ic
  also id·i·ot·i·cal

id·i·ot·i·cal·ly

id·i·ot sa·vant
  pl id·i·ots sa·vants
  or id·i·ot sa·vants

if-bet

ig·ne·ous

ig·nis fat·u·us
  pl ig·nes fat·ui

ig·nite

ig·nit·ed

ig·nit·ing

ig·ni·tion

ig·no·mi·ny
  pl ig·no·mi·nies

ig·no·ra·mus

ig·no·rance

ig·no·rant

ig·no·ran·tia fac·ti

ig·no·ran·tia ju·ris

ig·no·ra·tio elen·
  chi

ig·nore

ig·nored

ig·nor·ing

ig·nor·er

il·e·al
  also il·e·ac

il·e·um
  pl il·ea

il·e·us

il·i·ac

il·i·um
  pl il·ia

ill
  worse
    also ill·er
  worst

ill-ad·vised

ill-be·ing

ill-dis·posed

ill-do·ing

il·le·gal

il·le·gal·i·ty
  pl il·le·gal·i·ties

il·le·gal·iza·tion

il·le·gal·ize
  il·le·gal·ized
  il·le·gal·iz·ing

il·le·gal·ly

il·leg·i·bil·i·ty

il·leg·i·ble
  not readable
  (*see* eligible)

il·le·git·i·ma·cy
  pl il·le·git·i·ma·cies

il·le·git·i·mate
  il·le·git·i·mat·ed
  il·le·git·i·mat·ing
il·le·git·i·ma·tion

ill fame

ill-famed

ill-got·ten
  also ill-got

ill-gov·erned

il·lic·it
  not lawful
  (*see* elicit)

il·lic·ite

il·lic·it·ly

il·lic·i·tum
  col·le·gi·um

il·lit·er·a·cy
  pl il·lit·er·a·cies

il·lit·er·ate

il·lit·er·ate·ly

ill·ness

il·loc·able

ill re·pute

ill-treat

il·lude
  il·lud·ed
  il·lud·ing
  to deceive
  (*see* elude)

ill-us·age

ill-use
  ill-used
  ill-us·ing

il·lu·sion

il·lu·sion·al

il·lu·sion·ary

il·lu·sive

il·lu·so·ry

ill will

imag·i·nal

imag·i·nary

imag·i·na·tion

imag·i·na·tive

imag·ine
  imag·ined
  imag·in·ing

im·bal·ance

im·bar·go
  var of embargo

im·be·cile

im·be·cil·ic

im·be·cil·i·ty
  pl im·be·cil·i·ties

im·bibe
  im·bibed
  im·bib·ing

im·bib·er

im·bro·glio
  or em·bro·glio
  pl im·bro·glios
  or em·bro·glios

im·i·tate
  im·i·tat·ed
  im·i·tat·ing

im·i·tat·ee

im·i·ta·tion

im·i·ta·tive

im·i·ta·tor

im·ma·nence
  restricted to one do-
  main
  (*see* eminence, immi-
  nence)

im·ma·nent
  inherent
  (*see* eminent, immi-
  nent)

impedimentum

im·ma·te·ri·al
im·ma·te·ri·al·i·ty
  pl im·ma·te·ri·al·i·ties

im·ma·te·ri·al·ly
im·ma·te·ri·al·ness
im·ma·ture
im·ma·tu·ri·ty
  pl im·ma·tu·ri·ties

im·me·di·a·cy
  pl im·me·di·a·cies

im·me·di·ate
im·me·di·ate·ly
im·med·i·ca·ble
im·me·mo·ri·al
im·me·mo·ri·al·ly
im·meu·bles *n pl*
im·mi·grant
im·mi·grate
  im·mi·grat·ed
  im·mi·grat·ing
im·mi·gra·tion
im·mi·nence
  something imminent
  (see eminent, imma-
  nent*)*

im·mi·nent
  menacingly near
  (see eminent, imma-
  nent*)*

im·mi·nent·ly
im·mo·bil·i·ty
  pl im·mo·bil·i·ties

im·mo·bi·li·za·tion
im·mo·bi·lize
  im·mo·bi·lized
  im·mo·bi·liz·ing

im·mod·er·ate
im·mod·est
im·mor·al
im·mo·ral·i·ty
  pl im·mo·ral·i·ties

im·mor·al·ly
im·mov·able
  also im·move·able

im·mune
im·mun·ist
im·mu·ni·ty
  pl im·mu·ni·ties

im·mu·ni·za·tion
im·mu·nize
  im·mu·nized
  im·mu·niz·ing
im·mu·no·log·ic
  also im·mu·no·log·i·cal

im·mu·no·log·i·
  cal·ly
im·mu·nol·o·gy
  pl im·mu·nol·o·gies

im·mu·no·sup·
  pres·sant
im·mu·no·sup·
  pres·sion
im·mu·no·sup·
  pres·sive
im·pac·tion
im·pair
im·pair·ment
im·pan·el
  also em·pan·el
  im·pan·eled
  also em·pan·eled

im·pan·el·ing
  also em·pan·el·ing

im·par·i·ty
  pl im·par·i·ties

im·parl
  or em·parl

im·par·lance
im·part
im·par·ta·tion
im·par·tial
im·par·tial·i·ty
im·par·tial·ly
im·par·tial·ness
im·par·ti·bil·i·ty
im·par·ti·ble
im·par·ti·bly
im·pass·able
  not passable
  (see impassible*)*

im·pas·si·ble
  unable to feel
  (see impassable*)*

im·peach
im·peach·able
im·peach·ment
im·pec·ca·ble
im·pec·ca·bly
im·pe·cu·ni·os·i·ty
im·pe·cu·nious
im·pede
  im·ped·ed
  im·ped·ing
im·pe·di·ent
im·ped·i·ment
im·ped·i·men·tum
  pl im·ped·i·men·ta

im·pel
  im·pelled
  im·pel·ling
im·pend·ing
im·per·a·tive
im·per·cep·ti·ble
im·per·cep·ti·bly
im·per·fect
im·per·il
  im·per·iled
    or im·per·illed
  im·per·il·ing
    or im·per·il·ling
im·pe·ri·ous
im·pe·ri·um
im·pe·ri·um in im·
  pe·rio
im·per·son·ate
  im·per·son·at·ed
  im·per·son·at·ing
im·per·son·ation
im·per·ti·nence
  also im·per·ti·nen·cy
  pl im·per·ti·nenc·es
  also im·per·ti·nen·cies

im·per·ti·nent
im·pig·no·rate
  im·pig·no·rat·ed
  im·pig·no·rat·ing
im·pig·no·ra·tion
im·plant
im·plan·ta·tion
im·plead
  im·plead·ed
    or im·pled
  im·plead·ing

im·plead·er
im·ple·ment
im·ple·men·ta·tion
im·pli·cate
  im·pli·cat·ed
  im·pli·cat·ing
im·pli·ca·tion
im·plic·it
im·plied·ly
im·ply
  im·plied
  im·ply·ing
im·port
im·port·able
im·por·ta·tion
im·por·tee
im·port·er
im·por·tune
  im·por·tuned
  im·por·tun·ing
im·por·tu·ni·ty
  pl im·por·tu·ni·ties

im·pose
  im·posed
  im·pos·ing
im·po·si·tion
im·pos·si·bil·i·ty
  pl im·pos·si·bil·i·ties

im·pos·si·ble
im·post
im·pos·tor
im·pos·ture
im·po·tence
  also im·po·ten·cy
  pl im·po·tenc·es
  also im·po·ten·cies

im·po·tent
im·po·tent·ly
im·pound
im·pound·able
im·pound·ment
  also im·pound·age
im·prac·ti·ca·bil·
  i·ty
    pl im·prac·ti·ca·bil·i·
    ties

im·prac·ti·ca·ble
  not feasible
  (*see* impractical)

im·prac·ti·cal
  not practical
  (*see* impracticable)

im·preg·nate
  im·preg·nat·ed
  im·preg·nat·ing
im·preg·na·tion
im·pre·scrip·ti·bil·
  i·ty
im·pre·scrip·ti·ble
im·pres·sion
im·pri·ma·tur
im·pri·mis
im·pris·on
  im·pris·oned
  im·pris·on·ing
im·pris·on·ment
im·prob·a·ble
im·pro·ba·tion
im·pro·ba·tive
  also im·pro·ba·to·ry

im·pro·bi·ty
  pl im·pro·bi·ties

im·prop·er
im·prop·er·ly
im·prove
  im·proved
  im·prov·ing
im·prove·ment
im·prov·er
im·prov·i·dence
im·prov·i·dent
im·prov·i·dent·ly
im·pru·dence
im·pru·dent
im·pu·ber·ty
im·pu·bic
im·pugn
im·pugn·able
im·pugn·er
im·pugn·ment
im·pulse
im·pul·sion
im·pul·sive
im·pu·ni·ty
im·put·able
im·pu·ta·tion
im·pute
  im·put·ed
  im·put·ing
in·abil·i·ty
in ab·sen·tia
in·ac·ces·si·ble
in·ac·ti·vate
  in·ac·ti·vat·ed
  in·ac·ti·vat·ing
in·ac·ti·va·tion
in·ac·tive

in·ad·e·qua·cy
  pl in·ad·e·qua·cies

in·ad·e·quate
in·ad·mis·si·bil·i·ty
  also in·ad·mis·sa·bil·i·ty

in·ad·mis·si·ble
  also in·ad·mis·sa·ble

in ad·ver·sum
in·ad·ver·tence
in·ad·ver·tent
in·ad·ver·tent·ly
in ae·qua·li ju·re
in·alien·abil·i·ty
in·alien·able
in·alien·ably
in ali·e·no so·lo
in·ar·tic·u·late
in·ar·tic·u·late·ly
in ar·ti·cu·lo mor·tis
in·as·much as
in ban·co
in bo·nis
in bo·nis de·func·ti
in cam·era
in·ca·pa·bil·i·ty
in·ca·pa·ble
in·ca·pa·bly
in·ca·pac·i·tant
in·ca·pac·i·tate
  in·ca·pac·i·tat·ed
  in·ca·pac·i·tat·ing
in·ca·pac·i·ta·tion

in·ca·pac·i·ty
  pl in·ca·pac·i·ties

in·ca·pax
in ca·pi·te
in·car·cer·ate
  in·car·cer·at·ed
  in·car·cer·at·ing
in·car·cer·a·tion
in·car·cer·a·tor
in cau·sa
in·cau·tious
in·cen·di·a·rism
in·cen·di·a·rist
in·cen·di·ary
  pl in·cen·di·ar·ies

in·cen·tive
in·cep·tion
in·cest
in·ces·tu·ous
in·ces·tu·ous·ly
in·ces·tu·ous·ness
Inch·ma·ree clause
in·cho·ate
in·cho·ate·ly
in·ci·dence
in·ci·dent
in·ci·den·tal
in·ci·den·tal·ly
in·ci·dent·less
in·ci·dent·ly
in·cip·i·en·cy
  pl in·cip·i·en·cies

in·cip·i·ent
in·ci·pi·tur

in·cit·ant
in·ci·ta·tion
in·cite
  in·cit·ed
  in·cit·ing
  to urge on
  (*see* insight)

in·cite·ment
in·cit·er
in·cit·ing·ly
in·ci·tive
in·ci·to·ry
in·cli·na·tion
in·close
  var of enclose

in·clo·sure
  var of enclosure

in·clude
  in·clud·ed
  in·clud·ing
in·clu·sive
in·cog·ni·to
  pl in·cog·ni·tos

in·co·her·ent
in·co·in·ci·dence
in·co·in·ci·dent
in·com·bus·ti·ble
in·come
in·come·less
in·com·ing
in com·men·dam
in·com·mu·ni
in·com·mu·ni·ca·
  do
in·com·mut·able

in·com·pat·i·bil·i·
  ty
  pl in·com·pat·i·bil·i·
  ties

in·com·pat·i·ble
in·com·pat·i·bly
in·com·pe·tence
in·com·pe·ten·cy
  pl in·com·pe·ten·cies

in·com·pe·tent
in·com·plete
in·com·pli·ance
  or in·com·pli·an·cy
  pl in·com·pli·anc·es
  or in·com·pli·an·cies

in·com·pli·ant
in·con·ceal·able
in·con·clu·si·ble
in·con·clu·sive
in·con·gru·ence
in·con·gru·ent
in·con·gru·ent·ly
in·con·gru·i·ty
  pl in·con·gru·i·ties

in·con·gru·ous
in·con·gru·ous·ly
in·con·se·quence
in·con·se·quent
in·con·se·quen·tial
in·con·se·quen·ti·
  al·i·ty
in·con·se·quen·
  tial·ly
in·con·sid·er·able

in·con·sid·er·able·
  ness
in con·si·mi·li
  ca·su
in·con·sist·able
in·con·sis·ten·cy
  also in·con·sis·tence
  pl in·con·sis·ten·cies
  also in·con·sis·tenc·es

in·con·sis·tent
in·con·sis·tent·ly
in·con·sis·tent·ness
in·con·test·abil·i·ty
  pl in·con·test·abil·i·ties

in·con·test·able
  or in·con·test·ible

in·con·ti·nence
in·con·ti·nen·cy
  pl in·con·ti·nen·cies

in·con·ti·nent
in con·ti·nen·ti
in·con·tro·vert·ible
in·con·vert·ibil·i·ty
in·con·vert·ible
in·co·or·di·nate
in·co·or·di·na·tion
in·cor·po·ra·ble
in·cor·po·rate
  in·cor·po·rat·ed
  in·cor·po·rat·ing
  in·cor·po·rat·ed·
  ness
in·cor·po·ra·tion
in·cor·po·ra·tor

in·cor·po·ra·tor·
　ship
in·cor·po·re·al
in·cor·po·re·al·i·ty
in·cor·po·re·al·ly
in·cor·po·re·i·ty
in·cor·ri·gi·bil·i·ty
in·cor·ri·gi·ble
in·cor·ri·gi·ble·ness
in·cor·ri·gi·bly
in·cor·rupt
　also in·cor·rupt·ed

in·cor·rupt·ibil·i·ty
in·cor·rupt·ible
in·cor·rupt·ible·
　ness
in·cor·rupt·ibly
in·cor·rup·tion
in·cor·rupt·ly
in·creas·able
in·crease
　in·creased
　in·creas·ing
in·cred·ibil·i·ty
　pl in·cred·ibil·i·ties
　unbelievableness
　(*see* incredulity)

in·cred·i·ble
in·cred·i·bly
in·cre·du·li·ty
　disbelief
　(*see* incredibility)

in·cre·ment
in·cre·men·tal
in·crim·i·nate

in·crim·i·nat·ed
in·crim·i·nat·ing
in·crim·i·na·tion
in·crim·i·na·tor
in·crim·i·na·to·ry
in·cu·bate
　in·cu·bat·ed
　in·cu·bat·ing
in·cu·ba·tion
in·cul·pa·bil·i·ty
in·cul·pa·ble
in·cul·pate
　in·cul·pat·ed
　in·cul·pat·ing
in·cul·pa·to·ry
in·cum·ben·cy
　pl in·cum·ben·cies

in·cum·bent
in·cum·bent·ly
in·cum·ber
　var of encumber

in·cum·brance
　var of encumbrance

in·cum·branc·er
　var of encumbrancer

in·cur
　in·curred
　in·cur·ring
in·cur·able
　not curable
　(*see* incurrable)

in·cur·ably
in·cu·ria
in·cur·ment

in·cur·rable
　that can be incurred
　(*see* incurable)

in·cur·sion
in cus·to·dia le·gis
in·de·bi·ta·tus
　as·sump·sit
in·debt·ed
in·debt·ed·ness
in·de·cen·cy
　pl in·de·cen·cies

in·de·cent
in·de·fea·si·bil·i·ty
　pl in·de·fea·si·bil·i·ties

in·de·fea·si·ble
in·de·fea·si·bly
in·de·fen·si·bil·i·ty
in·de·fen·si·ble
in·def·i·nite
in de·lic·to
in·dem·ni·fi·ca·tion
in·dem·ni·fi·ca·tor
in·dem·nif·i·ca·to·
　ry
in·dem·ni·fi·er
in·dem·ni·fy
　in·dem·ni·fied
　in·dem·ni·fy·ing
in·dem·ni·tee
in·dem·ni·tor
in·dem·ni·ty
　pl in·dem·ni·ties

in·dem·ni·za·tion
in·den·i·za·tion
in·dent

in·den·tor
also in·dent·er

in·den·ture
  in·den·tured
  in·den·tur·ing
in·de·pen·dence
in·de·pen·dent
in·de·pen·dent·ly
in·de·struc·ti·ble
in·de·ter·min·able
in·de·ter·mi·na·cy
in·de·ter·mi·nate
in·de·ter·mi·na·
  tion
in·dex
  pl in·dex·es
  or in·di·ces

in·di·cate
  in·di·cat·ed
  in·di·cat·ing
in·di·ca·tion
in·dic·a·tive
in·di·ca·vit
in·di·cia
in·dict
  to accuse formally
  (see indite*)*

in·dict·able
in·dict·ably
in·dict·ee
in·dict·ment
in·dict·or
  or in·dict·er

in·dif·fer·ent
in·di·gence
in·di·gent

in·dig·ni·ty
  pl in·dig·ni·ties

in·di·rect
in·di·rect·ly
in·dis·creet
in·dis·creet·ly
in·dis·cre·tion
in·dis·crim·i·nate
in·dis·crim·i·nate·
  ly
in·dis·pens·abil·i·
  ty
in·dis·pens·able
in·dis·pens·ably
in·dis·posed
in·dis·po·si·tion
in·dis·put·able
in·dis·put·able·
  ness
in·dis·put·ably
in·dis·sol·u·bil·i·ty
in·dis·sol·u·ble
in·dite
  in·dit·ed
  in·dit·ing
  to put in writing
  (see indict*)*

in·di·vid·u·al
in·di·vis·i·bil·i·ty
in·di·vis·i·ble
in·di·vis·i·bly
in·do·lence
in·do·lent
in·dorse
  in·dorsed
  in·dors·ing

in·dors·ee
in·dorse·ment
in·dors·er
in du·bio
in·du·bi·ta·ble
in·du·bi·ta·bly
in·duce
  in·duced
  in·duc·ing
in·duce·ment
in·du·ci·ae
  or in·du·ci·ae le·ga·les

in·duct
in·duc·tion
in·duc·tor
in·dul·gence
in·du·rate
  in·du·rat·ed
  in·du·rat·ing
in·du·ra·tion
in·du·ra·tive
in·dus·tri·al
in·dus·tri·al·ly
in·dus·try
  pl in·dus·tries

ine·bri·ant
ine·bri·ate
  ine·bri·at·ed
  ine·bri·at·ing
ine·bri·a·tion
in·ebri·ety
in·ebri·ous
in·ed·u·ca·bil·i·ty
in·ed·u·ca·ble
in·ef·fec·tu·al

in·ef·fi·cien·cy
  pl in·ef·fi·cien·cies

in·ef·fi·cient
in·el·i·gi·bil·i·ty
in·el·i·gi·ble
in·equa·ble
in·equal·i·ty
  pl in·eqal·i·ties

in·eq·ui·ta·ble
in·eq·ui·ta·ble·ness
in·eq·ui·ta·bly
in·eq·ui·ty
  pl in·eq·ui·ties
  lack of equity
  (*see* iniquity)

in·es·cap·able
in es·se
in·ev·i·ta·bil·i·ty
  pl in·ev·i·ta·bil·i·ties

in·ev·i·ta·ble
in·ev·i·ta·ble·ness
in·ev·i·ta·bly
in·ex·cus·abil·i·ty
in·ex·cus·able
in·ex·cus·able·ness
in·ex·cus·ably
in·ex·e·cut·able
in·ex·e·cu·tion
in ex·ten·so
in ex·tre·mis
in fa·cie cu·ri·ae
in·fa·mia fac·ti
in·fa·mia ju·ris
in·fa·mous
in·fa·my
  pl in·fa·mies

in·fan·cy
  pl in·fan·cies

in·fant
in·fan·ti·ci·dal
in·fan·ti·cide
in·farct
in·farct·ed
in·farc·tion
in·fect
in·fec·tion
in·fec·tious
in·fec·tious·ly
in·fec·tive
in·fec·tiv·i·ty
  pl in·fec·tiv·i·ties

in·feft
in·feft
  also in·feft·ed
in·feft·ing
in·feft·ment
in·fer
in·ferred
in·fer·ring
in·fer·able
  also in·fer·ible
  or in·fer·ri·ble

in·fer·ence
in·fer·en·tial
in·fer·en·tial·ly
in·fe·ri·or
in·fe·ri·or·i·ty
  pl in·fe·ri·or·i·ties

in·fi·del
in·fi·del·i·ty
  pl in·fi·del·i·ties

in fi·eri

in·fi·ni·tum
in·firm
in·firm·able
in·fir·ma·tion
  invalidation
  (*see* information)

in·fir·ma·tive
in·fir·mi·ty
  pl in·fir·mi·ties

in·firm·ness
in fla·gran·te
de·lic·to
in·flame
in·flamed
in·flam·ing
in·flam·ma·bil·i·ty
  pl in·flam·ma·bil·i·ties

in·flam·ma·ble
in·flam·ma·tion
in·flam·ma·tive
in·flam·ma·to·ri·ly
in·flam·ma·to·ry
in·fla·tion
in·fla·tion·ary
in·flict
in·flict·able
in·flict·er
  or in·flic·tor

in·flic·tion
in·flic·tive
in·flu·ence
  in·flu·enced
  in·flu·enc·ing
in·flu·ence·abil·i·ty
in·flu·ence·able
in·flu·enc·er

in·form
in·for·mal
in·for·mal·i·ty
   pl in·for·mal·i·ties
in·for·mal·ly
in·for·mant
in for·ma pau·per·
   is
in·for·ma·tion
in·for·ma·tion·al
in·form·er
in fo·ro
in fo·ro con·sci·
   en·ti·ae
in fo·ro con·ten·
   tio·so
in·for·tu·ni·um
in·fra
in·fract
in·fract·ible
in·frac·tion
in·frac·tor
in·fra fu·ro·rem
in·fra hos·pi·ti·um
in·fran·gi·bil·i·ty
in·fran·gi·ble
in·fran·gi·bly
in·fra prae·si·dia
in frau·dem cre·di·
   to·rum
in frau·dem le·gis
in·fringe
   in·fringed
   in·fring·ing
in·fringe·ment

in·fring·er
in fu·tu·ro
in·gath·er
in·ge·nious
   notably apt or clever
   (*see* ingenuous)

in·gen·u·ous
   naively frank
   (*see* ingenious)

in·ger·ence
in·gra·ves·cent
in gre·mio le·gis
in·gress
in·gres·sion
in·gres·sive
in gross
   existing independently
   (*see* engross)

in·gui·nal
in·hab·it
in·hab·it·abil·i·ty
in·hab·it·able
in·hab·it·ance
in·hab·it·an·cy
   pl in·hab·it·an·cies

in·hab·it·ant
in·hab·i·ta·tion
in·hab·it·ed
in·hab·it·er
in·hab·i·tress
in haec ver·ba
in·hal·ant
in·ha·la·tion
in·hale
   in·haled

in·hal·ing
in·here
   in·hered
   in·her·ing
in·her·ence
in·her·ent
in·her·ent·ly
in·her·it
in·her·it·abil·i·ty
   pl in·her·it·abil·i·ties

in·her·it·able
in·her·it·ably
in·her·i·tance
in·her·i·tor
in·her·i·tress
in·hib·it
in·hib·it·able
in·hi·bi·tion
in·hib·i·tive
in·hib·i·to·ry
in·hold·ing
in·hu·man
in·hu·mane
in·hu·mane·ly
in·hu·man·ly
in·im·i·ca·bil·i·ty
in·im·i·ca·ble
in·im·i·cal
in·im·i·cal·ly
in in·vi·tum
in·iq·ui·ty
   pl in·iq·ui·ties
   wickedness
   (*see* inequity)

ini·tial

ini·tialed
  or ini·tialled
ini·tial·ing
  or ini·tial·ling
ini·tial·ly
ini·ti·ate
  ini·ti·at·ed
  ini·ti·at·ing
ini·ti·a·tion
ini·tia·tive
in iti·ne·re
in ju·di·cio
in·junct
in·junc·tion
in·junc·tive
in ju·re
  according to law
  (*see* injure)

in·jure
  in·jured
  in·jur·ing
  to do harm to
  (*see* in jure)

in·jur·er
in·ju·ria
in·ju·ria abs·que
  dam·no
in·ju·ri·ous
in·ju·ri·ous·ly
in·ju·ri·ous·ness
in·ju·ry
  pl in·ju·ries
in·jus·tice
in·land
in·law
  pl in-laws

in lieu of
in li·mi·ne
in li·mi·ne li·tis
in li·tem
in lo·co
in lo·co pa·ren·tis
in lo·co tu·to·ris
in-lot
in·mate
in me·di·as res
in-mi·grant
in-mi·grate
  in-mi·grat·ed
  in-mi·grat·ing
in mi·ti·o·ri sen·su
inn
in·nav·i·ga·bil·i·ty
in·nav·i·ga·ble
in·ner
in·ner·va·tion
inn·hold·er
inn·keep·er
in·no·cence
in·no·cen·cy
in·no·cent
in·no·cent·ly
in·noc·u·ous
inn of court
in·no·tes·ci·mus
in·no·va·tion
in·nox·ious
in nu·bi·bus
in·nu·en·do
  pl in·nu·en·dos
  or in·nu·en·does

in·nu·mer·able
  too many to count
  (*see* enumerable)

in·oc·u·late
in·oc·u·lat·ed
in·oc·u·lat·ing
in·oc·u·la·tion
in·oc·u·lum
  pl in·oc·u·la

in·of·fi·cial
in·of·fi·cious
in·op·er·a·ble
in·op·er·a·tive
in·ops con·si·lii
in pais
in pa·ri cau·sa
in pa·ri de·lic·to
in pa·ri ma·te·ria
in pa·ri pas·su
in par·ti·ceps
  cri·mi·nis
in·pa·tient
in pec·to·re
  ju·di·cis
in per·pe·tu·um
in per·so·nam
in pos·se
in prae·sen·ti
in pro·pria
  per·so·na
in·quest
in·quire
  also en·quire
in·quired
  also en·quired

in·quir·ing
also en·quir·ing

in·qui·ren·do
pl in·qui·ren·dos

in·qui·ry
also en·qui·ry
pl in·qui·ries
also en·qui·ries

in·qui·si·tion
in·qui·si·tion·al
in·quis·i·tor
in·quis·i·to·ri·al
in·quis·i·to·ri·al·ly
in·quis·i·to·ry

in re
in the matter of
(see in rem)

in rem
against a thing
(see in re)

in re·spect of
in re·spect to
in·sa·lu·bri·ous
in·sa·lu·bri·ty
pl in·sa·lu·bri·ties

in·sane
in·san·i·tary
in·san·i·ta·tion
in·san·i·ty
pl in·san·i·ties

in·scribe
in·scribed
in·scrib·ing
in·scrib·er
in·scrip·tio
in·scrip·tion

in·sec·ti·cid·al
in·sec·ti·cid·al·ly
in·sec·ti·cide
in·se·cure
in·se·cu·ri·ty
pl in·se·cu·ri·ties

in·sem·i·nate
in·sem·i·nat·ed
in·sem·i·nat·ing
in·sem·i·na·tion
in·sen·si·ble
in·sert
in·side
in·sid·er
in·sid·i·ous
in·sight
discernment
(see incite)

in·sin·u·ate
in·sin·u·at·ed
in·sin·u·at·ing
in·sin·u·a·tion
in·so·far
in·so·far as
in·so·far that
in·so·lent
in·so·lent·ly
in so·li·do
also in so·li·dum

in·sol·ven·cy
pl in·sol·ven·cies

in·sol·vent
in spe·cie
in·spect
in·spec·tion
in·spec·tor

in·spec·tor·ate
in·spec·to·ri·al
or in·spec·tor·al

in·sta·bil·i·ty
in·sta·ble
in·stall
also in·stal

in·stalled
in·stall·ing
in·stal·lant
in·stal·la·tion
in·stall·er
in·stall·ment
also in·stal·ment

in·stance
in·stant
in·stan·ta·ne·ous
in·stan·ta·ne·ous·ly
in·stan·ter
in·stant·ly
in·state
in·stat·ed
in·stat·ing
in·state·ment
in sta·tu quo
in·sti·gate
in·sti·gat·ed
in·sti·gat·ing
in·sti·gat·ing·ly
in·sti·ga·tion
in·sti·ga·tive
in·sti·ga·tor
in stir·pes
in·sti·tor
in·sti·tute

in·sti·tut·ed
in·sti·tut·ing
in·sti·tu·tion
in·sti·tu·tion·al
in·sti·tu·tion·al·ize
in·sti·tu·tion·al·
    ized
in·sti·tu·tion·al·
    iz·ing
in store
in stric·tu ju·re
in·struct
in·struc·tion
in·stru·ment
in·stru·men·tal
in·stru·men·tal·i·ty
    pl in·stru·men·tal·i·ties
in·stru·men·ta·ry
in·sub·mis·sive
in·sub·or·di·nate
in·sub·or·di·na·
    tion
in sub·stance
in·suf·fi·cien·cy
    pl in·suf·fi·cien·cies
in·suf·fi·cient
in·su·late
in·su·lat·ed
in·su·lat·ing
in·su·la·tion
in·sult
in·su·per·a·ble
in·sup·port·able
in·sur·abil·i·ty
in·sur·able
in·sur·ance

in·sur·ant
in·sure
in·sured
in·sur·ing
in·sur·er
in·sur·gence
in·sur·gen·cy
in·sur·gent
in·sur·ges·cence
in·sur·rect
in·sur·rec·tion
in·sur·rec·tion·al·ly
in·sur·rec·tion·ary
    also in·sur·rec·tion·al
in·sur·rec·tion·ist
in sus·pen·so
in·tact
in·tan·gi·bil·i·ty
    pl in·tan·gi·bil·i·ties
in·tan·gi·ble
in·te·gral
in·te·grate
in·te·grat·ed
in·te·grat·ing
in·te·gra·tion
in·teg·ri·ty
in·tel·lec·tu·al
in·tel·lec·tu·al·ly
in·tel·li·gence
in·tel·li·gent
in·tel·li·gi·bil·i·ty
    pl in·tel·li·gi·bil·i·ties
in·tel·li·gi·ble
in·tel·li·gi·bly
in·tem·per·ance

in·tem·per·ate
in·tem·per·ate·ly
in·tend
in·tend·ment
in·tent
in·ten·tion
in·ten·tion·al
in·ten·tion·al·ly
in·ten·tioned
in·ter·agen·cy
    pl in·ter·agen·cies

in·ter·agent
in·ter alia
in·ter ali·os
in·ter ali·os ac·ta
in·ter·bank
in·ter·bor·ough
in·ter·bourse
in·ter·cede
in·ter·ced·ed
in·ter·ced·ing
in·ter·ced·er
in·ter·cept
in·ter·cep·tion
in·ter·ces·sion
in·ter·change
in·ter·changed
in·ter·chang·ing
in·ter·change·able
in·ter·change·ably
in·ter·cit·i·zen·ship
in·ter·city
in·ter·com·pa·ny
in·ter·cor·po·rate
in·ter·coun·try
in·ter·course

in·ter·dict
in·ter·dic·tion
in·ter·dic·tive
in·ter·dic·tor
in·ter·dic·to·ry
in·ter·dic·tum
  pl in·ter·dic·ta

in·ter·es·se
in·ter·es·se
  ter·mi·ni
in·ter·est
in·ter·est·ed
in·ter·fer·ant
in·ter·fere
  in·ter·fered
  in·ter·fer·ing
in·ter·fer·ence
in·ter·firm
in·ter·gov·ern·men·tal
in·ter·im
in·ter·in·dus·tri·al
  or in·ter·in·dus·try

in·ter·in·sur·ance
in·ter·in·sur·er
in·te·ri·or
in·ter·line
  in·ter·lined
  in·ter·lin·ing
in·ter·lin·ea·tion
in·ter·lock
in·ter·lo·cu·tion
in·ter·loc·u·tor
in·ter·loc·u·to·ry

in·ter·loc·u·tress
  or in·ter·loc·u·trice
  pl in·ter·loc·u·tress·es
  or in·ter·loc·u·tri·ces

in·ter·lope
  in·ter·loped
  in·ter·lop·ing
  in·ter·lop·er
in·ter·ma·rine
in·ter·mar·riage
in·ter·mar·ry
  in·ter·mar·ried
  in·ter·mar·ry·ing
in·ter·med·dle
  in·ter·med·dled
  in·ter·med·dling
  in·ter·med·dler
in·ter·me·di·ary
  pl in·ter·me·di·ar·ies

in·ter·me·di·ate
in·ter·me·di·at·ed
in·ter·me·di·at·ing
in·ter·me·di·a·tion
in·ter·me·di·a·tor
in·ter·me·di·a·to·ry
in·ter·ment
  burial
  (*see* internment)

in·ter·mit·tent
in·ter·mix·ture
in·tern
in·ter·nal
in·ter·nal·ly

in·ter·na·tion·al
in·tern·ee
in·ter·nist
in·tern·ment
  confinement or im-
  pounding
  (*see* interment)

in·ter·own·er·ship
in·ter par·tes
in·ter·pel
  in·ter·pelled
  in·ter·pel·ling
in·ter·pel·late
  in·ter·pel·lat·ed
  in·ter·pel·lat·ing
  to question formally
  (*see* interpolate)

in·ter·pel·la·tion
in·ter·plea
in·ter·plead
  in·ter·plead·ed
  or in·ter·pled
  in·ter·plead·ing

in·ter·plead·er
in·ter·po·late
  in·ter·po·lat·ed
  in·ter·po·lat·ing
  to insert words in a
  text
  (*see* interpellate)

in·ter·po·la·tion
in·ter·pos·al
in·ter·pose
  in·ter·posed
  in·ter·pos·ing
in·ter·po·si·tion

in·ter·pret
in·ter·pret·able
in·ter·pre·ta·tion
in·ter·pre·ta·tive
in·ter·pret·er
in·ter·pre·tive
in·ter·pro·vin·cial
in·ter·ra·cial
  or in·ter·race

in·ter·reg·num
  pl in·ter·reg·nums
  or in·ter·reg·na

in·ter·reign
in·ter·rex
  pl in·ter·re·ges

in·ter·ro·ga·ble
in·ter·ro·gant
in·ter·ro·gate
  in·ter·ro·gat·ed
  in·ter·ro·gat·ing
in·ter·ro·ga·tion
in·ter·rog·a·tive
in·ter·ro·ga·tor
in·ter·rog·a·to·ry
  pl in·ter·rog·a·to·ries

in·ter·ro·gee
in ter·ro·rem
in·ter·rupt
in·ter·rup·tion
in·ter se
in·ter·sect
in·ter·sec·tion
in·ter se·se
in·ter·sex
in·ter·sex·u·al

in·ter·sex·u·al·ism
in·ter·sex·u·al·i·ty
  pl in·ter·sex·u·al·i·ties

in·ter·sex·u·al·ly
in·ter·state
  involving more than
  one state
  (*see* intestate, intra-
  state)

in·ter·sti·tial
  also in·ter·sti·cial

in·ter·trade
in·ter·traf·fic
in·ter·ur·ban
in·ter·vene
  in·ter·vened
  in·ter·ven·ing
in·ter·ven·er
  or in·ter·ve·nor

in·ter·ve·nience
in·ter·ve·nient
in·ter·ven·tion
in·ter·ver·te·bral
in·ter·view
in·ter·view·ee
in·ter·view·er
in·ter vi·rum et
  ux·o·rem
in·ter vi·vos
in·tes·ta·ble
in·test·ta·cy
in·tes·tate
  leaving no valid will
  (*see* interstate, intra-
  state)

in tes·ti·mo·ni·um

in·tes·ti·nal
in·tes·ti·nal·ly
in·tes·tine
in the per
in·ti·ma·cy
  pl in·ti·ma·cies

in·ti·mate
  in·ti·mat·ed
  in·ti·mat·ing
in·ti·mate·ly
in·ti·mate·ness
in·ti·ma·tion
in·tim·i·date
  in·tim·i·dat·ed
  in·tim·i·dat·ing
in·tim·i·da·tion
in·tim·i·da·tor
in·tim·i·da·to·ry
in·to
in·tol·er·a·ble
in·tol·er·ance
in to·to
in·tox·i·cant
in·tox·i·cate
  in·tox·i·cat·ed
  in·tox·i·cat·ing
in·tox·i·cat·ed·ly
in·tox·i·ca·tion
in·tox·i·ca·tive
in·tra
in·tra·city
in·tra·coast·al
in·tra·com·pa·ny
in·trac·ta·ble
in·tra fi·dem

in·tra·lim·i·nal
in·tra·na·tion·al
in·trans·fer·able
in tran·sit *adv*
in tran·sit *adj*
in tran·si·tu
in·tra·shop
in·tra·state
  existing in a state
  (see interstate, intestate)

in·tra vi·res
in·tri·cate
in·trin·sic
in·trin·si·cal·ly
in·tro·duce
  in·tro·duced
  in·tro·duc·ing
in·tro·duc·ible
in·tro·duc·tion
in·troi·tal
in·troi·tus
  pl in·troi·tus

in·tro·mis·sion
in·tro·mit
  in·tro·mit·ted
  in·tro·mit·ting
in·tro·mit·tent
in·tro·mit·ter
in·tro·ver·sion
in·tro·ver·sive
in·tro·vert
in·trude
  in·trud·ed
  in·trud·ing
in·trud·er

in·trud·ing·ly
in·tru·sion
in·tru·sive
in·tru·sive·ly
in·trust
  var of entrust

in·tu·i·to
  mat·ri·mo·nii
in·tu·i·tu mor·tis
in·ure
  or en·ure
  in·ured
  or en·ured
  in·ur·ing
  or en·ur·ing

in·ure·ment
in ute·ro
in vac·uo
in·vad·able
in·vade
  in·vad·ed
  in·vad·ing
in vain
in·va·lid
  sickly or disabled

in·val·id
  not valid

in·val·i·date
  in·val·i·dat·ed
  in·val·i·dat·ing
in·val·i·da·tion
in·va·lid·ism
in·va·lid·i·ty
in·val·id·ness
in·va·sion
in·va·sive

in·va·sive·ness
in·vec·ta et il·la·ta
in·vei·gle
  in·vei·gled
  in·vei·gling
in·vei·gle·ment
in·vent
in·ven·tion
in·ven·tive
in·ven·tor
  also in·vent·er
in·ven·to·ry
  in·ven·to·ried
  in·ven·to·ry·ing
in·ven·to·ry
  pl in·ven·to·ries

in ven·tra sa mère
in·vert
in·vest
in·vest·able
  also in·vest·ible

in·vest·ed
in·ves·ti·gat·able
in·ves·ti·gate
  in·ves·ti·gat·ed
  in·ves·ti·gat·ing
in·ves·ti·ga·tion
in·ves·ti·ga·tion·al
in·ves·ti·ga·tive
in·ves·ti·ga·tor
in·ves·ti·ga·to·ry
in·ves·ti·tive
in·ves·ti·ture
in·vest·ment
in·ves·tor
in·vid·i·ous

in vin·cu·lis
in·vi·o·la·bil·i·ty
in·vi·o·la·ble
in·vi·o·la·bly
in·vi·o·la·cy
in·vi·o·late
  also in·vi·o·lat·ed

in·vi·o·late·ness
in·vi·ta·tion
in·vite
  in·vit·ed
  in·vit·ing
in·vi·tee
in·vi·to do·mi·no
in·vi·tor
  also in·vit·er

in·vo·ca·ble
in·vo·ca·tion
in·vo·ca·tor
in·voice
  in·voiced
  in·voic·ing
in·voke
  in·voked
  in·vok·ing
in·vol·un·tari·ly
in·vol·un·tary
in·volve
  in·volved
  in·volv·ing
in·volve·ment
io·dine
  also io·din

ip·e·cac
  or ipe·ca·cu·a·nha

ipro·ni·a·zid
ip·se dix·it
ip·se fe·cit
ip·sis·si·mis ver·bis
ip·so fac·to
ip·so ju·re
iri·do·cho·roid·itis
iri·do·cy·cli·tis
iri·tis
iron
ir·ra·di·ate
  ir·ra·di·at·ed
  ir·ra·di·at·ing
ir·ra·di·a·tion
ir·ra·tio·nal·i·ty
  pl ir·ra·tio·nal·i·ties

ir·ra·tio·nal
ir·ra·tio·nal·ly
ir·re·but·ta·ble
ir·re·claim·able
ir·rec·on·cil·abil·i·ty
ir·rec·on·cil·able
ir·rec·on·cil·able·
  ness
ir·rec·on·cil·ably
ir·re·cov·er·able
ir·re·cov·er·ably
ir·re·cu·sa·ble
ir·re·deem·abil·i·ty
ir·re·deem·able
ir·re·deem·ably
ir·re·duc·ible
ir·re·form·able
ir·re·fra·ga·ble

ir·re·fut·abil·i·ty
ir·re·fut·able
ir·re·fut·ably
ir·reg·u·lar
ir·reg·u·lar·i·ty
  pl ir·reg·u·lar·i·ties

ir·rel·e·vance
  or ir·rel·e·van·cy
  pl ir·rel·e·vanc·es
  or ir·rel·e·van·cies

ir·rel·e·vant
ir·rel·e·vant·ly
ir·re·me·di·able
ir·re·me·di·able·
  ness
ir·re·me·di·ably
ir·re·mis·si·ble
ir·re·mov·able
ir·rep·a·ra·ble
ir·rep·a·ra·ble·ness
ir·rep·a·ra·bly
ir·re·pa·tri·able
ir·re·peal·abil·i·ty
ir·re·peal·able
ir·re·plevi·able
ir·re·sist·ible
ir·re·sist·ibly
ir·re·spec·tive
ir·re·spec·tive·ly
ir·re·spon·si·bil·i·ty
ir·re·spon·si·ble
ir·re·spon·si·ble·
  ness
ir·re·spon·si·bly
ir·re·triev·abil·i·ty
ir·re·triev·able

ir·re·triev·ably
ir·re·vers·ibil·i·ty
ir·re·vers·ible
ir·re·vers·ibly
ir·re·vo·ca·bil·i·ty
ir·re·vo·ca·ble
ir·re·vo·ca·bly
ir·ri·gate
  ir·ri·gat·ed
  ir·ri·gat·ing
ir·ri·ga·tion
ir·ri·tan·cy
  pl ir·ri·tan·cies

ir·ri·tant
ir·ri·tate
  ir·ri·tat·ed
  ir·ri·tat·ing
ir·ri·ta·tion
ir·ri·ta·tive
isch·emia
  also isch·aemia

isch·emic
is·chi·um
  pl is·chia

ish
iso·lat·ed
ison·omy
iso·pol·i·ty
  pl iso·pol·i·ties

iso·tope
iso·to·pic
is·sei
  pl is·sei
  also is·seis

is·su·able
is·su·ance

is·sue
is·sued
is·su·ing
is·sue·less
is·su·er
ita est
ita quod
item
item·iza·tion
item·ize
  item·ized
  item·iz·ing
itin·er·ant
ius
  var of jus

J

ja·cens
ja·cens
  hae·re·di·tas
jack·knife
  pl jack·knives

jack·pot
jack·roll
jack·roll·er
Jack·so·ni·an
Ja·cob·son's
  car·ti·lage
   or Ja·cob·son's
   tur·bi·nal

jac·ti·tate
  jac·ti·tat·ed
  jac·ti·tat·ing
jac·ti·ta·tion

jac·ti·vus
jac·tu·ra
jac·tus
jail
jail·bait
jail·bird
jail·break
jail·break·er
jail break·ing
jail de·liv·ery
  pl jail de·liv·er·ies

jail·er
  or jail·or

jail·house
jail·keep·er
jake leg
jal·ap
  also ja·la·pa

Ja·mai·ca gin·ger
James·town weed
  var of jimsonweed

Jane Doe
Ja·nus-faced plea
jar·gon
jar·gon·ize
  jar·gon·ized
  jar·gon·iz·ing
Ja·risch-Herx·
  hei·mer
  re·ac·tion
Ja·son clause
jaun·dice
jaun·diced
Ja·velle wa·ter
  or Ja·vel wa·ter

ja·vell·iza·tion
jaw·bone
jaw·line
jay·walk
jay·walk·er
jay·walk·ing
jeal·ous
jeal·ous·ly
jeal·ous·ness
jeal·ou·sy
  pl jeal·ou·sies

Jed·burgh cast
Jed·burgh jus·tice
  or Jed·dart jus·tice

je·ju·nal
je·ju·ni·tis
je·ju·no·il·e·itis
je·ju·num
  pl je·ju·na

Jen·ne·ri·an
jeop·ard
jeop·ar·dize
  jeop·ar·dized
  jeop·ar·diz·ing
jeop·ar·dous
jeop·ar·dy *n*
  pl jeop·ar·dies

jeop·ar·dy *vb*
  jeop·ar·died
  jeop·ar·dy·ing
jer·ry-build
  jer·ry-built
  jer·ry-build·ing
jer·ry-build·er
jet·sam

jet·ti·son
jim·my
  pl jim·mies

jim·my
  jim·mied
  jim·my·ing
jim·son·weed
  or James·town weed
  or jimp·son
  or jimp·son·weed

job
  jobbed
  job·bing
job ac·tion
job·ber
job·bery
  pl job·ber·ies

job·less
job lot
John Doe
john·ny
  also john·nie
  pl john·nies

join
join·der
joint
joint ad·ven·ture
joint and sev·er·al
joint·ist
joint·ly
join·tress
  or join·tur·ess

joint stock *n*
joint-stock *adj*
join·ture
  join·tured

join·tur·ing
jos·tle
  jos·tled
  jos·tling
jos·tle·ment
jour·nal
jour·nal·ize
  jour·nal·ized
  jour·nal·iz·ing
joy·pop
  joy·popped
  joy·pop·ping
  joy·pop·per
joy ride
joy·ride
  joy·rode
  joy·rid·den
  joy·rid·ing
  joy·rid·er
ju·dex
  pl ju·di·ces

ju·dex ad quem
ju·dex a quo
ju·dex de·le·ga·tus
  pl ju·di·ces de·le·ga·ti

ju·dex fis·ca·lis
ju·dex
  or·di·na·ri·us
    pl ju·di·ces or·di·na·rii

ju·dex se·lec·tus
  pl ju·di·ces·se·lec·ti

judge
  judged
  judg·ing

judge ad·vo·cate
 pl judge ad·vo·cates

judge-made
judge-ship
judg·mat·ic
 or judg·mat·i·cal

judg·mat·i·cal·ly
judg·ment
 or judge·ment

judg·men·tal
ju·di·ca·re
ju·di·ca·tio
ju·di·ca·to·ry
 pl ju·di·ca·to·ries

ju·di·ca·ture
ju·di·cia
ju·di·cial
ju·di·cial·ize
 ju·di·cial·ized
 ju·di·cial·iz·ing
ju·di·cial·ly
ju·di·cia pu·bli·ca
ju·di·cia·ry
 pl ju·di·cia·ries

ju·di·cious
ju·di·cious·ly
ju·di·cious·ness
ju·di·ci·um
ju·gal
ju·gal point
 also ju·ga·le

jug·u·lar
ju·gum
 pl ju·ga
 or ju·gums

ju·jube
jump
junc·tion·al
junc·tu·ra
 pl junc·tu·rae

junc·ture
Jung·ian
ju·nior
jun·ket
junk·ie
 or junky
 pl junk·ies

jun·ta
 pl jun·tas

ju·ra
ju·ra ad
 per·so·nam
ju·ra fis·ca·lia
ju·ra in
 per·so·nam
ju·ra in rem
ju·ral
ju·ral·ly
ju·ra ma·jes·ta·tis
ju·ra·men·tum
 pl ju·ra·men·ta

ju·ra
 per·so·na·rum
ju·ra pu·bli·ca
ju·ra·re
ju·ra re·ga·lia
ju·ra re·rum
ju·ra sum·ma
 im·pe·rii
ju·rat
ju·ra·tion

ju·ra·tor
ju·ra·to·ry
jure
 jured
 jur·ing
ju·re bel·li
ju·re ci·vi·le
ju·re co·ro·nae
ju·re di·vi·no
ju·re gen·ti·um
ju·re im·pe·rii
ju·re ma·ri·ti
ju·re na·tu·rae
ju·re pro·pin·qui·
 ta·tis
ju·re re·pre·sen·
 ta·tio·nes
ju·re ux·o·ris
ju·rid·i·cal
 or ju·rid·ic

ju·rid·i·cal·ly
ju·rid·i·cal per·son
ju·ris
ju·ris·con·sult
ju·ris·dic·tion
ju·ris·dic·tion·al
ju·ris·dic·tion·al·ly
ju·ris·dic·tive
ju·ris et de ju·re
ju·ris gen·ti·um
ju·ris po·si·ti·vi
ju·ris pri·va·ti
ju·ris·prude
ju·ris·pru·dence
ju·ris·pru·dent
ju·ris·pru·den·tia

ju·ris·pru·den·tial
ju·ris·pru·den·tial·ly
ju·ris pu·bli·ci
ju·rist
ju·ris·tic
ju·ris·ti·cal·ly
ju·ris·tic per·son
ju·ris utrum
ju·ror
ju·ry
   pl ju·ries

ju·ry box
ju·ry·less
ju·ry·man
   pl ju·ry·men

ju·ry-pack·ing
ju·ry·wom·an
   pl ju·ry·wom·en

jus
   or ius
   pl ju·ra
   or iu·ra

jus ab·u·ten·di
jus ac·cre·scen·di
jus ad rem
   pl ju·ra ad rem

jus bel·li
jus ca·non·i·cum
jus ci·vi·le
jus ci·vi·ta·tis
jus com·mer·cii
jus com·mu·ne
jus co·nu·bii
   or jus con·nu·bii

jus da·re

jus de·li·be·ran·di
jus di·ce·re
jus dis·po·nen·di
jus dis·tra·hen·di
jus di·vi·den·di
jus du·pli·ca·tum
jus ec·cle·si·as·
   ti·cum
jus em·mins
jus fi·du·ci·a·ri·um
jus fru·en·di
jus fu·tu·rum
jus gen·ti·um
jus ha·ben·di
jus hae·re·di·ta·tes
jus im·mu·ni·ta·tis
jus in·cog·ni·tum
jus in·di·vi·du·um
jus in per·so·nam
jus in re
   or jus in rem
   pl ju·ra in re

jus in·ter gen·tes
jus le·gi·ti·mum
jus ma·ri·ti
jus na·tu·rae
jus na·tu·ra·le
jus non scrip·tum
jus per·so·na·rum
jus pos·ses·si·o·nes
jus pos·si·den·di
jus post·li·mi·ni
jus prae·sens
jus pre·ca·ri·um
jus pre·sen·ta·ti·
   o·nes

jus pri·va·tum
jus pro·pri·e·ta·tis
jus pub·li·cum
jus quae·si·tum
jus re·lic·tae
jus re·lic·ti
jus rep·re·sen·ta·ti·
   o·nes
jus re·rum
jus san·gui·nis
jus scrip·tum
jus so·li
jus spa·ti·an·di
jus stric·tum
just
juste-mi·lieu
   pl juste-mi·lieux

jus ter·tii
jus·tice
jus·tice court
   or jus·tice's court
   pl jus·tice courts
   or jus·tice's courts

jus·tice gen·er·al
   pl jus·tices gen·er·al

jus·tice in eyre
   pl jus·tices in eyre

jus·tice of the
  peace
   pl jus·tices of the
   peace

jus·tice·ship
jus·ti·cia·bil·i·ty
jus·ti·cia·ble
jus·ti·ci·ar
jus·ti·ci·ar·ship

jus·ti·ci·ary
  pl jus·ti·ci·ar·ies

jus·ti·ci·a·tus
jus·ti·ci·es
  pl jus·ti·ci·es

jus·ti·fi·able
jus·ti·fi·ably
jus·ti·fi·ca·tion
jus·ti·fi·ca·tive
jus·ti·fi·ca·tor
jus·ti·fi·ca·to·ry
jus·ti·fi·er
jus·ti·fy
  jus·ti·fied
  jus·ti·fy·ing
Jus·tin·i·an
  or Jus·tin·i·a·ni·an
  or Jus·tin·i·a·ne·an

Jus·tin·i·an·ist
jus·ti·tia
jus·ti·ti·um
just·ly
just·ness
jus uten·di
ju·ve·nile
ju·ve·nil·i·ty
  pl ju·ve·nil·i·ties

jux·ta
jux·ta-ar·tic·u·lar
jux·ta·epiph·y·se·al
jux·ta for·mam sta·tu·ti
jux·tan·gi·na
jux·ta·pose

jux·ta·posed
jux·ta·pos·ing
jux·ta·po·si·tion
jux·ta·py·lo·ric
jux·ta·spi·nal

K

Kahn test
  or Kahn re·ac·tion
  or Kahn

kak·is·toc·ra·cy
  pl kak·is·toc·ra·cies

kak·o·gen·ic
ka·na·my·cin
kan·ga·roo *adj*
ka·olin
  also ka·oline

ka·o·lin·osis
  pl ka·o·lin·oses
  or ka·o·lin·osis·es

kary·ol·y·sis
  pl kary·ol·y·ses

karyo·lyt·ic
karyo·type
kat
  or khat
  or qat
  also quat

ka·tab·o·lism
  var of catabolism

ka·thar·sis
  var of catharsis

ka·thar·tic
  var of cathartic

kat·zen·jam·mer
keel·age
Kee·ler poly·graph
keep
  kept
  keep·ing
keep·er
kef
  or kif

ke·loid
  or che·loid

ke·loi·dal
ke·lo·ma
  pl ke·lo·mas
  or ke·lo·ma·ta

kelp-shore
Ken·ny meth·od
  or Ken·ny treat·ment

ke·no
Ken·tucky rule
ker·a·tal·gia
ker·a·tin
  also cer·a·tin

ke·ra·ti·ni·za·tion
ke·ra·tin·ize
  ke·ra·tin·ized
  ke·ra·tin·iz·ing
ke·ra·ti·no·phil·ic
ke·ra·ti·nous
ker·a·ti·tis
  also cer·a·ti·tis
  pl ker·a·tit·i·des
  also cer·a·tit·i·des

ker·a·to·con·junc·
  ti·vi·tis
  or cer·a·to·con·junc·
    ti·vi·tis

ker·a·to·der·ma
ker·a·toid
ker·a·to·iri·tis
ker·a·tol·y·sis
  pl ker·a·tol·y·ses

ker·a·to·lyt·ic
ker·a·to·ma
  pl ker·a·to·mas
  or ker·a·to·ma·ta

ker·a·to·ma·la·cia
ker·a·to·rhex·is
  pl ker·a·to·rhex·es

ker·a·to·scle·ri·tis
ker·a·to·sis
  pl ker·a·to·ses

ker·a·tot·ic
ker·o·sene
  or ker·o·sine

ke·to·ac·i·do·sis
  pl ke·to·ac·i·do·ses

ke·to·nu·ria
ke·to·sis
  pl ke·to·ses

ke·tot·ic
key·age
keyed
key·man in·sur·
  ance

key mon·ey
key·note ad·dress

khat
  var of kat

ki·bei
  pl ki·bei
  also ki·beis

kick back *vb*
kick·back *n*
kick up *vb*
kick·up *n*
kid·nap
  kid·napped
  or kid·naped
  kid·nap·ping
  or kid·nap·ing

kid·nap·ee
kid·nap·per
  or kid·nap·er

kid·ney
kif
  var of kef

kill
kill·er
kill·ing
Kim·bell-Di·a·
  mond rule

kin
kind
kin·dred
kin·dred·less
kin·dred·ness
kin·dred·ship
kin·e·plas·ty
  var of cineplasty

kin·e·sal·gia

kin·es·the·sia
  or kin·es·the·sis
  also kin·aes·the·sia
  or kin·aes·the·sis
  pl kin·es·the·sias
  or kin·es·the·ses
  also kin·aes·the·sias
  or kin·aes·the·ses

kin·es·thet·ic
  also kin·aes·thet·ic

kin·es·thet·i·cal·ly
  also kin·aes·thet·i·
    cal·ly

ki·net·ic
kin·e·to·sis
  pl kin·e·to·ses

kin·folk
  or kins·folk

king
king·dom
King's Bench
kin·less
kin·ship
kins·man
  pl kins·men

kins·man·ship
kins·peo·ple
kins·wom·an
  pl kins·wom·en

kite
  kit·ed
  kit·ing
kit·er
kith
kith and kin
kit·ty
  pl kit·ties

Klebs-Löff·ler ba·
cil·lus
klep·to·lag·nia
klep·to·ma·nia
or clep·to·ma·nia

klep·to·ma·ni·ac
or clep·to·ma·ni·ac

klep·to·pho·bia
Kline re·ac·tion
or Kline test

knave
knav·ery
pl knav·er·ies

knav·ish
knav·ish·ly
knav·ish·ness
knee
kneed
knee·ing
knee·cap
knee jerk
knee·pan
knife n
pl knives

knife vb
knifed
knif·ing
knif·er
knock
knock down vb
knock·down n
knock-down-and-
drag-out adj
or knock-down,
drag-out

knock-knee
knock-kneed
knock off
knock out vb
knock·out n or adj
knock·out drops
know
knew
known
know·ing
know-how
know·ing·ly
know-it-all
or know-all
pl know-it-alls
or know-alls

knowl·edge
knowl·edge·abil·i·ty
or knowl·edg·abil·i·ty

knowl·edge·able
also knowl·edg·able

knowl·edge·able·
ness
also knowl·edg·
able·ness

knowl·edge·ably
also knowl·edg·ably

knowl·edge and
be·lief
knowl·edged
knowl·edge·less
knuck·le
knuck·led
knuck·ling
knuck·le·bone
knuck·le·dust

knuck·le-dust·er
Koch
phe·nom·e·non
Koch's ba·cil·lus
or Koch ba·cil·lus

Koch-Weeks
ba·cil·lus
koil·onych·ia
Kol·mer
or Kol·mer re·ac·tion
or Kol·mer test
or Kol·mer's test

ko·ni·ol·o·gy
or co·ni·ol·o·gy

Kor·sa·koff's psy·
cho·sis
or Kor·sa·koff's
syn·drome
also Kor·sa·kow's
psy·cho·sis
or Kor·sa·kow's
syn·drome

krau·ro·sis
pl krau·ro·ses

krau·rot·ic
kum·shaw
Kuss·maul
breath·ing
or Kuss·maul res·pi·
ra·tion

kwash·i·or·kor
ky·pho·sco·li·o·sis
pl ky·pho·sco·li·o·ses

ky·pho·sis
pl ky·pho·ses

ky·phot·ic

L

la·bel *n*
la·bi·al
la·bi·al·ly
la·bia ma·jo·ra
la·bia mi·no·ra
la·bile
la·bil·i·ty
  pl la·bil·i·ties

la·bio·den·tal
la·bio·glos·so·la·
  ryn·geal
la·bio·glos·so·pha·
  ryn·geal
la·bio·na·sal
la·bio·pal·a·tine
la·bi·um
  pl la·bia

la·bor
lab·o·ra·to·ri·al
lab·o·ra·to·ri·al·ly
lab·o·ra·to·ri·an
lab·o·ra·to·ry
  pl lab·o·ra·to·ries

la·bo·ri·ous
lab·y·rinth
lab·y·rin·thine
lab·y·rin·thi·tis
lac·er·a·bil·i·ty
lac·er·a·ble
lac·er·ate
  lac·er·at·ed
  lac·er·at·ing
lac·er·a·tion

la·ches
  pl la·ches
lach·ry·mal
  or lac·ri·mal
lac·ri·ma·tion
  also lach·ry·ma·tion
lac·ri·ma·tor
  or lach·ry·ma·tor
lac·ri·ma·to·ry
  or lach·ry·ma·to·ry
lact·al·bu·min
lac·tate
  lac·tat·ed
  lac·tat·ing
lac·ta·tion
lac·ta·tion·al
lac·ta·tion·al·ly
lac·ti·fuge
lac·to·ba·cil·lus
  pl lac·to·ba·cil·li
lac·to·gen·ic
lac·to·glob·u·lin
lac·to·pro·tein
lac·tor·rhea
lac·tose
la·cu·na
  pl la·cu·nae
  or la·cu·nas
la·cu·na·ry
Laen·nec's
  cir·rho·sis
lae·sa ma·jes·tas
  pl lae·sae ma·jes·ta·
    tis
la·e·trile
lag

lagged
lag·ging
lag·an
  also lag·end
  or lag·on
  or li·gan
  or li·gen
  or lo·gan
lag·oph·thal·mos
  or lag·oph·thal·mus
la grippe
lais·sez-faire
  also lais·ser-faire

lais·sez-faire·ism
lais·sez-pas·ser
lake
  laked
  lak·ing
lam
  lammed
  lam·ming
lame
  lamed
  lam·ing
lame duck
la·mel·la
  pl la·mel·lae
  also la·mel·las

la·mel·lar
la·mel·lar·ly
lam·i·na
  pl lam·i·nae
  or lam·i·nas

lam·i·nar
lam·i·nate
  lam·i·nat·ed
  lam·i·nat·ing

lam·i·nec·to·my
  pl lam·i·nec·to·mies

lance
  lanced
  lanc·ing
lan·cet
lan·ci·nate
  lan·ci·nat·ed
  lan·ci·nat·ing
land
land·ed
land·fill
land·grab·ber
land·hold·er
land·hold·ing
land·la·dy
  pl land·la·dies

land·less
land·less·ness
land·look·er
land·lord
land·lord·ism
land·lord·ly
land·lord·ship
land·mark
land·oc·ra·cy
  pl land·oc·ra·cies

land·own·er
land·own·er·ship
land·own·ing
land·poor
land·right
land·slide
land·tax par·ish
land·wait·er
land·ward

lan·o·lin
  also lan·o·line

lan·qui·dus
lap·a·ror·rhaphy
  pl lap·a·ror·rhaphies

lap·a·rot·o·my
  pl lap·a·rot·o·mies

lap·i·da·tion
lap·page
lapse
  lapsed
  laps·ing
lar·cen·able
lar·ce·ner
lar·ce·nist
lar·ce·nous
lar·ce·nous·ly
lar·ce·ny
  pl lar·ce·nies

lar·es and
  pe·na·tes
lar·va
  pl lar·vae
  also lar·vas

lar·val
lar·vi·cide
  also lar·va·cide

la·ryn·geal
la·ryn·geal·ly
lar·yn·gec·to·mee
lar·yn·gec·to·mize
  lar·yn·gec·to·
   mized
  lar·yn·gec·to·
   miz·ing

lar·yn·gec·to·my
  pl lar·yn·gec·to·mies

lar·yn·git·ic
lar·yn·gi·tis
  pl lar·yn·git·i·des

la·ryn·go·fis·sure
la·ryn·go·pa·ral·y·
  sis
   pl la·ryn·go·pa·ral·y·
   ses

la·ryn·go·pha·ryn·
  geal
la·ryn·go·plas·ty
  pl la·ryn·go·plas·ties

la·ryn·go·ple·gia
la·ryn·go·scope
la·ryn·go·scop·ic
lar·yn·gos·co·py
  pl lar·yn·gos·co·pies

la·ryn·go·tra·che·al
la·ryn·go·tra·che·
  itis
la·ryn·go·tra·che·
  ot·o·my
   pl la·ryn·go·tra·che·
   ot·o·mies

lar·ynx
  pl la·ryn·ges
  also lar·ynx·es

las·civ·i·ous
las·civ·i·ous·ly
las·civ·i·ous·ness
la·ser
last·age
last in, first out
la·ta cul·pa

la·ten·cy
  pl la·ten·cies

la·tent
la·tent·ly
lat·er·ad
lat·er·al
lat·er·al·ly
lat·ero·de·vi·a·tion
lat·ero·po·si·tion
lat·ero·ver·sion
la·tis·si·mus dor·si
  pl la·tis·si·mi dor·si

lat·ro·ci·na·tion
lat·ter
lau·da·num
laugh·ing gas
la·vage
law
law-abid·ing
law-abid·ing·ness
law blank
law·book
law·break·er
law·break·ing
law·court
law·ful
law·ful·ly
law·ful·ness
law·giv·er
law·less
law·less·ly
law·less·ness
law·like
law·mak·er
law·mak·ing

law·man
  pl law·men

law·suit
law·yer
law·yer·ess
  pl law·yer·ess·es

law·yer·ing
law·yer·like
law·yer·ly
lax·a·tion
lax·a·tive
lay
  laid
  lay·ing
lay·day
lay·man
  pl lay·men

lay off *vb*
lay·off *n*
laz·a·ret·to
  or laz·a·ret
  also laz·a·rette
  pl laz·a·ret·tos
  or laz·a·rets
  also laz·a·rettes

lead
  led
  lead·ing
lead·er
lead·er·less
lead·er·ship
lead·ing-up
leap·frog
  leap·frogged
  leap·frog·ging
learn·er
learn·ing

lease
  leased
  leas·ing
lease·back
lease·hold
lease·hold·er
lease·less
lease·man
  pl lease·men

leave
  left
  leav·ing
lec·i·thin
led·ger
left
  past of leave

left-hand·ed
leg·a·cy
  pl leg·a·cies

le·gal
le·gal·ese
le·gal·ism
le·gal·ist
le·gal·is·tic
le·gal·is·ti·cal·ly
le·gal·i·ty
  pl le·gal·i·ties

le·gal·iza·tion
le·gal·ize
  le·gal·ized
  le·gal·iz·ing
le·gal·ly
le·gal mem·o·ry
le·gal·ness
leg·ate *n*

le·gate *vb*
　le·gat·ed
　le·gat·ing
leg·a·tee
leg·a·tine
le·ga·tion
le·ga·tor
le·ga·to·ry
leg·i·bil·i·ty
　pl leg·i·bil·i·ties

leg·i·ble
leg·is·late
　leg·is·lat·ed
　leg·is·lat·ing
leg·is·la·tion
leg·is·la·tive
leg·is·la·tive·ly
leg·is·la·tor
leg·is·la·to·ri·al
leg·is·la·tor·ship
leg·is·la·tress
　also leg·is·la·trix
　pl leg·is·la·tress·es
　also leg·is·la·trix·es
　or leg·is·la·tri·ces

leg·is·la·ture
le·gist
le·git
le·git·i·ma·cy
　pl le·git·i·ma·cies

le·git·i·mate
　le·git·i·mat·ed
　le·git·i·mat·ing
le·git·i·mate·ly
le·git·i·mate·ness

le·git·i·ma·tion
le·git·i·ma·tize
　le·git·i·ma·tized
　le·git·i·ma·tiz·ing
leg·i·time
　or leg·i·tim

le·git·i·mism
le·git·i·mist
le·git·i·mi·za·tion
le·git·i·mize
　le·git·i·mized
　le·git·i·miz·ing
le·git·i·miz·er
leg·work
lend
　lent
　lend·ing
lend·er
le·nien·cy
　pl le·nien·cies

le·nient
len·i·tive
lens
　pl lens·es

len·tic·u·lar
len·ti·go
　pl len·tig·i·nes

le·o·nine
　part·ner·ship
lep·er
lep·rid
lep·roid
lep·ro·ma
　pl lep·ro·mas
　or lep·ro·ma·ta

lep·ro·ma·tous
lep·ro·sar·i·um
　pl lep·ro·sar·i·ums
　or lep·ro·sar·ia

lep·ro·sy
　pl lep·ro·sies

lep·rot·ic
lep·rous
lep·to·men·in·ge·al
lep·to·men·in·
　ges *n pl*
lep·to·men·in·gi·tis
　pl lep·to·men·in·git·
　i·des

lep·to·pho·nia
lep·to·spi·ra
　pl lep·to·spi·ra
　also lep·to·spi·ras
　or lep·to·spi·rae

lep·to·spir·al
le·re·sis
les·bi·an
les·bi·an·ism
lese maj·es·ty
　or lèse ma·ges·té
　pl lèse maj·es·ties
　or lèse ma·ges·tés

le·sion
les·see
less·er
　smaller
　(*see* lessor)

les·sor
　the grantor of a lease
　(*see* lesser)

le·thal

le·thal·i·ty
  pl le·thal·i·ties

le·thal·ly
le·thar·gic
leth·ar·gy
let off
  let off
  let·ting off
let·ter
let·ter·head
let·ter mis·sive
  pl let·ters mis·sive

let·ters close *n pl*
let·ters overt *n pl*
let·ters pat·ent *n pl*
let·ters ro·ga·to·
  ry *n pl*
let·ters tes·ta·men·
  ta·ry *n pl*
leu·cae·mia,
  leu·ce·mia
  vars of leukemia

leu·co·cyte
  var of leukocyte

leu·co·cyt·ic
  var of leukocytic

leu·co·cy·to·sis
  var of leukocytosis

leu·co·cy·tot·ic
  var of leukocytotic

leu·co·ma
  var of leukoma

leu·co·pe·nia
  var of leukopenia

leu·cor·rhea,
  leu·cor·rhoea
  vars of leukorrhea

leu·co·tox·ic
  var of leukotoxic

leu·ke·mia
  also leu·kae·mia
  or leu·ce·mia
  also leu·cae·mia

leu·ke·mic
  also leu·kae·mic

leu·ke·mo·gen
leu·ke·mo·gen·e·sis
  pl leu·ke·mo·gen·ses

leu·ke·mo·gen·ic

leu·ko·cyte
  also leu·co·cyte

leu·ko·cyt·ic
  also leu·co·cyt·ic

leu·ko·cy·to·sis
  or leu·co·cy·to·sis
  pl leu·ko·cy·to·ses
  or leu·co·cy·to·ses

leu·ko·cy·tot·ic
  or leu·co·cy·tot·ic

leu·ko·ma
  also leu·co·ma

leu·kom·a·tous
leu·ko·pe·nia
  or leu·co·pe·nia

leu·ko·pe·nic
leu·ko·pla·kia
leu·kor·rha·gia
leu·kor·rhea
  also leu·kor·rhoea
  or leu·cor·rhea
  or leu·cor·rhoea

leu·kor·rhe·al
leu·ko·tox·ic
  or leu·co·tox·ic

leu·ko·tox·in
lev·ance and
  cou·chance
  also lev·an·cy and
  cou·chan·cy

lev·ant and
  cou·chant
le·va·ri fa·ci·as
lev·ee
  *a reception or an em-
  bankment*
  (see levy)

le·ver·age
  le·ver·aged
  le·ver·ag·ing
levi·able
levi·a·tion
le·vi·rate
le·vis cul·pa
le·vis·si·ma cul·pa
Le·vit·i·cal
  de·grees
levy *n*
  pl lev·ies
  *the imposition or
  amount of a charge*
  (see levee)

levy *vb*
  lev·ied
  lev·y·ing
levy en masse
  also le·vée en masse
  or levy in mass
  pl lev·ies en masse
  also le·vées en masse
  or lev·ies in mass

lewd

lewd·ly

lewd·ness

lex
  pl le·ges

lex ac·tus

lex com·mis·so·ria

lex com·mu·nis

lex de fu·ga

lex do·mi·ci·lii

lex fo·ri

lex ge·ne·ra·lis

lex lo·ci

lex lo·ci ac·tus

lex lo·ci ce·le·bra·ti·o·nis

lex lo·ci con·trac·tus

lex lo·ci de·lic·ti

lex lo·ci rei si·tae

lex lo·ci so·lu·ti·o·nis

lex mer·ca·to·ria
  or lex mer·ca·to·rum

lex na·tu·ra·le

lex non scrip·ta

lex or·di·nan·di

lex pri·va·ta

lex pu·bli·ca

lex scrip·ta

lex si·tus

lex ta·li·o·nis

lex ter·rae

li·a·bil·i·ty
  pl li·a·bil·i·ties

li·a·ble
  *obligated by law or
  equity*
  (see libel)

li·aise

li·aised

li·ais·ing

li·ai·son

li·ar

li·bel

li·beled
  or li·belled

li·bel·ing
  or li·bel·ling
  *make libelous state-
  ments*
  (see liable)

li·bel·ant
  or li·bel·lant

li·bel·ee
  or li·bel·lee

li·bel·er
  or li·bel·ler

li·bel·ous
  or li·bel·lous

li·bel·ous·ly
  or li·bel·lous·ly

lib·er·al

lib·er·al·ism

lib·er·al·i·ty
  pl lib·er·al·i·ties

lib·er·al·ize

lib·er·al·ized

lib·er·al·iz·ing

lib·er·al·ly

lib·er·ate

lib·er·at·ed

lib·er·at·ing

lib·er·a·tion

lib·er·a·tor

lib·er·ty
  pl lib·er·ties

li·be·rum
  te·ne·men·tum

li·bid·i·nal

li·bid·i·nal·ly

li·bid·i·nous

li·bid·i·nous·ly

li·bi·do
  pl li·bi·dos

lice
  pl of louse

li·cens·able

li·cense
  also li·cence

li·censed
  also li·cenced

li·cens·ing
  also li·cenc·ing

li·cens·ee

li·cense·less

li·cense plate
  or li·cense tag

li·cens·er

li·cen·sor

li·cen·sure

li·cen·ti·ate

li·cen·ti·ate·ship

li·cen·tious

li·cen·tious·ly

li·cen·tious·ness

li·chen

li·chen·i·fi·ca·tion

li·chen·oid
li·chen pla·nus
lic·it
lic·i·ta·tion
lic·it·ly
li·do·caine
lie
  lay
  lain
  ly·ing
  to be admissible

lie
  lied
  ly·ing
  to practice deceit

lie de·tec·tor
liege pou·stie
lien
lien·able
lien·ee
lien·hold·er
lien·or
lieu
lieu·ten·an·cy
  pl lieu·ten·an·cies

lieu·ten·ant
life
  pl lives

life-and-death
life·less
lif·er
life·rent
life·rent·er
life·rent·rix
  pl life·rent·rix·es
  or life·rent·ri·ces

life-span
life-sup·port
  sys·tem
lig·a·ment
lig·a·men·ta·ry
lig·a·men·tous
li·gan
  var of lagan
li·gate
  li·gat·ed
  li·gat·ing
li·ga·tion
lig·a·ture
li·geance
  also li·gean·cy
light
ligh·ter·age
light-fin·gered
light-head·ed
light·ing
li·gon,
  li·gen
  vars of lagan

like·li·hood
like-mind·ed
like·ness
like·wise
lim·it
lim·it·able
lim·i·ta·tion
lim·i·ta·tive
lim·it·ed
li·moph·thi·sis
  pl li·moph·thi·ses

lin·ea al·ba
  pl lin·e·ae al·bae

lin·eage
lin·eal
lin·ea·ment
lin·gual
lin·gual·ly
lin·i·ment
lip·i·do·sis
  pl lip·i·do·ses

li·po·ma
  pl li·po·mas
  or li·po·ma·ta

li·po·sar·co·ma
  pl li·po·sar·co·mas
  or li·po·sar·co·ma·ta

Lip·pes loop
li·pu·ria
li·ques·cent
liq·ui·date
  liq·ui·dat·ed
  liq·ui·dat·ing
liq·ui·da·tion
liq·ui·da·tor
li·quid·i·ty
  pl li·quid·i·ties

li·quor
li·quor am·nii
lis
  pl li·tes

lis ali·bi pen·dens
lis mo·ta
lis pen·dens
list
list·ing
li·te pen·den·te
lit·er·al
li·tera le·gis

li·tharge
lith·i·um
lith·o·pe·di·on
litho·scope
lit·i·ga·ble
lit·i·gant
lit·i·gate
  lit·i·gat·ed
  lit·i·gat·ing
lit·i·ga·tion
lit·i·ga·tor
li·ti·gi·os·i·ty
li·ti·gious
li·ti·gious·ly
li·ti·gious·ness
li·tis·con·test
li·tis con·tes·ta·tio
li·tis·con·tes·ta·tion
li·tis ma·gis·ter
lit·mus
liv·abil·i·ty
  also live·abil·i·ty

liv·able
  also live·able

live
  lived
  liv·ing
live-born
live·li·hood
liv·er
liv·ery
  pl liv·er·ies

liv·id
li·vid·i·ty
  pl li·vid·i·ties

liv·ing-apart
liv·ing trust
load
load·ing
load line
loan
loan·er
loan shark *n*
loan-shark *vb*
lo·bar
lob·by
  lob·bied
  lob·by·ing
lob·by·er
lob·by·ism
lob·by·ist
lo·bec·to·my
  pl lo·bec·to·mies
lo·be·line
lo·bot·o·mize
  lo·bot·o·mized
  lo·bot·o·miz·ing
lo·bot·o·my
  pl lo·bot·o·mies
lob·u·lar
lob·u·late
  also lob·u·lat·ed
lob·ule
lo·cal
lo·cal·i·ty
  pl lo·cal·i·ties
lo·cal·iza·tion
lo·cal·ize
  lo·cal·ized
  lo·cal·iz·ing

lo·ca·tio
lo·ca·tio
  con·duc·tio
  or lo·ca·tio et
  con·duc·tio

lo·ca·tion
lo·ca·tio ope·ris
  fa·ci·en·di
lo·ca·tio rei
loc·a·tive
lo·ca·tor
lo·chia
  pl lo·chia
lo·ci
  pl of locus
lock·age
lock·jaw
lo·co ci·ta·to
lo·co·ism
lo·co·mo·tive
lo·co·mo·tor
  also lo·co·mo·to·ry
lo·co pa·ren·tis
lo·co tu·to·ris
lo·co·weed
lo·cum-te·nen·cy
  pl lo·cum-te·nen·cies
lo·cum te·nens
  pl lo·cum te·nen·tes
lo·cus
  pl lo·ci
lo·cus clas·si·cus
  pl lo·ci clas·si·ci
lo·cus con·trac·tus
lo·cus cri·mi·nis

lo·cus cus·to·di·ae

lo·cus de·lic·ti

lo·cus in quo

lo·cus pe·ni·ten·
   ti·ae
    pl lo·ci pe·ni·ten·ti·ae

lo·cus poe·ni·ten·
   ti·ae
    pl lo·ci poe·ni·ten·
    ti·ae

lo·cus pu·bli·cus

lo·cus si·gil·li
   pl lo·ci si·gil·li

lo·cus stan·di
   pl lo·ci stan·di

lodge
   lodged
   lodg·ing

lodg·er

log·ag·no·sia

log·am·ne·sia

lo·gan
   var of lagan

log·apha·sia

log·book

log·op·a·thy
   pl log·op·a·thies

logo·ple·gia

loi·ter

loi·ter·er

lon·gis·si·mus
   dor·si

lon·gi·tu·di·nal

long-term

long-term·er

look·out

loop·hole

loot

loot·er

lop·wood

lor·do·sis
   pl lor·do·ses

lor·dot·ic

lord·ship

loss

lo·tion

lot·tery
   pl lot·ter·ies

louse
   pl lice

lous·i·ness

lousy
   lous·i·er
   lous·i·est

loy·al

loy·al·ty
   pl loy·al·ties

loz·enge

lu·cid in·ter·val

lu·cid·i·ty
   pl lu·cid·i·ties

lu·cra·tive

lu·cra·tive·ly

lu·cri cau·sa

lu·crum ces·sans

lu·crum in·ter·
   cep·tum

Lud·wig's an·gi·na

lu·es
   pl lu·es

lu·et·ic

lug·gage

lum·ba·go
   pl lum·ba·gos

lum·bar

lum·bo·cos·tal

lum·bo·in·gui·nal

lum·bo·sa·cral

lu·men
   pl lu·mi·na
   or lu·mens

lu·mi·nal
   also lu·me·nal

lu·na·cy
   pl lu·na·cies

lu·nar

lu·na·tic

lu·pus

lu·pus er·y·the·
   ma·to·sus

lu·pus vul·gar·is

lust

lust·ful

lust·ful·ly

lust·ful·ness

lu·sus na·tu·rae

lu·tein

lu·tein·iza·tion

lu·tein·ize
   lu·tein·ized
   lu·tein·iz·ing

lux·ate
   lux·at·ed
   lux·at·ing

lux·a·tion

ly·ing-in
  pl ly·ings-in
  or ly·ing-ins
lymph
lymph·ad·e·ni·tis
lymph·a·gogue
lym·phat·ic
lym·pha·tol·y·sis
lym·pho·cy·to·ma
  pl lym·pho·cy·to·mas
  or lym·pho·cy·to·ma·ta
lym·pho·cy·to·sis
  pl lym·pho·cy·to·ses
lym·pho·gran·u·lo·
  ma
    pl lym·pho·gran·u·
      lo·mas
    or lym·pho·gran·u·
      lo·ma·ta
lym·pho·gran·u·lo·
  ma in·gui·na·le
lym·pho·gran·u·lo·
  ma·tous
lym·pho·gran·u·
  lo·ma
  ve·ne·re·um
lym·phoid
lym·pho·sar·co·ma
  pl lym·pho·sar·co·mas
  or lym·pho·sar·co·ma·
    ta
lym·pho·sar·co·ma·
  tous
lynch
lynch·er
lynch·ing
lyo·phile
  also lyo·phil

lyo·phil·ic
ly·oph·i·li·za·tion
ly·oph·i·lize
  ly·oph·i·lized
  ly·oph·i·liz·ing
lyo·pho·bic
  also lyo·phobe
lyo·trop·ic
ly·ser·gic ac·id
  di·eth·yl·am·ide
ly·sin
ly·sis
  pl ly·ses
ly·so·gen
ly·so·gen·e·sis
  pl ly·so·gen·e·ses
ly·so·gen·ic
lyt·ic

M

Mc·Bur·ney's
  point
mace
  symbol of authority
Mace
  *trademark for a
    disabling liquid*
mace-bear·er
mace-proof
mac·er
mac·er·ate
  mac·er·at·ed
  mac·er·at·ing

mac·er·a·tion
mac·er·a·tor
Ma·chi·a·vel·lian
Ma·chi·a·vel·lian·ly
ma·chin·abil·i·ty
ma·chin·able
  also ma·chine·able
mach·i·nate
  mach·i·nat·ed
  mach·i·nat·ing
mach·i·na·tion
mach·i·na·tor
ma·chine
ma·chin·ery
ma·chin·ist
ma·chin·ize
  ma·chin·ized
  ma·chin·iz·ing
Mc·Nagh·ten rule
  also M'Nagh·ten rule
mac·ro·ceph·a·lous
  or mac·ro·ce·phal·ic
mac·ro·ceph·a·lus
  pl mac·ro·ceph·a·li
mac·ro·ceph·a·ly
mac·ro·eco·nom·ic
mac·ro·eco·nom·ics
mac·ro·ma·nia
mac·ro·pro·ce·dure
mac·ro·scop·ic
  also mac·ro·scop·i·cal
mac·ro·scop·i·cal·ly
mac·ro·struc·tur·al
mac·ro·struc·ture
mac·u·lar

mac·u·late
mac·u·la·tion
mac·u·lo·pap·u·lar
mac·u·lo·pap·u·le
mad
  mad·der
  mad·dest
mad·am
  pl mad·ams

ma·dame
  pl ma·dames
  or mes·dames

mad·a·ro·sis
  pl mad·a·ro·ses

mad·a·rot·ic
made-to-mea·sure
made-to-or·der
mad·man
  pl mad·men

mad·ness
mad·wom·an
  pl mad·wom·en

Mae·ce·nas
  pl Mae·ce·nas·es

Ma·fia
  or Maf·fia

ma·fi·o·so
  pl ma·fi·o·si

mag·got
ma·gis
mag·is·te·ri·al
mag·is·te·ri·al·ly
mag·is·te·ri·al·ness
ma·gis·ter li·tis
ma·gis·ter na·vis

ma·gis·ter
  so·ci·e·ta·tis
mag·is·tra·cy
  pl mag·is·tra·cies

mag·is·trate
mag·is·trate's
  court
mag·is·trate·ship
mag·is·trat·i·cal
mag·is·trat·i·cal·ly
mag·is·tra·ture
mag·na ave·na
mag·na com·po·
  ne·re par·vis
mag·na cul·pa
mag·na neg·li·
  gen·tia
mag·nate
mag·nate·ship
mag·ne·sia
mag·ne·sian
mag·ne·sium
mag·ne·sium
  bomb
mag·net
mag·ni·fi·ca·tion
mag·ni·fy
  mag·ni·fied
  mag·ni·fy·ing
mag·num opus
mags·man
  pl mags·men

maid·en·head
mail
mail·abil·i·ty

mail·able
mail·cert
maills and du·ties
mail-or·der house
maim
  maimed
  maim·ing
maim·er
main line *n*
main·line *vb*
  main·lined
  main·lin·ing
main·lin·er
main·per·na·ble
main·per·nor
main·prise
  also main·prize
  main·prised
  also main·prized
  main·pris·ing
  also main·priz·ing

main·pri·sor
main·sworn
main·tain
main·tain·able
main·tain·er
main·tain·or
main·te·nance
main·te·nance
  cu·ri·a·lis
main·te·nance of
  mem·ber·ship
main·te·nance
  ru·ra·lis
ma·jor
ma·jor·i·ty
  pl ma·jor·i·ties

ma·jor·i·ty-owned
make
  made
  mak·ing
make over *vb*
make-over *n*
mak·er
make·shift
make up *vb*
make·up *n or adj*
make·weight
make-work
mak·ing-up *adj*
mal
ma·la
  pl of malum

ma·la ani·mo
mal·ad·just·ed
mal·ad·jus·tive
mal·ad·just·ment
mal·ad·min·is·ter
mal·ad·min·is·tra·
  tion
mal·a·dy
  pl mal·a·dies

ma·la fi·de *adj*
ma·la fi·des *n*
ma·la in se
mal·aise
  or mal·ease

ma·la mens
ma·la prax·is
ma·la pro·hi·bi·ta
ma·lar
ma·lar·ia
ma·lar·i·al

ma·lar·i·ous
mal·a·thi·on
mal·be·hav·ior
mal·con·duct
mal·con·struc·tion
mal·con·tent
mal de mer
male
ma·le ap·pre·ti·
  a·ta
mal·ease
  var of malaise

male·dic·tion
male·dic·tive
male·dic·to·ry
male·fac·tion
male·fac·tor
male·fac·tress
ma·lef·ic
ma·lef·i·cence
ma·lef·i·cent
ma·lev·o·lence
ma·lev·o·lent
mal·fea·sance
mal·fea·sant
mal·for·ma·tion
mal·formed
mal·func·tion
mal gra·to
mal·ice
mal·ice afore·
  thought
mal·ice pre·pense
ma·li·cious
ma·li·cious·ly
ma·li·cious·ness

ma·lign
ma·lig·nance
ma·lig·nan·cy
  pl ma·lig·nan·cies

ma·lig·nant
ma·lig·nant·ly
ma·lig·ni·ty
  pl ma·lig·ni·ties

ma·lin·ger
ma·lin·ger·er
mal·in·vest·ment
ma·li·tia im·pli·
  ca·ta
ma·li·tia prae·co·
  gi·ta·ta
mal·lea·bil·i·ty
mal·lea·ble
mal·le·o·lar
mal·le·o·lare
mal·le·o·lus
  pl mal·le·o·li

mal·le·us
  pl mal·lei

mal·nour·ished
mal·nour·ish·ment
mal·nu·tri·tion
ma·lo ani·mo
mal·oc·clu·sion
ma·lo gra·to
ma·lo sen·su
mal·posed
mal·po·si·tion
mal·prac·tice
  mal·prac·ticed
  mal·prac·tic·ing

mal·prac·ti·tio·ner
mal·prax·is
Mal·ta fe·ver
mal·treat
mal·treat·ment
ma·lum
  pl ma·la

ma·lum in se
ma·lum pro·hi·
  bi·tum
mal·union
mal·unit·ed
ma·lus ani·mus
mal·ver·sa·tion
mam·ma
  pl mam·mae

mam·ma·ry
man·a·cle
  man·a·cled
  man·a·cling
man·age
  man·aged
  man·ag·ing
man·age·abil·i·ty
man·age·able
man·age·able·ness
man·age·ably
man·age·ment
man·age·men·tal
man·ag·er
man·ag·er·ess
man·a·ge·ri·al
man·a·ge·ri·al·ly
man·ag·er·ship
man·da·mus *n*
  pl man·da·mus·es

man·da·mus *vb*
  man·da·mused
  man·da·mus·ing
man·dant
man·da·tary
  pl man·da·tar·ies
  one holding a mandate
  (*see* mandatory)

man·date
  man·dat·ed
  man·dat·ing
man·da·tee
man·da·tor
man·da·to·ri·ly
man·da·to·ry
  obligatory
  (*see* mandatary)

man·da·tum
  pl man·da·ta

man·da·vi bal·li·vo
man·day
man·di·ble
man·dib·u·lar
man·dib·u·lary
ma·neu·ver
  also ma·noeu·vre
  or ma·noeu·ver
  ma·neu·vered
  also ma·noeu·vred
  or ma·noeu·vered
  ma·neu·ver·ing
  also ma·noeu·vre·ing
  or ma·noeu·ver·ing
ma·neu·ver·abil·
  i·ty
  pl ma·neu·ver·abil·
    i·ties

ma·neu·ver·able

ma·neu·ver·er
man·ga·nese
man·ga·ne·sian
man·gle
  man·gled
  man·gling
man·gler
man·han·dle
  man·han·dled
  man·han·dling
man·hole
man·hood
man-hour
man·hunt
ma·nia
ma·nia a po·tu
ma·ni·ac
  or ma·ni·a·cal

ma·ni·a·cal·ly
man·ic
man·i·cal·ly
man·ic-de·pres·
  sive
man·i·fest
man·i·fest·able
man·i·fes·ta·tion
man·i·fes·ta·tive
man·i·fest·ly
man·i·fes·to *vb*
  man·i·fes·toed
  man·i·fes·to·ing
  man·i·fes·toes
man·i·fes·to *n*
  man·i·fes·tos
  or man·i·fes·toes
ma·nip·u·la·bil·i·ty

ma·nip·u·la·ble
ma·nip·u·lat·able
ma·nip·u·late
  ma·nip·u·lat·ed
  ma·nip·u·lat·ing
ma·nip·u·la·tion
ma·nip·u·la·tive
ma·nip·u·la·tor
ma·nip·u·la·to·ry
ma·nit
man-made
man·ner
ma·noeu·ver,
  ma·noeu·vre
  vars of maneuver
man-of-all-work
man of straw
man·or
man·pow·er
man·sion
man·slaugh·ter
man·slay·er
man·steal·ing
man·su·e·tae na·
  tu·rae *n pl*
man·sue·tude
Man·toux test
man·trap
  pl man·traps
man·u·al
man·u·al·ly
ma·nu·bri·al
ma·nu·bri·um
  pl ma·nu·bria
  also ma·nu·bri·ums

ma·nu·cap·tio

man·u·cap·tion
man·u·cap·tor
man·u·cap·ture
man·u·fac·to·ry
  pl man·u·fac·to·ries
man·u·fac·tur·able
man·u·fac·tur·al
man·u·fac·ture
  man·u·fac·tured
  man·u·fac·tur·ing
  man·u·fac·tur·er
ma·nu for·ti
man·u·mis·sion
man·u·mit
  man·u·mit·ted
  man·u·mit·ting
ma·nu ope·ra
manu·script
manu·scrip·tion
ma·nus mor·tua
map·per
ma·ras·mic
ma·ras·moid
ma·ras·mus
ma·raud
ma·raud·er
ma·re al·tum
ma·re li·be·rum
ma·re no·strum
ma·re·tum
  or ma·ret·tum

mar·gin
mar·gin·al
mar·gin of safe·ty
mar·i·jua·na
  or mar·i·hua·na

ma·ri·na
ma·rine
mar·i·ner
mar·i·schal
mar·i·tage
  also mar·i·ta·gi·um
  pl mar·i·tag·es
  also mar·i·ta·gia
mar·i·tal
mar·i·tal·ly
ma·rit·i·cid·al
ma·rit·i·cide
ma·ri·ti·ma
  in·cre·men·ta
mar·i·time
mark
mark down *vb*
mark·down *n*
mark·er
mar·ket
  mar·ket·ed
  mar·ket·ing
mar·ket·abil·i·ty
mar·ket·able
mar·ke·teer
mar·ket·er
mar·ket overt
mar·ket·place
mark-on
marks·man
  pl marks·men

marks·man·ship
mark up *vb*
mark·up *n*
mar·plot
marque

mar·riage
mar·riage·abil·i·ty
mar·riage·able
mar·riage por·tion
mar·ri·er
mar·ry
  mar·ried
  mar·ry·ing
mar·shal
  mar·shaled
    or mar·shalled
  mar·shal·ing
    or mar·shal·ling

mar·shal·cy
  pl mar·shal·cies

Marsh test
  also Marsh's test

mart
mar·tial
mar·tial·ly
mar·tyr
mar·tyr·dom
Marx·ian
Marx·ism
Marx·ism-Le·nin·ism
Marx·ist
mas·cu·lin·i·za·tion
mas·cu·lin·ize
  mas·cu·lin·ized
  mas·cu·lin·iz·ing
mash·er
mash·gi·ah
  or mash·gi·ach
  pl mash·gi·him
  or mash·gi·chim

mash·ing
mas·och·ism
mas·och·ist
mas·och·is·tic
mas·och·is·ti·cal·ly
ma·son
ma·son·ry
  pl ma·son·ries

ma·son·work
mas·quer·ade
  mas·quer·ad·ed
  mas·quer·ad·ing
mass
Mas·sa·chu·setts rule
Mas·sa·chu·setts trust
mas·sa·cre
  mas·sa·cred
  mas·sa·cring
mas·sage
  mas·saged
  mas·sag·ing
mas·sage par·lor
mas·se·ter
mas·seur
mas·seuse
mass-pro·duce
  mass-pro·duced
  mass-pro·duc·ing
mass-pro·duc·er
mass pro·duc·tion
mast
mas·tec·to·my
  pl mas·tec·to·mies

mas·ter
mas·ter build·er
mas·ter·ful
mas·ter·ful·ly
mas·ter·ful·ness
mas·tery
mas·ti·cate
  mas·ti·cat·ed
  mas·ti·cat·ing
mas·tit·ic
mas·ti·tis
  pl mas·tit·i·des

mas·toid
mas·toid·ec·to·my
  pl mas·toid·ec·to·mies

mas·toid·itis
  pl mas·toid·it·i·des

mas·toid·ot·o·my
  pl mas·toid·ot·o·mies

mas·tur·bate
  mas·tur·bat·ed
  mas·tur·bat·ing
mas·tur·bat·ic
mas·tur·ba·tion
mas·tur·ba·tor
mas·tur·ba·tory
match
ma·te·lo·tage
ma·ter·fa·mil·i·as
  pl ma·ter·fa·mil·i·as·es

ma·te·ria
ma·te·ri·al
  adj having relevance
    or importance
  n that of which
    something is made
  (*see* matériel)

ma·te·ri·al·i·ty
  pl ma·te·ri·al·i·ties

ma·te·ri·al·ly
ma·te·ri·al·man
  pl ma·te·ri·al·men

ma·te·ri·al·ness
ma·te·ria med·i·ca
ma·té·ri·el
  or ma·te·ri·el
  equipment and supplies
  (see material)

ma·ter·nal
ma·ter·nal·ism
ma·ter·nal·ly
ma·ter·ni·ty
ma·ter·te·ra
ma·ter·te·ra
  mag·na
ma·ter·te·ra
  ma·jor
ma·ter·te·ra
  max·i·ma
ma·ti·ma
ma·tri·arch
ma·tri·ar·chal
ma·tri·cid·al
ma·tri·cide
ma·tri·lat·er·al
ma·tri·line
ma·tri·lin·eage
ma·tri·lin·eal
ma·tri·lin·eal·ly
ma·tri·lin·ear
ma·tri·lin·ear·ly
ma·tri·liny
  pl ma·tri·li·nies

ma·tri·lo·cal

ma·tri·lo·cal·i·ty
  pl ma·tri·lo·cal·i·ties

mat·ri·mo·ni·al
mat·ri·mo·ni·al·
  i·ter
mat·ri·mo·nial·ly
mat·ri·mo·ni·um
mat·ri·mo·ny
mat·ri·po·tes·tal
ma·trix
  pl ma·tri·ces
  or ma·trix·es

ma·tron
mat·ter
mat·ter in pais
mat·tery
mat·u·ra·tion
ma·ture *vb*
ma·tured
ma·tur·ing
ma·ture *adj*
ma·tur·er
ma·tur·est
ma·tu·ri·ty
  pl ma·tu·ri·ties

max·il·la
  pl max·il·lae
  also max·il·las

max·il·lary
max·im
max·i·mal
max·i·mal·ly
max·i·mi·za·tion
max·i·mize
max·i·mized
max·i·miz·ing

max·i·mum
  pl max·i·mums
  or max·i·ma

may·hem
may·hemed
  or may·hemmed
may·hem·ing
  or may·hem·ming

may·he·ma·vit
may·or
may·or·al
may·or·al·ty
  pl may·or·al·ties

may·or·coun·cil
may·or·do·mo
may·or·ship
mea cul·pa
  pl mea cul·pas

mead·ow
mean
me·an·der
me·an·dered
me·an·der·ing
mean·ing
means *n pl*
mean·time
mean·while
mea·sles
mea·sly
mea·sli·er
mea·sli·est
mea·sur·abil·i·ty
mea·sur·able
mea·sur·ably
mea·sur·age
mea·sure

mea·sured
mea·sur·ing
mea·sure·ment
mea·sure·ment
  car·go
    also mea·sure·ment
    goods
    or mea·sure·ment
    freight
me·atus
  pl me·atus·es
  or me·atus
me·chan·ic
me·chan·i·cal
me·chan·i·cal·ly
me·chan·ic's lien
mech·a·nism
med·dle
  med·dled
  med·dling
med·dler
med·dle·some
med·dle·some·ly
me·dia con·clu·
  den·di
me·di·ad
me·di·al
me·di·al·ly
me·di·an
me·di·as·ti·nal
me·di·as·ti·num
  pl me·di·as·ti·na
me·di·ate
  me·di·at·ed
  me·di·at·ing
me·di·ate da·tum
  pl me·di·ate da·ta
  or me·di·ate da·tums

me·di·ate·ly
me·di·a·tion
me·di·a·tive
me·di·a·tor
me·di·a·to·ri·al
me·di·a·tor·ship
me·di·a·to·ry
me·di·a·tress
med·ic·aid
med·i·cal
med·i·ca·ment
medi·care
med·i·cate
  med·i·cat·ed
  med·i·cat·ing
med·i·ca·tion
med·i·ca·tive
med·ic·i·nal
med·ic·i·nal·ly
med·i·cine
med·i·co·le·gal
me·di·o·cre
me·di·oc·ri·ty
  pl me·di·oc·ri·ties

med·i·tate
  med·i·tat·ed
  med·i·tat·ing
me·di·ta·tio fu·gae
med·i·ta·tion
me·di·um
  pl me·di·ums
  or me·dia

me·di·um con·clu·
  den·di
  pl me·dia con·clu·
    den·di

me·dul·la
  pl me·dul·las
  or me·dul·lae

me·dul·la ob·lon·
  ga·ta
  pl me·dul·la ob·lon·
    ga·tas
  or me·dul·lae ob·
    lon·ga·tae

med·ul·lary
meet
meet·ing
meg·a·lo·car·dia
meg·a·lo·ma·nia
meg·a·lo·ma·ni·ac
meg·a·lo·ma·ni·a·
  cal
meg·a·lo·ma·ni·a·
  cal·ly
Mei·bo·mian cyst
Mei·licke sys·tem
meith
me·lae·na
  var of melena

mel·an·cho·lia
  pl mel·an·cho·li·as
  also mel·an·cho·li·ae

mel·an·cho·li·ac
mel·an·chol·ic
mel·an·choly
  pl mel·an·chol·ies

mel·a·no·ma
  pl mel·a·no·mas
  or mel·a·no·ma·ta

mel·a·no·ma·to·sis
  pl mel·a·no·ma·to·ses

mel·a·no·sis
  pl mel·a·no·ses

mel·a·not·ic
me·le·na
  or me·lae·na

me·lio·rate
  me·lio·rat·ed
  me·lio·rat·ing
me·lio·ra·tion
me·lio·ra·tive
me·li·or res
mel·i·tu·ria
  or mel·li·tu·ria

mel·on-seed body
mel·o·plas·ty
  pl mel·o·plas·ties

mem·ber
mem·ber·ship
mem·bra·na
  pl mem·bra·nae

mem·bra·na·ceous
mem·brane
mem·bra·nous
mem·brum
  pl mem·bra

mem·o·ran·dum
  pl mem·o·ran·dums
  or mem·o·ran·da

mem·o·ran·dum
  check
    pl mem·o·ran·dum
    checks

me·mo·ri·al
me·mo·ri·al·ist
me·mo·ri·al·ize
  me·mo·ri·al·ized
  me·mo·ri·al·iz·
    ing

me·mo·ri·ter
mem·o·ri·za·tion
mem·o·rize
  mem·o·rized
  mem·o·riz·ing
mem·o·ry
  pl mem·o·ries

men·ace
  men·aced
  men·ac·ing
men·a·di·one
mé·nage
mé·nage à trois
men·arche
men·ar·che·al
  also men·ar·chi·al

men·da·cious
men·dac·i·ty
  pl men·dac·i·ties

men·di·can·cy
  pl men·di·can·cies

men·di·cant
me·nial
me·nial·ly
Mé·nière's dis·ease
  or Mé·nière's syn·
  drome

men·in·ge·al
men·in·git·ic
men·in·gi·tis
  pl men·in·git·i·des

me·nin·go·coc·cal
  also me·nin·go·coc·cic

me·nin·go·coc·cus
  pl me·nin·go·coc·ci

me·nin·go·en·ceph·
  a·lit·ic
me·nin·go·en·ceph·
  a·li·tis
    pl me·nin·go·en·
    ceph·a·lit·i·des

me·nin·go·en·ceph·
  a·lo·my·eli·tis
    pl me·nin·go·en·
    ceph·a·lo·my·elit·
    i·des

me·nin·go·my·
  eli·tis
    pl me·nin·go·my·
    elit·i·des

me·ninx
  pl me·nin·ges

me·nis·cus
  pl me·nis·ci

meno·paus·al
meno·pause
men·or·rha·gia
men·or·rhag·ic
mens
  pl men·tes

men·sa
  pl men·sas
  or men·sae

men·sa et tho·ro
men·ses
mens le·ges
mens rea
men·stru·al
men·stru·ant
men·stru·ate
  men·stru·at·ed
  men·stru·at·ing

men·stru·a·tion
men·stru·ous
men·su·ra·bil·i·ty
men·su·ra·ble
men·su·ra·tion
men·tal
men·tal·i·ty
  pl men·tal·i·ties

men·tal·ly
men·te cap·tus
men·ti·cide
men·tion
  men·tioned
  men·tion·ing
  men·tion·able
men·tum
  pl men·ta

me·per·i·dine
me·pho·bar·bi·tal
mep·ro·bam·ate
mer·bro·min
mer·can·tile
mer·can·til·ism
mer·can·til·is·tic
mer·cap·tan
mer·ce·nary
  pl mer·ce·nar·ies

mer·chan·dis·able
mer·chan·dise n
mer·chan·dise vb
  also mer·chan·dize
  mer·chan·dised
  also mer·chan·dized
  mer·chan·dis·ing
  also mer·chan·diz·ing

mer·chan·dis·er

mer·chant
mer·chant·abil·i·ty
mer·chant·able
mer·chant·man
  pl mer·chant·men
mer·chant·ry
  pl mer·chant·ries

mer·cia·ment
mer·ci·ful
mer·ci·ful·ly
mer·ci·less
mer·ci·less·ly
mer·cu·ri·al
mer·cu·ri·al·ism
mer·cu·ri·al·iza·
  tion
mer·cu·ri·al·ize
  mer·cu·ri·al·ized
  mer·cu·ri·al·iz·
  ing
mer·cu·ric chlo·
  ride
mer·cu·ry
mer·cu·ry chlo·
  ride
mer·cy
  pl mer·cies

mere
mere droit
mere jus
mere·ly
meres·man
  pl meres·men
mer·e·tri·cious
mer·e·tri·cious·ly
mer·e·tri·cious·ness

mer·e·trix
  pl mer·e·tri·ces

merge
  merged
  merg·ing
mer·gence
merg·er
me·rid·i·an
mer·it
mer·it·able
mer·i·to·ri·ous
mer·i·to·ri·ous·ly
mer·i·to·ri·ous·ness
mes·ad
  or mesi·ad
me·sal
  var of mesial

mes·al·liance
  a poor marriage
  (see misalliance)

me·sal·ly
  var of mesially

mes·cal
mes·ca·line
mes·cal·ism
mes·en·ter·ic
mes·en·tery
  pl mes·en·ter·ies

mesi·ad
  var of mesad

me·sial
  also me·sal

me·si·al·ly
  also me·sal·ly

mesne

me·so·co·lon
mesque
mes·sage
mes·sen·ger
mes·sen·ger-at-
  arms
mes·suage
mes·ti·za
mes·ti·zo
  pl mes·ti·zos
  or mes·ti·zoes
met·a·bol·ic
  also met·a·bol·i·cal
met·a·bol·i·cal·ly
me·tab·o·lism
me·tab·o·lite
me·tab·o·liz·abil·
  i·ty
  pl me·tab·o·liz·
    abil·i·ties
me·tab·o·liz·able
me·tab·o·lize
  me·tab·o·lized
  me·tab·o·liz·ing
meta·car·pal
meta·car·pus
  pl meta·car·pi
meta·chro·nism
met·age
met·al
meta·law
me·tal·lic
met·al·lif·er·ous
met·al·lur·gi·cal
  also met·al·lur·gic
met·al·lur·gi·cal·ly

met·al·lur·gist
met·al·lur·gy
me·taph·y·se·al
me·taph·y·sis
  pl me·taph·y·ses
meta·pla·sia
meta·plas·tic
me·tas·ta·sis
  pl me·tas·ta·ses
me·tas·ta·size
  me·tas·ta·sized
  me·tas·ta·siz·ing
met·a·stat·ic
met·a·stat·i·cal·ly
meta·tar·sal
meta·tar·sal·gia
meta·tar·sus
  pl meta·tar·si
me·ta·yer
mete
  met·ed
  met·ing
me·te·or·ism
me·ter
metes and bounds
mete·wand
  or mete·yard
meth·a·done
  or meth·a·don
meth·am·phet·
  amine
meth·a·nol
me·tha·qua·lone
met·he·mo·glo·bin
met·he·mo·glo·bin·
  emia

met·he·mo·glo·bin·
  uria
meth·od
meth·o·mania
meth·o·trex·ate
me·thoxy·chlor
meth·yl
meth·yl·do·pa
me·tic·u·lous
me·tic·u·lous·ly
met·o·pon
me·tra
  pl me·trae
me·tric
me·tri·tis
me·trop·o·lis
  pl me·trop·o·lis·es
met·ro·pol·i·tan
met·ro·pol·i·tan·ize
  met·ro·pol·i·tan·
    ized
  met·ro·pol·i·tan·
    iz·ing
me·tror·rha·gia
me·tror·rha·gic
meu·bles *n pl*
me·um et tu·um
mi·as·ma
  also mi·asm
  pl mi·as·mas
  or mi·as·ma·ta
  also mi·asms
mi·as·mal
mi·as·mat·ic
mi·as·mic
mi·crobe

mi·cro·bi·al
  also mi·cro·bic

mi·cro·bi·ci·dal
mi·cro·bi·cide
mi·cro·ce·phal·ic
mi·cro·ceph·a·ly
mi·cro·cul·ture
mi·cro·de·ter·mi·
  na·tion
mi·cro·dis·sec·tion
mi·cro·log·i·cal
  or mi·cro·log·ic

mi·crol·o·gist
mi·crol·o·gy
  pl mi·crol·o·gies

mi·cro·meth·od
mi·cro·nu·tri·ent
mi·cro·or·gan·ism
mi·cro·pho·to·
  graph
mi·cro·pho·to·
  graph·ic
mi·cro·pho·tog·ra·
  phy
  pl mi·cro·pho·tog·
    ra·phies

mi·cro·pro·ce·dure
mi·cro·scope
mi·cro·scop·ic
  or mi·cro·scop·i·cal

mi·cro·scop·i·cal·ly
mi·cro·spec·tro·
  pho·to·met·ric
  also mi·cro·spec·
    tro·pho·to·met·
    ri·cal

mi·cro·spec·tro·
  pho·to·met·ri·
  cal·ly
mi·cro·spec·tro·
  pho·tom·e·try
  pl mi·cro·spec·tro·
    pho·tom·e·tries

mi·cro·struc·tur·al
mi·cro·struc·ture
mi·cro·sur·gery
  pl mi·cro·sur·ger·ies

mi·cro·sur·gi·cal
mid-chan·nel
mid·dle·man
  pl mid·dle·men

mid·dle·man·ism
mid·riff
mid·sag·it·tal
mid·sec·tion
mid·ship·man
  pl mid·ship·men

mid·way
mid·wife *n*
  pl mid·wives

mid·wife *vb*
  mid·wifed
  or mid·wived
  mid·wif·ing
  or mid·wiv·ing
  mid·wifes
  or mid·wives

mid·wife·ry
  pl mid·wife·ries

mi·graine
mi·grain·oid
mi·grain·ous

mi·grant
mi·grate
  mi·grat·ed
  mi·grat·ing
mi·gra·to·ry
mile·age
  also mil·age
  travel allowance
  (see millage)

mile·stone
mil·i·ary
mil·i·tan·cy
mil·i·tant
mil·i·tant·ly
mil·i·tant·ness
mil·i·tary
mi·li·tia
mi·li·tia·man
  pl mi·li·tia·men

mill·age
  rate in mills
  (see mileage)

mil·li·gram
mil·li·li·ter
mil·li·me·ter
mill·work
mill·wright
min·able
mind·ful
mind·ful·ly
mine
  mined
  min·ing
min·er
  worker of a mine
  (see minor)

min·er·al

min·er·al·og·i·cal
  also min·er·al·og·ic

min·er·al·og·i·
  cal·ly
min·er·al·o·gist
min·er·al·o·gy
mine-run
min·im
min·i·mal
min·i·mal·ly
min·i·ment
  var of muniment

min·i·mize
  min·i·mized
  min·i·miz·ing
min·i·mum
  pl min·i·ma
  or min·i·mums

min·ion
min·is·ter
min·is·te·ri·al
min·is·te·ri·al·ly
min·is·tra·tion
min·is·try
  pl min·is·tries

mi·nor
  n   one of less than
     legal age
  adj   not important
     or serious
  (*see* miner)

mi·nor ae·tas
mi·nor·i·ty
  pl mi·nor·i·ties

mint
mint·age
mint·er

mint·mark
mint·mas·ter
mi·nus
min·ute
min·ute book
mi·nu·tia
  pl mi·nu·ti·ae
  also mi·nu·tia

mi·o·sis
  also my·o·sis
  pl mi·o·ses
  also my·o·ses

mi·ot·ic
  or my·ot·ic

mis·ad·dress
mis·ad·ven·ture
mis·ad·vise
  mis·ad·vised
  mis·ad·vis·ing
mis·al·lege
  mis·al·leged
  mis·al·leg·ing
mis·al·li·ance
  an improper alliance
  (*see* mesalliance)

mis·ap·pli·ca·tion
mis·ap·pli·er
mis·ap·ply
  mis·ap·plied
  mis·ap·ply·ing
mis·ap·pre·hen·sion
mis·ap·pro·pri·ate
  mis·ap·pro·pri·
  at·ed
  mis·ap·pro·pri·
  at·ing

mis·ap·pro·pri·a·
  tion
mis·be·get
  mis·be·got
  mis·be·got·ten
  mis·be·get·ting
mis·be·have
  mis·be·haved
  mis·be·hav·ing
mis·be·hav·ior
mis·brand
  mis·brand·ed
  mis·brand·ing
mis·cal·cu·late
  mis·cal·cu·lat·ed
  mis·cal·cu·lat·
  ing
mis·cal·cu·la·tion
mis·call
mis·car·riage
mis·car·ry
  mis·car·ried
  mis·car·ry·ing
mis·cast
  mis·cast
  mis·cast·ing
mis·ce·ge·na·tion
mis·ce·ge·na·
  tion·al
mis·ce·ge·net·ic
mis·cel·la·neous
mis·cel·la·ny
  pl mis·cel·la·nies

mis·chance
mis·charge

mis·charged
mis·charg·ing
mis·chief
mis·chie·vous
mis·cog·ni·zant
mis·con·duct
mis·con·struc·tion
mis·con·strue
  mis·con·strued
  mis·con·stru·ing
mis·con·tin·u·ance
mis·cre·an·cy
  mis·cre·an·cies
mis·cre·ant
mis·date
  mis·dat·ed
  mis·dat·ing
mis·deal·ing
mis·deed
mis·de·liv·ery
  pl mis·de·liv·er·ies

mis·de·mean·ant
mis·de·mean·or
mis·de·scribe
  mis·de·scribed
  mis·de·scrib·ing
mis·de·scrip·tion
mis·de·scrip·tive
mis·di·ag·nose
  mis·di·ag·nosed
  mis·di·ag·nos·ing
mis·di·ag·no·sis
  pl mis·di·ag·no·ses

mis·di·rect
mis·di·rec·tion

mise
mi·seri·cor·dia
mis·fea·sance
mis·fea·sor
mis·for·tune
mis·giv·ing
mis·guid·ed
mis·han·dle
  mis·han·dled
  mis·han·dling
mis·in·form
mis·in·for·ma·tion
mis·in·struct
mis·in·tel·li·gence
mis·in·ter·pret
  mis·in·ter·
    pret·ed
  mis·in·ter·pret·
    ing
  mis·in·ter·pre·ta·
    tion
mis·join·der
mis·judge
  mis·judged
  mis·judg·ing
mis·lay
  mis·laid
  mis·lay·ing
mis·lead
  mis·led
  mis·lead·ing
mis·lead·er
mis·lead·ing·ly
mis·man·age
  mis·man·aged
  mis·man·ag·ing

mis·man·age·ment
mis·man·ag·er
mis·name
  mis·named
  mis·nam·ing
mis·no·mer
mis·per·form
mis·place
  mis·placed
  mis·plac·ing
mis·place·ment
mis·plead·ing
mis·pri·sion
mis·punc·tu·ate
mis·quo·ta·tion
mis·quote
  mis·quot·ed
  mis·quot·ing
mis·read
  mis·read
  mis·read·ing
mis·re·ci·tal
mis·re·port
mis·rep·re·sent
mis·rep·re·sen·ta·
  tion
mis·rep·re·sen·ta·
  tive
mis·rep·re·sen·tee
mis·rep·re·sent·er
mis·sion
mis·sion·ary
  pl mis·sion·ar·ies
mis·sive
miss·mail
mis·spell

mis·spell·ing
mis·spend
  mis·spent
  mis·spend·ing
mis·state
  mis·stat·ed
  mis·stat·ing
mis·state·ment
mis·tak·able
mis·take
  mis·took
  mis·tak·en
  mis·tak·ing
mis·tak·en·ly
mis·tran·scribe
  mis·tran·scribed
  mis·tran·scrib·
    ing
mis·tran·scrip·tion
mis·trans·late
  mis·trans·lat·ed
  mis·trans·lat·ing
mis·trans·la·tion
mis·treat
mis·treat·ment
mis·tress
mis·tri·al
mis·trust
mis·un·der·stand
  mis·un·der·stood
  mis·un·der·
    stand·ing
mis·us·age
mis·use
  mis·used
  mis·us·ing

mis·us·er
mi·ti·cid·al
mi·ti·cide
mit·i·gant
mit·i·gate
  mit·i·gat·ed
  mit·i·gat·ing
  mit·i·gat·ing cir·
    cum·stance
  mit·i·ga·tion
  mit·i·ga·tive
  mit·i·ga·tor
  mit·i·ga·to·ry
mi·ti·or sen·sus
mi·tral
mit·ti·mus
  pl mit·ti·mus·es
mixed
mix·tion
M'Nagh·ten rule
  var of McNaghten rule
mob
  mobbed
  mob·bing
mo·bi·lia *n pl*
mo·bil·i·ary
mo·bi·lia se·quun·
  tur per·so·nam
mo·bles *n pl*
mob·ster
mode
model
  mod·eled
    or mod·elled
  mod·el·ing
    or mod·el·ling

mod·er·ate
  mod·er·at·ed
  mod·er·at·ing
mo·de·ra·te
  cas·ti·ga·vit
mod·er·ate·ly
mod·er·ate·ness
mod·er·a·tion
mod·er·a·tor
mod·er·a·to·ri·al
mod·er·a·tor·ship
mod·i·cum
  pl mod·i·cums
mod·i·fi·ca·tion
mod·i·fi·er
mod·i·fy
  mod·i·fied
  mod·i·fy·ing
mo·do et for·ma
mo·dus
  pl mo·di
mo·dus ope·ran·di
mo·dus va·can·di
mo·dus vi·ven·di
moi·ety
  pl moi·eties
mois·ture·proof
mo·lar
mo·lest
mo·les·ta·tion
mo·lest·er
mol·li·fy
  mol·li·fied
  mol·li·fy·ing
mol·li·ter ma·nus
  im·po·su·it

mo·men·tari·ly
mo·men·tary
mo·men·tum
  pl mo·men·ta
  or mo·men·tums

mo·ne·ta
mon·e·tari·ly
mon·e·tary
mon·e·ti·za·tion
mon·e·tize
  mon·e·tized
  mon·e·tiz·ing
mon·ey *n*
  pl mon·eys
  or mon·ies

mon·ey *vb*
  mon·eyed
    also mon·ied
  mon·ey·ing
mon·ey·lend·er
mon·gol·ism
  or mon·go·lian·ism

mon·gol·oid
mon·i·ment
mon·ish
mo·nism
mo·nis·tic
  or mo·nis·ti·cal

mo·ni·tion
mon·i·to·ry
  pl mon·i·to·ries

mon·oc·u·lar
mon·oc·u·lar·ly
mono·gam·ic
mo·nog·a·mist
mo·nog·a·mis·tic

mo·nog·a·mous
mo·nog·a·mous·ly
mo·nog·a·mous·
  ness
mo·nog·a·my
  pl mo·nog·a·mies

mono·graph
mo·nog·y·nous
mo·nog·y·ny
  pl mo·nog·y·nies
mono·ma·nia
mono·ma·ni·ac
mono·pho·bia
mono·ple·gia
mono·ple·gic
mo·nop·o·lism
mo·nop·o·list
mo·nop·o·lis·tic
mo·nop·o·lis·ti·
  cal·ly
mo·nop·o·li·za·tion
mo·nop·o·lize
  mo·nop·o·lized
  mo·nop·o·liz·ing
mo·nop·o·liz·er
mo·nop·o·ly
  pl mo·nop·o·lies
mo·nop·so·nist
mo·nop·so·nis·tic
mo·nop·so·ny
  pl mo·nop·so·nies
mono·sex·u·al
mono·sex·u·al·i·ty
  pl mono·sex·u·al·i·ties

mons pu·bis
mon·ster

mon·strans de
  droit
mon·stros·i·ty
  pl mon·stros·i·ties

mons ve·ne·ris
  pl mon·tes ve·ne·ris

month
month·ly
mon·u·ment
moon·light
  moon·light·ed
  moon·light·ing
moon·light·er
moon·shine
  moon·shined
  moon·shin·ing
moon·shin·er
moor
moor·age
moor·ing
moot
moot·ing
mo·ra
  pl mo·rae
  or mo·ras

mor·al
mo·rale
mo·ral·i·ty
mor·al·ly
mor·a·to·ri·um
  pl mor·a·to·ri·ums
  or mor·a·to·ria

mor·a·to·ry
mo·ra·tur in le·ge
mor·bid

mor·bid·i·ty
  pl mor·bid·i·ties

mor·bif·ic
mor·bil·li
more or less
more·over
mo·res *n pl*
mor·ga·nat·ic
mor·ga·nat·i·cal·ly
morgue
mor·i·bund
mo·ron
mo·ron·ic
mor·phia
mor·phine
mor·phin·ic
mor·phin·ism
mor·phin·ize
  mor·phin·ized
  mor·phin·iz·ing
mor·phi·no·ma·nia
  also mor·phi·o·ma·nia

mor·phi·no·ma·
  ni·ac
Mor·ris Plan
  com·pa·ny
mort
mor·tal
mor·tal·i·ty
  pl mor·tal·i·ties

mor·tal·ly
mort·gage
  mort·gaged
  mort·gag·ing
mort·gage·able

mort·gag·ee
mort·gag·or
  also mort·gag·er

mor·ti·fi·ca·tion
mor·ti·fy
  mor·ti·fied
  mor·ti·fy·ing
mor·tis cau·sa
mort·ling
mort·main
Mor·ton's toe
  also Mor·ton's dis·ease

mor·tua ma·nu
mor·tu·ary
  pl mor·tu·ar·ies

mor·tu·um va·
  di·um
mor·tu·us
mor·tu·us si·ne
  pro·le
moth·er
moth·er-in-law
moth·er·less
mo·til·i·ty
  pl mo·til·i·ties

mo·tion
mo·ti·vate
  mo·ti·vat·ed
  mo·ti·vat·ing
mo·ti·va·tion
mo·tive
mo·tor
mo·tor·cy·cle
mo·tor-driv·en
mo·tor·drome
mo·tor·ist

mo·tu pro·prio
mou·lage
moun·te·bank
mouth·piece
mouth-to-mouth
mov·abil·i·ty
  or move·abil·i·ty

mov·able
  or move·able

mov·able·ness
mov·ably
mov·ant
  or mov·ent

move
  moved
  mov·ing
move·ment
move·over
mu·co·pu·ru·lent
mu·co·pus
mu·co·sa
  pl mu·co·sae
  or mu·co·sas

mu·co·sal
mu·co·san·guin·
  e·ous
mu·co·se·rous
mu·cous *adj*
  (*see* mucus)

mu·cus *n*
  (*see* mucous)

muf·fler
mug
  mugged
  mug·ging
mug·ger

mug·gles
  pl mug·gles
muir·burn
mu·lat·to
  pl mu·lat·toes
  or mu·lat·tos
mulct
mu·li·ebria
mu·li·eb·ri·ty
mu·li·er
mu·li·e·ra·tus
mu·li·er puis·ne
  or mu·li·er young·er
  pl mu·li·ers puis·ne
  or mu·li·ers young·er
mul·ti·far·i·ous
mul·ti·far·i·ous·ly
mul·ti·far·i·ous·ness
mul·ti·grav·i·da
  pl mul·ti·grav·i·das
  or mul·ti·grav·i·dae
mul·ti·lat·er·al
mul·ti·lat·er·al·ly
mul·tip·a·ra
  pl mul·tip·a·ras
  or mul·tip·a·rae
mul·ti·par·i·ty
  pl mul·ti·par·i·ties
mul·tip·a·rous
mul·ti·par·tite
mul·ti·par·ty
mul·ti·ple
mul·ti·plic·i·ty
  pl mul·ti·plic·i·ties
mul·ti·ply vb
  mul·ti·plied

mul·ti·ply·ing
mul·ti·ply adj
mul·ti·re·cid·i·vism
mul·ti·tude
mul·ti·tu·di·nous
mul·ti·tu·di·nous·ly
mul·to for·ti·o·ri
mul·ture
mul·tur·er
mum·mi·fi·ca·tion
mum·mi·fy
  mum·mi·fied
  mum·mi·fy·ing
mum·my
  pl mum·mies
mun·cu·pate
mu·nic·i·pal
mu·nic·i·pal·i·ty
  pl mu·nic·i·pal·i·ties
mu·nic·i·pal·ly
mu·ni·ment
  also min·i·ment
mur·der
  mur·dered
  mur·der·ing
mur·der·ee
mur·der·er
mur·der·ess
mur·der·ous
mur·der·ous·ly
mur·der·ous·ness
mur·mur
mus·ca·rine
mus·ca·rin·ic
mus·ca·rin·ism

mus·cle
mus·cled
mus·cling
mus·cu·lar
mus·cu·lar·i·ty
  pl mus·cu·lar·i·ties
mus·cu·la·ture
mus·cu·lo·skel·e·tal
mus·tard gas
mu·ta·fa·cient
mu·ta·gen
mu·ta·ge·nic·i·ty
  pl mu·ta·ge·nic·i·ties
mu·ta·tion
mu·ta·tis mu·tan·dis
mute
mu·ti·late
  mu·ti·lat·ed
  mu·ti·lat·ing
mu·ti·la·tion
mu·ti·la·tive
mu·ti·la·tor
mu·ti·neer
mu·ti·nous
mu·ti·nous·ly
mu·ti·nous·ness
mu·ti·ny
  pl mu·ti·nies
mu·ti·ny
  mu·ti·nied
  mu·ti·ny·ing
mu·tu·al
mu·tu·al·i·ty
  pl mu·tu·al·i·ties

mu·tu·al·iza·tion
mu·tu·al·ly
mu·tu·ant
mu·tu·ary
  pl mu·tu·ar·ies

mu·tus
mu·tus et sur·dus
mu·tu·um
  pl mu·tua

muz·zle
  muz·zled
  muz·zling
my·al·gia
my·al·gic
my·as·the·nia
my·as·the·nia
  gra·vis
my·as·then·ic
my·a·to·nia
  muscular flabbiness
  (see myotonia)

my·ce·li·al
my·ce·li·um
  pl my·ce·lia

my·co·sis
  pl my·co·ses

my·co·tox·in
my·dri·a·sis
  pl my·dri·a·ses

myd·ri·at·ic
my·elit·ic
my·eli·tis
  pl my·elit·i·des

my·elo·gram
my·elo·graph·ic

my·elog·ra·phy
  pl my·elog·ra·phies

my·elo·ma
  pl my·elo·mas
  or my·elo·ma·ta

my·elo·ma·to·sis
  pl my·elo·ma·to·ses

my·elo·ma·tous
my·elo·path·ic
my·elop·a·thy
  pl my·elop·a·thies

myo·car·di·tis
myo·car·di·um
  pl myo·car·dia

myo·clo·nia
my·oc·lo·nus
myo·fi·bro·ma
  pl myo·fi·bro·mas
  also myo·fi·bro·ma·ta

my·o·ma
  pl my·o·mas
  or my·o·ma·ta

myo·me·tri·al
myo·me·tri·um
myo·pa·ral·y·sis
  pl myo·pa·ral·y·ses

myo·pa·re·sis
  pl myo·pa·re·ses

myo·path·ic
my·op·a·thy
  pl my·op·a·thies

my·o·pia
my·o·pic
my·o·sis
  var of miosis

my·o·si·tis

my·ot·ic
  var of miotic

myo·to·nia
  tonic muscular spasm
  (see myatonia)

myo·ton·ic
mys·te·ri·ous
mys·tery
  pl mys·ter·ies

myx·ede·ma
  pl myx·ede·mas
  or myx·ede·ma·ta

myx·o·ma
  pl myx·o·mas
  or myx·o·ma·ta

N

nae·void
  var of nevoid

nae·vus
  var of nevus

na·ked
na·lor·phine
nal·ox·one
name
  named
  nam·ing
name·less
name·ly
naph·tha
naph·thol
Na·po·le·on·ic
  Code
nap·ra·path
na·prap·a·thy

nar·cism
nar·cis·sism
nar·cis·sist
nar·cis·sis·tic
nar·co·anal·y·sis
   pl nar·co·anal·y·ses
nar·co·an·es·the·
   sia
     also nar·co·an·aes·
      the·sia
nar·co·di·ag·no·sis
   pl nar·co·di·ag·no·ses
nar·co·hyp·no·sis
   pl nar·co·hyp·no·ses
nar·co·lep·sy
   pl nar·co·lep·sies
nar·co·ma
   pl nar·co·mas
   also nar·co·ma·ta
nar·co·ma·nia
nar·cose
   also nar·cous
nar·co·sis
   pl nar·co·ses
nar·co·syn·the·sis
   pl nar·co·syn·the·ses
nar·co·ther·a·py
   pl nar·co·ther·a·pies
nar·cot·ic
nar·cot·i·cal·ly
nar·cot·i·cism
nar·co·tism
nar·co·ti·za·tion
nar·co·tize
   nar·co·tized
   nar·co·tiz·ing

nar·cous
   var of narcose
na·ris
   pl na·res
nar·ra·tio
   pl nar·ra·tio·nes
nar·ra·tion
nar·ra·tive
na·so·lac·ri·mal
na·so·pal·a·tine
na·so·pha·ryn·geal
na·so·phar·yn·gi·tis
   pl na·so·phar·yn·git·
   i·des
na·so·phar·ynx
na·so·si·nus·itis
   also na·so·si·nu·itis
na·tal
na·tal·ly
na·tes
na·tion
na·tion·al
na·tion·al·i·ty
   pl na·tion·al·i·ties
na·tion·al·iza·tion
na·tion·al·ize
   na·tion·al·ized
   na·tion·al·iz·ing
na·tion·less
nat·u·ral
nat·u·ral-born
nat·u·ral·iza·tion
nat·u·ral·ize
   nat·u·ral·ized
   nat·u·ral·iz·ing
nat·u·ral person

na·tu·ro·path
na·tu·ro·path·ic
na·tu·rop·a·thy
nau·sea
nau·se·ant
nau·se·ate
   nau·se·at·ed
   nau·se·at·ing
nau·se·at·ing·ly
nau·seous
nau·seous·ly
nau·ti·cal
na·val
   relating to a navy
   (*see* navel)
na·vel
   umbellicus
   (*see* naval)
nav·i·cert
nav·i·ga·bil·i·ty
nav·i·ga·ble
nav·i·gate
   nav·i·gat·ed
   nav·i·gat·ing
nav·i·ga·tion
nav·i·ga·tion·al
nav·i·ga·tor
nay
né
neap tide
near
   near·er
   near·est
near·by
near·ly
near·ness

near·sight·ed
near·sight·ed·ness
ne·ar·thro·sis
  pl ne·ar·thro·ses

neb·u·la
  pl neb·u·las
  or neb·u·lae

nec·es·sar·i·ly
nec·es·sary
  pl nec·es·saries

ne·ces·si·tate
  ne·ces·si·tat·ed
  ne·ces·si·tat·ing
ne·ces·si·tous
ne·ces·si·ty
  pl ne·ces·si·ties

neck
nec·ro·fe·tish·ism
nec·ro·gen·ic
  or ne·crog·e·nous

nec·ro·log·i·cal
  or nec·ro·log·ic

ne·crol·o·gist
ne·crol·o·gy
  pl ne·crol·o·gies

nec·ro·phile
nec·ro·phil·ia
nec·ro·phil·ic
ne·croph·i·lism
ne·croph·i·lous
nec·rop·sy
  pl nec·rop·sies

nec·rop·sy
  nec·rop·sied
  nec·rop·sy·ing

ne·cro·sis
  pl ne·cro·ses

ne·crot·ic
née
  or nee

need
need·ful
nee·dle
need·less
need·less·ly
needy
ne'er-do-well
ne ex·e·at
ne ex·e·at reg·no
ne ex·e·at
  re·pub·li·ca
ne·far·i·ous
ne·far·i·ous·ly
ne·far·i·ous·ness
ne·gate
  ne·gat·ed
  ne·gat·ing
ne·ga·tion
neg·a·tive
neg·a·tive preg·
  nant
    pl neg·a·tives preg·
    nant

neg·a·tiv·ism
neg·a·tiv·is·tic
ne·glect
ne·glect·ed
ne·glect·er
  also ne·glec·tor
ne·glect·ful
neg·li·gence

neg·li·gence per se
neg·li·gent
neg·li·gent·ly
neg·li·gi·ble
  also neg·lige·able

neg·li·gi·bly
ne·go·tia·bil·i·ty
ne·go·tia·ble
ne·go·tiant
ne·go·ti·ate
  ne·go·ti·at·ed
  ne·go·ti·at·ing
ne·go·ti·a·tion
ne·go·ti·a·tor
ne·go·tia·to·ry
ne·go·ti·a·tress
ne·go·ti·a·trix
  pl ne·go·ti·a·trix·es

ne·go·ti·o·rum
  ges·tio
ne·go·ti·o·rum
  ges·tor
ne·go·ti·um
Ne·gri body
neigh·bor
neigh·bor·hood
neigh·bor·ing
Neis·se·ria
nei·ther
Nem·bu·tal
ne·mi·ne con·tra·
  di·cen·te
ne·mi·ne dis·sen·
  ti·en·te
neo·la·lia
neo·my·cin

neo·na·tal
neo·na·tal·ly
ne·o·nate
neo·phyte
neo·pla·sia
neo·plasm
neo·plas·tic
neph·a·lism
neph·a·list
neph·e·lom·e·ter
neph·e·lo·met·ric
neph·e·lom·e·try
neph·ew
ne·phrec·to·mize
  ne·phrec·to·
   mized
  ne·phrec·to·miz·
   ing
ne·phrec·to·my
  pl ne·phrec·to·mies
neph·ric
ne·phrit·ic
ne·phri·tis
  pl ne·phrit·i·des
  or ne·phri·tis·es
neph·ro·gen·ic
  also ne·phrog·e·nous
neph·ro·lith
neph·ro·li·thi·a·sis
  pl neph·ro·li·thi·a·ses
ne·phrop·a·thy
  pl ne·phrop·a·thies
ne·phro·sis
  pl ne·phro·ses
ne·phrot·ic
neph·ro·tox·ic

neph·ro·tox·ic·i·ty
  pl neph·ro·tox·ic·i·ties
ne·pos
  pl ne·po·tes
ne·po·tal
ne·pot·ic
nep·o·tism
nep·o·tist
nep·o·tis·tic
  or nep·o·tis·ti·cal
nep·tis
nerve
ner·vous
  break·down
   also ner·vous pros·
   tra·tion
net
  net·ted
  net·ting
net·tle rash
neu·ral
neu·ral·gia
neu·ral·gic
neu·ral·gi·form
neu·ral·ly
neur·as·the·nia
neur·as·then·ic
neur·as·then·i·cal·
  ly
neu·rit·ic
neu·ri·tis
  pl neu·rit·i·des
  or neu·ri·tis·es
neu·ro·ac·tive
neu·ro·anat·o·mist
neu·ro·anat·o·my
  pl neu·ro·anat·o·mies

neu·ro·der·ma·tit·ic
neu·ro·der·ma·ti·tis
  pl neu·ro·der·ma·ti·
   tis·es
  or neu·ro·der·ma·tit·
   i·des
neu·ro·fi·bro·ma
  pl neu·ro·fi·bro·mas
  also neu·ro·fi·bro·
   ma·ta
neu·ro·gen·ic
neu·ro·gen·i·cal·ly
neu·ro·lept·an·al·
  ge·sia
  or neu·ro·lept·to·
   an·al·ge·sia
neu·ro·lept·an·al·
  ge·sic
neu·ro·lep·tic
neu·ro·log·i·cal
neu·ro·log·i·cal·ly
neu·rol·o·gist
neu·rol·o·gy
  pl neu·rol·o·gies
neu·ro·ma
  pl neu·ro·mas
  or neu·ro·ma·ta
neu·ro·mo·tor
neu·ro·mus·cu·lar
neu·ron
  also neu·rone
neu·ro·nal
  also neu·ron·ic
neu·ro·path
neu·ro·path·ic
neu·ro·patho·log·ic
neu·ro·pa·thol·o·
  gist

neu·ro·pa·thol·o·gy
  pl neu·ro·pa·thol·o·gies

neu·rop·a·thy
  pl neu·rop·a·thies

neu·ro·psy·chi·at·ric

neu·ro·psy·chi·at·ri·cal·ly

neu·ro·psy·chi·a·trist

neu·ro·psy·chi·a·try
  pl neu·ro·psy·chi·a·tries

neu·ro·sis
  pl neu·ro·ses

neu·rot·ic

neu·rot·i·cal·ly

neu·rot·i·cism

neu·roto·gen·ic

neu·ro·tox·ic

neu·ro·tox·ic·i·ty
  pl neu·ro·tox·ic·i·ties

neu·ro·tox·in

neu·ter

neu·tral

neu·tral·ism

neu·tral·ist

neu·tral·is·tic

neu·tral·i·ty
  pl neu·tral·i·ties

neu·tral·iza·tion

neu·tral·ize
  neu·tral·ized
  neu·tral·iz·ing

neu·tron

ne va·ri·e·tur

nev·er·the·less

ne·void
  also nae·void

ne·vus
  also nae·vus
  pl ne·vi
  also nae·vi

new·born
  pl new·born
  or new·borns

new town

next friend

next·ly

next of kin
  pl next of kin

nex·us
  pl nex·us·es
  or nex·us

nic·o·tine

nic·o·tin·ic

nic·o·tin·ism

nic·o·tin·ize
  nic·o·tin·ized
  nic·o·tin·iz·ing

ni·dus
  pl ni·di
  or ni·dus·es

niece

night-blind

night blind·ness

night bolt

night·man
  pl night·men

night·time

ni·hil de·bet

ni·hil di·cit

ni·hil est

ni·hil ha·bet

ni·hil ha·bu·it

ni·hil·ism

ni·hil·ist

nil

nil de·bet

nil di·cit

nip·ple

ni·sei
  pl ni·sei
  also ni·seis

ni·si

ni·si pri·us

ni·tro·ben·zene

ni·tro·cel·lu·lose

ni·tro·cel·lu·los·ic

ni·tro·gen

ni·tro·gen nar·co·sis

ni·trog·e·nous

ni·tro·glyc·er·in

ni·tro·mer·sol

ni·tro·starch

ni·trous

nixe

nob·i·le of·fi·ci·um

no·bill

no·blesse oblige

noct·am·bu·la·tion

noct·am·bule

noct·am·bu·lic
  also noct·am·bu·lis·tic

noct·am·bu·lism

noct·am·bu·list

noc·tiv·a·gant

noc·tiv·a·ga·tion

noc·tu·ria

no·cu·me·tum
noc·u·ous
noc·u·ous·ly
node
nod·ule
no-holds-barred
no·lens vo·lens
no·li me tan·ge·re
   pl no·li mi tan·ge·res
nol·le
  con·ten·de·re
nol·le pros
  nol·le prossed
  nol·le pros·sing
nol·le pro·se·qui
no·lo con·ten·de·re
nol-pros
  nol-prossed
  nol-pros·sing
no·ma
nom de plume
  pl noms de plume
  also nom de plumes

no·men
  pl no·mi·na

no·men
  col·lec·ti·vum
no·men
  gen·er·al·is·si·
  mum
nom·ic
nom·i·nal
nom·i·nate
  nom·i·nat·ed
  nom·i·nat·ing
nom·i·nate·ly

nom·i·na·tim
nom·i·na·tion
nom·i·na·tum
  pl nom·i·na·ta
nom·i·nee
no·moc·ra·cy
no·mog·ra·pher
no·mog·ra·phy
no·mo·log·i·cal
no·mos
  pl no·moi
no·mo·thet·ic
non·abat·able
non·abil·i·ty
  pl non·abil·i·ties
non·ab·so·lute
non·ac·ced·ing
non·ac·cep·tance
non·ac·cept·ed
non·ac·cess
non·ac·qui·es·cence
non·ac·tive
non·ad·min·is·tra·
  tive
non·ad·mit·ted
non·age
non·ag·gre·ga·ble
non·agree·ment
non·ag·ri·cul·tur·al
non·al·co·hol·ic
non·an·ces·tral
non·ap·par·ent
non·ap·pear·ance
non·ap·pli·ca·bil·
  i·ty

non·as·sess·able
non·as·sign·able
non as·sump·sit
non as·sump·sit
  in·fra
non·at·ten·dance
non·bank
non·board
non·busi·ness
non·call·able
non·can·cel·able
  or non·can·cel·la·ble

non·can·cel·la·tion
non·cash
non·cat·e·go·ry
non ce·pit
non·cit·i·zen
non·claim
non·co·hab·i·ta·tion
non·col·lect·ible
non·com·bus·ti·ble
non·com·mer·cial
non·com·mu·nist
  or non-Com·mu·nist

non·com·mu·ni·ty
non·com·pear·ance
non·com·pen·sa·ble
non·com·pen·sa·
  tion
non·com·pen·sa·
  to·ry
non·com·pe·tent
non·com·pet·i·tive
non·com·ple·tion
non·com·pli·ance

non com·pos
  pl non·com·pos·es
  or non·com·pos·ses

non com·pos men·
  tis
non·con·cur
  non·con·curred
  non·con·cur·ring
non·con·cur·rence
non·con·cur·ren·cy
non·con·cur·rent
non·con·fi·dence
non·con·fin·ing
non·con·fis·ca·to·ry
non·con·form·ing
non con·stat
non·con·sum·ma·
  tion
non·con·ten·tious
non·con·test·able
non·con·tig·u·ous
non·con·tin·u·ous
non·con·tra·band
non·con·trac·tu·al
non·con·tra·dic·
  tion
non·con·tra·dic·
  to·ry
non·con·trib·u·
  to·ry
non·crim·i·nal
non·cu·mu·la·tive
non·cus·to·di·al
non dam·ni·fi·ca·
  tus

non·de·duct·ibil·
  i·ty
non·de·duct·ible
non·de·fam·a·to·ry
non·del·e·ga·ble
non·de·lin·quent
non·de·liv·ery
  pl non·de·liv·er·ies

non de·mis·it
non de·pre·cia·ble
non·de·script
non·de·tach·able
non de·ti·net
non·di·rec·tion
non·dis·clo·sure
non·dol·lar
non·du·ra·bles *n pl*
  or non·du·ra·ble goods

non·ef·fec·tive
non·em·ployed
non·em·ploy·ment
non·es·sen·tial
non est
non est fac·tum
  pl non est fac·tums

non est in·ven·tus
  pl non est in·ven·tus·es

none·the·less
non·ex·clud·able
non·ex·clu·sive
non·ex·empt
non·ex·is·tent
non·ex·pert
non·ex·pi·ry
non·ex·plo·sive

non·fea·sance
non·fi·nan·cial
non·flam·ma·ble
non·for·feit·able
non·for·fei·ture
non·free·hold
non·func·tion·al
non·fund·able
non·game
non·gam·ing
non·gov·ern·ment
non·gov·ern·men·
  tal
non gra·ta
non·gra·tu·itous
non·haz·ard·ous
non·im·mi·grant
non·im·por·ta·tion
non·im·put·abil·i·ty
non·im·put·able
non·in·dict·able
non·in·fec·tious
non·in·flam·ma·to·
  ry
non·in·sane
non·in·sti·tu·tion·
  al
non·in·ter·course
non·in·ter·ven·tion
non·in·tox·i·cant
non·in·tox·i·cat·ing
non·in·tru·sion
non in·ven·tus
  pl non in·ven·tus·es

non·in·volve·ment
non·is·su·able

non·join·der
non·ju·di·cial
non·ko·sher
non·law·yer
non·led·ger
non·le·gal
non·li·bel·lous
non li·quet
  pl non li·quets

non·lit·i·gat·ed
non·load-bear·ing
non·mail·able
non·ma·lig·nant
non·ma·rine
non·mar·i·time
non·mar·ket·able
non·med·i·cal
non·mem·ber
non·mer·chant·
  able
non·me·tered
non·mon·e·tary
non·nat·u·ral
non·nav·i·ga·ble
non·ne·ces·si·ty
  pl non·ne·ces·si·ties

non·ne·go·tia·ble
non·neo·plas·tic
non·no·ti·fi·ca·tion
non·oblig·a·to·ry
non·ob·ser·vance
non ob·stan·te
non ob·stan·te ve·
  re·dic·to
non·oc·cu·pa·tion·
  al

non·oc·cu·pi·er
non·oc·cu·py·ing
non·of·fi·cial
non·op·er·at·ing
non·own·er
non·own·ing
non·par
non·par·tic·i·pant
non·par·tic·i·pat·
  ing
non·par·ti·san
non·par·ty
non·pa·ter·ni·ty
non·patho·gen·ic
non·pay·ment
non·pe·cu·ni·ary
non·per·for·mance
non·per·sis·tent
non pla·cet
  pl non pla·cets

non-pla·cet
  non-pla·cet·ed
  non-pla·cet·ing
non pos·su·mus
  pl non pos·su·mes

non·pref·er·ence
non·preg·nant
non·pre·scrip·tion
non·pro·duc·tion
non·prof·it
non·pro·pri·etary
non·pros
  non·prossed
  non·pros·sing
non pro·se·qui·tur
  pl non pro·se·qui·turs

non·prov·en
non·quo·ta
non·re·ceipt
non·re·course
non·rec·ti·fi·ca·tion
non·reg·is·tra·tion
non·reg·u·la·tion
non·re·im·burs·able
non·re·pair
non·res·i·dence
non·res·i·dent
non·res·i·den·tial
non res ju·di·ca·ta
non·re·turn·able
non·rev·e·nue
non·sched·uled
non·self-gov·ern·
  ing
non·sen·si·tive
non·sep·a·ra·ble
non·sep·a·rate
non se·qui·tur
  pl non se·qui·turs

non·spouse
non·stat·u·to·ry
non sui ju·ris
non·suit
non·suit·abil·i·ty
non sum
  in·for·ma·tus
non·sup·port
non·sur·gi·cal
non·tax·able
non-tax-paid
non·ten·ant
non·ten·ure

non·term
non·tox·ic
non·trad·ing
non·trans·fer·able
non·union
non·union·ist
non·use
non·us·er
non·vot·ing
non vult con·ten·
  de·re
    or non vult
    pl non vult con·ten·
      de·res
    or non vults

non·waiv·er
no-par
  or no-par-val·ue
nor·mal
nor·mal·cy
  pl nor·mal·cies
nor·mal·i·ty
  pl nor·mal·i·ties
nor·mal·iza·tion
nor·mal·ize
  nor·mal·ized
  nor·mal·iz·ing
nor·mal·ly
Nor·man-French
nor·mo·ten·sion
nor·mo·ten·sive
north·bound
north·east
north·east·er·ly
north·east·ern
north·east·ward

north·east·ward·ly
north·er·ly
north·ern
north·ward
north·ward·ly
north·west
north·west·er·ly
north·west·ern
north·west·ward
north·west·ward·ly
nos·ci·tur a so·ci·is
nos·o·co·mi·al
noso·geo·graph·ic
  or noso·geo·graph·i·cal
noso·ge·og·ra·phy
  pl noso·ge·og·ra·phies
nos·tril
nos·trum
no·tan·dum
  pl no·tan·da
  also no·tan·dums
no·tar·i·al
no·tar·i·al·ly
no·ta·ri·za·tion
no·ta·rize
  no·ta·rized
  no·ta·riz·ing
no·ta·ry
  pl no·ta·ries
no·ta·ry pub·lic
  pl no·ta·ries pub·lic
  or no·ta·ry pub·lics
no·ta·ry·ship
no·tate
  no·tat·ed
  no·tat·ing

no·ta·tion
note
  not·ed
  not·ing
note of hand
note pay·able
  pl notes pay·able

note re·ceiv·able
  pl notes re·ceiv·able

not guilty
no·tice
  no·ticed
  no·tic·ing
no·ti·fi·able
no·ti·fi·ca·tion
no·ti·fy
  no·ti·fied
  no·ti·fy·ing
no·tion·al
no·tion·al·ly
no·to·ri·ety
  pl no·to·ri·eties
no·to·ri·ous
no·to·ri·ous·ly
no·tour
not proved
  or not prov·en

not·with·stand·ing
no·va·lia *n pl*
no·vate
  no·vat·ed
  no·vat·ing

no·va·tion
nov·el
nov·el·ty
   pl nov·el·ties

no·vo·caine
no·wise
noxa
   pl nox·ae

nox·ae de·di·tio
nox·al
nox·ious
nox·ious·ness
nu·bile
nu·bil·i·ty
   pl nu·bil·i·ties

nu·cha
   pl nu·chae

nu·cle·ar
nu·cle·us
   pl nu·clei
   also nu·cle·us·es

nude
nu·dum pac·tum
   pl nu·da pac·ta

nu·ga·to·ry
nui·sance
null
nul·la bo·na
null and void
nul·li·fi·ca·tion
nul·li·fi·ca·tor
nul·li·fi·er
nul·li·fy
   nul·li·fied
   nul·li·fy·ing

nul·li·grav·i·da
   pl nul·li·grav·i·das
   also nul·li·grav·i·dae

nul·lip·a·ra
   pl nul·lip·a·ras
   also nul·lip·a·rae

nul·lip·a·rous
nul·li·ty
   pl nul·li·ties

nul·li·us fi·li·us
nul·li·us ju·ris
nul·lo est er·ra·tum
nul tiel rec·ord
nul tort
numb
num·bers game
   also num·bers pool
   or num·bers rack·et

numb·ness
nu·me·rus clau·sus
num·mu·lar
nun·cio
   pl nun·ci·os

nunc pro tunc
nun·cu·pan·do
nun·cu·pate
   nun·cu·pat·ed
   nun·cu·pat·ing

nun·cu·pa·tion
nun·cu·pa·tive
nun·quam in·deb·i·ta·tus
nup·tial
nur·ture
   nur·tured

nur·tur·ing
nu·tri·ent
nu·tri·ment
nu·tri·tion
nu·tri·tion·al
nu·tri·tion·al·ly
nu·tri·tion·ist
nu·tri·tious
nu·tri·tive
nux vom·i·ca
   pl nux vom·i·ca

nym·pha
   pl nym·phae

nymph·et
nym·pho·ma·nia
nym·pho·ma·ni·ac
   also nym·pho·ma·ni·a·cal

nys·tag·mic
nys·tag·moid
nys·tag·mus
nyx·is
   pl nyx·es

O

oath
   pl oaths

ob con·tin·gen·ti·am
ob·du·ra·cy
   pl ob·du·ra·cies

ob·du·rate
ob·du·rat·ed
ob·du·rat·ing

ob·du·rate·ness
ob·du·ra·tion
obe·ah
obe·di·ence
obe·di·ent
obe·di·en·tial
obe·di·ent·ly
obe·si·ty
   pl obe·si·ties

obey
  obeyed
  obey·ing
obey·able
obey·ance
obey·er
ob·fusc
ob·fus·ca·ble
ob·fus·cate
  ob·fus·cat·ed
  ob·fus·cat·ing
ob·fus·ca·tion
ob·fus·ca·tor
ob·fus·ca·to·ry
obit
obi·ter
obi·ter dic·tum
  pl obi·ter dic·ta

obit·u·al
obit·u·ary
  pl obit·u·ar·ies

ob·ject
ob·ject·ant
ob·jec·tee
ob·jec·tion
ob·jec·tion·abil·i·ty
  pl ob·jec·tion·abil·i·ties

ob·jec·tion·able
ob·jec·tion·al
ob·jec·tive
ob·jec·tive·ly
ob·jec·tive·ness
ob·jec·tiv·i·ty
ob·jec·tor
ob·ji·cient
ob·ju·ra·tion
obla·tio
  pl obla·tio·nes

ob·li·ga·bil·i·ty
ob·li·ga·ble
ob·li·gant
ob·li·gate
  ob·li·gat·ed
  ob·li·gat·ing
ob·li·ga·tio ci·vi·lis
ob·li·ga·tion
ob·li·ga·tion·al
ob·li·ga·tive
ob·li·ga·tor
oblig·a·to·ry
oblige
  obliged
  oblig·ing
ob·li·gee
oblige·ment
oblig·er
  one who obliges
  (see obligor)

ob·li·gor
  one who writes a
  surety bond
  (see obliger)

oblique

oblit·er·ate
  oblit·er·at·ed
  oblit·er·at·ing
oblit·er·a·tion
oblit·er·a·tive
oblit·er·a·tor
obliv·i·on
obliv·i·ous
ob·li·vis·cence
ob·lo·cu·tor
ob·lo·quy
  pl ob·lo·quies

ob·nox·i·e·ty
  pl ob·nox·i·e·ties

ob·nox·ious
ob·rep·tion
ob·rep·ti·tious
ob·ro·gate
  ob·ro·gat·ed
  ob·ro·gat·ing
  to alter or repeal
  (see abrogate)

ob·ro·ga·tion
ob·scene
ob·scen·i·ty
  pl ob·scen·i·ties

ob·scur·ant
ob·scu·ran·tism
  also ob·scu·ran·ti·cism

ob·scu·ra·tion
ob·scu·ra·tive
ob·scure
  ob·scured
  ob·scur·ing
ob·scure·ment

ob·scu·ri·ty
  pl ob·scu·ri·ties

ob·serv·able

ob·ser·vance
  pl ob·ser·vanc·es

ob·ser·vant

ob·ser·va·tion

ob·serve
  ob·served
  ob·serv·ing

ob·serv·er

ob·sess

ob·ses·sion

ob·ses·sion·al

ob·ses·sive

ob·ses·sive·ly

ob·ses·sive·ness

ob·sig·na·tion

ob·sig·na·to·ry
  pl ob·sig·na·to·ries

ob·so·les·cence

ob·so·les·cent

ob·so·lete

ob·sta·cle

ob·stan·te

ob·sta prin·ci·pi·is

ob·stet·ric

ob·stet·ri·cal

ob·ste·tri·cian

ob·stet·rics

ob·sti·na·cy
  pl ob·sti·na·cies

ob·sti·nate

ob·strep·er·ous

ob·struct

ob·struc·tion

ob·struc·tion·ist

ob·struc·tive

ob·struc·tive·ness

ob·struc·tor

ob·tain

ob·tain·ment

ob·tem·per

ob·ten·tion

ob·test

ob·tes·ta·tion

ob·ven·tio

ob·ven·tion

ob·vi·ous

oc·ca·sion

oc·ca·sion·al

oc·cip·i·tal

oc·ci·put
  pl oc·ci·puts
  or oc·cip·i·ta

oc·clude
  oc·clud·ed
  oc·clud·ing

oc·clu·sal

oc·clu·sion

oc·cult

oc·cu·pance

oc·cu·pan·cy
  pl oc·cu·pan·cies

oc·cu·pant

oc·cu·pa·tile

oc·cu·pa·tio bel·li

oc·cu·pa·tion

oc·cu·pa·tion·al

oc·cu·pa·tion·al
  dis·ease

oc·cu·pa·tion·al·ly

oc·cu·pa·tio pa·ci·
  fi·ca

oc·cu·pa·tive

oc·cu·pi·able

oc·cu·pi·er

oc·cu·py
  oc·cu·pied
  oc·cu·py·ing

oc·cur
  oc·curred
  oc·cur·ring

oc·cur·rence

ocean·go·ing

och·loc·ra·cy

och·lo·crat·ic

oc·ta·vo

oc·to·dec·i·mo

oc·to·ge·nar·i·an

oc·to·roon

oc·to ta·les

oc·troi

oc·troy
  oc·troyed
  oc·troy·ing

oc·u·lar

oc·u·lau·di·to·ry

oc·u·list

odd-job

odd lot

odd·ment

odi·ous

odi·um

odon·toid

oe·de·ma
  var of edema

oe·di·pal

Oe·di·pus com·
   plex
   pl Oe·di·pus com·
   plex·es

oe·soph·a·ge·al
   var of esophageal

oe·soph·a·gus
   var of esophagus

oes·tro·gen
   var of estrogen

oes·tro·gen·ic
   var of estrogenic

oes·tru·al
   var of estrual

oes·trus,
   oes·trum
   vars of estrus

of course
of·fal
off-board
off-col·or
   or off-col·ored

off·cut
of·fend
of·fend·er
of·fense
   or of·fence

of·fense·less
of·fen·sive
of·fer
   of·fered
   of·fer·ing
of·fer·able
of·fer·ee
of·fer·er
   or of·fer·or

off-fla·vor
off-go·ing
off-grade
off hire
off-hour
of·fice
of·fice copy
of·fice found
of·fice·hold·er
of·fi·cer
of·fi·cial
of·fi·ci·al·i·ty
   pl of·fi·ci·al·i·ties

of·fi·cial·ly
of·fi·ci·ate
   of·fi·ci·at·ed
   of·fi·ci·at·ing

of·fi·ci·a·tion
of·fi·ci·a·tor
of·fi·ci·na jus·ti·
   ti·ae
of·fi·ci·nal
of·fi·ci·nal·ly
of·fi·cious
off-li·cense
off lim·its
off-list
off-odor
off-peak
off-sale
off·set
   off·set
   off·set·ting

off·set well
off·shore
off·spring

off-street
off-take
off-taste
oil and gas lease
oint·ment
old-line
ole·an·der
olec·ra·nal
olec·ra·non
ole·om·e·ter
oleo·tho·rax
   pl oleo·tho·rax·es
   or oleo·tho·ra·ces

ol·fac·tion
ol·fac·to·met·ric
ol·fac·tom·e·try
   pl ol·fac·tom·e·tries

ol·fac·to·ry
oli·gar·chy
   pl oli·gar·chies

ol·i·ge·mia
ol·i·ge·mic
oli·go·cy·the·mia
oli·go·cy·the·mic
oli·gop·o·list
oli·gop·o·ly
   pl oli·gop·o·lies

oli·gop·so·nist
oli·gop·so·ny
   pl oli·gop·so·nies

oli·go·sper·mat·ic
oli·go·sper·mia
ol·i·gu·ria
olo·graph
omen·tum
   pl omen·ta
   or omen·tums

omis·sion
omit
  omit·ted
  omit·ting
omit·tance
om·nia per·for·
  ma·vit
om·ni·bus
om·ni·com·pe·tence
om·ni·com·pe·tent
om·ni·um
om·ni·um
  bo·no·rum
onan·ism
onan·ist
onan·is·tic
on·co·gen·e·sis
  pl on·co·gen·e·ses

on·co·gen·ic
on·co·ge·nic·i·ty
  pl on·co·ge·nic·i·ties

on·cot·o·my
  pl on·cot·o·mies

one-par·ty
oner·os·i·ty
  pl oner·os·i·ties

oner·ous
oner·ous·ly
oner·ous·ness
one-to-one
on·li·cense
on lim·its
on·o·mas·tic
on pain of
  or un·der pain of
  also up·on pain of

on-sale
on-shore
onus
onus pro·ban·di
onus pro·cen·di
on·y·mous
oo·pho·rec·to·mize
oo·pho·rec·to·
  mized
oo·pho·rec·to·
  miz·ing
oo·pho·rec·to·my
  pl oo·pho·rec·to·mies

opaci·fi·ca·tion
opac·i·ty
  pl opac·i·ties

ope et con·si·lio
  or ope con·si·lio

open
open-and-shut
open door *n*
open-door *adj*
open-end
open-heart
open·ing
open·ly
open mar·ket *n*
open-mar·ket *adj*
open sea
open shop
op·er·a·bil·i·ty
  pl op·er·a·bil·i·ties

op·er·a·ble
op·er·a·bly
op·er·ance

op·er·ate
  op·er·at·ed
  op·er·at·ing
op·er·a·tion
op·er·a·tion·al
op·er·a·tive
op·er·a·tor
ope·re ci·ta·to
ophe·lim·i·ty
oph·thal·mia
oph·thal·mia neo·
  na·to·rum
oph·thal·mic
oph·thal·mo·log·ic
  also oph·thal·mo·log·
  i·cal

oph·thal·mol·o·gist
oph·thal·mol·o·gy
  pl oph·thal·mol·o·gies

opi·ate
  opi·at·ed
  opi·at·ing
opine
  opined
  opin·ing
opin·ion
opis·tho·ton·ic
opis·thot·o·nos
opi·um
op·pi·dan
op·po·nent
op·por·tune
op·por·tun·ism
op·por·tu·ni·ty
  pl op·por·tu·ni·ties

op·pos·abil·i·ty
  pl op·pos·abil·i·ties

op·pos·able
op·pose
  op·posed
  op·pos·ing
op·po·site
op·po·si·tion
op·press
op·pres·sion
op·pres·sive
op·pres·sor
op·pro·bri·ate
  op·pro·bri·at·ed
  op·pro·bri·at·ing
op·pro·bri·ous
op·pro·bri·um
op·pugn
op·ti·cal
op·ti·cian
op·tion
op·tion·al
op·tion·ee
op·tion·or
op·tom·e·ter
op·to·met·ric
  also op·to·met·ri·cal

op·tom·e·trist
op·tom·e·try
  pl op·tom·e·tries

opus ci·ta·tum
  pl ope·ra ci·ta·ta

opus ope·ran·tis
  pl ope·ra ope·ran·tes

opus ope·ra·tum
  pl ope·ra ope·ra·ta

oral

oral·ly
or·bit
or·bit·al
or·chi·dec·to·my
  pl or·chi·dec·to·mies

or·chi·ec·to·my
  also or·chec·to·my
  pl or·chi·ec·to·mies
  also or·chec·to·mies

or·chit·ic
or·chi·tis
or·dain
or·der
or·der-in-coun·cil
or·der pro con·
  fes·so
or·di·nance
  a law, rule, or decree
  (see ordnance, ordon-
  nance*)*

or·di·nan·di lex
or·di·nary
  pl or·di·nar·ies

ord·nance
  military supplies
  (see ordinance, ordon-
  nance*)*

or·don·nance
  a compilation of laws
  (see ordinance, ord-
  nance*)*

ore-leave
ore te·nus
or·gan
or·gan·ic
or·gan·i·cal·ly
or·ga·ni·za·tion
or·ga·nize

or·ga·nized
or·ga·niz·ing
or·ga·niz·er
or·gan·o·lep·tic
or·gan·o·ther·a·
  peu·tic
or·gan·o·ther·a·py
  pl or·gan·o·ther·a·pies

or·gasm
or·gas·mic
  or or·gas·tic

or·gi·as·tic
  also or·gi·as·ti·cal

or·gy
  pl or·gies

or·i·fice
or·i·fi·cial
or·i·gin
orig·i·nal
orig·i·nal·i·ty
  pl orig·i·nal·i·ties

orig·i·nate
  orig·i·nat·ed
  orig·i·nat·ing
orig·i·na·tion
or·i·gin-of-in·tent
  test
oro·pha·ryn·geal
oro·phar·ynx
  pl oro·pha·ryn·ges
  also oro·phar·ynx·es

or·phan
  or·phaned
  or·phan·ing
or·phan's court
orth·odon·tia

orth·odon·tic
orth·odon·tics
orth·odon·tist
or·tho·pe·dic
  also or·tho·pae·dic

or·tho·pe·dics
  also or·tho·pae·dics

or·tho·pe·dist
or·thop·nea
  also or·thop·noea

or·thop·ne·ic
  also or·thop·noe·ic

or·tho·praxy
  pl or·tho·prax·ies

or·tho·sis
  pl or·tho·ses

or·thot·ic
or·thot·ics
or·tho·tist
or·to·la·gi·um
os
  pl os·sa
  bone

os
  pl ora
  mouth

os cox·ae
  pl os·sa cox·ae

os·phre·sis
os·phret·ic
os·seo·car·ti·lag·i·nous
os·se·ous
os·si·cle
os·si·cu·lec·to·my
  pl os·si·cu·lec·to·mies

os·si·cu·lot·o·my
  pl os·si·cu·lot·o·mies

os·sic·u·lum
  pl os·sic·u·la

os·si·fi·ca·tion
os·si·fy
  os·si·fied
  os·si·fy·ing
os·tal·gia
os·te·it·ic
os·te·itis
  pl os·te·it·i·des

os·te·itis
  de·for·mans
os·te·itis fi·bro·sa
os·ten·si·bil·i·ty
  pl os·ten·si·bil·i·ties

os·ten·si·ble
os·teo·ar·thrit·ic
os·teo·ar·thri·tis
  pl os·teo·ar·thrit·i·des

os·teo·car·ti·lag·i·nous
os·teo·chon·dri·tis
os·teo·chon·dro·ma
  pl os·teo·chon·dro·mas
  also os·teo·chon·dro·ma·ta

os·teo·chon·dro·ma·to·sis
os·teo·chon·dro·sar·co·ma
  pl os·teo·chon·dro·sar·co·mas
  or os·teo·chon·dro·sar·co·ma·ta

os·teo·chon·dro·sis
  pl os·teo·con·dro·ses

os·teo·chon·drot·ic
os·te·oc·la·sis
os·teo·dyn·ia
os·te·o·log·ic
  or os·te·o·log·i·cal

os·te·o·log·i·cal·ly
os·te·ol·o·gist
os·te·ol·o·gy
  pl os·te·ol·o·gies

os·teo·ma·la·cia
os·teo·my·eli·tis
os·teo·path
os·teo·path·ic
os·teo·path·i·cal·ly
os·te·op·a·thist
os·te·op·a·thy
  pl os·te·op·a·thies

os·teo·po·ro·sis
  pl os·teo·po·ro·ses

os·teo·po·rot·ic
os·teo·ra·dio·ne·cro·sis
  pl os·teo·ra·dio·ne·cro·ses

os·teo·sar·co·ma
  pl os·teo·sar·co·mas
  or os·teo·sar·co·ma·ta

os·tra·cism
os·tra·cize
  os·tra·cized
  os·tra·ciz·ing
os uteri
otal·gia

otal·gic
oth·er·wise
otic
otit·ic
oti·tis
   pl otit·i·des

oto·lar·yn·go·log·
  i·cal
oto·lar·yn·gol·o·
  gist
oto·lar·yn·gol·o·gy
  pl oto·lar·yn·gol·o·gies

oto·log·ic
  also oto·log·i·cal

oto·log·i·cal·ly
otol·o·gist
otol·o·gy
  pl otol·o·gies

oto·rhi·no·lar·yn·
  gol·o·gy
    pl oto·rhi·no·lar·yn·
    gol·o·gies

oust
oust·er
oust·er in pais
oust·er le main
out
out·age
out·board
out·bound
out-bound·ary
  pl out-bound·aries

out·break
out·build·ing
out·cast

out·come-
  de·ter·mi·
  na·tive
out·crop
out·cry
  pl out·cries

out·go
  pl out·goes

out·go·er
out·go·ings
out·house
  pl out·hous·es

out·law
out·law·ry
  pl out·law·ries

out·lay
out·let
out·li·er
out·line
out·lot
out·ly·ing
out-of-court
out-of-pock·et
out-of-state
out·pa·tient
out·pay·ment
out·put
out·rage
  out·raged
  out·rag·ing
out·ra·geous
out·right
out·set
out·side
out·stand·ing

out·stroke
out·work·er
ovar·i·al
ovar·i·an
ovari·ec·to·mize
  ovari·ec·to·
  mized
  ovari·ec·to·miz·
  ing
ovari·ec·to·my
  pl ovari·ec·to·mies

ovari·o·hys·ter·ec·
  to·my
    pl ovari·o·hys·ter·ec·
    to·mies

ovari·ot·o·my
  pl ovari·ot·o·mies

ova·ry
  pl ova·ries

over·age
over and above
over·as·sess·ment
over·breadth
over·bur·den
over·charge
  over·charged
  over·charg·ing
over·claim
over·come
  over·came
  over·come
  over·com·ing
over·com·pen·sate
  over·com·pen·
  sat·ed

over·com·pen·
  sat·ing
over·com·pen·sa·
  tion
over·cor·rect
over·cor·rec·tion
over·dos·age
over·dose
  over·dosed
  over·dos·ing
over·draft
over·draw
  over·drew
  over·drawn
  over·draw·ing
over·due
over·ex·er·tion
over·ex·tend
over·ex·ten·sion
over·flow
over·freight
over·head
over·in·sur·ance
over·in·sured
over·is·sue
  over·is·sued
  over·is·su·ing
over·lap
  over·lapped
  over·lap·ping
over·lease
over·lie
  over·lay
  over·lain
  over·ly·ing
over·load

over·look
over·man
  pl over·men

over·pay
  over·paid
  over·pay·ing
  over·pay·ment
over·plus
over·rate
  over·rat·ed
  over·rat·ing
over·reach
over·ride
  over·rode
  over·rid·den
  over·rid·ing
over·rule
  over·ruled
  over·rul·ing
over·run
  over·ran
  over·run·ning
over·see
  over·saw
  over·seen
  over·see·ing
over·seer
over·seer·ship
over·sell
  over·sold
  over·sell·ing
over·sight
overs·man
  pl overs·men

overt
  not concealed
  (*see* avert)

over-the-count·er
over-the-road
over·throw
  over·threw
  over·thrown
  over·throw·ing
over·throw·al
over·throw·er
over·time
over·trade
  over·trad·ed
  over·trad·ing
over·ture
over·turn
over·valu·ation
over·val·ue
  over·val·ued
  over·valu·ing
over·writ·ing
  com·mis·sion
owe
  owed
  ow·ing
ow·el·ty
  pl ow·el·ties

own
own·er
own·er·less
own·er pro hac
  vi·ce
own·er·ship
ox·y·gen·ize
oxy·he·mo·glo·bin

oxy·myo·glo·bin
oy·er
oy·er and
  ter·mi·ner
oyez
  pl oyes·ses

oys·tery
  pl oys·ter·ies

P

pace·mak·er
pachy·men·in·gi·tis
  pl pachy·men·in·git·i·
    des

pachy·me·ninx
  pl pachy·me·nin·ges

pac·i·fi·ca·tion
pac·i·fism
pac·i·fist
pack
pack·age
pack·aged
packed
  filled to capacity
  (*see* pact)

pact
  an agreement or un-
    derstanding
  (*see* packed)

pac·tion
pac·tum
  also pac·tio
  pl pac·ta
  also pac·tio·nes

paed·er·ast
  var of pederast

paed·er·as·ty
  var of pederasty

pae·di·at·ric
  var of pediatric

pae·di·at·rics
  var of pediatrics

paed·i·ca·tio
  var of pedicatio

pae·do·phil·ia
  var of pedophilia

Pag·et's dis·ease
paid-up
pain
pain·kill·er
pain·kill·ing
pais
pal·a·tal
pal·ate
pal·a·tine
pal·a·to·max·il·lary
pal·a·to·na·sal
pal·a·to·pha·ryn·
  geal
pal·a·to·prox·i·mal
pali·la·lia
pal·in·drom·ic
pal·in·drom·i·cal·ly
pall·an·es·the·sia
pall·es·the·sia
pal·li·ate
  pal·li·at·ed
  pal·li·at·ing
pal·li·a·tion

pal·lia·tive
pal·lia·tive·ly
pal·mar
palm·ing off
  doc·trine
palm·ist·ry
pal·pa·ble
pal·pa·bly
pal·pate
  pal·pat·ed
  pal·pat·ing
pal·pa·tion
pal·pe·bra
  pl pal·pe·brae

pal·pe·bral
pal·pi·tate
  pal·pi·tat·ed
  pal·pi·tat·ing
pal·pi·ta·tion
pal·sied
pal·sy
  pl pal·sies

pal·try
  also paul·try

pam·a·quine
  also pam·a·quin

pam·phlet
pan·ag·glu·ti·na·
  bil·i·ty
  pl pan·ag·glu·ti·na·
    bil·i·ties

pan·ag·glu·ti·na·ble
pan·ag·glu·ti·na·
  tion
pan·ar·thri·tis
  pl pan·ar·thrit·i·des

pan·at·ro·phy
  pl pan·at·ro·phies
pan·car·di·tis
pan·cre·as
pan·cre·at·ic
pan·cre·ati·tis
  pl pan·cre·atit·i·des
pan·cy·to·pe·nia
pan·cy·to·pe·nic
pan·dem·ic
pan·der
  or pan·der·er
  also pan·dor
pan·der·ing
pan·der·ism
pan·el
pan·en·do·scope
pan·en·do·scop·ic
pan·en·dos·co·py
  pl pan·en·dos·co·pies
pan·glos·sia
pan·hys·ter·ec·to·
  my
  pl pan·hys·ter·ec·to·
    mies
pan·my·eloid
pan·my·elop·a·thy
  pl pan·my·elop·a·thies
pan·nage
pan·to·the·nate
pan·to·then·ic
pa·pa·in
Pa·pa·ni·co·laou
  test
pa·pav·er·ine
pa·per

pa·pil·la
  pl pa·pil·lae
pap·il·lar
pap·il·lary
pa·pil·late
  or pa·pil·lat·ed
pap·ill·ede·ma
  also pap·ill·oe·de·ma
  pl pap·ill·ede·mas
  or pap·ill·ede·ma·ta
  also pap·ill·oe·de·mas
  or pap·ill·oe·de·ma·ta
pap·il·li·tis
pap·il·lo·ma
  pl pap·il·lo·mas
  or pap·il·lo·ma·ta
Pap smear
  also Pap test
pap·u·lar
pap·u·la·tion
pap·ule
pap·u·lo·pus·tu·lar
para
  pl par·as
  or par·ae
para-ami·no·ben·
  zo·ic
para·an·es·the·sia
para·bu·lia
para·cen·te·sis
  pl para·cen·te·ses
pa·rach·ro·nism
para·col·pi·tis
par·a·col·pi·um
par·acu·sia
  or par·acu·sis
  pl par·acu·sias
  or par·acu·ses

par·a·dox
par·aes·the·sia
  var of paresthesia
par·aes·thet·ic
  var of paresthetic
par·af·fin
  also par·af·fine
par·af·fin·oma
  pl par·af·fin·omas
  or par·af·fin·oma·ta
para·func·tion
para·gam·ma·cism
  also para·gam·ma·cis·
    mus
  pl para·gam·ma·cisms
  also para·gam·ma·cis·
    mus·es
par·age
para·geu·sia
para·gram·ma·tism
para·graph
para·graph·ia
para·in·flu·en·za
para·ki·ne·sia
  or para·ki·ne·sis
  pl para·ki·ne·sias
  or para·ki·ne·ses
para·ki·net·ic
para·la·lia
par·al·de·hyde
para·lex·ia
para·lex·ic
par·al·ge·sia
par·al·ge·sic
par·al·lel
pa·ral·y·sis
  pl pa·ral·y·ses

pa·ral·y·sis agi·
tans
par·a·lyt·ic
  also par·a·lyt·i·cal

par·a·ly·zant
  also par·a·ly·sant

par·a·ly·za·tion
par·a·lyze
  also par·a·lyse
par·a·lyzed
  also par·a·lysed
par·a·lyz·ing
  also par·a·lys·ing

para·mas·toid
para·med·ic
para·med·i·cal
para·metha·di·one
par·am·ne·sia
par·a·mount
par·amour
para·noia
para·noi·ac
para·no·ic
para·noid
para·no·mia
para·nor·mal
para·nor·mal·i·ty
para·nor·mal·ly
para·pa·re·sis
  pl para·pa·re·ses

pa·raph
par·a·pha·sia
par·a·pha·sic
par·a·pher·na
par·a·pher·nal
par·a·pher·na·lia

para·phil·ia
para·phil·i·ac
para·pho·nia
  pl para·pho·nias
  also para·phon·i·ae

para·ple·gia
para·ple·gic
par·ap·o·plexy
  pl par·ap·o·plex·ies

para·prax·ia
  or para·prax·is
  pl para·prax·ias
  or para·prax·es

para·psy·cho·log·
  i·cal
para·psy·chol·o·
  gist
para·psy·chol·o·gy
  pl para·psy·chol·o·gies

para·sa·cral
para·sex·u·al
para·sex·u·al·i·ty
  pl para·sex·u·al·i·ties

par·a·site
par·a·sit·ic
  also par·a·sit·i·cal

par·a·sit·i·cal·ly
par·a·sit·i·cid·al
  also par·a·sit·i·cid·ic

par·a·sit·i·cide
par·a·sit·ism
par·a·sit·ize
  par·a·sit·ized
  par·a·sit·iz·ing
para·sym·pa·thet·ic

para·sym·pa·thet·i·
  co·mi·met·ic
para·sym·pa·tho·
  lyt·ic
para·sym·pa·tho·
  mi·met·ic
para·syph·i·lit·ic
para·thi·on
para·tu·ber·cu·lo·
  sis
para·ure·thral
para·vag·i·nal
para·vag·i·ni·tis
par·cel
  par·celed
  or par·celled
  par·cel·ing
  or par·cel·ling

par·ce·nary
  pl par·ce·na·ries

par·ce·ner
par·co frac·to
par de·lic·tum
par·don
  par·doned
  par·don·ing
par·don·able
par·ec·ta·sis
  or par·ec·ta·sia
  pl par·ec·ta·ses
  or par·ec·ta·sias

par·e·gor·ic
par·en·chy·ma
  also par·en·chyme

par·en·chy·ma·tous
  or par·en·chy·mat·ic

pa·rens pa·tri·ae
par·ent
par·ent·age
pa·ren·tal
par·en·te·la
par·en·tel·ic
par·en·ter·al
par·en·ter·al·ly
par·en·the·sis
   pl par·en·the·ses

par·en·thet·i·cal
par·ent·hood
pa·ren·ti·cide
par·ent-in-law
   pl par·ents-in-law

pa·re·sis
   pl pa·re·ses

par·es·the·sia
   also par·aes·the·sia

par·es·thet·ic
   also par·aes·thet·ic

pa·ret·ic
pa·ri cau·sa
pa·ri de·lic·to
pa·ri·etal
pa·ri ma·te·ria
pari-mu·tu·el
   pl pari-mu·tu·els
   or par·is-mu·tu·els

pa·ri pas·su
par·ish
pa·rish·io·ner
par·i·ty
   pl par·i·ties

pa·ri·um ju·di·cium

park
park·ing
par·kin·so·nian
par·kin·son·ism
park·way
par·lay
par·lia·ment
par·lia·men·ta·ry
pa·ro·chi·al
par·odon·tal
par·odon·ti·tis
   pl par·odon·tit·i·des

par·ol
   an oral statement
   (*see* parole)

pa·rol·able
pa·role
   conditional release
   (*see* parol)

pa·rol·ee
par·o·nych·ia
par·o·nych·i·al
par·oph·thal·mia
par·o·rex·ia
par·os·mia
par·ot·id
par·ous
par·ox·ysm
par·ox·ys·mal
par·ox·ys·mic
par·ri·cid·al
par·ri·cide
pars
   pl par·tes

pars pro to·to
par·tial

par·tial·i·ty
   pl par·tial·i·ties

par·tial·ly
par·ti·bil·i·ty
par·ti·ble
par·ti·ceps
   cri·mi·nis
par·ti·ceps do·li
par·tic·i·pant
par·tic·i·pate
   par·tic·i·pat·ed
   par·tic·i·pat·ing
par·tic·i·pa·tion
par·tic·u·lar
par·ti·do
par·ties
   pl of party

par·ti-mort·gage
par·ti·san
   or par·ti·zan

par·tite
par·ti·tion
part·ner
part·ner in com·
   men·dam
part·ner·ship
part-time
part-tim·er
par·tu·ri·ent
par·tu·ri·fa·cient
par·tu·ri·tion
par·ty
   pl parties

par·ty wall
pass·able
pass·ably

pas·sage
pas·sage·way
pass·book
pas·sen·ger
pass·er·by
  pl pass·ers·by

pas·sion
pas·sive
pass·port
pass·way
pas·teu·rel·la
  pl pas·teu·rel·las
  or pas·teu·rel·lae

pas·teu·rel·lo·sis
  pl pas·teu·rel·lo·ses

pas·teur·iza·tion
pas·teur·ize
  pas·teur·ized
  pas·teur·iz·ing
pas·teur·iz·er
Pas·teur treat·
  ment
pas·tur·age
pas·ture
  pas·tured
  pas·tur·ing
pa·tel·la
  pl pa·tel·lae
  or pa·tel·las

pa·tel·lar
pat·el·lec·to·my
  pl pat·el·lec·to·mies

pa·ten·cy
  pl pa·ten·cies

pa·tens
pat·ent

pat·ent·abil·i·ty
pat·ent·able
pat·ent·ably
pat·en·tee
pat·ent·ly
pat·en·tor
pa·ter·fa·mil·i·as
  pl pa·tres·fa·mil·i·as

pa·ter·nal
pa·ter·nal·ism
pa·ter·ni·ty
  pl pa·ter·ni·ties

patho·gen
  also patho·gene

patho·gen·e·sis
  pl patho·gen·e·ses

patho·ge·net·ic
patho·gen·ic
patho·gen·i·cal·ly
patho·ge·nic·i·ty
  pl patho·ge·nic·i·ties

patho·log·i·cal
  or patho·log·ic

patho·log·i·cal·ly
pa·thol·o·gist
pa·thol·o·gy
  pl pa·thol·o·gies

patho·phys·i·o·log·
  i·cal
    or patho·phys·i·o·
    log·ic

patho·phys·i·ol·
  o·gy
    pl patho·phys·i·ol·
    o·gies

pa·tho·sis
  pl pa·tho·ses

pa·tient
pat·ri·cid·al
pat·ri·cide
pat·ri·lin·eal
pat·ri·lin·ear
pat·ri·li·ny
  pl pat·ri·li·nies

pat·ri·lo·cal
pat·ri·lo·cal·i·ty
pat·ri·mo·ni·al
pat·ri·mo·ni·al·ly
pat·ri·mo·ny
  pl pat·ri·mo·nies

pa·trol
  pa·trolled
  pa·trol·ling
pa·trol·man
  pl pa·trol·men

pa·trol·wom·an
  pl pa·trol·wom·en

pa·tron
pa·tron·age
pa·tron·ize
  pa·tron·ized
  pa·tron·iz·ing
paul·try
  var of paltry

pau·per
pave
  paved
  pav·ing
pave·ment
pawn

pawn·age
pawn·bro·ker
pawn·bro·king
pay
    paid
    pay·ing
pay·abil·i·ty
pay·able
pay-as-you-go
pay back *vb*
pay·back *n*
pay·ee
pay·er
    also pay·or
pay·mas·ter
pay·ment
pay off *vb*
pay·off *n or adj*
pay out *vb*
pay·out *n*
pay·roll
Pea·body-Dim·mock for·mu·la
peace
peace·able
peace·ably
peace·ful
peace·ful·ly
pec·to·ral
pec·tor·al·gia
pec·u·late
    pec·u·lat·ed
    pec·u·lat·ing
pec·u·la·tion
pec·u·la·tor
pe·cu·liar

pe·cu·li·um
    pl pe·cu·lia

pe·cu·li·um
    ad·ven·ti·ci·um
pe·cu·nia
pe·cu·ni·ari·ly
pe·cu·ni·ary
ped·al
    *relating to the foot or a
    pedal*
    (*see* peddle)

ped·dle
    ped·dled
    ped·dling
    *to travel about and sell
    goods*
    (*see* pedal)

ped·dler
ped·er·ast
    also paed·er·ast

ped·er·as·tic
ped·er·as·ti·cal·ly
ped·er·as·ty
    also paed·er·as·ty
    pl ped·er·as·ties
    also paed·er·as·ties

pe·des·tri·an
pe·di·at·ric
    also pae·di·at·ric

pe·di·a·tri·cian
pe·di·at·rics
    also pae·di·at·rics

ped·i·ca·tio
    also paed·i·ca·tio

pe·dic·u·lar
pe·dic·u·lo·sis
    pl pe·dic·u·lo·ses

pe·dic·u·lous
pe·dic·u·lus
    pl pe·dic·u·li
    or pe·dic·u·lus

ped·i·gree
pe·dis pos·ses·sio
pe·do·phile
pe·do·phil·ia
    or pae·do·phil·ia

pe·do·phil·i·ac
    or pe·do·phil·ic

peep·ing tom
peer
    one of equal standing
    (*see* pier)

pel·la·gra
pel·la·grous
pel·vic
pel·vis
    pl pel·vis·es
    or pel·ves

pel·vi·sa·cral
pem·phi·gus
    pl pem·phi·gus·es
    or pem·phi·gi

pe·nal
    relating to punishment
    (*see* penial)

pe·nal·ize
    pe·nal·ized
    pe·nal·iz·ing
pen·al·ty
    pl pen·al·ties

pen·den·cy
pen·dent
    or pen·dant

pen·den·te li·te

pend·ing
pen·e·trate
  pen·e·trat·ed
  pen·e·trat·ing
pen·e·tra·tion
pe·ni·al
  relating to the penis
  (see penal)

pen·i·cil·lin
pe·nile
pe·nis
  pl pe·nes
  or pe·nis·es

pen·i·ten·tia·ry
  pl pen·i·ten·tia·ries

Penn·syl·va·nia
  rule
pen·sion
pen·sion·able
pen·sion·er
pe·on·age
peo·til·lo·ma·nia
pep·tic
per ac·ci·dens
per·acute
per·am·bu·late
  per·am·bu·lat·ed
  per·am·bu·lat·ing
per·am·bu·la·tion
per an·num
  by or for each year
  (see per anum)

per anum
  by way of the anus
  (see per annum)

per au·tre vie

per aver·si·o·nem
per cap·i·ta
per·ceiv·able
per·ceiv·ably
per cent
per·cent·age
per·co·late
  per·co·lat·ed
  per·co·lat·ing
per con·tra
per cu·ri·am
per di·em
per·du·ra·ble
pe·remp·tion
pe·remp·to·ry
  ending a right of ac-
  tion, debate, or
  delay
  (see preemptory)

pe·ren·ni·al
per eun·dem
per·fect
per·fect·ed
per·fect·ly
per·fid·i·ous
per·fid·i·ous·ly
per·fi·dy
  pl per·fi·dies
per·fo·rate
  per·fo·rat·ed
  per·fo·rat·ing
per·fo·ra·tion
per·form
per·form·able
per·for·mam do·ni
per·for·mance
per frau·dem

peri·anal
peri·car·dit·ic
peri·car·di·tis
  pl peri·car·dit·i·des

peri·car·di·um
  pl peri·car·dia

peri·cra·ni·al
peri·cra·ni·um
  pl peri·cra·nia

per·il
peri·na·tal
per in·cu·ri·am
per in·dus·tri·am
per·i·ne·al
per·i·ne·um
  also per·i·nae·um
  pl per·i·nea
  also per·i·naea

per in·for·tu·ni·um
peri·oc·u·lar
pe·ri·od
pe·ri·od·ic
pe·ri·od·i·cal
pe·ri·od·i·cal·ly
peri·oral
peri·or·bit·al
peri·os·te·al
peri·rec·tal
per·ish·abil·i·ty
per·ish·able
peri·to·ne·al
peri·to·ne·al·ly
peri·to·ne·um
  pl peri·to·ne·ums
  or peri·to·nea

peri·to·nit·ic

peri·to·ni·tis
per·jure
  per·jured
  per·jur·ing
per·jur·er
per·ju·ri·ous
per·ju·ri·ous·ly
per·ju·ry
  pl per·ju·ries

per le·gum ter·rae
per·ma·nen·cy
  pl per·ma·nen·cies

per·ma·nent
per·ma·nent·ly
per·mis·si·ble
per·mis·sion
per·mis·sive
per·mit
  per·mit·ted
  per·mit·ting
per·mit·tee
per my et per tout
per·nan·cy
  pl per·nan·cies

per·ni·cious
per·oral
per·oral·ly
per os
per pais
  or per pays

per·pe·trate
  per·pe·trat·ed
  per·pe·trat·ing
  to be guilty of
  (see perpetuate*)*

per·pe·tra·tion

per·pe·tra·tor
per·pet·u·al
per·pet·u·al·ly
per·pet·u·ate
  per·pet·u·at·ed
  per·pet·u·at·ing
  to make perpetual
  (see perpetrate*)*

per·pet·u·a·tion
per·pe·tu·ity
  pl per·pe·tu·ities

per pro·cu·ra·ti·o·
  nem
  also per proc·u·ra·tion

per·qui·site
  a right or privilege
  (see prerequisite*)*

per quod
per·rec·tal
per·rec·tal·ly
per rec·tum
per se
per·se·cute
  per·se·cut·ed
  per·se·cut·ing
  to harass injuriously
  (see prosecute*)*

per·se·cut·ee
per·se·cu·tion
per·se·cu·tor
per·sist
per·sis·tence
per·sis·tent
per·sis·tent·ly
per·son

per·so·na
  pl per·so·nae
  or per·so·nas

per·son·able
per·so·na de·sig·
  na·ta
per·so·na gra·ta
  pl per·so·nae gra·tae
  or per·so·na gra·ta

per·son·al
per·son·al·i·ty
  pl per·son·al·i·ties
  distinctive personal
  quality
  (see personalty*)*

per·son·al·ly
per·son·al·ty
  pl per·son·al·ties
  personal property
  (see personality*)*

per·so·na non grat·
  ta
  pl per·so·nae non
    gra·tae
  or per·so·na non
    gra·ta

per·son·ate
per·son·ation
per·spi·ca·cious
  very discerning
  (see perspicuous*)*

per·spic·u·ous
  easily understood
  (see perspicacious*)*

per stir·pes
per·suade
  per·suad·ed
  per·suad·ing

per·suad·er
per·sua·sion
per·sua·sive·ness
per·tain
per·ti·nence
per·ti·nen·cy
  pl per·ti·nen·cies

per·ti·nent
per·ti·nen·tia
per tout et non
  per my
per ver·ba de
  prae·sen·ti
per·verse
per·verse·ly
per·ver·sion
per·ver·si·ty
  pl per·ver·si·ties

per·vert
per·vert·ed
per·vert·er
pes·ti·cid·al
pes·ti·cide
pe·te·chia
  pl pe·te·chi·ae

pe·te·chi·al
Pe·ter Funk
pe·ter·man
  pl pe·ter·men

pet·it
pe·ti·tion
pe·ti·tion·al
pe·ti·tion·ee
pe·ti·tion·er
pe·ti·tio prin·ci·pii

pe·tit mal
pet·i·to·ry
pe·tits che·vaux
pet·ti·fog
  pet·ti·fogged
  pet·ti·fog·ging
pet·ti·fog·ger
pet·ti·fog·gery
pet·ty
pey·o·te
  or pey·otl

pha·go·ma·nia
pha·lange
pha·lan·ge·al
pha·lanx
  pl pha·lanx·es
  or pha·lan·ges

phal·lic
phal·li·cal·ly
phal·loi·dine
  also phal·loi·din

phal·lus
  pl phal·li
  or phal·lus·es

phar·ma·ceu·tic
phar·ma·ceu·ti·cal
phar·ma·ceu·ti·cal·
  ly
phar·ma·ceu·tics
phar·ma·cist
phar·ma·co·dy·
  nam·ic
phar·ma·co·dy·
  nam·i·cal·ly
phar·ma·co·dy·
  nam·ics

phar·ma·cog·nos·
  tic
phar·ma·cog·no·sy
phar·ma·co·log·i·
  cal
    or phar·ma·co·
    log·ic

phar·ma·co·log·i·
  cal·ly
phar·ma·col·o·gy
  also phar·ma·co·lo·gia
  pl phar·ma·col·o·gies
  also phar·ma·co·lo·gias

phar·ma·co·poe·ia
  also phar·ma·co·peia

phar·ma·co·ther·
  a·py
    pl phar·ma·co·ther·
    a·pies

phar·ma·cy
  pl phar·ma·cies

pha·ryn·geal
phar·ynx
  pl pha·ryn·ges
  also phar·ynx·es

phe·na·caine
  also phe·no·cain

phen·ac·e·tin
phe·no·bar·bi·tal
phe·no·bar·bi·tone
phe·nol
phe·no·lic
phe·nom·e·nal
phe·nom·e·non
  pl phe·nom·e·na
  or phe·nom·e·nons

phil·an·throp·ic

phil·an·thro·py
   pl phil·an·thro·pies

phle·bit·ic
phle·bi·tis
   pl phle·bit·i·des

pho·bia
pho·bic
pho·no·ma·nia
pho·no·re·cep·tion
pho·no·re·cep·tor
phos·gene
pho·tal·gia
pho·tic
pho·to·in·duced
pho·to·in·duc·tion
pho·to·in·duc·tive
pho·to·re·cep·tion
pho·to·re·cep·tive
pho·to·re·cep·tor
pho·to·sen·si·tive
pho·to·sen·si·tiv·i·
   ty
      pl pho·to·sen·si·tiv·i·
      ties

pho·to·sen·si·ti·za·
   tion
pho·to·sen·si·tize
  pho·to·sen·si·
    tized
  pho·to·sen·si·tiz·
    ing
pho·to·sen·si·tiz·er
phren·ic
phthi·ri·a·sis
   pl phthi·ri·a·ses

phthis·ic
  or phthis·i·cal

phys·ic
  phys·icked
  phys·ick·ing
  phys·ics
  or phys·icks

phys·i·cal
phys·i·cal·ly
phy·si·cian
phy·si·cian·ly
phys·i·og·nom·ic
  also phys·i·og·nom·i·cal

phys·i·og·no·my
   pl phys·i·og·no·mies

phys·i·o·log·i·cal
  or phys·i·o·log·ic

phys·i·o·log·i·cal·ly
phys·i·ol·o·gy
   pl phys·i·ol·o·gies

phys·io·ther·a·pist
phys·io·ther·a·py
   pl phys·io·ther·a·pies

phy·to·tox·ic
phy·to·tox·ic·i·ty
   pl phy·to·tox·ic·i·ties

phy·to·tox·in
pia
pia-arach·noid
  or pi·arach·noid

pia-arach·noi·dal
pi·al
pia ma·ter
pia-ma·tral
pick·age
  or pic·cage

pick·et
pick·et·er
pick·et·ing
pick·pock·et
piece·work
piece·work·er
pier
   bridge support
   (*see* peer)

pier·age
pig·no·rate
  pig·no·rat·ed
  pig·no·rat·ing
pig·no·ra·tive
pig·nus
  ju·di·ci·a·le
  or pig·nus
    prae·to·ri·um

pig·nus le·ga·le
pil·fer
pil·fer·age
pil·fer·er
pil·lage
pil·lag·er
pi·lot
pi·lot·age
pimp
pimp·ing
pi·o·neer
pi·ra·cy
   pl pi·ra·cies

pi·rate
pis·ca·ria
pis·ca·ri·al
pis·ca·ry
   pl pis·ca·ries

pitch·blende
pit·fall
pi·tu·itary
  pl pi·tu·itar·ies

pla·ca·bil·i·ty
pla·ca·ble
  easily placated
  (see placeable)

place·able
  that can be placed
  (see placable)

pla·ce·bo
  pl pla·ce·bos

pla·cen·ta
  pl pla·cen·tas
  also pla·cen·tae

pla·cen·tal
pla·cen·ta pre·via
  pl pla·cen·tae pre·vi·ae

pla·cen·ta·tion
pla·cen·ti·tis
  pl pla·cen·tit·i·des

pla·gia·rism
pla·gia·rist
pla·gia·ris·tic
pla·gia·rize
  pla·gia·rized
  pla·gia·riz·ing
pla·gia·ry
  pl pla·gia·ries

plain clothes *n*
plain·clothes *adj*
plain·clothes·man
  pl plain·clothes·men

plaint

plain·tiff
  *the complaining party
  in litigation*
  (see plaintive)

plain·tive
  expressive of sadness
  (see plaintiff)

plan·tar
plan·ta·tion
plat
  plat·ted
  plat·ting
plea
plea bar·gain·ing
plead
  plead·ed
  or pled
  plead·ing
plead·able
plead·er
pleas of the crown
ple·bi·sci·ta·ry
pleb·i·scite
  also pleb·e·scite

pleb·i·sci·tum
  pl pleb·i·sci·ta

pledge
  pledged
  pledg·ing
pledg·ee
pledge·hold·er
pledg·ery
pled·gor
  or pled·geor
ple·nary
ple·ne ad·mi·ni·
  stra·vit

ple·ne ad·mi·ni·
  stra·vit prae·tor
pleni·po·ten·tia·ry
  pl pleni·po·ten·tia·ries

pleu·ra
  pl pleu·rae
  or pleu·ras

pleu·ral
pleu·ri·sy
  pl pleu·ri·sies

pleu·rit·ic
pleu·ro·dyn·ia
pleu·ro·per·i·to·
  ne·um
    pl pleu·ro·per·i·to·
      ne·ums
    or pleu·ro·per·i·to·
      nea

plev·in
plex·us
plot
  plot·ted
  plot·ting
plot·tage
plow·bote
plum·bic
plum·bism
plun·der
plun·der·age
plu·ral
plu·ral·i·ty
  pl plu·ral·i·ties

plu·ri·es
  pl plu·ri·es

plu·rip·a·ra
  pl plu·rip·a·rae

plu·to·ni·um

ply
  plied
  ply·ing
pneu·mo·ba·cil·lus
  pl pneu·mo·ba·cil·li

pneu·mo·coc·cal
  also pneu·mo·coc·cic

pneu·mo·coc·cus
  pl pneu·mo·coc·ci

pneu·mo·co·ni·o·sis
  or pneu·mo·ko·ni·o·sis
  also pneu·mo·no·co·ni·
    o·sis
  or pneu·mo·no·ko·ni·o·
    sis
  pl pneu·mo·co·ni·o·ses
  or pneu·mo·ko·ni·o·ses
  also pneu·mo·no·co·ni·
    o·ses
  or pneu·mo·no·ko·ni·o·
    ses

pneu·mo·nia
pneu·mo·no·ul·
  tra·mi·cro·scop·
  ic·sil·i·co·vol·
  ca·no·co·ni·o·sis
  pl pneu·mo·no·ul·
    tra·mi·cro·scop·ic·
    sil·i·co·vol·ca·no·
    co·ni·o·ses

pneu·mo·tho·rax
  pl pneu·mo·tho·rax·es
  or pneu·mo·tho·ra·ces

poach
poach·er
poind
poind·er
poind·ing
poi·son
poi·son·er

poi·son·ing
poi·son·ous
pok·er
  a metal rod
po·ker
  a card game
po·lice
  po·liced
  po·lic·ing
po·lice·man
  pl po·lice·men

po·lice·wom·an
  pl po·lice·wom·en

pol·i·cy
  pl pol·i·cies

po·lio
po·lio·my·eli·tis
po·lit·i·cal
po·lit·i·cal·ly
pol·i·ti·cian
pol·i·ty
poll
poll·book
pol·len
pol·lex
  pl pol·li·ces

pol·li·cal
pol·lic·i·ta·tion
poll·ing
pol·li·no·sis
  or pol·len·o·sis
  pl pol·li·no·ses
  or pol·len·o·ses

pol·lute
  pol·lut·ed
  pol·lut·ing

pol·lu·tion
po·lo·ni·um
poly·an·dric
poly·an·drist
poly·an·drous
poly·an·dry
  pl poly·an·dries

poly·gam·ic
po·lyg·a·mist
po·lyg·a·mous
po·lyg·a·my
  pl po·lyg·a·mies

poly·gram
poly·graph
poly·graph·ic
poly·graph·i·cal·ly
po·lyg·y·nist
po·lyg·y·nous
po·lyg·y·ny
  pl po·lyg·y·nies

poly·neu·rit·ic
poly·neu·ri·tis
  pl poly·neu·rit·i·des
  or poly·neu·ri·tis·es

poly·opia
poly·opic
pol·yp
pol·yp·o·sis
  pl pol·yp·o·ses

pol·yp·ous
poly·vi·nyl
pons
  pl pon·tes

pon·tic
pool
pool·ing

pool·room
poor
  poor·er
  poor·est
pop·li·te·al
pop·u·lace
pop·u·lar
pop·u·la·tion
por·nog·ra·pher
por·no·graph·ic
por·no·graph·i·cal·
  ly
por·nog·ra·phy
  pl por·nog·ra·phies

po·ro·sis
  pl po·ro·ses
  or po·ro·sis·es

po·rot·ic
por·ta·ble
por·ta·ca·val
  also por·to·ca·val

por·tion
por·tion·er
po·si·tion
pos·i·tive
poso·log·ic
  also poso·log·i·cal

po·sol·o·gy
  pl po·sol·o·gies

pos·se
pos·se co·mi·ta·tus
pos·se·man
  pl pos·se·men

pos·sess
pos·sess·able
  also pos·sess·ible

pos·sessed
pos·ses·sion
pos·sess·or
pos·ses·so·ry
pos·si·bil·i·ty
  pl pos·si·bil·i·ties

pos·si·ble
post
post·age
post·al
post·an·es·thet·ic
post·ca·va
post·ca·val
post·co·ital
post·date
  post·dat·ed
  post·dat·ing
post di·em
post·ea
post·ed
pos·te·ri·ad
pos·te·ri·or
pos·te·ri·or·ly
pos·ter·i·ty
  pl pos·ter·i·ties

post-fac·tum
post hoc
post·hu·mous
post·hu·mous·ly
post·ing
post·lim·i·nary
  or post·li·min·i·ary

post·li·min·i·um
  or post·lim·i·ny
  pl post·li·min·ia
  or post·lim·i·nies

post li·tem mo·
  tam
post-mor·tem *adv*
post·mor·tem *adj or*
  n or vb

post·na·tal
post·na·tal·ly
post·na·tus
post·nup·tial
post-obit
post·op·er·a·tive
post·par·tum
  or post·par·tal

post·pone
  post·poned
  post·pon·ing
post·pone·ment
post·pu·ber·tal
post rem
  or post res

post·treat·ment
pos·tre·mo·gen·i·
  ture
po·ta·ble
po·ten·tial
po·ten·tial·ly
po·tes·ta·tive
po·to·ma·nia
Pott's frac·ture
pound
pound·age
pound breach
pound·keep·er
pour-over
pour·par·ler

prejudge

pour·par·ty
var of purparty

pour·pres·ture
var of purpresture

pour·vey·ance
var of purveyance

pow·er

prac·ti·ca·bil·i·ty
pl prac·ti·ca·bil·i·ties

prac·ti·ca·ble
feasible
(*see* practical)

prac·ti·ca·bly

prac·ti·cal
skilled through prac-
tice
(*see* practicable)

prac·ti·cal·ly

prac·tice

prac·ti·tio·ner

praecipe
or precipe

prae·ci·pe quod
red·dat

prae·di·al
or pre·di·al

prae·di·um
pl prae·dia

prae·di·um dom·
i·nans

prae·di·um
rus·ti·ca·num

prae·di·um
rus·ti·cum

prae·di·um
ser·vi·ens

prae·di·um
ur·ba·num
pl prae·dia ur·ba·na

pra·tique

pray
prayed
pray·ing

prayer

pre·ad·o·les·cence

pre·ad·o·les·cent

pre·ag·o·nal

pre·am·ble

pre·an·es·thet·ic

pre·can·cer·ous

pre·car·i·ous

prec·a·to·ry

pre·cau·tion

pre·ca·va
pl pre·ca·vae

pre·ca·val

pre·cede
pre·ced·ed
pre·ced·ing
to go or come before
(*see* proceed)

prec·e·dent

prec·e·dent·less

pre·cept

pre·cinct

pre·ci·pe
var of praecipe

pre·cise

pre·clin·i·cal

pre·clude
pre·clud·ed
pre·clud·ing

pre·cog·ni·tion

pre·con·demn

pre·con·di·tion

pre·con·tract

pre·cop·u·la·to·ry

pre·date
pre·dat·ed
pre·dat·ing

pred·a·tor

pre·de·cease
pre·de·ceased
pre·de·ceas·ing

pre·de·ces·sor

pre·di·al
var of praedial

pre·dis·pose
pre·dis·posed
pre·dis·pos·ing

pre·eclamp·sia

pre·eclamp·tic

pre·empt

pre·emp·tion

pre·emp·tive

pre·emp·to·ry
pre-emptive
(*see* peremptory)

pre·fer
pre·ferred
pre·fer·ring

pref·er·ence

pref·er·en·tial

preg·nan·cy
pl preg·nan·cies

preg·nant

pre·in·va·sive

pre·judge

pre·judged
pre·judg·ing
pre·judg·er
pre·judg·ment
prej·u·dice
prej·u·diced
prej·u·di·cial
prej·u·di·cial·ly
pre·law
pre·le·gal
pre·leu·ke·mic
pre·li·cense
pre·lim·i·nar·i·ly
pre·lim·i·nary
pre·ma·lig·nant
pre·mar·i·tal
pre·mat·ri·mo·nial
pre·ma·ture
pre·ma·ture·ly
pre·ma·tu·ri·ty
  pl pre·ma·tu·ri·ties

pre·med·i·cate
  pre·med·i·cat·ed
  pre·med·i·cat·ing
pre·med·i·ca·tion
pre·med·i·tate
  pre·med·i·tat·ed
  pre·med·i·tat·ing
pre·med·i·tat·ed·ly
pre·med·i·tat·ed·
  ness
pre·med·i·ta·tion
pre·med·i·ta·tive
pre·med·i·ta·tor
prem·ise
  also prem·iss
  pl prem·is·es
  also prem·iss·es

pre·mi·um
  pl pre·mi·ums
  also pre·mia

pre·mon·i·to·ry
  also pre·mon·i·tary

pre·mor·tal
pre·na·tal
pre·na·tal·ly
pre·nup·tial
prep·a·ra·tion
pre·pare
  pre·pared
  pre·par·ing
pre·pay
  pre·paid
  pre·pay·ing
pre·pay·ment
pre·pense
pre·pon·der·ance
pre·pon·der·ant
pre·pon·der·ate
  pre·pon·der·at·ed
  pre·pon·der·at·
    ing
pre·psy·chot·ic
pre·pu·ber·tal
  or pre·pu·ber·al
pre·pu·ber·tal·ly
  or pre·pu·ber·al·ly
pre·pu·ber·ty
  pl pre·pu·ber·ties
pre·puce
pre·pu·tial
  or pre·pu·cial
pre·req·ui·site
  *a necessary prelim-
  inary*
  (*see* perquisite)

pre·rog·a·tive
pre·scrib·able
pre·scribe
  pre·scribed
  pre·scrib·ing
  *to assert a prescrip-
  tive right or title*
  (*see* proscribe)

pre·scrip·tion
pre·scrip·tive
pres·ence
  *the fact of being pres-
  ent*
  (*see* presents)

pre·se·nile
pre·se·nil·i·ty
  pl pre·se·nil·i·ties

pre·sen·tence
pre·sen·ti·ment
  *a premonition or pre-
  judgment*
  (*see* presentment)

pres·ent·ly
pre·sent·ment
  *an offering of some-
  thing to be dealt
  with*
  (*see* presentiment)

pres·ents *n pl*
  *the present legal in-
  strument*
  (*see* presence)

pres·er·va·tion
pre·serve
  pre·served
  pre·serv·ing
pre·side
  pre·sid·ed
  pre·sid·ing
pres·i·dent

pre·sum·ably
pre·sume
  pre·sumed
  pre·sum·ing
pre·sump·tion
pre·sump·tive
pre·sump·tive·ly
pre·sup·pose
pre·tend
pre·tend·ed
pre·tense
  or pre·tence

pre·tensed
pre·ten·sion
  also pre·ten·tion

pre·ter·mi·nal
pre·tèr·mis·sion
pre·ter·mit
  pre·ter·mit·ted
  pre·ter·mit·ting
pre·text
pre·ti·um af·fec·
  tio·nis
    pl pre·tia af·fec·tio·
    nis

pre·treat·ment
pre·tri·al
pre·tu·ber·cu·lous
  or pre·tu·ber·cu·lar

pre·vail
pre·vail·ing
pre·var·i·cate
  pre·var·i·cat·ed
  pre·var·i·cat·ing
pre·var·i·ca·tion
pre·var·i·ca·tor
pre·vent

pre·vent·abil·i·ty
pre·vent·able
  also pre·vent·ible

pre·ven·ta·tive
pre·ven·tion
pre·ven·tive
pre·view
  an advance view
  (*see* purview)

pre·vi·ous
pre·vi·ous·ly
pri·a·pism
pri·a·pis·mic
pri·a·pus
  pl pri·a·pi
  or pri·a·pus·es

price
  priced
  pric·ing
pri·mae im·pres·
  sio·nis
pri·ma fa·cie
pri·mage
pri·mar·i·ly
pri·ma·ry
prime
pri·mi·grav·id
pri·mi·grav·i·da
  pl pri·mi·grav·i·das
  or pri·mi·grav·i·dae

pri·mip·a·ra
  pl pri·mip·a·ras
  or pri·mip·a·rae

pri·mi·par·i·ty
  pl pri·mi·par·i·ties

pri·mip·a·rous
pri·mo·gen·i·tal
pri·mo·gen·i·tary

pri·mo·gen·i·ture
prin·ci·pal
  main body of an es-
  tate; chief person or
  matter
  (*see* principle)

prin·ci·pal·ly
prin·ci·ple
  basic rule or assump-
  tion
  (*see* principal)

pri·or
pri·or·i·ty
  pl pri·or·i·ties

pris·on
pris·on·er
pri·va·cy
  pl pri·va·cies

pri·vate
pri·vate·ly
pri·va·tim
pri·va·tion
pri·va·tize
  pri·vat·ized
  pri·vat·iz·ing
priv·i·lege
  priv·i·leged
  priv·i·leg·ing
priv·i·ly
priv·i·ty
  pl priv·i·ties

privy
  pl priv·ies

prize
  prized
  priz·ing
prob·a·bil·i·ty
  pl prob·a·bil·i·ties

prob·a·ble
prob·a·bly
pro·band
pro·bate
  pro·bat·ed
  pro·bat·ing
pro·ba·tion
pro·ba·tion·al
pro·ba·tion·ary
pro·ba·tion·er
pro·ba·tive
pro·bi·ty
pro bo·no pu·bli·co
pro·caine
pro·ce·den·do
pro·ce·dur·al
pro·ce·dur·al·ly
pro·ce·dure
pro·ceed
  to go to law
  (see precede)

pro·ceed·ing
pro·ceeds *n pl*
pro·cess
pro·cess serv·er
pro·cès-ver·bal
  pl pro·cès-ver·baux

pro·chein ami
  or pro·chein amy

pro·claim
proc·la·ma·tion
pro con·fes·so
proct·al·gia
proc·ti·tis
proc·to·log·ic
  or proc·to·log·i·cal

proc·tol·o·gy
  pl proc·tol·o·gies

proc·tor
proc·to·ri·al
proc·u·ra·tion
proc·u·ra·tor
pro·cure
  pro·cured
  pro·cur·ing
pro·cure·ment
pro·cur·er
prod·i·gal
pro·duce
  pro·duced
  pro·duc·ing
pro·duc·er goods
prod·uct
pro·duc·tion
pro·fane
pro·fane·ly
pro·fane·ness
pro·fan·i·ty
  pl pro·fan·i·ties

pro·fert
pro·fert in cu·ria
pro·fessed·ly
pro·fes·sion
pro·fes·sion·al
prof·it
prof·it·abil·i·ty
prof·it·able
prof·it·ably
prof·it a pren·dre
  or profit à pren·dre
  pl profits a pren·dre
  or profits à pren·dre

prof·i·teer

pro·for·ma
prog·no·sis
  pl prog·no·ses

prog·nos·tic
pro·gram·ma
  pl pro·gram·ma·ta

pro·gres·sive
pro hac vi·ce
pro·hib·it
pro·hi·bi·tion
pro·hib·i·tive
pro·hib·i·tive·ly
pro·hib·i·tor
pro·hib·i·to·ry
pro in·di·vi·so
pro in·ter·es·se suo
proj·ect
pro lae·sio·ne
  fi·del
pro·lapse
  pro·lapsed
  pro·laps·ing
pro·lap·sus
pro·le·tar·i·an
pro·le·tar·i·at
  also pro·le·tar·i·ate
  pl pro·le·tar·i·at
  also pro·le·tar·i·ate

pro·li·cide
pro·lif·er·ate
  pro·lif·er·at·ed
  pro·lif·er·at·ing
pro·lif·er·a·tion
pro·lif·er·a·tive
pro·lix·i·ty
pro·mis·cu·i·ty
  pl pro·mis·cu·i·ties

pro·mis·cu·ous

prom·ise
  prom·ised
  prom·is·ing

prom·is·ee

prom·i·sor

prom·is·so·ry

pro·mote
  pro·mot·ed
  pro·mot·ing

pro·mot·er

pro·mo·tion

pro·mo·tion·al

prompt

prompt·ly

pro·mul·gate
  pro·mul·gat·ed
  pro·mul·gat·ing

pro·mul·ga·tion

pro·mul·ga·tor

pro·nounce
  pro·nounced
  pro·nounc·ing

pro·nun·ci·a·men·
to
  pl pro·nun·ci·a·
   men·tos
  or pro·nun·ci·a·men·
   toes

proof

pro·pa·gan·da

pro·pa·gan·dist

prop·a·gate
  prop·a·gat·ed
  prop·a·gat·ing

prop·a·ga·tion

prop·a·ga·tive

pro par·te

pro·pen·si·ty
  pl pro·pen·si·ties

prop·er

prop·er·ly

prop·er·ty
  pl prop·er·ties

pro·phy·lac·tic

pro·phy·lac·ti·cal·
ly

pro·phy·lax·is
  pl pro·phy·lax·es

pro·pin·qui·ty

pro·po·nent

pro·por·tion

pro·por·tion·al

pro·por·tion·al·ly

pro·por·tion·ate

pro·pos·al

pro·pose
  pro·posed
  pro·pos·ing

prop·o·si·tion

pro·pos·i·tus
  pl pro·pos·i·ti

pro·pound

pro·pri·etary
  pl pro·pri·etar·ies

pro·pri·etor

pro·pri·eto·ri·al

pro·pri·etor·ship

pro·prio mo·tu

pro·prio vi·go·re

prop·ter af·fec·
tum

prop·ter de·fec·
tum

prop·ter de·fec·
tum san·gui·nis

prop·ter de·lic·tum

prop·ter hoc

prop·ter ho·no·ris
re·spec·tum

pro que·ren·te

pro ra·ta

pro·rate
  pro·rat·ed
  pro·rat·ing

pro·rat·er

pro·ra·tion

pro re na·ta

pro·ro·gate
  pro·ro·gat·ed
  pro·ro·ga·ting

pro·ro·ga·tion

pro·rogue
  pro·rogued
  pro·rogu·ing

pro·scribe
  pro·scribed
  pro·scrib·ing
  to put outside the law
  (*see* prescribe)

pros·e·cut·able

pros·e·cute
  pros·e·cut·ed
  pros·e·cut·ing
  to proceed against at
  law
  (*see* persecute)

pros·e·cu·tion

pros·e·cu·tive

pros·e·cu·tor

pros·e·cu·trix
  pl pros·e·cu·tri·ces
  or pros·e·cu·trix·es

pros·pect
pro·spec·tive
pro·spec·tive·ly
pro·spec·tor
pro·spec·tus
  pl pro·spec·tus·es

pros·the·sis
  pl pros·the·ses

pros·thet·ic
pros·thet·i·cal·ly
pros·thet·ics
pros·ti·tute
  pros·ti·tut·ed
  pros·ti·tut·ing
pros·ti·tu·tion
pros·tra·tion
pro tan·to
pro·tect
pro·tec·tion
pro·tec·tive
pro tem·po·re
pro·test
pro·test·able
pro·tes·tan·do
pro·tes·ta·tion
pro·to·col
prov·abil·i·ty
prov·able
prove
  proved
  proved
    or prov·en
  prov·ing

pro·vide
  pro·vid·ed
  pro·vid·ing
prov·i·den·tial·ly
  hin·dered
pro·vi·sion
pro·vi·sion·al
pro·vi·sion·al·ly
pro·vi·so
  pl pro·vi·sos
  or pro·vi·soes

prov·o·ca·tion
pro·voc·a·tive
pro·voke
  pro·voked
  pro·vok·ing
pro·vost
prowl
prowl·er
prox·i·mal
prox·i·mate
prox·i·mate·ly
proxy
  pl prox·ies
pru·dence
pru·dent
pru·den·tial
pru·dent·ly
pru·rig·i·nous
pru·ri·go
  pl pru·ri·gos
pru·rit·ic
pru·ri·tus
pseu·do·graph
pseu·dog·ra·pher
pseud·onym
  also pseud·onyme

pseu·do·preg·nan·cy
  pl pseu·do·preg·nan·cies

pseu·do·preg·nant
psi·lo·cin
psi·lo·cy·bin
psy·chal·gia
psy·chi·at·ric
  also psy·chi·at·ri·cal

psy·chi·at·ri·cal·ly
psy·chi·a·trist
psy·chi·a·try
  pl psy·chi·a·tries
psy·chic
psy·cho·ac·tive
psy·cho·anal·y·sis
  also psych·anal·y·sis
  pl psy·cho·anal·y·ses
  also psych·anal·y·ses

psy·cho·an·a·lyst
  also psych·an·a·lyst

psy·cho·an·a·lyt·ic
  or psy·cho·an·a·lyt·i·cal
  also psych·an·a·lyt·ic
  or psych·an·a·lyt·i·cal

psy·cho·an·a·lyze
  psy·cho·an·a·lyzed
  psy·cho·an·a·lyz·ing

psy·cho·lep·sy
  pl psy·cho·lep·sies

psy·cho·lep·tic
psy·cho·log·i·cal
  also psy·cho·log·ic

psy·cho·log·i·cal·ly

psy·chol·o·gist
psy·chol·o·gize
  psy·chol·o·gized
  psy·chol·o·giz·ing
psy·chol·o·gy
  pl psy·chol·o·gies

psy·cho·neu·ro·sis
  pl psy·cho·neu·ro·ses

psy·cho·neu·rot·ic
psy·cho·path
psy·cho·path·ia
psy·cho·path·ic
psy·cho·path·i·cal·
  ly
psy·cho·patho·log·
  ic
    or psy·cho·patho·
    log·i·cal

psy·cho·pa·thol·o·
  gy
  pl psy·cho·pa·thol·
  o·gies

psy·chop·a·thy
  pl psy·chop·a·thies

psy·cho·quack
psy·cho·quack·ery
  pl psy·cho·quack·er·ies

psy·cho·sis
  pl psy·cho·ses

psy·cho·so·mat·ic
psy·cho·sur·gery
  pl psy·cho·sur·ger·ies

psy·cho·sur·gi·cal
psy·cho·ther·a·py
  pl psy·cho·ther·a·pies

psy·chot·ic

psy·chot·i·cal·ly
pto·maine
pu·ber·tal
  or pu·ber·al
pu·ber·ty
  pl pu·ber·ties

pu·bes
  pl pu·bes
  pubic hair or region
  (*see* pubis)

pu·bes
  pl of pu·bis

pu·bic
pu·bis
  pl pu·bes
  a pubic bone
  (*see* pubes)

pub·lic
pub·li·ca·tion
pub·li·ci ju·ris
pub·li·cist
pub·lic·i·ty
pub·lic·ly
pub·lish
pub·lish·able
pub·lish·er
pu·den·dal
pu·den·dum
  pl pu·den·da

pu·dic
pu·er·pera
  pl pu·er·pe·rae

pu·er·per·al
pu·er·pe·ri·um
  pl pu·er·pe·ria

puff·er
puff·ing

puis dar·rein con·
  tin·u·ance
puis·ne
pul·mo·nary
punc·ture
  punc·tured
  punc·tur·ing
pun·ish
pun·ish·abil·i·ty
pun·ish·able
pun·ish·ably
pun·ish·ment
pu·ni·tive
pu·ni·to·ry
pur au·tre vie
pur·chase
  pur·chased
  pur·chas·ing
pur·chas·er
pure
  pur·er
  pur·est
pure·ly
pur·ga·tion
purge
  purged
  purg·ing
pur·loin
pur·part
  purparty
  (*see* purport)

pur·par·ty
  or pour·par·ty
  pl pur·par·ties
  or pour·par·ties

pur·port
  meaning
  (*see* purpart)

pur·port·ed
pur·pose
  pur·posed
  pur·pos·ing
pur·pose·ly
pur·pres·ture
  or pour·pres·ture

purse
pur·su·ance
pur·su·ant
pur·su·ant to
pur·sue
  pur·sued
  pur·su·ing
pur·su·er
pur·suit
pu·ru·lence
  also pu·ru·len·cy
  pl pu·ru·lenc·es
  also pu·ru·len·cies

pu·ru·lent
pur·vey
pur·vey·ance
  also pour·vey·ance

pur·vey·or
pur·view
  a part or the scope of a
  statute
  (see preview*)*

push·er
push mon·ey
put
  put
  put·ting
pu·ta·tive

py·ar·thro·sis
  pl py·ar·thro·ses

py·elit·ic
py·eli·tis
py·emia
  or py·ae·mia

py·emic
pyg·ma·lion·ism
pyo·me·tra
pyo·sal·pinx
  pl pyo·sal·pin·ges

py·ro·ma·nia
py·ro·ma·ni·ac
py·ro·ma·ni·a·cal

Q

qat
  var of kat

quack
quack·ery
quack·ish
quack·ish·ly
quack·ish·ness
quack·ism
quack·sal·ver
quack·salv·ing
quack·ster
quacky
  quack·i·er
  quack·i·est
quad·ran·gle
quad·rant
quad·rate
qua·dra·to·man·dib·
  u·lar

quad·ri·ceps
  also quad·ri·ceps
    ex·ten·sor
  or quad·ri·ceps
    fem·o·ris

quad·ri·cip·i·tal
quad·ri·en·ni·um
  uti·le
qua·drig·a·mist
qua·drip·a·rous
quad·ri·par·tite
quad·ri·ple·gia
quad·ri·ple·gic
qua·droon
qua·drum·vir
qua·drum·vi·rate
qua·dru·ple
qua·dru·plet
qua·dru·pli·cate
  qua·dru·pli·cat·ed
  qua·dru·pli·cat·ing
qua·dru·pli·ca·tion
quae co·ram no·
  bis re·si·dant
quae est eadem
quae·re
quaes·tio
  pl quaes·tio·nes

quaes·tio vex·ata
qual·i·fi·ca·tion
qual·i·fi·ca·tor
qual·i·fied·ly
qual·i·fy
  qual·i·fied
  qual·i·fy·ing

qual·i·ty
pl qual·i·ties

quam diu
quan·do
ac·ci·de·rint
quan·ti mi·no·ris
quan·ti·ty
pl quan·ti·ties

quan·tum
pl quan·ta

quan·tum me·ru·it
quan·tum
va·le·bant
quar·an·tin·able
quar·an·tine
quar·an·tined
quar·an·tin·ing
qua·re clau·sum
fre·git
quar·rel
quar·reled
or quar·relled
quar·rel·ing
or quar·rel·ling
quar·ry
pl quar·ries

quar·ry·ing
quar·tan
quar·ter
quar·ter-breed
quar·ter·ly
quash
qua·si
qua·si-char·i·ta·ble
qua·si de·lict

qua·si ex
con·trac·tu
qua·si in rem
qua·si-ju·di·cial
qua·si-leg·is·la·tive
qua·si-pub·lic
qua·si-re·or·ga·ni·
za·tion
quat
var of kat

quay
quay·age
Queen's Coun·sel
que·re·la
pl que·re·lae

que·rens
quer·u·lous
ques·tion
quia
quia ti·met
quib·ble
quib·bled
quib·bling
quick
quick as·sets
quick·en
quick·ened
quick·en·ing
quick·lime
quick·sil·ver
quid pro quo
pl quid pro quos
or quids pro quos
also quids pro quo

qui·es·cence

qui·es·cent
qui·et
qui·et·er
qui·et·est
qui·e·ta non mo·
ve·re
qui·etus
pl qui·etus·es

quin·a·crine
also chin·a·crin
or chin·a·crine

quin·i·dine
qui·nine
quin·o·line
also chin·o·line

qui·none
quin·sy
pl quin·sies

quin·troon
quin·tu·ple
quin·tu·pled
quin·tu·pling
quin·tu·plet
quin·tu·pli·cate
quin·tu·pli·cat·
ed
quin·tu·pli·cat·
ing
quis·ling
quit
quit
also quit·ted

quit·ting
qui tam
quit·claim

quit·rent
quit·tance
quo
  pl quos

quo·ad
quo·ad hoc
quo ani·mo
quo·dam·mo·do
quod cog·no·vit in·
  dic·ta·men·tum
quod com·pu·tet
quod cum
quod no·ta
quod per·mit·tat
  pro·ster·ne·re
quod si con·tin·gat
quod vi·de
quo ju·re
quo·mo·do
quo·rum
  pl quo·rums

quo·ta
quo·ta·tion
quote
  quot·ed
  quot·ing
quo·tid·i·an
quo·tient
quous·que
quo war·ran·to

R

ra·bid
ra·bies

race
  raced
  rac·ing
race-bait·er
race-bait·ing
race·way
ra·chi·cen·te·sis
  pl ra·chi·cen·te·ses

ra·chit·ic
ra·chi·tis
  also rha·chi·tis
  pl ra·chit·i·des
  also rha·chit·i·des

rach·i·to·gen·ic
ra·cial
rac·ism
rac·ist
rack·et
rack·e·teer
rack·e·teer·ing
rack rent *n*
rack-rent *vb*
rack-rent·er
ra·dar
ra·dec·to·my
  pl ra·dec·to·mies

ra·di·al
ra·di·a·le
  pl ra·di·a·lia

ra·di·ant
ra·di·ate
  ra·di·at·ed
  ra·di·at·ing
ra·di·a·tion
rad·i·cal

ra·dic·u·lar
ra·dic·u·lec·to·my
  pl ra·dic·u·lec·to·mies

ra·dic·u·li·tis
ra·dif·er·ous
ra·dio·ac·tin·i·um
ra·dio·ac·tive
ra·dio·ac·tiv·i·ty
ra·dio·bi·o·log·i·cal
  or ra·dio·bi·o·log·ic

ra·dio·bi·o·log·i·
  cal·ly
ra·dio·bi·ol·o·gist
ra·dio·bi·ol·o·gy
  pl ra·dio·bi·ol·o·gies

ra·dio·car·bon
ra·dio·car·pal
ra·dio·chem·i·cal
ra·dio·chem·i·cal·ly
ra·dio·chem·ist
ra·dio·chem·is·try
  pl ra·dio·chem·is·tries

ra·dio·co·balt
ra·dio·der·ma·ti·tis
  pl ra·dio·der·ma·
  ti·ti·ses
  or ra·dio·der·ma·
  tit·i·des

ra·dio·don·tia
ra·di·odon·tic
ra·di·odon·tist
ra·dio·el·e·ment
ra·dio·gen·ic
ra·dio·hum·er·al

ra·dio·io·dine
ra·dio·iso·tope
ra·dio·iso·to·pic
ra·dio·log·i·cal
  or ra·dio·log·ic

ra·dio·log·i·cal·ly
ra·di·ol·o·gist
ra·di·ol·o·gy
  pl ra·di·ol·o·gies

ra·dio·sur·gery
  pl ra·dio·sur·ger·ies

ra·dio·ther·a·peu·
  tic
ra·dio·ther·a·peu·
  tics
ra·dio·ther·a·pist
ra·dio·ther·a·py
  pl ra·dio·ther·a·pies

ra·dio·ther·my
  pl ra·dio·ther·mies

ra·dio·tho·ri·um
ra·dio·ul·nar
ra·di·um
ra·di·us
  pl ra·dii
  also ra·di·us·es

ra·dix
  pl ra·di·ces
  or ra·dix·es

raf·fle
  raf·fled
  raf·fling
raft·age
rage
  raged

rag·ing
raid
raid·er
rail
rail·age
rail·head
rail·ing
rail·road
rail·side
rail·wa·ter
rail·way
rain
rain·fall
rain·wa·ter
raise
  raised
  rais·ing
rake-off
ra·mal
ram·i·fi·ca·tion
ram·i·fy
  ram·i·fied
  ram·i·fy·ing
ramp
ram·u·lus
  pl ram·u·li

ra·mus
  pl ra·mi

ra·mus com·mu·
  ni·cans
    pl ra·mi com·mu·
      ni·can·tes

ran·cel·man
  pl ran·cel·men

ran·cid

ran·cid·i·ty
  pl ran·cid·i·ties

ran·cor
ran·cored
ran·cor·ous
ran·dom
ran·dom·ly
range
  ranged
  rang·ing
rang·er
rank
ran·sack
ran·sack·er
ran·som
ran·som·able
ran·som·er
ran·u·la
ran·u·lar
rape
  raped
  rap·ing
rap·er
ra·phe
  or rha·phe

rap·ine
rap·ist
rap·per
rap·port à suc·
  ces·sion
rap·por·teur
rap·proche·ment
rap·ture of the
  deep
rap·tus

rar·efac·tion
rar·efy
 also rar·i·fy
 rar·efied
 also rar·i·fied
 rar·efy·ing
 also rar·i·fy·ing

rase
 rased
 ras·ing
ra·sure
rat·abil·i·ty
 or rate·abil·i·ty

rat·able
 or rate·able

rat·ably
 or rate·ably

rat-bite fe·ver
rate
 rat·ed
 rat·ing
rate·pay·er
rat·er
rat·i·fi·ca·tion
rat·i·fi·er
rat·i·fy
 rat·i·fied
 rat·i·fy·ing
ra·ti·ha·bi·tio
rat·i·ha·bi·tion
ra·tio
 pl ra·tios

ra·tio de·ci·den·di
 pl ra·ti·o·nes de·ci·den·di

ra·tio im·per·ti·nens
ra·tion
ra·tio·nal
 reasonable; sensible
 (*see* rationale)

ra·tio·nale
 underlying reason
 (*see* rational)

ra·tio·nal·i·ty
ra·tio·nal·iza·tion
ra·tio·nal·ize
 ra·tio·nal·ized
 ra·tio·nal·iz·ing
ra·tio·nal·ly
ra·tio·nal·ness
ra·ti·o·ne do·mi·ci·lii
ra·ti·o·ne rei si·tae
ra·tio per·ti·nens
rat·ten·ing
rau·wol·fia
rav·ish
rav·ish·er
rav·ish·ment
re
re·ac·cept
re·ac·cep·tance
re·ac·ces·sion
re·ac·count·ing
re·ac·cred·it
re·ac·cred·i·ta·tion
reach
reach·able
re·ac·quire
re·ac·qui·si·tion

re·act
re·ac·tion
re·ac·tive
re·ac·tiv·i·ty
 pl re·ac·tiv·i·ties

read·er
readi·ly
readi·ness
re·ad·journ
re·ad·just
re·ad·just·able
re·ad·just·ment
re·ad·min·is·ter
re·ad·mis·sion
re·ad·mit
 re·ad·mit·ted
 re·ad·mit·ting
re·ad·mit·tance
re·adopt
re·adop·tion
ready
re·af·firm
re·af·fir·ma·tion
re·agen·cy
 pl re·agen·cies

re·agent
real
re·al·i·ty
 pl re·al·i·ties
 actualness
 (*see* realty)

re·al·iz·abil·i·ty
re·al·iz·able
re·al·iza·tion
re·al·ize
 re·al·ized

re·al·iz·ing
re·al·iz·er
re·al·lege
re·al·lo·cate
  re·al·lo·cat·ed
  re·al·lo·cat·ing
re·al·lo·ca·tion
re·al·lot
  re·al·lot·ted
  re·al·lot·ting
re·al·lot·ment
Re·al·tor
re·al·ty
  pl re·al·ties
  real property
  (*see* reality)

re·amend
re·am·pu·ta·tion
re·an·nex
re·an·nex·ation
re·ap·peal
re·ap·pli·ca·tion
re·ap·pli·er
re·ap·ply
  re·ap·plied
  re·ap·ply·ing
re·ap·point
re·ap·point·ment
re·ap·por·tion
re·ap·por·tion·
  ment
re·ap·prais·al
re·ap·praise
  re·ap·praised
  re·ap·prais·ing
re·ap·praise·ment

re·ap·prais·er
re·ap·pre·hend
re·ap·pro·pri·ate
  re·ap·pro·pri·
    at·ed
  re·ap·pro·pri·
    at·ing
re·ap·pro·pri·a·
  tion
re·ar·gue
  re·ar·gued
  re·ar·gu·ing
re·ar·gu·ment
re·ar·rest
rea·son
rea·son·abil·i·ty
rea·son·able
rea·son·able·ness
rea·son·ably
rea·son·less
re·as·sert
re·as·sess
re·as·sess·ment
re·as·sign
re·as·sign·ment
re·as·sur·ance
re·as·sure
  re·as·sured
  re·as·sur·ing
re·at·tach
re·at·tach·ment
re·bate
  re·bat·ed
  re·bat·ing
re·bate·ment
re·bat·er

re·bel
  re·belled
  re·bel·ling
re·bel·lion
re·bel·lious
re·bel·lious·ly
re·bel·lious·ness
re·bill·ing
re·build
  re·built
  re·build·ing
re·bus sic stan·
  ti·bus
re·but
  re·but·ted
  re·but·ting
re·but·ment
re·but·ta·ble
re·but·ta·bly
re·but·tal
re·but·ter
re·cal·ci·trance
  or re·cal·ci·tran·cy
  pl re·cal·ci·tranc·es
  or re·cal·ci·tran·cies

re·cal·ci·trant
re·call
re·call·able
re·call·ment
re·cant
re·can·ta·tion
re·cant·er
re·cap·i·tal·iza·tion
re·cap·i·tal·ize
  re·cap·i·tal·ized

re·cap·i·tal·iz·
    ing
re·cap·tion
re·cap·tor
re·cap·ture
    re·cap·tured
    re·cap·tur·ing
re·cede
    re·ced·ed
    re·ced·ing
re·ceipt
re·ceipt·or
re·ceiv·abil·i·ty
re·ceiv·able
re·ceiv·ables
re·ceiv·al
re·ceive
    re·ceived
    re·ceiv·ing
re·ceiv·er
re·ceiv·er·ship
re·cent
re·cent·ly
re·cep·tion
re·cep·tor
re·cess
re·ces·sion
    a ceding back
    (*see* recision, rescis-
    sion)

re·ces·sus
re·cid·i·vate
    re·cid·i·vat·ed
    re·cid·i·vat·ing
re·cid·i·va·tion
re·cid·i·vism

re·cid·i·vist
re·cid·i·vis·tic
re·cid·i·vous
re·cip·ro·cal
re·cip·ro·cal·i·ty
re·cip·ro·cal·ly
re·cip·ro·cate
    re·cip·ro·cat·ed
    re·cip·ro·cat·ing
re·cip·ro·ca·tion
re·cip·ro·ca·tive
re·cip·ro·ca·tor
re·cip·ro·ca·to·ry
rec·i·proc·i·ty
    pl rec·i·proc·i·ties

re·ci·sion
    cancellation
    (*see* recession, rescis-
    sion)

re·cit·al
re·cite
    re·cit·ed
    re·cit·ing
reck·less
reck·less·ly
reck·less·ness
reck·on
    reck·oned
    reck·on·ing
re·claim
    to reform or better
    (*see* re-claim)

re-claim
    to claim back
    (*see* reclaim)

re·claim·able

re·claim·ant
rec·la·ma·tion
re·clas·si·fi·ca·tion
re·clas·si·fy
    re·clas·si·fied
    re·clas·si·fy·ing
re·clu·sion
re·cod·i·fi·ca·tion
re·cod·i·fy
    re·cod·i·fied
    re·cod·i·fy·ing
rec·og·ni·tion
rec·og·ni·tive
rec·og·ni·tor
rec·og·ni·to·ry
rec·og·niz·abil·i·ty
rec·og·niz·able
rec·og·niz·abiy
rec·og·ni·zance
rec·og·nize
    rec·og·nized
    rec·og·niz·ing
rec·og·ni·zee
rec·og·niz·er
    one that recognizes
    (*see* recognizor)

rec·og·ni·zor
    *one obligated under a
    recognizance*
    (*see* recognizer)

re·cog·nosce
    re·cog·nosced
    re·cog·nosc·ing
rec·ol·lect
rec·ol·lec·tion
re·com·mence

re·com·menced
re·com·menc·ing
rec·om·mend
rec·om·men·da·
  tion
rec·om·men·da·
  to·ry
re·com·mit
  re·com·mit·ted
  re·com·mit·ting
re·com·mit·ment
  also re·com·mit·tal
rec·om·pen·sa·ble
rec·om·pen·sa·tion
rec·om·pense
  rec·om·pensed
  rec·om·pens·ing
rec·om·pens·er
rec·om·pen·sive
rec·om·pres·sion
rec·on·cil·abil·i·ty
rec·on·cil·able
rec·on·cil·ably
rec·on·cile
  rec·on·ciled
  rec·on·cil·ing
rec·on·cile·ment
rec·on·cil·er
  also rec·on·ci·lor

rec·on·cil·i·ate
  rec·on·cil·i·at·ed
  rec·on·cil·i·at·ing
rec·on·cil·i·a·tion
rec·on·cil·i·a·tor
rec·on·cil·ia·to·ry
re·con·duc·tion

re·con·fess
re·con·firm
re·con·fir·ma·tion
re·con·fis·cate
  re·con·fis·cat·ed
  re·con·fis·cat·ing
re·con·fis·ca·tion
re·con·sid·er
re·con·sid·er·a·tion
re·con·sign
re·con·sign·ment
re·con·struct
re·con·struct·ible
re·con·struc·tion
re·con·struc·tive
re·con·tin·u·ance
re·con·tract
re·con·trol
  re·con·trolled
  re·con·trol·ling
re·con·ven·tion
re·con·ven·tion·al
re·con·ver·sion
re·con·vey
re·con·vey·ance
re·con·vict
re·con·vic·tion
re·cord *vb*
rec·ord *n*
re·cord·able
re·cor·dari
re·cor·da·tion
re·cord·er
re·cord·er·ship
re·cor·dum
  pl re·cor·da

re·count
re·coup
re·coup·ment
re·course
re·cov·er
  re·cov·ered
  re·cov·er·ing
  *to obtain a right in
    court*
  (see re-cover)

re·cov·er
  to cover again
  (see recover)

re·cov·er·able
re·cov·er·ee
re·cov·er·er
re·cov·ery
  pl re·cov·er·ies

rec·re·ant
re·crim·i·nate
  re·crim·i·nat·ed
  re·crim·i·nat·ing
re·crim·i·na·tion
re·crim·i·na·tor
re·crim·i·na·to·ry
re·cru·des·cence
re·cru·des·cent
re·cruit
rec·tal
rec·tal·ly
rec·ti·fi·able
rec·ti·fi·ca·tion
rec·ti·fy
  rec·ti·fied
  rec·ti·fy·ing
rec·to·uter·ine

rec·to·ves·i·cal

rec·tum
  pl rec·tums
  or rec·ta

rec·tus in cu·ria
re·cu·per·ate
  re·cu·per·at·ed
  re·cu·per·at·ing
re·cu·per·a·tion
re·cu·per·a·tive
re·cur
  re·curred
  re·cur·ring
re·cur·rence
re·cur·rent
rec·u·sa·tion
rec·u·sa·tor
re·cuse
  re·cused
  re·cus·ing
red·den·dum
  pl red·den·da

re·deem
re·deem·abil·i·ty
re·deem·able
re·de·liv·er
re·de·liv·ery
  re·de·liv·er·ies
re·de·mise
  re·de·mised
  re·de·mis·ing
re·demp·ti·ble
re·demp·tion
re·demp·tion·er
re·de·ter·mi·na·tion

red-green blind·ness
red-hand·ed
red her·ring
red·hi·bi·tion
red·hib·i·to·ry
red·in·te·gra·tion
red·in·te·gra·tive
re·di·rect
re·dis·count
re·dis·tri·bu·tion
re·dis·trict
re·di·tus qui·eti
red·out
re·draft
re·dress
re·dress·er
re·dress·ment
re·duce
  re·duced
  re·duc·ing
re·duc·ibil·i·ty
re·duc·ible
re·duc·tio ad ab·sur·dum
re·duc·tion
re·dun·dan·cy
  also re·dun·dance
  pl re·dun·dan·cies
  also re·dun·danc·es

re·dun·dant
re·dun·dant·ly
re·ed·u·ca·tion
re·elect
re·elec·tion
re·em·ploy

re·em·ploy·ment
re·en·act
re·en·act·ment
re·en·ter
re·en·try
  pl re·en·tries

re·es·tab·lish
reeve
re·ex·am·i·na·tion
re·ex·am·ine
  re·ex·am·ined
  re·ex·am·in·ing
re·ex·change
  re·ex·changed
  re·ex·chang·ing
re·ex·e·cu·tion
re·fer
  re·ferred
  re·fer·ring
ref·er·ee
  ref·er·eed
  ref·er·ee·ing
ref·er·ence
ref·er·en·dal
ref·er·en·da·ry
  pl ref·er·en·da·ries

ref·er·en·dum
  pl ref·er·en·da
  or ref·er·en·dums

re·fer·ral
re·fi·nance
  re·fi·nanced
  re·fi·nanc·ing
re·flex
re·flexo·gen·ic
  or re·flex·og·e·nous

re·flux
re·form
amend; amendment
(*see* re-form)

re-form
form again
(*see* reform)

re·form·abil·i·ty
re·form·able
ref·or·ma·tion
re·for·ma·to·ry
  pl re·for·ma·to·ries

re·fract
re·frac·tion
re·frac·tion·ist
re·frac·tive
re·frac·to·ry
re·frac·ture
  re·frac·tured
  re·frac·tur·ing
re·fresh·er
ref·uge
  ref·uged
  ref·ug·ing
re·fund
re·fund·able
re·fus·al
re·fuse *vb*
  re·fused
  re·fus·ing
  decline
  (*see* refuse *n*)

ref·use *n*
  waste
  (*see* refuse *vb*)

re·fus·er

re·fut·abil·i·ty
re·fut·able
re·fut·al
ref·u·ta·tion
re·fu·ta·to·ry
re·fute
  re·fut·ed
  re·fut·ing
re·fut·er
re·gal·i·ty
re·gen·cy
  pl re·gen·cies

re·gent
reg·i·cide
re·gie
re·gime
re·gion
re·gion·al
reg·is·ter
reg·is·ter·er
reg·is·ter·ship
reg·is·tra·bil·i·ty
reg·is·tra·ble
  also reg·is·ter·able

reg·is·trant
reg·is·trar
reg·is·trar-gen·er·
  al
  pl reg·is·trars-gen·
  er·al

reg·is·trar·ship
reg·is·tra·tion
reg·is·tra·tion·al
reg·is·try
  pl reg·is·tries

reg·nal year

re·grant
re·grate
  re·grat·ed
  re·grat·ing
re·grat·er
  also re·gra·tor

re·gress
re·gres·sion
re·gres·sive
re·grow
  re·grew
  re·grown
  re·grow·ing
reg·u·la·ble
reg·u·la ge·ne·ra·lis
  pl re·gu·lae ge·ne·ra·les

reg·u·lar
reg·u·lar·i·ty
  pl reg·u·lar·i·ties

reg·u·lar·iza·tion
reg·u·lar·ize
  reg·u·lar·ized
  reg·u·lar·iz·ing
reg·u·lar·ly
reg·u·lat·able
reg·u·late
  reg·u·lat·ed
  reg·u·lat·ing
reg·u·la·tion
reg·u·la·tive
reg·u·la·tive·ly
reg·u·la·to·ry
re·gur·gi·tant
re·gur·gi·tate
  re·gur·gi·tat·ed

re·gur·gi·tat·ing
re·gur·gi·ta·tion
re·gur·gi·ta·tive
re·ha·bil·i·tant
re·ha·bil·i·tate
  re·ha·bil·i·tat·ed
  re·ha·bil·i·tat·ing
re·ha·bil·i·ta·tion
re·ha·bil·i·ta·tive
re·ha·bil·i·ta·tor
re·ha·bil·i·tee
re·hear
  re·heard
  re·hear·ing
re·hy·drate
  re·hy·drat·ed
  re·hy·drat·ing
re·hy·dra·tion
rei in·ter·ven·tus
re·im·burs·able
re·im·burse
  re·im·bursed
  re·im·burs·ing
  re·im·burse·ment
re·im·pose
  re·im·posed
  re·im·pos·ing
re·im·po·si·tion
re·in·cor·po·rate
  re·in·cor·po·rat·ed
  re·in·cor·po·rat·ing
re·in·dict
re·in·fec·tion
re·in·state

re·in·stat·ed
re·in·stat·ing
re·in·state·ment
re·in·sur·ance
re·in·sure
  re·in·sured
  re·in·sur·ing
re·in·sur·er
re·in·vest
re·in·ves·ti·ture
re·in·vest·ment
re·is·su·able
re·is·sue
  re·is·sued
  re·is·su·ing
re·ject
re·ject·able
re·jec·tion
re·join
re·join·der
re·lapse
  re·lapsed
  re·laps·ing
re·lat·able
re·late
  re·lat·ed
  re·lat·ing
re·la·tion
re·la·tion·ship
rel·a·tive
re·la·tor
re·la·trix
  pl re·la·trix·es

re·lax
re·lax·ant
re·lax·ation

re·leas·abil·i·ty
  also re·leas·ibil·i·ty
re·leas·able
  also re·leas·ible

re·lease
  re·leased
  re·leas·ing
  to give up
  (*see* re-lease)

re-lease
  to lease again
  (*see* release)

re·leas·ee
re·lea·sor
re·les·see
re·les·sor
re·let
rel·e·van·cy
  also rel·e·vance
  pl rel·e·van·cies
  also rel·e·vanc·es
rel·e·vant
rel·e·vant·ly
re·li·abil·i·ty
re·li·able
re·li·able·ness
re·li·ably
re·li·ance
re·li·ant
rel·ic
  something remaining
  (*see* relict)

rel·ict
  widow
  (*see* relic)

re·lic·tion
re·lief

re·liev·able
re·lieve
  re·lieved
  re·liev·ing
re·li·gious
  cor·po·ra·tion
re·lin·quish
re·lin·quish·ment
re·lo·cate
  re·lo·cat·ed
  re·lo·cat·ing
re·lo·ca·tion
re·ly
  re·lied
  re·ly·ing
re·main
re·main·der
re·main·der·man
  pl re·main·der·men

re·mand
rem·a·net
re·mar·riage
re·mar·ry
  re·mar·ried
  re·mar·ry·ing
re·me·di·a·ble
re·me·di·al
re·me·di·al·ly
rem·e·di·less
rem·e·dy
  pl rem·e·dies

rem·e·dy
  rem·e·died
  rem·e·dy·ing
re·mise

re·mised
re·mis·ing
re·mis·sion
re·mit
  re·mit·ted
  re·mit·ting
re·mit·ment
re·mit·ta·ble
re·mit·tal
re·mit·tance
re·mit·tee
re·mit·tent
re·mit·tent·ly
re·mit·ter
re·mit·ti·tur
re·mon·strance
  pl re·mon·stranc·es

re·mon·strate
  re·mon·strat·ed
  re·mon·strat·ing
re·mote
re·mote·ness
re·mov·able
re·mov·al
re·move
  re·moved
  re·mov·ing
re·mov·er
re·mu·ner·able
re·mu·ner·ate
  re·mu·ner·at·ed
  re·mu·ner·at·ing
re·mu·ner·a·tion
re·mu·ner·a·tive
re·mu·ner·a·tive·ly

re·mu·ner·a·tive·
  ness
re·mu·ner·a·tor
re·nal
ren·der
ren·der·able
ren·di·tion
ren·e·gade
  ren·e·gad·ed
  ren·e·gad·ing
re·ne·go·tia·ble
re·ne·go·ti·ate
  re·ne·go·ti·at·ed
  re·ne·go·ti·at·ing
re·ne·go·ti·a·tion
re·ne·go·ti·a·tor
re·new
re·new·al
re·new·er
re·ni·por·tal
re·nounce
  re·nounced
  re·nounc·ing
re·nounce·able
re·nounce·ment
re·nounc·er
rent
rent·abil·i·ty
rent·able
rent·age
rent·al
rent charge
  pl rents charge

rente fon·ci·ère
rent·er
rent-roll

rent seck
  pl rents seck
re·nun·ci·a·tion
ren·voi
reo ab·sen·te
re·oc·cu·py
  re·oc·cu·pied
  re·oc·cu·py·ing
re·open
  re·opened
  re·open·ing
re·open·er
re·or·ga·ni·za·tion
re·or·ga·nize
  re·or·ga·nized
  re·or·ga·niz·ing
  re·or·ga·niz·er
re·pair
re·pair·able
rep·a·ra·ble
rep·a·ra·tion
re·par·a·tive
re·pa·tri·ate
  re·pa·tri·at·ed
  re·pa·tri·at·ing
  re·pa·tri·a·tion
re·pay
  re·paid
  re·pay·ing
re·pay·able
re·pay·ment
re·peal
re·peal·able
re·peal·er
re·peat
re·peat·er

rep·e·ti·tion
re·place·ment
re·plead
  re·plead·ed
    or re·pled
  re·plead·ing
  re·plead·er
re·pledge
  re·pledged
  re·pledg·ing
re·ple·gi·ate
  re·ple·gi·at·ed
  re·ple·gi·at·ing
re·plevi·able
re·plev·in
re·plev·i·sa·ble
re·plev·i·sor
re·plevy
  re·plev·ied
  re·plevy·ing
re·pli·ant
rep·li·cate
  rep·li·cat·ed
  rep·li·cat·ing
rep·li·ca·tion
rep·li·ca·tion de
  in·ju·ria
re·pli·er
re·ply
  re·plied
  re·ply·ing
re·pone
  re·poned
  re·pon·ing
re·port
re·port·able

re·port·er
re·po·si·tion
re·pos·sess
re·pos·ses·sion
re·pos·ses·sor
rep·re·sent
rep·re·sent·able
rep·re·sent·ant
rep·re·sen·ta·tion
rep·re·sen·ta·tion·al
rep·re·sen·ta·tive
rep·re·sen·tee
rep·re·sen·tor
re·price
  re·priced
  re·pric·ing
re·prieve
  re·prieved
  re·priev·ing
rep·ri·mand
rep·ri·sal
re·prise
re·pri·vat·iza·tion
rep·ro·bate
  rep·ro·bat·ed
  rep·ro·bat·ing
rep·ro·ba·tion
re·pro·duce
  re·pro·duced
  re·pro·duc·ing
re·pro·duc·tion
re·pub·li·ca·tion
re·pub·lish
re·pub·lish·er
re·pu·di·ate
  re·pu·di·at·ed

re·pu·di·at·ing
re·pu·di·a·tion
re·pu·di·a·tor
re·pug·nance
re·pug·nan·cy
re·pug·nant
re·pur·chase
  re·pur·chased
  re·pur·chas·ing
rep·u·ta·ble
rep·u·ta·tion
re·pute
re·put·ed
re·quest
re·quire
  re·quired
  re·quir·ing
re·quire·ment
req·ui·site
req·ui·si·tion
re·quit·al
res
  pl res

res ad·ju·di·ca·ta
re·sal·able
re·sale
res ali·e·na
re·scind
re·scind·able
re·scind·er
re·scind·ment
re·scis·si·ble
re·scis·sion
  a bringing to an end
  (*see* recession, recision)

re·scis·so·ry

res com·mu·nes
res cor·po·ra·les
res·cous
  pl res·cous·es

re·script
re·scrip·tion
res·cue
  res·cued
  res·cu·ing
res·cu·er
res de·re·lic·ta
res do·mi·nans
re·seal
re·sect
re·sect·abil·i·ty
  pl re·sect·abil·i·ties

re·sect·able
re·sec·tion
re·sell
  re·sold
  re·sell·ing
re·sen·tence
re·ser·pine
re·ser·pin·iza·tion
re·ser·pin·ized
res·er·va·tion
re·serve
  re·served
  re·serv·ing
  to keep back
  (*see* re-serve)

re-serve
  to serve again
  (*see* reserve)

re·set·tle
  re·set·tled

re·set·tling
re·set·tle·ment
res ges·tae
re·ship
  re·shipped
  re·ship·ping
re·ship·ment
re·ship·per
re·side
  re·sid·ed
  re·sid·ing
res·i·dence
res·i·den·cy
  pl res·i·den·cies

res·i·dent
res·i·den·tial
res·i·den·ti·ary
re·sid·u·al
re·sid·u·ary
res·i·due
re·sid·u·um
  pl re·sid·ua

re·sign
  to relinquish
  (*see* re-sign)

re-sign
  to sign again
  (*see* resign)

res·ig·na·tion
re·sign·ee
re·sign·er
re·sile
  re·siled
  re·sil·ing
res in·cor·po·ra·les
res in·te·gra

res in·ter ali·os
res in·ter ali·os
   ac·ta
res ip·sa lo·qui·tur
re·sip·sy
   pl re·sip·sies
re·sist
re·sis·tance
re·sis·tant
   also re·sis·tent
re·sist·er
re·sit·ting
res ju·di·ca·ta
res mo·bi·les
res no·va
res nul·li·us
res·o·lu·tion
res·o·lu·tive
res·o·lu·to·ry
re·solve
   re·solved
   re·solv·ing
res·or·cin
res·or·cin·ol
re·sort
re·source
re·spect·able
re·spect·ing
re·spec·tive
re·spec·tive·ly
re·spi·ra·ble
res·pi·ra·tion
re·spi·ra·to·ry
re·spire
   re·spired
   re·spir·ing

re·spite
   re·spit·ed
   re·spit·ing
re·spond
re·spon·de
re·spon·de·at
   oust·er
re·spon·de·at
   su·pe·ri·or
re·spon·dence
   also re·spon·den·cy
   pl re·spon·denc·es
   also re·spon·den·cies
re·spon·dent
re·spon·den·tia
re·sponse
re·spon·si·bil·i·ty
   pl re·spon·si·bil·i·ties
re·spon·si·ble
re·spon·sive
res pri·va·tae
res pu·bli·cae
res ser·vi·ens
rest
re·staur
   or re·stor

res·ti·tute
   res·ti·tut·ed
   res·ti·tut·ing
res·ti·tu·tio in
   in·te·grum
res·ti·tu·tion
res·ti·tu·tive
res·ti·tu·to·ry
re·stor·able
res·to·ra·tion

re·stor·ative
re·store
   re·stored
   re·stor·ing
re·strain
re·straint
re·strict
re·stric·tion
re·stric·tive
re·sult
re·sul·tant
re·sult·ing
re·sume
   re·sumed
   re·sum·ing
   to take up again
   (*see* résumé)
ré·su·mé
   or re·su·me
   or re·su·mé
   a summary
   (*see* resume)
re·sum·mon
   re·sum·moned
   re·sum·mon·ing
re·sum·mons
re·sump·tion
res uni·ver·si·ta·tis
re·sur·vey
re·sus·ci·tate
   re·sus·ci·tat·ed
   re·sus·ci·tat·ing
re·sus·ci·ta·tion
re·sus·ci·ta·tive
re·sus·ci·ta·tor
re·tail
re·tail·er

re·tail·ing
re·tain
re·tain·er
re·tain·ing
re·take
  re·took
  re·tak·en
  re·tak·ing
re·tal·i·a·tion
re·tal·i·a·tor
re·tal·i·a·to·ry
re·tar·date
re·tar·da·tion
re·tard·ed
re·ten·tion
re·ten·tive
ret·i·na
  pl ret·i·nas
  or ret·i·nae

ret·i·nal
ret·i·ni·tis
  pl ret·i·nit·i·des

ret·i·no·blas·to·ma
  pl ret·i·no·blas·to·mas
  or ret·i·no·blas·to·ma·ta

ret·i·no·cho·roid·i·tis
ret·i·nol
ret·i·no·pap·il·li·tis
ret·i·nop·a·thy
  pl ret·i·nop·a·thies

ret·i·no·scope
ret·i·no·scop·ic
ret·i·nos·co·py
  pl ret·i·nos·co·pies

re·tire
  re·tired
  re·tir·ing
re·tire·ment
re·tor·no
  ha·ben·do
re·tor·sio fac·ti
  pl re·tor·sio·nes fac·ti

ré·tor·sion de droit
  pl ré·tor·sions de droit

re·tor·tion
  or re·tor·sion

re·tour
re·tour·able
re·tract
re·trac·ta·tion
re·trac·tion
re·trax·it
re·tri·al
re·trib·ute
  re·trib·ut·ed
  re·trib·ut·ing
ret·ri·bu·tion
re·trib·u·tive
re·trib·u·tor
ret·ro·ac·tive
ret·ro·ac·tiv·i·ty
ret·ro·car·di·ac
ret·ro·ca·val
ret·ro·cede
  ret·ro·ced·ed
  ret·ro·ced·ing
ret·ro·ces·sion
ret·ro·ces·sion·al
ret·ro·ces·sive

ret·ro·dis·place·ment
ret·ro·gres·sion
ret·ro·per·i·to·ne·al
ret·ro·per·i·to·ne·al·ly
ret·ro·pu·bic
ret·ro·spec·tive
ret·ro·spec·tive·ly
ret·ro·ver·sion
ret·ro·vert·ed
re·try
  re·tried
  re·try·ing
re·turn
re·turn·abil·i·ty
re·turn·able
re·uni·ent
re·union
re·unite
  re·unit·ed
  re·unit·ing
re·us
  pl rei

re·val·i·date
  re·val·i·dat·ed
  re·val·i·dat·ing
re·val·i·da·tion
re·val·o·ri·za·tion
re·val·o·rize
  re·val·o·rized
  re·val·o·riz·ing
re·val·u·ate
  re·val·u·at·ed
  re·val·u·at·ing
re·val·u·a·tion

re·val·ue
  re·val·ued
  re·valu·ing
re·ven·di·cate
  re·ven·di·cat·ed
  re·ven·di·cat·ing
  to recover something
  (see revindicate)

re·ven·di·ca·tion
re·venge
  re·venged
  re·veng·ing
rev·e·nue
  rev·e·nued
  rev·e·nu·er
re·ver·i·fi·ca·tion
re·ver·i·fy
  re·ver·i·fied
  re·ver·i·fy·ing
re·ver·sal
re·verse
  re·versed
  re·vers·ing
re·vers·er
re·vers·ible
re·ver·sion
re·ver·sion·al
re·ver·sion·ary
re·ver·sion·er
re·ver·sion·ist
re·ver·sor
re·vert
re·vert·er
re·vert·ible
re·vest
re·view

re·view·abil·i·ty
re·view·able
re·view·al
re·vin·di·cate
  re·vin·di·cat·ed
  re·vin·di·cat·ing
  to vindicate again
  (see revendicate)

re·vin·di·ca·tion
re·vise
  re·vised
  re·vis·ing
re·vi·sion
re·vi·so·ry
re·viv·al
re·vive
  re·vived
  re·viv·ing
re·vi·vor
re·vo·ca·bil·i·ty
re·vo·ca·ble
re·vo·ca·tion
re·vo·ca·tive
re·vo·ca·to·ry
re·vo·ca·tur
re·voke
  re·voked
  re·vok·ing
re·vok·er
re·volt
re·volt·er
rev·o·lu·tion
rev·o·lu·tion·ary
rev·o·lu·tion·ist
re·volve
  re·volved

re·volv·ing
re·ward
re·way·bill
re·zone
  re·zoned
  re·zon·ing
rha·chi·tis
  var of rachitis

rha·phe
  var of raphe

rheu·mat·ic
rheu·mat·i·cal·ly
rheu·ma·tism
rheu·mat·o·gen·ic
rheu·ma·toid
rheu·ma·tol·o·gist
rheu·ma·tol·o·gy
rhi·ni·tis
  pl rhi·nit·i·des

rhi·no·lar·yn·gol·
  o·gy
    pl rhi·no·lar·yn·gol·
    o·gies

rhi·no·lar·yn·go·
  scope
rhi·no·log·ic
  or rhi·no·log·i·cal

rhi·nol·o·gist
rhi·nol·o·gy
  pl rhi·nol·o·gies

rhi·no·phar·ynx
  pl rhi·no·pha·ryn·ges
  or rhi·no·phar·ynx·es

rhi·no·plas·tic
rhi·no·plas·ty
  pl rhi·no·plas·ties

rhi·nor·rha·gia
rhi·nor·rhea
   or rhi·nor·rhoea

rhi·no·scope
rhi·no·scop·ic
rhi·nos·co·py
   pl rhi·nos·co·pies

Rh-neg·a·tive
rho·dop·sin
Rh-pos·i·tive
rhus
   pl rhus·es
   or rhus

rhyt·id·ec·to·my
rhyt·i·do·plas·ty
ri·bo·fla·vin
   also ri·bo·fla·vine

rich
   rich·er
   rich·est
Rich·ard Miles
Rich·ard Roe
ri·cin
ric·i·nus
rick·ets
rick·ett·sia
   pl rick·ett·si·as
   or rick·ett·si·ae

rick·ett·si·al
rick·ett·si·o·sis
   pl rick·ett·si·o·ses

rick·ety
ric·tal
ric·tus
   pl ric·tus
   or ric·tus·es

rid·er
rid·i·cule
   rid·i·culed
   rid·i·cul·ing
ri·ding
ri·fam·pi·cin
ri·fa·my·cin
rig
   rigged
   rig·ging
right
right·ful
right·ful·ly
right-hand
right-hand·ed
right·ly
right of way
   pl rights of way
   or right of ways

rig·or
rig·or ju·ris
rig·or mor·tis
rig·or·ous
rig·or·ous·ly
ring·er
ri·ot
ri·ot·er
ri·ot·ous
ri·ot·ous·ly
ri·par·i·an
rise
   rose
   ris·en
   ris·ing
risk
riv·er·ain

road
road·bed
road·stead
road·way
rob
   robbed
   rob·bing
rob·ber
rob·bery
   pl rob·ber·ies

ro·den·ti·cide
roent·gen
   also rönt·gen

roent·gen·iza·tion
   also rönt·gen·iza·tion

roent·gen·ize
   also rönt·gen·ize
   roent·gen·ized
   also rönt·gen·ized
   roent·gen·iz·ing
   also rönt·gen·iz·ing

roent·gen·o·gram
roent·gen·o·graph
roent·gen·o·graph·
ic
roent·gen·o·graph·
i·cal·ly
roent·gen·og·ra·phy
   pl roent·gen·og·ra·
phies

roent·gen·o·log·ic
   or roent·gen·o·log·i·
cal

roent·gen·o·log·i·
cal·ly
roent·gen·ol·o·gist

roent·gen·ol·o·gy
  pl roent·gen·ol·o·gies

ro·ga·tio tes·ti·um

ro·ga·to·ry

rogue

rogu·ery
  pl rogu·er·ies

roll

rolled-up

Rom·berg sign
  or Rom·berg's sign

ron·geur

rönt·gen
  var of roentgen

rönt·gen·iza·tion
  var of roentgenization

rönt·gen·ize
  var of roentgenize

root of ti·tle

Ror·schach test
  or Ror·schach ink·blot
  test

ro·se·o·la

ro·ta

ro·tate
  ro·tat·ed
  ro·tat·ing
ro·ta·tion

ro·te·none

rou·lette

roup

rout

roy·al

roy·al·ty
  pl roy·al·ties

rub·ber check

ru·bel·la

ru·be·o·la

ru·be·o·lar

ru·big·i·nous

ru·bor

ru·bric

rul·able

rule
  ruled
  rul·ing
  rul·er

rum·mage
  rum·maged
  rum·mag·ing
  rum·mag·er

ru·mor

rum·run·ner

rum·run·ning

run
  ran
  run
  run·ning

run·away

run·ner

run off *vb*

run·off *n*

rup·ture
  rup·tured
  rup·tur·ing

ru·ral

rus·ti·cum fo·rum

rus·ti·cum jus
  or rus·ti·cum ju·di·
  ci·um

ruth·er·ford

S

sab·bath

sab·bat·i·cal
  or sab·bat·ic

sab·o·tage
  sab·o·taged
  sab·o·tag·ing

sab·o·teur

sa·bur·ra

sa·bur·ral

sac·cade

sac·cad·ic

sac·cha·rase

sac·cha·ride

sac·char·i·fi·ca·tion

sac·char·i·fy
  sac·char·i·fied
  sac·char·i·fy·ing

sac·cha·rin
  artificial sweetener
  (*see* saccharine)

sac·cha·rine
  sugary
  (*see* saccharin)

sack

sack·er

sa·crad

sa·cral

sa·cral·gia

sac·ra·men·tum
  pl sac·ra·men·ta

sa·cred

sac·ri·fice
  sac·ri·ficed
  sac·ri·fic·ing

sa·cro·coc·cy·geal
sa·cro·dyn·ia
sa·cro·il·i·ac
sa·cro·lum·bar
sa·cro·sci·at·ic
sa·cro·spi·na·lis
sa·cro·spi·nous
sa·cro·ver·te·bral
sa·crum
   pl sa·cra

sa·dism
sa·dist
sa·dis·tic
sa·dis·ti·cal·ly
sa·do·mas·och·ism
sa·do·mas·och·ist
sa·do·mas·och·is·tic
saec·u·lar
   var of secular

sae·ve·tia
safe
safe-con·duct
safe·crack·er
safe·crack·ing
safe·de·pos·it
safe·guard
safe·keep·ing
safe·ly
safe·ness
safe·ty
   pl safe·ties

safe·ty is·land
   also safe·ty isle

sag·it·tal
sag·it·tal·ly

said *adj*
sail
Saint An·tho·ny's
   fire
Saint Lou·is
   en·ceph·
   a·li·tis
Saint Vi·tus'
   dance
   or Saint Vi·tus's
    dance

sal·abil·i·ty
   pl sal·abil·i·ties

sal·able
   also sale·able

sal·a·cious
sa·lac·i·ty
   pl sa·lac·i·ties

sal·a·ry
   pl sal·a·ries

sal·a·ry
   sal·a·ried
   sal·a·ry·ing
sale
sa·le per
   ad·ver·sio·nem
sales agent
sales·man
   pl sales·men

sales·peo·ple
sales·per·son
sales·room
   also sale·room

sales·wom·an
   pl sales·wom·en

sale·yard
sal·i·cyl·am·ide
sa·lic·y·late
sa·lic·y·lat·ed
sal·i·cyl·ic
sal·i·cyl·ism
sal·i·cyl·iza·tion
sal·i·cyl·ize
   sal·i·cyl·ized
   sal·i·cyl·iz·ing
sa·line
sa·li·va
sal·i·vant
sal·i·vary
sal·i·vate
   sal·i·vat·ed
   sal·i·vat·ing
sal·i·va·tion
sal·mo·nel·la
   pl sal·mo·nel·lae
   or sal·mo·nel·las
   or sal·mo·nel·la

sal·mo·nel·lo·sis
   pl sal·mo·nel·lo·ses

sal·pin·gec·to·my
   pl sal·pin·gec·to·mies

sal·pin·gi·tis
sal·pin·go·cele
sal·pin·go·cy·e·sis
   pl sal·pin·go·cy·e·ses

sal·pin·go·oo·pho·
   rec·to·my
   pl sal·pin·go·oo·pho·
    rec·to·mies

sal·pin·go·oo·pho·
   ri·tis

sal·pin·go·peri·
  to·ni·tis
sal·pin·go·pexy
  pl sal·pin·go·pexies
sal·pin·gys·tero·cy·
  e·sis
    pl sal·pin·gys·tero·
    cy·e·ses
sal·pinx
  pl sal·pin·ges
salt·pe·ter
  also salt·pe·tre
sa·lu·bri·ous
sa·lu·bri·ous·ly
sa·lu·bri·ty
  pl sa·lu·bri·ties
sal·u·tari·ly
sal·u·tary
salv·able
sal·vage
  sal·vaged
  sal·vag·ing
sal·vage·abil·i·ty
sal·vage·able
sal·vag·er
salve
  salved
  salv·ing
sal·vo
  pl sal·vos
sal·vor
sa·mar·i·tan
same
sam·ple
  sam·pled
  sam·pling

sam·pler
sa·nae men·tis
san·a·tar·i·um
  pl san·a·tar·i·ums
  or san·a·tar·ia
san·a·tive
san·a·to·ri·um
  pl san·a·to·ri·ums
  or san·a·to·ria
san·a·to·ry
sanc·tion
  sanc·tioned
  sanc·tion·ing
sanc·tion·ative
sanc·tion·er
sanc·tu·ary
  pl sanc·tu·ar·ies
sane
  san·er
  san·est
san·guine
san·guin·e·ous
san·guin·o·lent
san·gui·no·pu·ru·
  lent
sa·ni·es
  pl sa·ni·es
san·i·fi·ca·tion
sa·ni·ous
san·i·tar·i·an
san·i·tari·ly
san·i·tar·i·um
  pl san·i·tar·i·ums
  or san·i·tar·ia
san·i·tary
san·i·tate

san·i·tat·ed
san·i·tat·ing
san·i·ta·tion
san·i·ta·tion·ist
san·i·ti·za·tion
san·i·tize
  san·i·tized
  san·i·tiz·ing
san·i·tiz·er
san·i·to·ri·um
  pl san·i·to·ri·ums
  also san·i·to·ria
san·i·ty
  pl san·i·ties
san·sei
  pl san·sei
  also san·seis
sans jour
sans re·cours
sa·phe·nous
sa·po·ge·nin
sa·po·nin
sap·o·tox·in
sap·phic
sap·phism
sar·co·cele
sar·coid
sar·coid·osis
  pl sar·coid·oses
sar·co·ma
  pl sar·co·mas
  or sar·co·ma·ta
sar·co·ma·gen·ic
sar·co·ma·toid
sar·co·ma·to·sis
  pl sar·co·ma·to·ses

sar·co·ma·tous
sar·to·ri·us
  pl sar·to·rii

sa·sine
sa·tan·o·pho·bia
sat·is·fac·tion
sat·is·fac·to·ri·ly
sat·is·fac·to·ri·ness
sat·is·fac·to·ry
sat·is·fi·able
sat·is·fi·er
sat·is·fy
  sat·is·fied
  sat·is·fy·ing
sat·ur·nine
sat·urn·ism
sa·ty·ri·a·sis
  pl sa·ty·ri·a·ses

sau·cer·iza·tion
sau·cer·ize
  sau·cer·ized
  sau·cer·iz·ing
sav·able
  or save·able

save
  saved
  sav·ing
save harm·less
sav·er
sav·ings *n pl*
saxi·tox·in
say
  said
  say·ing
say·able

say·ee
say·er
say-so
scab
  scabbed
  scab·bing
scab·by
  scab·bi·er
  scab·bi·est
sca·bies
  pl sca·bies

sca·bi·et·ic
  also sca·bet·ic

sca·bi·ous
sca·brous
sca·brous·ly
sca·brous·ness
scaf·fold
scaf·fold·age
scaf·fold·ing
scal·age
scald
scale
  scaled
  scal·ing
scale-down
scale·man
  pl scale·men

scale·pan
scal·er
scales·man
  pl scales·men

scale-up
scalp
scalp·er

scam·mo·ny
  pl scam·mo·nies

scamp
scamp·ing
scan
  scanned
  scan·ning
scan·dal
scan·dal·iza·tion
scan·dal·ize
  scan·dal·ized
  scan·dal·iz·ing
scan·dal·iz·er
scan·dal·mon·ger
scan·dal·ous
scan·dal·ous·ly
scan·dal·ous·ness
scan·da·lum mag·
na·tum
  pl scan·da·la mag·na·
  tum

scape·goat
scape·goat·er
scape·goat·ism
scaph·oid
scap·u·la
  pl scap·u·lae
  or scap·u·las

scap·u·lal·gia
scap·u·lar
scar
  scarred
  scar·ring
scare
  scared
  scar·ing

scar·i·fi·ca·tion
scar·i·fy
  scar·i·fied
  scar·i·fy·ing
scar·la·ti·na
scar·la·ti·nal
scarp·er
scat·o·log·i·cal
  also scat·o·log·ic
sca·tol·o·gy
  also ska·tol·o·gy
  pl sca·tol·o·gies
  also ska·tol·o·gies
scav·enge
  scav·enged
  scav·eng·ing
scav·eng·er
scav·en·gery
sched·u·lar
sched·ule
  sched·uled
  sched·ul·ing
sched·ul·er
scheme
  schemed
  schem·ing
schem·er
sche·mery
  pl sche·mer·ies

Schick test
Schiff re·ac·tion
schism
schis·mat·ic
schis·ma·tize
  schis·ma·tized
  schis·ma·tiz·ing

schis·to·sis
schizo
  pl schiz·os

schizo·af·fec·tive
schiz·oid
schiz·oid·ism
schiz·oid·ma·nic
  also schizo·man·ic
schizo·ki·ne·sis
  pl schizo·ki·ne·ses
schizo·pha·sia
schizo·phre·nia
schizo·phren·ic
schizo·phren·i·
  cal·ly
schizo·thyme
schizo·thy·mia
schizo·thy·mic
  also schizo·thy·mous

schol·ar
schol·ar·ship
scho·las·tic
school
school·house
school·room
school·teach·er
school·teach·ing
Schül·ler-Chris·
tian dis·ease
sci·at·ic
sci·at·i·ca
sci·ent
sci·en·ter
sci·li·cet
scin·ti·gram

scin·ti·graph·ic
scin·tig·ra·phy
  pl scin·tig·ra·phies

scin·til·la
  pl scin·til·las
  also scin·til·lae

scin·til·la ju·ris
scin·ti·scan
sci·on
  also ci·on

sci·re fa·cias
sci·re fa·cias sur
  mort·gage
scle·ra
  pl scler·as
  or scler·ae

scler·al
scle·ri·tis
sclero·cho·roi·di·tis
sclero·con·junc·ti·
  val
sclero·cor·nea
sclero·cor·ne·al
sclero·iri·tis
sclero·ker·a·ti·tis
scle·ro·ma
  pl scle·ro·mas
  or scle·ro·ma·ta

sclero·nych·ia
scle·rose
  scle·rosed
  scle·ros·ing
scle·ro·sis
  pl scle·ro·ses

sclero·ste·no·sis
  pl sclero·ste·no·ses

scle·rot·ic
scle·rot·i·co·chor·
   doidi·tis
sclero·ti·tis
scle·rot·o·my
   pl scle·rot·o·mies

scoff·law
scold
scold·ing
sco·li·o·sis
   pl sco·li·o·ses

sco·li·ot·ic
scoot
scope
sco·pine
sco·pol·amine
sco·po·phil·ia
   or scop·to·phil·ia

sco·po·phil·i·ac
   or scop·to·phil·i·ac

sco·po·phil·ic
   or scop·to·phil·ic

scor·bu·tic
scor·bu·ti·cal·ly
scor·bu·ti·gen·ic
scor·bu·tus
score
   scored
   scor·ing
scot
   scot·ted
   scot·ting
Scotch
scot-free
scoun·drel

scoun·drel·ly
scout
scram·bling
   pos·ses·sion
scrap
   scrapped
   scrap·ping
scrap·page
screen
screw
scrip
script
scriv·en·er
scriv·en·ery
scrof·u·la
scrof·u·lo·der·ma
scrof·u·lo·der·mic
scrof·u·lous
scroll
scro·tal
scro·tum
   pl scro·ta
   or scro·tums

scru·ple
   scru·pled
   scru·pling
scru·pu·lous
scru·pu·lous·ly
scru·pu·lous·ness
scru·ta·ble
scru·ta·tor
scru·ti·nize
   also scru·ti·nise
   scru·ti·nized
   also scru·ti·nised
   scru·ti·niz·ing
   also scru·ti·nis·ing

scru·ti·niz·er
   also scru·ti·nis·er

scru·ti·niz·ing·ly
scru·ti·ny
   pl scru·ti·nies

scul·dug·gery,
   scull·dug·gery
   vars of skulduggery

scur·rile
scur·ril·i·ty
   pl scur·ril·i·ties

scur·ri·lous
scur·vy
   pl scur·vies

scut·tle
   scut·tled
   scut·tling
scut·tler
sea
sea·bed
sea·board
sea·borne
sea·coast
sea·craft
sea·far·ing
sea·front
sea·go·ing
sea·keep·ing
sea·kind·ly
seal
seal·able
sea-lane
sealed
seal·er
seal·ing

seam
sea·man
 pl sea·men

sea·man·like
sea·man·ly
sea·man·ship
sea·mark
sea·port
search
search·able
search·er
sea·sick·ness
sea·son
sea·son·able
sea·son·ably
sea·son·al
sea·son·al·i·ty
seat
seat·ed land
sea·wall
sea-walled
sea·way
sea·wor·thi·ness
sea·wor·thy
se·cede
 se·ced·ed
 se·ced·ing
se·ced·er
se·ces·sion
se·clude
 se·clud·ed
 se·clud·ing
se·clu·sion
se·clu·sion·ist
seco·bar·bi·tal
sec·o·nal

sec·ond
sec·ond·ari·ly
sec·ond·ary
sec·ond-class
sec·ond-de·gree
sec·ond·er
sec·ond·hand
se·con·dines
 var of secundines

sec·ond·ly
sec·ond-rate
sec·ond-rate·ness
sec·ond-rat·er
se·cre·cy
 pl se·cre·cies

se·cret
sec·re·tary
 pl sec·re·tar·ies

se·cre·tion
se·cre·tive
se·cre·tive·ly
se·cre·tive·ness
se·cret·ly
se·cret·ness
se·cre·tum
 pl se·cre·ta

sec·tar·i·an
sec·tion
sec·tion·al
sec·tion·ize
 sec·tion·ized
 sec·tion·iz·ing
sec·u·lar
 also saec·u·lar

sec·u·lar·ism
sec·u·lar·i·ty

sec·u·lar·iza·tion
sec·u·lar·ize
 sec·u·lar·ized
 sec·u·lar·iz·ing
se·cun·di·grav·i·da
 pl se·cun·di·grav·i·das
 or se·cun·di·grav·i·dae

se·cun·dines
 or se·con·dines

se·cun·dip·a·ra
 pl se·cun·dip·a·ras
 or se·cun·dip·a·rae

se·cun·dip·a·rous
se·cun·do·gen·i·
 ture
se·cun·dum
se·cun·dum al·le·
 ga·ta
se·cun·dum bo·nos
 mo·res
se·cun·dum for·
 mam sta·tu·ti
se·cun·dum le·gem
se·cur·able
se·cur·ance
se·cure
 se·cured
 se·cur·ing
se·cure·ly
se·cure·ment
se·cure·ness
se·cu·ri·ty
 pl se·cu·ri·ties

se·cus
se·date
 se·dat·ed

se·dat·ing
se·da·tion
sed·a·tive
se de·fen·den·do
sed·en·tary
se·de·runt
sed·i·ment
sed·i·men·ta·tion
se·di·tion
se·di·tion·ary
se·di·tion·ist
se·di·tious
sed per cu·ri·am
sed quae·re
se·duce
  se·duced
  se·duc·ing
se·duc·ee
se·duce·ment
se·duc·er
se·duc·ible
  or se·duce·able

se·duc·ing·ly
se·duc·tion
se·duc·tive
se·duc·tress
sed vi·de
seek
  sought
  seek·ing
seem·ing·ly
seep
seep·age
seg·re·gate
  seg·re·gat·ed
  seg·re·gat·ing

seg·re·ga·tion
seg·re·ga·tive
seiche
sei·gnior·age
  or sei·gnor·age
  also sei·gneur·age
seised
  also seized
sei·sin
  also sei·zin
seize
  seized
  seiz·ing
seiz·er
sei·zor
sei·zure
se·junc·tion
se·lect
se·lect·ee
se·lec·tion
se·lec·tive
se·lec·tive·ly
se·lect·man
  pl se·lect·men
se·lec·tor
se·le·ni·um
sel·e·no·sis
self-abuse
self-ac·cu·sa·tion
self-anal·y·sis
  pl self-anal·y·ses
self-an·a·lyt·i·cal
self-aware
self-aware·ness
self-con·tra·dic·
  to·ry

self-deal·ing
self-de·fense
self-ev·i·dence
self-ev·i·dent
self-ex·e·cut·ing
self-hyp·no·sis
  pl self-hyp·no·ses
self-iden·ti·fi·ca·
  tion
self-im·age
self-in·crim·i·na·
  tion
self-in·flict·ed
self-in·sur·ance
self-in·sured
self-in·sur·er
self-liq·ui·dat·ing
self-pol·lu·tion
self-serv·ing
self-treat·ment
sell
  sold
  sell·ing
sell·able
sel·la tur·ci·ca
  pl sel·lae tur·ci·cae
sell·er
sell off *vb*
sell-off *n*
sell out *vb*
sell·out *n*
sema·phore
Se·mayne's case
sem·ble
  sem·bled
  sem·bling

semi·an·nu·al
semi·an·nu·al·ly
semi·au·ton·o·
  mous
semi·cir·cu·lar
semi·co·ma
semi·co·ma·tose
semi·con·scious
semi·con·scious·ly
semi·con·scious·
  ness
semi·de·tached
semi·gov·ern·
  men·tal
semi·in·de·pen·
  dent
semi·job·ber
semi·ju·di·cial
semi·le·gal
semi·month·ly
sem·i·nal
sem·i·nal·ly
sem·i·nate
  sem·i·nat·ed
  sem·i·nat·ing
sem·i·na·tion
semi·nau·fra·gi·um
sem·i·nif·er·ous
  also sem·i·nif·er·al

semi·of·fi·cial
semi·pri·vate
semi·proof
semi·pub·lic
semi·skilled
semi·week·ly
sem·per pa·ra·tus

sen·ate
sen·a·tor
sen·a·to·ri·al
sen·a·to·ri·an
sen·a·tor·ship
send
  sent
  send·ing
send·ee
send·er
send up
se·ne·cio
  pl se·ne·cios
se·ne·ci·osis
  pl se·ne·ci·oses

se·nes·cence
se·nes·cent
sen·e·schal
se·nile
se·nile·ly
se·nil·i·ty
  pl se·nil·i·ties
se·nior
se·nior·i·ty
  pl se·nior·i·ties

se·ni·um
sen·sa·tion
sen·sa·tion·al
sen·si·bil·i·ty
  pl sen·si·bil·i·ties
sen·si·ble
sen·si·tive
sen·si·tive·ly
sen·si·tive·ness
sen·si·tiv·i·ty
  pl sen·si·tiv·i·ties

sen·si·ti·za·tion
sen·si·tize
  sen·si·tized
  sen·si·tiz·ing
sen·so·ri·al
sen·so·ri·um
  pl sen·so·ri·ums
  or sen·so·ria

sen·so·ry
  pl sen·so·ries

sen·su·al
sen·su·al·ism
sen·su·al·i·ty
  pl sen·su·al·i·ties

sen·su·al·ly
sen·su ho·nes·to
sen·sus
sen·tence
  sen·tenced
  sen·tenc·ing
sen·ti·nel
sen·try
  pl sen·tries

sen·try
  sen·tried
  sen·try·ing
sep·a·ra·bil·i·ty
sep·a·ra·ble
sep·a·ra·ble·ness
sep·a·rate
  sep·a·rat·ed
  sep·a·rat·ing
sep·a·rate·ly
sep·a·ra·tion
sep·to·na·sal

sep·tum
pl sep·ta
or sep·tums

se·quela
pl se·quel·ae

se·ques·ter
se·ques·tra·ble
se·ques·trate
se·ques·trat·ed
se·ques·trat·ing
se·ques·tra·tion
se·ques·tra·tor
se·ques·tra·trix
pl se·ques·tra·tri·ces

se·ques·trec·to·my
pl se·ques·trec·to·mies

se·ques·trum
pl se·ques·trums
also se·ques·tra

se·ra
pl of serum

ser·gean·cy
also ser·jean·cy
or ser·geant·cy
or ser·jeant·cy
pl ser·gean·cies
also ser·jean·cies
or ser·geant·cies
or ser·jeant·cies

ser·geant
also ser·jeant

ser·geant at arms
ser·geant-at-law
var of serjeant-at-law

ser·geant·ship
also ser·jeant·ship

se·ri·al

se·ri·al·i·ty
se·ri·al·iza·tion
se·ri·al·ize
se·ri·al·ized
se·ri·al·iz·ing
se·ri·al·ly
se·ri·ary
se·ri·a·tim
se·ri·a·tion
se·ries
pl se·ries

se·ri·ous
se·ri·ous·ly
se·ri·ous·ness
ser·jean·cy,
ser·jeant·cy
vars of sergeancy

ser·jeant
var of sergeant

ser·jeant-at-law
also ser·geant-at-law
pl ser·jeants-at-law
also ser·geants-at-law

ser·jeant·ship
var of sergeantship

se·ro·di·ag·no·sis
pl se·ro·di·ag·
no·ses

se·ro·di·ag·nos·tic
se·ro·log·i·cal
or se·ro·log·ic

se·ro·log·i·cal·ly
se·rol·o·gist
se·rol·o·gy
pl se·rol·o·gies

se·ro·neg·a·tive

se·ro·neg·a·tiv·i·ty
se·ro·pos·i·tive
se·ro·pos·i·tiv·i·ty
se·ro·pu·ru·lent
se·ro·re·ac·tion
se·ro·sa
pl se·ro·sas
also se·ro·sae

se·ro·sal
se·ro·ther·a·py
se·rous
se·rum
pl se·rums
or se·ra

se·rum·al
ser·vant
ser·vant·ship
serve
served
serv·ing
ser·vice
ser·viced
ser·vic·ing
ser·vice·abil·i·ty
ser·vice·able
ser·vice·able·ness
ser·vice·ably
ser·vi·ent
ser·vile
ser·vil·i·ty
pl ser·vil·i·ties

ser·vi·tude
ser·vo·mech·a·nism
ses·sion
ses·sion·al
ses·sion·ary

set
  set
  set·ting
set aside *vb*
set-aside *n*
set back
  set back
  set·ting back
set·back *n*
set off *vb*
set-off *n*
se·ton
set·ter
set·tle
  set·tled
  set·tling
set·tle·abil·i·ty
set·tle·ment
set·tler
  one who settles some-
    thing or somewhere
  (see settlor)

set·tlor
  one who makes a
    settlement
  (see settler)

set up *vb*
set·up *n*
sev·er
sev·er·abil·i·ty
sev·er·able
sev·er·al
sev·er·al·ize
  sev·er·al·ized
  sev·er·al·iz·ing
sev·er·al·ly

sev·er·al·ty
  pl sev·er·al·ties
sev·er·ance
sev·er·a·tion
se·vere
  se·ver·er
  se·ver·est
se·ver·i·ty
sew·age
sew·er
sew·er·age
sex
sex·o·log·i·cal
sex·ol·o·gist
sex·ol·o·gy
  pl sex·ol·o·gies
sex·tip·a·ra
  pl sex·tip·a·ras
  or sex·tip·a·rae
sex·u·al
sex·u·al·i·ty
  pl sex·u·al·i·ties
sex·u·al·iza·tion
sex·u·al·ize
  sex·u·al·ized
  sex·u·al·iz·ing
sex·u·al·ly
shack
shack·er
shack·le
  shack·led
  shack·ling
shaft
shake down *vb*
  shook down
  shak·en down

shak·ing down
shake·down *n*
shake out *vb*
shake-out *n*
sham
  shammed
  sham·ming
shape-up
share
  shared
  shar·ing
share·abil·i·ty
share·able
  or shar·able
share·crop
  share·cropped
  share·crop·ping
share·crop·per
share·hold·er
share·job·ber
share·man
  pl share·men
share out *vb*
share-out *n*
share·own·er
share·push·er
shar·er
shares·man
  pl shares·men
share-ten·ant
  also share-rent·er
shark
sharp
sharp·er
shave
  shaved

shav·ing
shav·er
shead·ing
shear
  sheared
  sheared
    or shorn
  shear·ing
sheathe
  sheathed
  sheath·ing
Shel·ley's case
shell-shock
shel·ter
sher·iff
sher·iff·al·ty
  pl sher·iff·al·ties
sher·iff·cy
  pl sher·iff·cies
sher·iff·dom
sher·iff·wick
shift
shift·abil·i·ty
shift·able
shift boss
shift·ing
shift·man
  pl shift·men
Shi·ga ba·cil·lus
  also Shi·ga dys·en·tery
  ba·cil·lus
shi·gel·la
  pl shi·gel·lae
  also shi·gel·las
shig·el·lo·sis
  pl shig·el·lo·ses
shill

shin·bone
shin·gles
shin·splints
ship
  shipped
  ship·ping
ship·board
ship-break·er
ship-break·ing
ship·build·ing
ship·keep·er
ship·load
ship·mas·ter
ship·ment
ship·own·er
ship·pa·ble
ship·page
ship·per
ship's hus·band
ship·side
ship·way
ship·wreck
ship·wright
ship·yard
shire
shock
shoe·string
shoot
  shot
  shoot·ing
shoot·ee
shoot·er
shoot out *vb*
shoot-out *n*
shop
shop·break·er

shop·keep·er
shop·lift
shop·lift·er
shop·lift·ing
shore
  shored
  shor·ing
shore·line
short
short·age
short·change
  short·changed
  short·chang·ing
short-dat·ed
short·fall
short·ly
short-paid
short sight
short·sight·ed
short·sight·ed·ly
short·sight·ed·ness
short-term
short weight *n*
short-weight *vb*
short-wind·ed
shoul·der
shoul·der blade
show
  showed
  shown
  show·ing
show·case mer·
  chan·dise
show up *vb*
show·up *n*
shrie·val

shrie·val·ty
shunt·er
shunt·ing
shut down *vb*
  shut down
  shut·ting down
shut·down *n*
shut in *vb*
shut-in *n*
shy·lock
shy·ster
si
si ac·tio
sib
sib·ling
sib·ship
sic
sick
sick·en
  sick·ened
  sick·en·ing
sick·le
  sick·led
  sick·ling
sick·le-cell ane·
  mia
sickl·emia
sickl·emic
sick·ness
sick·room
side
side-bar
side ef·fect
side-end
side·line
sid·ero·sil·i·co·sis

sid·er·o·sis
  pl sid·er·o·ses

sid·er·ot·ic
side·slip
  side·slipped
  side·slip·ping
side·swipe
  side·swiped
  side·swip·ing
side·walk
sid·ing
sight
  payable on
  presentation
  (*see* cite, site)

sig·moid
  also sig·moi·dal

sig·moid·ec·to·my
  pl sig·moid·ec·to·mies

sig·moid·itis
sig·moid·o·scope
sig·moid·o·scop·ic
sig·moid·os·co·py
  pl sig·moid·os·co·pies

sig·moid·os·to·my
  pl sig·moid·os·to·mies

sign
sign·able
sig·nal
  sig·naled
  or sig·nalled
  sig·nal·ing
  or sig·nal·ling
sig·nal·er
  or sig·nal·ler

sig·nal·i·za·tion

sig·nal·ize
  sig·nal·ized
  sig·nal·iz·ing
sig·nal·man
  pl sig·nal·men

sig·nal·ment
sig·na·tary
  pl sig·na·tar·ies

sig·na·to·ry
  pl sig·na·to·ries

sig·na·tur·al
sig·na·ture
  sig·na·tured
  sig·na·tur·ing
sig·na·ture by
  mark
sig·na·ture·less
sign·board
signed
sign·ee
sign·er
sig·net
sig·nif·i·cant
sig·nif·i·cant·ly
sig·nif·i·cate
sig·nif·i·ca·tion
sig·nif·i·ca·tive
sig·nif·i·ca·vit
sig·ni·fi·er
sig·ni·fy
  sig·ni·fied
  sig·ni·fy·ing
sign off *vb*
sign-off *n*
sig·num
  pl sig·na

si·lence
  si·lenced
  si·lenc·ing
si·lent
si·len·ti·ary
  pl si·len·ti·ar·ies

sil·i·ca
sil·i·cate
si·li·ceous
  or si·li·cious

sil·i·con
si·li·co·si·der·osis
sil·i·co·sis
  pl sil·i·co·ses

sil·i·co·tu·ber·cu·lo·sis
sil·ver
sim·i·lar
sim·i·lar·ly
si·mil·i·ter
si·mil·i·ter di·ce·re
si·mil·i·tude
Sim·monds' dis·ease
si·mo·ny
  pl si·mo·nies

sim·ple
  sim·pler
  sim·plest
sim·ple-mind·ed
sim·plex ob·li·ga·to
sim·pli·ci·ter
sim·u·late
  sim·u·lat·ed

sim·u·lat·ing
sim·u·la·tion
si·mul·ta·ne·ity
si·mul·ta·ne·ous
si·mul·ta·ne·ous·ly
si·mul·ta·ne·ous·ness
si·nal
sin·a·lag·mat·ic
  var of synallagmatic

sin·cip·i·tal
sin·ci·put
  pl sin·ci·puts
  or sin·cip·i·ta

si·ne·cure
  easy job
  (*see* cynosure)

si·ne die
si·ne prae·ju·di·cio
si·ne pro·le
si·ne qua non
sin·ew
sin·gle
sin·gu·lar
sink
  sank
    or sunk
  sunk
  sink·ing
sink·able
si·no·atri·al
  also si·nu·atri·al

si·no·au·ric·u·lar
  or si·nu·au·ric·u·lar

si·nus
si·nus·itis

sire
  sired
  sir·ing
sire·less
si·ri·a·sis
  pl si·ri·a·ses

sis·ter
sis·ter-ger·man
  pl sis·ters-ger·man

sis·ter-in-law
  pl sis·ters-in-law

sit
  sat
  sit·ting
sit down *vb*
sit-down *n or adj*
sit-down·er
site
  a piece of land
  (*see* cite, sight)

sit in *vb*
sit-in *n*
si·to·ma·nia
si·tu
sit·u·ate
  sit·u·at·ed
  sit·u·at·ing
sit·u·a·tion
sit·u·a·tion·al
si·tus
  pl si·tus

ska·tol·o·gy
  var of scatology

skel·e·tal
skel·e·tal·ly
skel·e·to·mus·cu·lar

skel·e·ton
skill
skilled
skill·ful
  or skil·ful

skill·ful·ly
skill·ful·ness
skim
  skimmed
  skim·ming
skin
  skinned
  skin·ning
skin·ner
skip
  skipped
  skip·ping
skip·per·age
skul·dug·ger·y
  or skull·dug·ger·y
  also scul·dug·ger·y
  or scull·dug·ger·y
  pl skul·dug·ger·ies
  or skull·dug·ger·ies
  also scul·dug·ger·ies
  or scull·dug·ger·ies

sky·lark·ing
sky·light
sky·way
slack
slack·age
slack·en
  slack·ened
  slack·en·ing
slack·er
slan·der
slan·der·er

slan·der·ing
slan·der·ous
slap
  slapped
  slap·ping
slate
  slat·ed
  slat·ing
slave
  slaved
  slav·ing
slav·ery
slay
  slew
  slain
  slay·ing
slay·er
sleep
  slept
  sleep·ing
sleep·ing pill
sleep·walk
sleep·walk·er
sleight of hand
slid·ing scale
slight
  slight·er
  slight·est
slight·ly
slip
slip·page
slip·pery
  slip·peri·er
  slip·peri·est
slip·shod
slip·shod·di·ness

slip·shod·ness
slob·ber
  slob·bered
  slob·ber·ing
slot ma·chine
slough
  a side channel of
  a river
  (*see* slough *or* sluff)

slough
  or sluff
  dead tissue separating
  from an ulcer
  (*see* slough)

slow·down
sludge
slug
  slugged
  slug·ging
sluice
sluice·way
slum
slum·lord
slur
  slurred
  slur·ring
slush fund
small
  small·er
  small·est
small·hold·er
small-scale
smart mon·ey
smash·able
smash-and-grab
smash up *vb*
smash·up *n*

smear

smol·der
　　or smoul·der

smoth·er

smug·gle
　　smug·gled
　　smug·gling
　　smug·gler

snake·bite

snare
　　snared
　　snar·ing

snar·er

snatch

snatch·er

sneak thief

snipe
　　sniped
　　snip·ing

snip·er

soak·age

so·ber
　　so·ber·er
　　so·ber·est

so·bri·ety

so·bri·quet
　　or sou·bri·quet

so·cage
　　or soc·cage

so·cag·er

so·called

so·cial

so·ci·e·tas
　　pl so·ci·e·ta·tes

so·ci·e·tas le·o·
　　ni·na

so·ci·e·tas na·va·lis

so·ci·e·tas uni·ver·
　　so·rum
　　bo·no·rum

so·cié·té ano·nyme

so·cié·té en com·
　　man·dite

so·ci·ety
　　pl so·ci·et·ies

so·cio·med·i·cal

so·cio·path

so·cio·path·ic

so·ci·op·a·thy
　　pl so·ci·op·a·thies

so·cio·sex·u·al

so·cio·sex·u·al·i·ty

so·ci·us
　　pl so·cii

so·ci·us cri·mi·nis

sock·et

so·di·um

so·di·um pen·to·
　　thal

so·di·um se·co·nal

sod·om·ite

sod·om·it·i·cal

sod·omy
　　pl sod·om·ies

soft·core

soft goods

so·journ

so·journ·er

so·journ·ing

so·journ·ment

so·la
　　or so·la bill

so·la·nine
　　or so·la·nin

so·lar plex·us
　　pl so·lar plex·us·es

so·la·ti·um
　　pl so·la·tia

sol·dier

sole

sole·ly

sol·emn

sol·em·ni·za·tion

sol·em·nize
　　sol·em·nized
　　sol·em·niz·ing

sol·emn·ly

sol·emn·ness

sole·print

so·le·us
　　pl so·lei
　　also so·le·us·es

so·lic·it

so·lic·i·tant

so·lic·i·ta·tion

so·lic·i·tor

so·lic·i·tor·ship

so·lic·i·tress

sol·id
　　sol·id·er
　　sol·id·est

sol·i·dar·i·ty
　　pl sol·i·dar·i·ties

sol·i·dary

sol·i·tary

so·lon

so long as

so·lo·ni·an

so·lu·tio
so·lu·tion
solv·abil·i·ty
solv·able
solve
  solved
  solv·ing
sol·ven·cy
sol·ven·do es·se
sol·vent
sol·vent·ly
so·mas·the·nia
so·mat·ic
so·mat·i·cal·ly
so·ma·to·log·i·cal
so·ma·tol·o·gy
  pl so·ma·tol·o·gies
so·mato·path·ic
so·mato·psy·chic
so·mato·sen·so·ry
som·es·the·sia
  also som·es·the·sis
  pl som·es·the·sias
  also som·es·the·ses
som·nam·bu·lant
som·nam·bu·lar
som·nam·bu·late
som·nam·bu·lat·
  ed
som·nam·bu·lat·
  ing
som·nam·bu·la·tion
som·nam·bu·la·tor
som·nam·bu·lism
som·nam·bu·list
som·nam·bu·lis·tic
som·nam·bu·lis·ti·
  cal·ly

som·ni·fa·cient
som·nif·er·ous
som·nif·u·gous
som·nil·o·quist
som·no·lence
  also som·no·len·cy
  pl som·no·lenc·es
  also som·no·len·cies
som·no·lent
som·no·lent·ly
son
son as·sault de·
  mesne
son·i·ca·tion
son-in-law
  pl sons-in-law
so·phis·ti·cate
  so·phis·ti·cat·ed
  so·phis·ti·cat·ing
so·phis·ti·ca·tion
so·phis·ti·ca·tor
so·pite
  so·pit·ed
  so·pit·ing
so·po·rif·er·ous
so·po·rif·er·ous·
  ness
so·po·rif·ic
so·po·rose
sor·des
  pl sor·des
sor·or·i·cide
sou·bri·quet
  var of sobriquet
souf·flé
sound
sound·ly
sound·ness

source
south·bound
south·east
south·east·er·ly
south·east·ern
south·east·ward
south·east·ward·ly
south·er·ly
south·ern
south·ward
south·ward·ly
south·west
south·west·er·ly
south·west·ern
south·west·ward
south·west·ward·
  ly
sov·er·eign
sov·er·eign·ly
sov·er·eign·ty
  pl sov·er·eign·ties

Span·ish fly
spare
  spared
  spar·ing
spar·go·sis
  pl spar·go·ses
  or spar·go·sis·es
spasm
spas·mat·ic
  or spas·mat·i·cal
spas·mod·ic
  or spas·mod·i·cal
spas·mod·i·cal·ly
spas·mo·gen·ic
spas·mo·lyt·ic
spas·tic

spas·tic·i·ty
  pl spas·tic·i·ties

speak
  spoke
  spo·ken
  speak·ing

speak·easy
  pl speak·eas·ies

speak·er

spe·cial

spe·cial·ist

spe·cial·ize
  spe·cial·ized
  spe·cial·iz·ing

spe·cial·ly

spe·cial·ty
  spe·cial·ties

spe·cie
  pl species
  coined money
  (*see* species)

spe·cies
  pl spe·cies
  class of individuals
  (*see* specie)

spe·cies fac·ti

spe·cif·ic

spe·cif·i·cal·i·ty

spe·cif·i·cal·ly

spe·cif·i·cate
  spe·cif·i·cat·ed
  spe·cif·i·cat·ing

spec·i·fi·ca·tion

spec·i·fi·ca·tive

spec·i·fic·i·ty

spe·cif·i·cize
  spe·cif·i·cized
  spe·cif·i·ciz·ing

spec·i·fy
  spec·i·fied
  spec·i·fy·ing

spe·ci·os·i·ty
  pl spe·ci·os·i·ties

spe·cious

spec·u·late
  spec·u·lat·ed
  spec·u·lat·ing

spec·u·la·tion

spec·u·la·tive

spec·u·la·tor

speech

speed
  sped
    or speed·ed
  speed·ing

speed·er

speed·i·ly

speed up *vb*

speed·up *n*

speedy
  speed·i·er
  speed·i·est

spend
  spent
  spend·ing

spend·able

spend·er

spend·thrift

spend·thrift·i·ness

spend·thrifty

spe·rate

sperm

sper·mat·ic

sper·mato·cid·al
  or sper·mi·cid·al

sper·mato·cide
  or sper·mi·cide

sper·ma·to·zo·on
  pl sper·ma·to·zoa

spes phthis·i·ca

sphac·e·late
  sphac·e·lat·ed
  sphac·e·lat·ing

sphac·e·la·tion

sphen·eth·moid

sphe·ni·on

sphe·no·bas·i·lar
  or sphe·no·bas·i·lic

sphe·no·eth·moid

sphe·no·fron·tal

sphe·noid
  also sphe·noi·dal

sphe·noid·itis

sphe·no·man·dib·u·lar

sphe·no·max·il·lary

sphe·no·oc·cip·i·tal

sphe·no·pal·a·tine

sphe·no·pa·ri·etal

sphe·no·pe·tro·sal

sphe·no·sis

sphe·no·squa·mo·sal

sphen·otic

sphe·no·tur·bi·nal

sphinc·ter

sphinc·ter·al

spi·ca
  pl spi·cae
  or spi·cas

spiff

spill
  spilled
    also spilt
  spill·ing
spill·age
spill·er
spi·na
  pl spi·nae

spi·nal
spi·na·lis
  pl spi·na·les

spi·nal·ly
spine
spin off *vb*
  span off
  spun off
  spin·ning off
spin-off *n*
spin·ster
spi·ril·li·ci·dal
spi·ril·lo·sis
  pl spi·ril·lo·ses
  or spi·ril·lo·sis·es

spi·ril·lum
  pl spi·ril·la

spir·it
spir·i·tu·ous
spir·i·tus
spir·i·tus fru·men·
ti
spi·ro·chae·ta
  or spi·ro·che·ta
  pl spi·ro·chae·tae
  or spi·ro·che·tae

spi·ro·chet·al
  or spi·ro·chaet·al

spi·ro·chete
  or spi·ro·chaete

spi·ro·chet·emia
spi·ro·che·ti·ci·dal
spi·ro·che·ti·cide
  or spi·ro·chae·ti·cide

spi·ro·chet·osis
  or spi·ro·chaet·osis
  pl spi·ro·chet·oses
  or spi·ro·chaet·oses

spite fence
spite-work
spiv
spiv·ery
  or spiv·very
  pl spiv·er·ies
  or spiv·ver·ies

splint
  splint·ed
  splint·ing
splint·age
split
split off *vb*
  split off
  split·ting off
split-off *n*
split up *vb*
  split up
  split·ing up
split-up *n*
spoil
  spoiled
    or spoilt
  spoil·ing
spoil·able
spoil·age
spoil·a·tion

spoils·man
  pl spoils·men

spo·li·ate
  spo·li·at·ed
  spo·li·at·ing
spo·li·a·tion
spo·li·a·tor
spo·li·a·to·ry
spo·li·um
  pl spo·lia

spon·dy·lit·ic
spon·dy·li·tis
spon·dy·lop·a·thy
  pl spon·dy·lop·a·thies

spon·sion
spon·sor
spon·so·ri·al
spon·sor·ship
spon·ta·ne·ous
spon·ta·ne·ous·ly
spot
spot check *n*
spot-check *vb*
spot·ter
spouse
spouse·less
sprag
  spragged
  sprag·ging
spread
  spread
  spread·ing
spring
  sprang
    or sprung
  sprung

spring·ing
spring tide
sprin·kler
spu·ri·ous
spu·ri·ous·ly
spu·ri·ous·ness
spu·tum
  pl spu·ta

spy *n*
  pl spies

spy *vb*
  spied
  spy·ing
squad
squat
  squat·ted
  squat·ting
squat·ter
squeal
squeal·er
squeeze
  squeezed
  squeez·ing
squeeze play
squire
stab
  stabbed
  stab·bing
sta·bil·i·ty
  pl sta·bil·i·ties

sta·bi·li·za·tion
sta·bi·lize
  sta·bi·lized
  sta·bi·liz·ing
sta·ble
sta·ble·ness

staff
stage
stag·ger
  stag·gered
  stag·ger·ing
stag·num
  pl stag·na

stair·way
stair·well
stake
  staked
  stak·ing
stake·hold·er
stake out *vb*
stake·out *n*
stale
stale·ness
stall
stall·age
stamp
stand
  stood
  stand·ing
stan·dard
stan·dard·iz·able
stan·dard·iza·tion
stan·dard·ize
  stan·dard·ized
  stan·dard·iz·ing
stand by *vb*
stand·by *n*
  pl stand·bys
stan·na·ry
  pl stan·na·ries
stan·te ma·tri·mo·
  nio

sta·pe·dec·to·mized
sta·pe·dec·to·my
  pl sta·pe·dec·to·mies

sta·pe·di·al
sta·pes
  pl sta·pes
  or sta·pe·des

staph·y·lo·coc·cal
staph·y·lo·coc·cic
staph·y·lo·coc·cus
  pl staph·y·lo·coc·ci

staph·y·lo·der·ma·
  ti·tis
  pl staph·y·lo·der·
    ma·ti·tis·es
  or staph·y·lo·der·ma·
    tit·i·des

staph·y·lo·coc·ce·
  mia
sta·ple
star·board
star-cham·ber
sta·re de·ci·sis
sta·re in ju·di·cio
sta·sis
  pl sta·ses

stat·able
  or state·able

stat·al
state
  stat·ed
  stat·ing
state·hood
state·house
state·less
state·less·ness

state·ment
state·way
sta·tio itur·ve
  na·vi·gio
sta·tion
sta·tion·ary
  still
  (see stationery)

sta·tio·ner
sta·tio·nery
  pl sta·tio·ner·ies
  writing material
  (see stationary)

sta·tis·ti·cal
sta·tis·tics
sta·tus
sta·tus quo
stat·ut·able
stat·ut·able·ness
stat·ut·ably
stat·ute
  stat·ut·ed
  stat·ut·ing
stat·ute of
  lim·i·ta·tions
stat·u·to·ri·ly
stat·u·to·ry
stax·is
stay
  stayed
    or staid
  stay·ing
stay-in
stead
steal
  stole

sto·len
steal·ing
steal·able
steal·age
stealth
stealthy
  stealth·i·er
  stealth·i·est
steer
steer·age
steer·er
stel·lion·ate
steno·car·dia
ste·nog·ra·pher
steno·graph·ic
steno·graph·i·cal·ly
ste·nog·ra·phy
Ste·no's duct
ste·nose
  ste·nosed
  ste·nos·ing
ste·no·sis
  pl ste·no·ses

ste·not·ic
sten·tor
step
  stepped
  step·ping
step·broth·er
step·child
  pl step·chil·dren
step·daugh·ter
step·fa·ther
step·moth·er
step·page
step·par·ent

step·sis·ter
step·son
ste·re·og·no·sis
ste·re·og·nos·tic
ster·ile
ste·ril·i·ty
  pl ste·ril·i·ties
ster·il·iza·tion
ster·il·ize
  ster·il·ized
  ster·il·iz·ing
ster·il·iz·er
ster·no·cla·vic·u·lar
ster·no·clei·do·mas·
  toid
ster·no·cos·tal
ster·no·hy·oid
ster·no·mas·toid
ster·no·thy·roid
ster·num
  pl ster·nums
  or ster·na

ster·nu·ta·tion
ster·nu·ta·tor
ster·nu·ta·to·ry
  or ster·nu·ta·tive

ster·tor
ster·to·rous
ster·to·rous·ly
stetho·scope
stet pro·ces·sus
ste·ve·dore
  ste·ve·dored
  ste·ve·dor·ing
stew·ard
stew·ard·ship

stib·i·um

stick up *vb*
 stuck up
 stick·ing up
stick·up *n*
stig·ma·ti·za·tion
stig·ma·tize
 stig·ma·tized
 stig·ma·tiz·ing
stil·bes·trol
 also stil·boes·trol

still
still·age
still·birth
still·born
stim·u·lant
stim·u·late
 stim·u·lat·ed
 stim·u·lat·ing
stim·u·la·tion
stim·u·la·tive
stim·u·lus
 pl stim·u·li

stint
sti·pend
sti·pen·di·ary mag·
 is·trate
stip·u·la·ble
stip·u·late
 stip·u·lat·ed
 stip·u·lat·ing
stip·u·la·tion
stip·u·la·tor
stip·u·la·to·ry
stir·pi·tal

stirps
 pl stir·pes

stock
stock·a·teer
stock·bro·ker
stock·brok·ing
 or stock·bro·ker·age

stock·hold·er
stock·hold·ing
stock·job·ber
stock·job·bing
stock·keep·er
stock·man
 pl stock·men

stock·tak·ing
sto·len
stom·ach
stom·ach·ache
sto·mach·ic
 also sto·mach·i·cal

sto·ma·ti·tis
 pl sto·ma·tit·i·des
 or sto·ma·ti·tis·es

sto·ma·to·gas·tric
sto·ma·to·log·i·cal
sto·ma·tol·o·gist
sto·ma·tol·o·gy
 pl sto·ma·tol·o·gies

stone-blind
stone-blind·ness
stone-deaf
stone-deaf·ness
stool pi·geon
stop
 stopped
 stop·ping

stope
stop·gap
stop·light
stop-loss
stop·page
stop·page in
 tran·si·tu
stor·able
stor·age
store
 stored
 stor·ing
store·break·ing
store·house
store·keep·er
store·room
stouth·rief
 also stouth·rife

stow·age
stow·away
stra·bis·mal
stra·bis·mus
strad·dle
 strad·dled
 strad·dling
strag·gler
straight
straight-line
straight time *n*
straight-time *adj*
strait·jack·et
 or straight·jack·et
stra·mo·ni·um
strand
strang·er
strang·er in blood

stran·gle
  stran·gled
  stran·gling
stran·gler
stran·gu·late
  stran·gu·lat·ed
  stran·gu·lat·ing
stran·gu·la·tion
strat·a·gem
strat·e·gy
  pl strat·e·gies

stra·tum
  pl stra·ta
  also stra·tums

straw man
  pl straw men

stray
street
street·walk·er
street·walk·ing
strepho·sym·bo·lia
strepho·sym·bol·ic
strep·to·coc·cal
  or strep·to·coc·cic

strep·to·coc·ce·mia
strep·to·coc·co·sis
strep·to·coc·cus
  pl strep·to·coc·ci

strep·to·my·ces
  pl strep·to·my·ces
  or strep·to·my·ce·tes

strep·to·my·cin
strep·to·thri·cin
strep·to·thrix
  pl strep·to·thri·ces

strep·to·tri·cho·sis
  also strep·to·thri·co·sis

stretch
stretch-out
stria
  pl stri·ae

strick·en
strict
  strict·er
  strict·est
stric·ti ju·ris
stric·tis·si·mi ju·ris
strict·ly
stric·to ju·ri
stric·tum jus
  or stric·tum ius

stric·ture
stri·dent
stri·dor
strike
  struck
  strik·ing
strike·break·er
strike·break·ing
strik·er
strin·gent
strin·gent·ly
strip mine *n*
strip-mine *vb*
  strip-mined
  strip-min·ing
strip min·er
stroke
stro·ma
  pl stro·ma·ta

stro·mal
stro·ma·tal
stro·mat·ic
strong arm *n*
  also strong·arm·er

strong-arm *adj or vb*
strong·box
stron·tium
stro·phan·thin
struc·tur·al
struc·ture
strych·nine
strych·nin·ism
strych·nin·iza·tion
stub·born
stub·born·ly
stump·age
stu·pe·fa·cient
stu·pe·fac·tion
stu·pe·fac·tive
stu·pe·fy
  stu·pe·fied
  stu·pe·fy·ing
stu·por
stu·por·ous
styp·sis
styp·tic
su·abil·i·ty
su·able
su·ably
sua·si·ble
sua·sion
sua·sive
sua·sive·ly
sua·sive·ness
sua spon·te

sub
  subbed
  sub·bing
sub·ab·dom·i·nal
sub·ac·count
sub·acute
sub·acute·ly
sub·agen·cy
  sub·agen·cies
sub·agent
sub·al·lo·cate
  sub·al·lo·cat·ed
  sub·al·lo·cat·ing
sub·al·lo·ca·tion
sub·arach·noid
sub·as·sign·ee
sub·chap·ter
sub·claim
sub·clause
sub·cla·vi·an
sub·cla·vi·us
  pl sub·cla·vii

sub·clin·i·cal
sub·clin·i·cal·ly
sub co·lo·re ju·ris
sub·co·ma
sub·com·mis·sion
sub·com·mis·sion·er
sub·com·mit·tee
sub·com·pa·ny
  pl sub·com·pa·nies

sub con·di·ti·o·ne
sub·con·scious
sub·con·scious·ly
sub·con·scious·ness
sub·con·tract

sub·con·trac·tor
sub·cor·tex
  pl sub·cor·ti·ces
  or sub·cor·tex·es

sub·cor·ti·cal
sub·cu·ta·ne·ous
sub·del·e·gate
  sub·del·e·gat·ed
  sub·del·e·gat·ing
sub·del·e·ga·tion
sub·der·mal
sub·dis·trict
sub·di·vid·able
sub·di·vide
  sub·di·vid·ed
  sub·di·vid·ing
sub·di·vid·er
sub·di·vis·i·ble
sub·di·vi·sion
sub·en·dorse
  sub·en·dorsed
  sub·en·dors·ing
sub·ja·cent
sub·ject
sbu·jec·tion
sub·jec·tion·al
sub·jec·tive
sub ju·di·ce
sub·lease
  sub·leased
  sub·leas·ing
sub·les·see
sub·les·sor
sub·let
  sub·let
  sub·let·ting

sub·le·thal
sub·le·thal·ly
sub·li·cense
  sub·li·censed
  sub·li·cens·ing
sub·li·cens·ee
sub·lux·a·tion
sub·merge
  sub·merged
  sub·merg·ing
sub·mer·gence
sub·mis·sion
sub·mit
  sub·mit·ted
  sub·mit·ting
sub·mit·tal
sub·mit·tance
sub·mit·ter
sub mo·do
sub·mu·co·sa
sub·mu·co·sal
sub·nar·cot·ic
sub no·mi·ne
sub·nor·mal
sub·nor·mal·ly
sub·or·di·nate
  sub·or·di·nat·ed
  sub·or·di·nat·ing
sub·or·di·na·tion
sub·orn
sub·or·na·tion
sub·orn·er
sub·part·ner·ship
sub pe·de si·gil·li
sub poe·na *adv*
sub·poe·na
  also sub·pe·na

sub·poe·na ad tes·
ti·fi·can·dum
pl sub·poe·nas ad tes·
ti·fi·can·dum

sub·poe·na du·ces
te·cum
pl sub·poe·nas du·ces
te·cum

sub·poe·nal
sub·po·ten·cy
pl sub·po·ten·cies

sub·po·tent
sub·rep·tion
sub·rep·ti·tious
sub·ro·gate
sub·ro·gat·ed
sub·ro·gat·ing
sub·ro·ga·tion
sub·ro·gee
sub·ro·gor
sub ro·sa *adv*
sub·ro·sa *adj*
sub·scribe
sub·scribed
sub·scrib·ing
sub·scrib·er
sub·scrip·tion
sub·sec·tion
sub·se·quent
sub·se·quen·tial
sub·se·quent·ly
sub·ser·vi·ent
sub·si·dence
sub·sid·iary
pl sub·sid·iar·ies

sub·si·diz·able

sub·si·di·za·tion
sub·si·dize
sub·si·dized
sub·si·diz·ing
sub·si·dy
pl sub·si·dies

sub si·len·tio
sub·sist
sub·sis·tence
sub·stance
sub·stance·less
sub·stan·dard
sub·stan·tia·ble
sub·stan·tial
sub·stan·ti·a·lia
sub·stan·ti·al·i·ty
sub·stan·tial·ize
sub·stan·tial·ized
sub·stan·tial·iz·
ing
sub·stan·tial·ly
sub·stan·tial·ness
sub·stan·ti·ate
sub·stan·ti·at·ed
sub·stan·ti·at·ing
sub·stan·ti·a·tion
sub·stan·ti·a·tor
sub·stan·tive
sub·stan·tive·ly
sub·stan·tive·ness
sub·sti·tute
sub·sti·tut·ed
sub·sti·tut·ing
sub·sti·tut·er
sub·sti·tu·tion
sub·sti·tu·tion·al

sub·sti·tu·tion·ary
sub·sti·tu·tive
sub·strac·tion
sub·sure·ty·ship
sub·ten·an·cy
pl sub·ten·an·cies

sub·ten·ant
sub·ter·fuge
sub·tract
sub·trac·tion
sub·val·u·a·tion
sub·ven·tion
sub·ver·sion
sub·ver·sion·ary
sub·ver·sive
sub·vert
sub·vert·er
sub·vert·ible
suc·ce·da·ne·um
pl suc·ce·da·ne·ums
or suc·ce·da·nea

suc·ceed
suc·ceed·ing
suc·cess·ful
suc·cess·ful·ly
suc·ces·sion
suc·ces·sive
suc·ces·sive·ly
suc·ces·sor
suc·ces·sor·ship
suc·cinct
su·da·tion
sud·den
sud·den·ly
sue
sued

su·ing
su·er
suf·fer
suf·fer·ance
suf·fer·er
suf·fer·ing
suf·fi·cien·cy
  pl suf·fi·cien·cies
suf·fi·cient
suf·fo·cate
  suf·fo·cat·ed
  suf·fo·cat·ing
suf·fo·ca·tion
suf·frage
sug·gest
sug·ges·tio fal·si
sug·ges·tion
sug·gil·la·tion
sui·cid·al
sui·cid·al·ly
sui·cide
sui·cid·ol·o·gist
sui·cid·ol·o·gy
  pl sui·cid·ol·o·gies

sui ge·ner·is
sui ju·ris
suit
suit·able
suit·ably
suit·or
sul·fa
sul·fa·di·a·zine
sul·fa·gua·ni·dine
sul·fa·mer·a·zine
sul·fa·meth·a·zine
sul·fa·mez·a·thine

sul·fa·nil·amide
sul·fa·nil·ic
sul·fa·pyr·azine
sul·fa·pyr·i·dine
sul·fa·qui·nox·a·
  line
sulf·ars·phen·a·
  mine
sul·fate
  sul·fat·ed
  sul·fat·ing
sul·fa·thi·a·zole
sul·fide
sul·fite
sul·fon·amide
sul·fur
sul·fu·rate
sul·fu·rize
  sul·fu·rized
  sul·fu·riz·ing
sul·lage
sul·phate
sul·phide
sul·phite
sul·phur
sul·phu·rate
sul·phu·rize
sum
  summed
  sum·ming
sum·mari·ly
sum·ma·rize
  sum·ma·rized
  sum·ma·riz·ing
sum·ma·ry
  pl sum·ma·ries

sum·ming-up
  pl sum·mings-up
sum·mon
sum·mon·er
sum·mons n
  pl sum·mons·es
  also sum·mons

sum·mons vb
  sum·monsed
  sum·mons·ing
sum·mum bo·num
sum·mum jus
sun·dries n pl
sun·dry
sun·stroke
suo no·mi·ne
suo pe·ri·cu·lo
su·per·an·nu·able
su·per·an·nu·ate
  su·per·an·nu·at·
  ed
  su·per·an·nu·at·
  ing
su·per·an·nu·a·tion
su·per·an·nu·i·tant
su·per·an·nu·ity
  pl su·per·an·nu·ities
su·per·car·go
  pl su·per·car·gos
  or su·per·car·goes

su·per·cede
  var of supersede

su·per·fi·ci·ary
su·per·fi·cies
  pl su·per·fi·cies
su·per·in·tend

su·per·in·ten·dence
su·per·in·ten·den·cy
su·per·in·ten·dent
su·per·in·ten·dent·
ship
su·pe·ri·or
su·pe·ri·or·i·ty
    pl su·pe·ri·or·i·ties

su·per·na·tion·al
su·per·na·tion·al·
ism
su·per·se·cret
su·per·sede
    or su·per·cede
    su·per·sed·ed
    or su·per·ced·ed
    su·per·sed·ing
    or su·per·ced·ing

su·per·se·de·as
    pl su·per·se·de·as

su·per·sed·ence
su·per·sed·er
su·per·se·de·re
su·per·se·dure
su·per·se·nior·i·ty
    pl su·per·se·nior·i·ties

su·per·ser·vice·able
su·per·ses·sion
su·per·ses·sive
su·per·ses·sor
su·per·tax
su·per·vene
    su·per·vened
    su·per·ven·ing
su·per·ve·nience
su·per·ve·nient

su·per·ven·tion
su·per·vis·al
su·per·vise
    su·per·vised
    su·per·vis·ing
su·per·vis·ee
su·per·vi·sion
su·per·vi·sor
su·per·vi·so·ri·al
su·per·vi·sor·ship
su·per·vi·so·ry
sup·plant
sup·plant·er
sup·ple·ment
sup·ple·men·tal
sup·ple·men·tar·i·ly
sup·ple·men·ta·ry
sup·ple·men·ta·tion
sup·ple·ment·er
sup·ple·to·ry
sup·pli·able
sup·pli·ance
sup·pli·ant
sup·pli·ca·vit
sup·pli·er
sup·ply *vb*
    sup·plied
    sup·ply·ing
sup·ply *n*
    pl sup·plies

sup·port
sup·port·able
sup·port·ance
sup·port·er
sup·port·less
sup·pose

sup·posed
sup·pos·ing
sup·pos·ed·ly
sup·po·si·tion
sup·po·si·tion·al
sup·pos·i·ti·tious
sup·pos·i·tive
sup·press
sup·press·ible
sup·pres·sion
sup·pres·sio ve·ri
sup·pres·sive
su·pra
su·pra·na·tion·al
su·pra·pro·test
su·preme
sur
sur·charge
    sur·charged
    sur·charg·ing
sure·ty
    pl sure·ties

sure·ty·ship
sur·face wa·ter
sur·geon
sur·geon gen·er·al
    pl sur·geons gen·er·al

sur·gery
    pl sur·ger·ies

sur·gi·cal
sur·mis·able
sur·mise
    sur·mised
    sur·mis·ing
sur·name

sur·named
sur·nam·ing
sur·plus
sur·plus·age
sur·prise
sur·prised
sur·pris·ing
sur·re·but
sur·re·but·ted
sur·re·but·ting
sur·re·but·ter
also sur·re·but·tal

sur·re·join
sur·re·join·der
sur·ren·der
sur·ren·der·ee
sur·ren·der·or
sur·rep·ti·tious
sur·rep·ti·tious·ly
sur·ro·ga·cy
pl sur·ro·ga·cies

sur·ro·gate
sur·tax
sur·veil·lance
sur·veil·lant
sur·vey
sur·vey·able
sur·vey·ance
sur·vey·ing
sur·vey·or
sur·viv·abil·i·ty
sur·viv·able
sur·viv·al
sur·viv·ance
sur·vive
sur·vived

sur·viv·ing
sur·vi·vor
sur·vi·vor·ship
sus·cep·ti·bil·i·ty
pl sus·cep·ti·bil·i·ties

sus·cep·ti·ble
sus·cep·ti·bly
sus·pect
sus·pect·able
sus·pect·ed·ly
sus·pect·ed·ness
sus·pect·er
sus·pend
sus·pend·er
sus·pense
sus·pen·sion
sus·pen·sive
sus·pen·so·ry
sus·pi·cion
sus·pi·cious
sus·tain
sus·tain·able
sus·tain·ment
sus·te·nance
sus·te·nant
su·us he·res
su·zer·ain
su·zer·ain·ty
swear
swore
sworn
swear·ing
swear·er
swear·er-in
sweat
sweat·shop

sweep·stakes
sweet·heart agree·
ment
or sweet·heart con·
tract

swin·dle
swin·dled
swin·dling
swin·dle·able
swin·dler
syl·la·bus
pl syl·la·bi
or syl·la·bus·es

sym·bol·ic
sym·bol·i·cal
sym·pa·thet·ic
sym·pa·thy
pl sym·pa·thies

sym·phy·sis
pl sym·phy·ses

symp·tom
symp·tom·at·ic
symp·tom·at·i·cal·
ly
symp·tom·at·o·log·
i·cal
or symp·tom·at·o·
log·ic

symp·tom·at·o·log·
i·cal·ly
symp·tom·atol·o·gy
symp·tom·less
syn·aes·the·sia
var of synesthesia

syn·aes·thet·ic
var of synesthetic

syn·al·lag·mat·ic
  or sin·a·lag·mat·ic

syn·dic
syn·di·cal
syn·di·cate
  syn·di·cat·ed
  syn·di·cat·ing
  syn·di·ca·tor
syn·drome
syn·er·get·ic
syn·er·gic
  also syn·er·gi·cal

syn·er·gi·cal·ly
syn·er·gism
syn·er·gist
syn·er·gis·tic
  also syn·er·gis·ti·cal

syn·er·gis·ti·cal·ly
syn·er·gy
  pl syn·er·gies

syn·es·the·sia
  or syn·aes·the·sia

syn·es·thet·ic
  or syn·aes·thet·ic

syn·os·tose
  syn·os·tosed
  syn·os·tos·ing
syn·os·to·sis
  also syn·os·te·osis
  pl syn·os·to·ses
  also syn·os·te·oses

syn·os·tot·ic
syn·os·tot·i·cal·ly
sy·no·via
sy·no·vi·al
sy·no·vi·tis

syn·thet·ic
  also syn·thet·i·cal

syn·thet·i·cal·ly
syph·il·e·mia
syph·i·lid
syph·i·lis
syph·i·lit·ic
syph·i·li·za·tion
syph·i·lize
  syph·i·lized
  syph·i·liz·ing
syph·i·lo·derm
  or syph·i·lo·der·ma
  pl syph·i·lo·derms
  or syph·i·lo·der·ma·ta

syph·i·lol·o·gy
  pl syph·i·lol·o·gies

syph·i·lo·phobe
syph·i·lo·pho·bia
syph·i·lo·psy·cho·sis
  pl syph·i·lo·psy·cho·ses

syph·i·lo·ther·a·py
  pl syph·i·lo·ther·a·pies

sy·ringe
  sy·ringed
  sy·ring·ing
sys·tem
sys·tem·at·ic
  also sys·tem·at·i·cal

sys·tem·at·i·cal·ly
sys·tem·ati·za·tion
sys·tem·atize
  sys·tem·atized

sys·tem·atiz·ing
sys·tem·ic
sys·tem·i·cal·ly
sys·to·le
sys·tol·ic

T

tab
tab·a·co·sis
ta·bes
ta·bes·cent
ta·bes dor·sa·lis
ta·bet·ic
ta·ble
  ta·bled
  ta·bling
ta·boo
  or ta·bu
  ta·booed
  or ta·bued
  ta·boo·ing
  or ta·bu·ing
ta·bo·pa·re·sis
  pl ta·bo·pa·re·ses

tab·u·la·ble
tab·u·la in
  nau·fra·gio
tab·u·lar
tab·u·late
  tab·u·lat·ed
  tab·u·lat·ing
tab·u·la·tion

tache noire
  pl taches noires

tachy·car·dia

tachy·car·di·ac

tachy·pnea
  also tachy·pnoea

tachy·pne·ic

tac·it

ta·cite

tac·it·ly

tac·it·ness

tac·i·tur·ni·ty
  pl tac·i·tur·ni·ties

tack

tack·er

tack·ing

tacks·man
  pl tacks·men

tac·tics

tac·tile

tae·di·um vi·tae

tag
  tagged
  tag·ging

tah·sil

tail

tail·age
  var of tallage

tai·la·gi·um

tail·ings

taint

tak·able
  or take·able

take
  took

tak·en

tak·ing

take-home

take-in

take over *vb*

take-over *n*

tak·er

take up *vb*
  took up
  tak·en up
  tak·ing up

take-up *n*

tak·ing in in·vi·
  tum

ta·lal·gia

tale·bear·er

tale·bear·ing

ta·les

ta·les de cir·cum·
  stan·ti·bus

ta·les·man
  pl ta·les·men

tali·pes

talk

tal·lage
  or tail·age
  also tal·li·age

tal·la·gi·um

tal·ly *n*
  pl tal·lies

tal·ly *vb*
  tal·lied
  tal·ly·ing

tal·ly·man
  pl tal·ly·men

tal qual

tam·per

tam·per·er

tam·per·ing

tam·pon

tam·pon·ade
  or tam·pon·age

tan·gi·bil·i·ty

tan·gi·ble

tan·gi·ble·ness

tan·gi·bly

tan·gle
  tan·gled
  tan·gling

tan·go
  pl tan·gos

tank

tank·age

tank·er

tan·ta·lum

tan·ta·mount

tan·tième

tan·trum

tap
  tapped
  tap·ping

tape
  taped
  tap·ing

tape-re·cord

tape re·cord·er

tar·de ve·nit

tar·dy
  tar·di·er
  tar·di·est

tare
  tared

tar·ing
tar·iff
tar·iff·less
tar·nish
tar·ry
  tar·ri·er
  tar·ri·est
tar·sal
tar·sa·le
  pl tar·sa·lia

tar·sal·gia
tar·so·meta·tar·sal
tar·so·pha·lan·ge·al
task
task·mas·ter
task·set·ter
task·work
tat·too
  also ta·too
  pl tat·toos
  also ta·toos

taunt
tav·ern
tax
  pl tax·es

tax·abil·i·ty
tax·able
tax·a·tion
tax·a·tion·al
tax·er
tax·ex·empt
tax-free
taxi *n*
  pl tax·is
  or tax·ies

taxi *vb*

tax·ied
taxi·ing
  or taxy·ing

taxi·cab
taxi·man
  pl taxi·men

taxi·me·ter
taxi·plane
tax·less
tax-loss com·pa·ny
tax-paid
tax·pay·er
teach
  taught
  teach·ing
teach·er
teach·er·age
team
team·er
team·ing
team·ster
tear
  tore
  torn
  tear·ing
tear gas *n*
tear·gas *vb*
  tear·gassed
  tear·gas·sing
tease
  teased
  teas·ing
tech·ne·tium
tech·ni·cal
tech·ni·cal·i·ty
  pl tech·ni·cal·i·ties

tech·ni·cal·ly
tech·ni·cian
tech·nique
tech·nol·o·gist
tech·nol·o·gy
  pl tech·nol·o·gies

teen·age
  or teen-aged

teen·ag·er
teens *n pl*
tee·ny·bop·per
teethe
  teethed
  teeth·ing
teg·men
  pl teg·mi·na

teg·men·tal
teind
teind·able
tel·al·gia
tel·an·gi·ec·ta·sia
  or tel·an·gi·ec·ta·sis
  pl tel·an·gi·ec·ta·sias
  or tel·an·gi·ec·ta·ses

tele·gram
tele·graph
tell
  told
  tell·ing
tell·er
tell·tale
tem·per
tem·per·ance
tem·per·ate
tem·pest
tem·po·ral

terminological

tem·po·ral·i·ty
pl tem·po·ral·i·ties

tem·po·ral·ty
pl tem·po·ral·ties

tem·po·rari·ly
tem·po·rari·ness
tem·po·rary
tem·po·re
tem·po·rize
  tem·po·rized
  tem·po·riz·ing
tem·po·riz·er
tempt
tempt·able
temp·ta·tion
tem·pus de·li·be·
  ran·di
ten·a·bil·i·ty
ten·a·ble
te·na·cious
te·na·cious·ly
te·nac·i·ty
pl te·nac·i·ties

ten·an·cy
pl ten·an·cies

ten·ant
ten·ant·able
ten·ant·less
ten·ant·like
ten·ant·right
ten·ant·ry
pl ten·ant·ries

ten·ant·ship
tend
ten·den·cy
pl ten·den·cies

ten·der
ten·der·abil·i·ty
ten·der·able
ten·der·er
ten·der·ness
ten·di·ni·tis
ten·di·nous
ten·do
pl ten·di·nes

ten·dol·y·sis
pl ten·dol·y·ses

ten·don
ten·don·itis
ten·do·plas·ty
pl ten·do·plas·ties

ten·e·ment
ten·e·men·tal
ten·e·men·ta·ry
ten·e·ment·ed
ten·e·men·tum
te·nen·das
te·nen·dum
te·nens
te·ne·re
possess
(*see* teneri)

te·ne·ri
a clause in a bond
(*see* tenere)

te·net
ten·nis el·bow
te·no·de·sis
pl te·no·de·ses

ten·o·dyn·ia
ten·on

ten·or
general character or
sense
(*see* tenure)

te·no·re prae·sen
ti·um
ten·os·to·sis
pl ten·os·to·ses
or ten·os·to·sis·es

te·no·sy·no·vi·tis
teno·vag·i·ni·tis
ten-per·cent·er
ten·sile
ten·ta·tive
ten·u·it
ten·ure
the act or right of
holding property
(*see* tenor)

te·nur·ial
terce
terc·er
term
term·er
ter·mi·na·bil·i·ty
ter·mi·na·ble
ter·mi·nal
ter·mi·nal·ly
ter·mi·nate
  ter·mi·nat·ed
  ter·mi·nat·ing
ter·mi·na·tion
ter·mi·na·tive
ter·mi·na·tor
ter·mi·na·to·ry
ter·mi·no·log·i·cal

ter·mi·no·log·i·cal·
ly
ter·mi·nol·o·gy
  pl ter·mi·nol·o·gies
ter·mi·nus
  or ter·mi·ni
  or ter·mi·nus·es
ter·mi·nus ad
quem
  also ter·mi·nus an·
  te quem
ter·mi·nus a que
  also ter·mi·nus post
  quem
term·less
ter·mon
ter·mor
term-trot·ter
ter·ra nul·li·us
terre-ten·ant
  or ter·ten·ant
ter·ri·ble
ter·ri·er
ter·ri·to·ri·al
ter·ri·to·ri·al·iza·
tion
ter·ri·to·ri·al·ize
  ter·ri·to·ri·al·ized
  ter·ri·to·ri·al·iz·
  ing
ter·ri·to·ry
  pl ter·ri·to·ries
ter·ror
ter·ror·ism
ter·ror·ist
ter·ror·iza·tion

ter·ror·ize
  ter·ror·ized
  ter·ror·iz·ing
ter·ten·ant
  var of terre-tenant
ter·tia·ry
  pl ter·tia·ries
ter·ti·um quid
ter·ti·us
test
test·abil·i·ty
test·able
tes·ta·cy
  pl tes·ta·cies
tes·ta·ment
tes·ta·men·tal
tes·ta·men·ta·ry
tes·ta·men·tum
  pl tes·ta·men·ta
tes·tate
tes·ta·tion
tes·ta·tor
tes·ta·trix
  pl tes·ta·tri·ces
tes·ta·tum
  pl tes·ta·ta
tes·ta·tum ca·pi·as
  or tes·ta·tum ca·pi·as
  ad sa·tis·fa·ci·en·
  dum
tes·te
test·er
tes·ti·cle
tes·tic·u·lar
tes·ti·fy
  tes·ti·fied

tes·ti·fy·ing
tes·ti·mo·ni·al
tes·ti·mo·nio
tes·ti·mo·ni·um
  pl tes·ti·mo·nia
tes·ti·mo·ny
  pl tes·ti·mo·nies
tes·tis
  pl tes·tes
tes·tos·ter·one
test tube *n*
test-tube *adj*
tet·a·nal
te·tan·ic
te·tan·i·cal·ly
te·tan·i·form
tet·a·nism
tet·a·ni·za·tion
tet·a·nize
  tet·a·nized
  tet·a·niz·ing
tet·a·nus
tet·a·ny
  pl tet·a·nies
tet·ra·caine
tet·ra·chlo·ride
tet·ra·chlo·ro·eth·
ane
  also tet·ra·chlor·eth·
  ane
tet·ra·chlo·ro·eth·
yl·ene
tet·ra·cy·cline
tet·ra·eth·yl·am·
mo·ni·um

tet·ra·eth·yl·thi·u·
  ram
tet·ra·hy·dro·can·
  nab·i·nol
tet·ra·ple·gia
te·tro·do·tox·in
  or te·tra·odon·tox·in

Tex·as Rang·er
text
tex·tu·al
tex·tu·al·ly
tex·tu·ary
thal·am·en·ce·phal·
  ic
thal·am·en·ceph·a·
  lon
    pl thal·am·en·ceph·
    a·la

tha·lam·ic
thal·am·i·cal·ly
thal·a·mus
    pl thal·a·mi

thal·id·o·mide
thal·li·um
thal·lo·tox·i·co·sis
    pl thal·lo·tox·i·co·ses

thal·weg
tham·uria
tha·na
tha·na·dar
the·ater
  or the·atre

the·ca
    pl the·cae

the·cal
  or the·cate

the·co·steg·no·sis
theft
theft·bote
theft·proof
thef·tu·ous
thence
thence·forth
theo·bro·mine
theo·ma·nia
theo·o·ret·i·cal
theo·o·ret·i·cal·ly
theo·o·ri·za·tion
the·o·rize
  the·o·rized
  the·o·riz·ing
the·o·ry
    pl the·o·ries

ther·a·peu·sis
    pl ther·a·peu·ses

ther·a·peu·tic
  also ther·a·peu·ti·cal

ther·a·peu·ti·cal·ly
ther·a·peu·tics
ther·a·pist
ther·a·py
    pl ther·a·pies

there·abouts
  also there·about

there·af·ter
there·against
there·among
there·anent
there·at
there·be·tween
there·by

there·for
  for that
  (*see* therefore)

there·fore
  for that reason
  (*see* therefor)

there·from
there·in
there·in·af·ter
there·in·be·fore
there·of
there·on
there·out
there·through
there·to
there·to·fore
there·un·der
there·un·til
there·un·to
there·up·on
there·with
there·with·al
ther·mal
therm·al·ge·sia
therm·es·the·sia
ther·mo·an·al·ge·
  sia
ther·mo·cau·tery
    pl ther·mo·cau·ter·ies

ther·mo·hy·per·al·
  ge·sia
ther·mo·hy·per·es·
  the·sia
ther·mo·hyp·es·
  the·sia
ther·mo·ple·gia

ther·mo·re·cep·tor
ther·mo·reg·u·la·
  tion
ther·mo·reg·u·la·
  tor
ther·mo·reg·u·la·
  to·ry
ther·mo·ther·a·py
  pl ther·mo·ther·a·pies
ther·mo·tra·che·ot·
  o·my
  pl ther·mo·tra·che·
  ot·o·mies
the·sau·ro·sis
  pl the·sau·ro·ses
  or the·sau·ro·sis·es
the·sis
  pl the·ses
thi·a·mine
  also thi·a·min
thi·a·zide
thief
  pl thieves
thief bote
thief·tak·er
thieve
  thieved
  thiev·ing
thiev·ery
  thiev·er·ies
thiev·ish
thigh·bone
thin
thing
thing·li·a·bil·i·ty
thio·cy·a·nate

thio·pen·tal
thio·te·pa
thio·ura·cil
thio·urea
third-de·gree burn
third par·ty *n*
  pl third par·ties
third-par·ty *adj*
thirds *n pl*
third-tier
30-day let·ter
Thom·as splint
tho·ra·cen·te·sis
  pl tho·ra·cen·te·ses
tho·ra·co·dyn·ia
tho·ra·co·lum·bar
tho·ra·co·plas·ty
  pl tho·ra·co·plas·ties
tho·ra·cos·to·my
  pl tho·ra·cos·to·mies
tho·ra·cot·o·my
  pl tho·ra·cot·o·mies
tho·rax
  pl tho·rax·es
  or tho·ra·ces
tho·ri·um
thor·ough
thor·ough·fare
thor·ough·ly
thought·ful
thought·less
thought·less·ly
thought·less·ness
thread
thread·worm
threat

threat·en
threat·en·er
threat·en·ing
threat·en·ing·ly
threat·ful
three-card mon·te
three-way
thrift
thrift·less
thrift·less·ness
thrifty
throb
  throbbed
  throb·bing
throm·bec·to·my
  pl throm·bec·to·mies
throm·bi
  pl of thrombus
throm·bo·an·gi·itis
throm·bo·an·gi·itis
  ob·lit·er·ans
throm·bo·ar·ter·i·
  tis
throm·bo·em·bo·
  lec·to·my
  pl throm·bo·em·bo·
  lec·to·mies
throm·bo·em·bol·
  ic
throm·bo·em·bo·
  lism
throm·bo·en·dar·
  ter·ec·to·my
  pl throm·bo·en·dar·
  ter·ec·to·mies

throm·bol·y·sis
  pl throm·bol·y·ses

throm·bo·lyt·ic
throm·bo·phle·bi·
  tis
throm·bose
  throm·bosed
  throm·bos·ing
throm·bo·sis
  pl throm·bo·ses

throm·bot·ic
throm·bus
  pl throm·bi

throt·tle
  throt·tled
  throt·tling
through
through·out
through·put
  also thru·put

through·way
  also thru·way

throw
  threw
  thrown
  throw·ing
throw-off
thug
thug·gee
thug·gery
  pl thug·ger·ies

thumb·print
thy·mic
thy·mi·co·lym·
  phat·ic

thy·mus
  pl thy·mus·es
  or thy·mi

thy·ro·epi·glot·tic
thy·ro·glos·sal
thy·ro·hy·al
thy·ro·hy·oid
  also thy·ro·hy·oid·ean

thy·roid
thy·roi·dal
thy·roid·ec·to·mize
  thy·roid·ec·to·
    mized
  thy·roid·ec·to·
    miz·ing
thy·roid·ec·to·my
  pl thy·roid·ec·to·mies

thy·roid·itis
thy·roid·ot·o·my
  pl thy·roid·ot·o·mies

thy·ro·tox·ic
thy·ro·tox·ic·i·ty
  pl thy·ro·tox·ic·i·ties

thy·ro·tox·i·co·sis
tib·ia
  pl tib·i·ae
  also tib·i·as

tib·i·al
tib·io·fib·u·la
  pl tib·io·fib·u·lae
  or tib·io·fib·u·las

tib·io·fib·u·lar
tib·io·tar·sal
tic
tic dou·lou·reux
tick·et

tick·et·ed
tick·et·ing
tick·et-of-leave
tid·al
tide
tide·land
tide·wait·er
tide·wa·ter
tide·way
tie
  tied
  ty·ing
  or tie·ing

tie-in
tie-up
tight
till
till·able
till·age
tim·ber
  tim·bered
  tim·ber·ing
tim·ber·land
time
  timed
  tim·ing
time char·ter
time im·me·mo·
  ri·al
time·keep·er
time·keep·ing
time-lapse
time·ly
time·ous
time·ous·ly
tim·er

time·serv·er
time·work
time·work·er
tin·ea bar·bae
tin·ea ca·pi·tis
tin·ea cor·po·ris
tin·ea cru·ris
tip
  tipped
  tip·ing
tip-off
tip·pee
tip·per
tip·ple
  tip·pled
  tip·pling
tip·pler
tip·staff
tip·ster
tis·sue
ti·ta·ni·um
tith·able
tithe
  tithed
  tith·ing
tith·ing·man
  pl tith·ing·men

tit·il·late
  tit·il·lat·ed
  tit·il·lat·ing
tit·il·la·tion
tit·il·la·tive
ti·tle
  ti·tled
  ti·tling
ti·tle·hold·er

tit·u·lar
T-man
  pl T-men

to-ar·rive
toch·er
toch·er-good
to·col·o·gy
  also to·kol·o·gy
  pl to·col·o·gies
  also to·kol·o·gies

toe·nail
to·geth·er
to·ken
tol·er·able
tol·er·a·bly
tol·er·ance
tol·er·ant
tol·er·ate
  tol·er·at·ed
  tol·er·at·ing
tol·er·a·tion
toll
toll·age
toll·bar
toll·er
toll·gate
toll·gath·er·er
toll·house
toll·man
  pl toll·men

toll-through
toll-tra·verse
toll·way
tol·sey
  or tol·zey
  pl tol·seys
  or tol·zeys

tomb·stone
ton
tongue
ton-mile
ton·nage
ton·sil
ton·sil·lar
ton·sil·lec·to·my
  pl ton·sil·lec·to·mies

ton·sil·li·tis
ton·sil·lot·o·my
  pl ton·sil·lot·o·mies

ton·tine
ton·tin·er
tooth
  pl teeth

tooth·ache
  pl tooth·aches

top
  topped
  top·ping
top·ag·no·sis
  pl top·ag·no·ses

to·pal·gia
top·es·the·sia
top-heavy
to·phus
  pl to·phi

top·i·cal
top·i·cal·ly
top-lev·el
top·man
  pl top·men

topo·nar·co·sis
  pl topo·nar·co·ses

topo·neu·ro·sis
  pl topo·neu·ro·ses

top se·cret

top spit

torch

tor·ment

tor·ment·ing·ly

tor·men·tor

tor·por

Tor·rens cer·tif·i·cate

Tor·rens sys·tem

tor·sion

tor·so
  pl tor·sos
  or tor·si
  also tor·soes

tort
  a wrongful act
  (*see* torte)

torte
  pl tor·ten
  or tortes
  a rich cake or pastry
  (*see* tort)

tort-fea·sor

tor·ti·col·lis

tor·tious
  involving tort
  (*see* tortuous, torturous)

tor·tious·ly

tor·tu·ous
  lacking in straightforwardness
  (*see* tortious, torturous)

tor·tu·os·i·ty
  pl tor·tu·os·i·ties

tor·tu·ous·ly

tor·ture

  tor·tured

  tor·tur·ing

tor·tur·er

tor·tur·ous
  very painful or distressing
  (*see* tortious, tortuous)

tot

  tot·ted

  tot·ting

total

  to·taled
  or to·talled

  to·tal·ing
  or to·tal·ling

to·tal·i·tar·i·an

to·tal·i·tar·i·an·ism

to·tal·i·ty
  pl to·tal·i·ties

to·tal·iza·tion

to·tal·iza·tor
  or to·tal·isa·tor

to·tal·ize

  to·tal·ized

  to·tal·iz·ing

to·tal·iz·er

to·tal·ly

to·ti·dem ver·bis

to·ti·es quo·ti·es

Tot·ten trust

tot·ter

tot·tery

tot·ting-up

touch

touch·er·ism

tou·cheur

touch·ing

tour

tour·ist

tour·ni·quet

tout

tout temps prist et en·core prist

tow

tow·abil·i·ty

tow·able

tow·age

to·ward
  or to·wards

tow·boat

to wit

town

town·ship

town·site

towns·man
  pl towns·men

towns·peo·ple *n pl*

towns·wom·an
  pl towns·wom·en

tox·emia
  also tox·ae·mia

tox·emic
  also tox·ae·mic

tox·ic

tox·i·cal·ly

tox·i·cant

tox·ic·i·ty
  pl tox·ic·i·ties

tox·i·co·der·ma
pl tox·i·co·der·mas
or tox·i·co·der·ma·ta

tox·i·co·der·ma·ti·
tis
pl tox·i·co·der·ma·ti·
tis·es
or tox·i·co·der·ma·
tit·i·des

tox·i·co·log·i·cal
or tox·i·co·log·ic

tox·i·col·o·gist
tox·i·col·o·gy
pl tox·i·col·o·gies

tox·i·co·ma·nia
tox·i·co·sis
pl tox·i·co·ses

tox·i·fy
tox·i·fied
tox·i·fy·ing
tox·in
trace
traced
trac·ing
trace·abil·i·ty
trace·able
trace·able·ness
trace·ably
trac·er
tra·chea
pl tra·che·ae
also tra·che·as

tra·che·al
tra·che·al·gia
tra·che·itis
tra·cheo·bron·chi·
al

tra·cheo·bron·chi·
tis
tra·cheo·esoph·a·
ge·al
tra·che·os·chi·sis
pl tra·che·os·chi·
ses
also tra·che·os·chi·
sis·es

tra·che·os·to·my
pl tra·che·os·to·mies

tra·che·ot·o·mize
tra·che·ot·o·
mized
tra·che·ot·o·miz·
ing
tra·che·ot·o·my
pl tra·che·ot·o·mies

tra·cho·ma
tra·cho·ma·tous
track
track·age
track·man
pl track·men

track·way
tract
trac·tion
trac·tor
trad·able
also trade·able

trad·al
trade
trad·ed
trad·ing
trade-in
trade·mark

trad·er
trad·er·ship
trades·man
pl trades·men

tra·di·tio
tra·di·tion
tra·di·tion·al
tra·di·tion·al·ly
tra·di·tion·ary
tra·di·tur in bal·li·
um
tra·duce
tra·duced
tra·duc·ing
tra·duce·ment
tra·duc·er
tra·duc·tion
traf·fic
also traf·fick

traf·ficked
traf·fick·ing
traf·fics
also traf·ficks

traf·fic·able
traf·fick·er
traf·fic·way
trail
trail·er
train
train·able
train·ee
train·er
train·ing school
train·load
train·man
pl train·men

train·mas·ter
trai·tor
trai·tor·ism
trai·tor·ous
trai·tor·ous·ly
trai·tor·ous·ness
trai·tress
   or trai·tor·ess

tram·mer
tramp
tramp·er
tramp·ing
tram·ple
   tram·pled
   tram·pling
tram·road
tram·way
tranche
tran·quil·ize
   or tran·quil·lize
   tran·quil·ized
     or tran·quil·lized
   tran·quil·iz·ing
     or tran·quil·liz·ing

tran·quil·iz·er
   or tran·quil·liz·er

trans·ab·dom·i·nal
trans·act
trans·ac·tio
trans·ac·tion
trans·ac·tion·al
trans·ac·tor
trans·an·i·ma·tion
trans·at·lan·tic
tran·scribe
   tran·scribed

tran·scrib·ing
tran·scrib·er
tran·script
tran·scrip·tion
trans·fer
   trans·ferred
   trans·fer·ring
trans·fer·abil·i·ty
trans·fer·able
   or trans·fer·ra·ble

trans·fer·al
   or trans·fer·ral

trans·fer·ee
trans·fer·ence
trans·fer·rer
   also trans·fer·er
   or trans·fer·or
   or trans·fer·ror

trans·fix
trans·fuse
   trans·fused
   trans·fus·ing
trans·fu·sion
trans·fu·sion·al
trans·gress
trans·gres·sion
trans·gres·sive
trans·gres·sor
tran·ship
   var of transship

tran·ship·ment
   var of transshipment

tran·sience
tran·sien·cy
   pl tran·sien·cies

tran·sient

trans·i·re
tran·sit
tran·sit·able
tran·si·tion·al
tran·si·tive
tran·si·to·ri·ly
tran·si·to·ry
tran·si·tus
trans·late
   trans·lat·ed
   trans·lat·ing
trans·la·tion
trans·la·tive
trans·mis·si·bil·i·ty
   pl trans·mis·si·bil·i·ties

trans·mis·si·ble
trans·mis·sion
trans·mis·sive
trans·mit
   trans·mit·ted
   trans·mit·ting
trans·mit·ta·ble
trans·mit·tal
trans·mit·tance
trans·mit·ter
trans·ocean
trans·oce·an·ic
trans·pa·cif·ic
tran·spire
   tran·spired
   tran·spir·ing
trans·plant
trans·plan·ta·tion
trans·port
trans·port·abil·i·ty
trans·port·able

trans·port·al
trans·por·ta·tion
trans·por·ta·tion·al
trans·port·ee
trans·port·er
trans·ship
  also tran·ship
  trans·shipped
   also tran·shipped
  trans·ship·ping
   also tran·ship·ping

trans·ship·ment
  also tran·ship·ment

tran·sumpt
tran·sump·tion
trans·ves·tism
trans·ves·tite
trap
  trapped
  trap·ping
tra·pe·zi·al
tra·pe·zi·um
  pl tra·pe·zi·ums
  or tra·pe·zia

tra·pe·zi·us
trap·per
trash
trau·ma
  pl trau·ma·ta
  or trau·mas

trau·mat·ic
trau·mat·i·cal·ly
trau·ma·tism
trau·ma·ti·za·tion
trau·ma·tize
  trau·ma·tized
  trau·ma·tiz·ing

tra·vail
trav·el
trav·eled
  or trav·elled
trav·el·ing
  or trav·el·ling

trav·el·able
  or trav·el·la·ble

trav·el·er
  or trav·el·ler

tra·vers·able
tra·vers·al
tra·verse
  tra·versed
  tra·vers·ing
trav·ers·er
trav·es·ty
  pl trav·es·ties

treach·er·ous
treach·er·ous·ly
treach·er·ous·ness
treach·ery
  pl treach·er·ies

trea·son
trea·son·able
trea·son·ably
trea·son·ous
trea·sure
trea·sur·er
trea·sur·er·ship
trea·sury
  pl trea·sur·ies

trea·sury·ship
treat
treat·abil·i·ty
  pl treat·abil·i·ties

treat·able
treat·ment
trea·ty
  pl trea·ties

tre·ble
trem·or
trem·u·lous
tre·pan
  tre·panned
  tre·pan·ning
trep·a·na·tion
treph·i·na·tion
tre·phine
  tre·phined
  tre·phin·ing
trep·i·da·tion
trepo·ne·ma
  pl trepo·ne·ma·ta
  or trep·o·ne·mas

trepo·ne·ma·to·sis
  pl trepo·ne·ma·to·ses

trepo·neme
tres·pass
tres·pass·er
tres·pas·so·ry
tres·pass qua·re
  clau·sum fre·git
tri·able
tri·al
tri·an·gle
tri·an·gu·lar
tri·an·gu·late
  tri·an·gu·lat·ed
  tri·an·gu·lat·ing
tri·an·gu·la·tion
tri·an·gu·la·tor

tri·bade
tri·bad·ic
trib·a·dism
trib·a·dy
 pl trib·a·dies

tri·bu·na
tri·bu·nal
tri·bu·nate
tri·bune
tri·bune·ship
trib·u·tary
 pl trib·u·tar·ies

trib·ute
trib·ut·er
 or trib·u·tor

tri·chi·na
 pl tri·chi·nae
 also tri·chi·nas

trich·i·niza·tion
trich·i·nize
 trich·i·nized
 trich·i·niz·ing
trich·i·no·sis
 pl trich·i·no·ses

tri·chi·nous
tricho·my·co·sis
 pl tricho·my·co·ses

trich·op·a·thy
 pl trich·op·a·thies

tricho·phyt·o·sis
tri·cho·sis
 pl tri·cho·ses

trick
trick·er
trick·ery
 pl trick·er·ies

trick·i·ly
trick·i·ness
trick·ing·ly
frick·ish
trick·ish·ness
trick·ster
tricky
 trick·i·er
 trick·i·est
tri·er
tri·eth·yl·amine
tri·eth·yl·ene·mel·
 amine
tri·fa·cial
trig·a·mist
trig·a·my
tri·gem·i·nal
tri·lat·er·al
tril·o·gy
 pl tril·o·gies

tri·ni·tro·glyc·er·in
tri·ni·tro·phe·nol
tri·ni·tro·tol·u·ene
tri·ol·ism
tri·or
tri·par·tite
tri·plex
trip·li·cate
 trip·li·cat·ed
 trip·li·cat·ing
trip·li·ca·tion
tris·mus
trit·an·ope
trit·an·opia
tri·um·vir
 pl tri·um·virs
 also tri·um·vi·ri

tri·um·vi·ral
tri·um·vi·rate
triv·i·al
tro·chan·ter
tro·chan·ter·ic
troch·lea
troch·le·ar
troop
troop·er
tro·pho·neu·ro·sis
 pl tro·pho·neu·ro·ses

tro·pho·neu·rot·ic
trou·ble
trove
tro·ver
tru·an·cy
 pl tru·an·cies

tru·ant
tru·ant·ry
truce
truck
truck·age
truck·er
truck·line
truck·load
truck·man
 pl truck·men

true
trumped-up
trun·cus ar·te·ri·
 o·sus
trunk
trunk·way
trust
trust·abil·i·ty
trust·able

trust·bust·er
trust-bust·ing
trust·ee *n*
  one entrusted with
    something
  (*see* trusty)

trust·ee
  var of trusty

trust·ee *vb*
  trust·eed
  trust·ee·ing
trust·ee·ship
trust·er
trust·ifi·ca·tion
trust·ify
  trust·if·ied
  trust·ify·ing
trust·man
  pl trust·men

trus·tor
trust·wom·an
  pl trust·wom·en

trust·wor·thi·ly
trust·wor·thi·ness
trust·wor·thy
trusty *adj*
  trust·i·er
  trust·i·est
trusty *n*
  also trust·ee
  pl trust·ies
  also trust·ees
  a convict allowed spe-
    cial privileges
  (*see* trustee)

truth
truth·ful

truth·less
try
  tried
  try·ing
tryst
tu·ber·cle
tu·ber·cled
tu·ber·cu·lar
tu·ber·cu·lid
  or tu·ber·cu·lide

tu·ber·cu·lin
tu·ber·cu·lo·cid·al
tu·ber·cu·lo·derm
  also tu·ber·cu·lo·der-
    ma

tu·ber·cu·lo·fi·
  broid
tu·ber·cu·loid
tu·ber·cu·lo·ma
  pl tu·ber·cu·lo·mas
  also tu·ber·cu·lo·ma·ta

tu·ber·cu·lo·sis
  pl tu·ber·cu·lo·ses

tu·ber·cu·lo·stat·ic
tu·ber·cu·lous
tu·ber·cu·lous·ly
tu·ber·os·i·ty
  pl tu·ber·os·i·ties

tu·bo·cu·ra·rine
tu·bo·ovar·i·an
tu·bo·uter·ine
tu·bo·vag·i·nal
tug
  tugged
  tug·ging
tug·boat

tug·man
  pl tug·men

tu·la·re·mia
tu·la·re·mic
tu·me·fac·tion
tu·me·fy
  tu·me·fied
  tu·me·fy·ing
tu·mes·cence
tu·mes·cent
tu·mor
  also tu·mour

tu·mor·al
tu·mor·i·gen·e·sis
  pl tu·mor·i·gen·e·ses

tu·mor·i·gen·ic
tu·mor·i·ge·nic·i·ty
  pl tu·mor·i·ge·nic·i·ties

tu·mor·ous
tun·nel
  tun·neled
  or tun·nelled
  tun·nel·ing
  or tun·nel·ling

tu quo·que
tur·ba·ry
  pl tur·ba·ries

tur·bu·lence
tur·bu·len·cy
tur·bu·lent
tur·bu·lent·ly
tur·ges·cence
tur·ges·cent
tur·gid
tur·gid·i·ty
  pl tur·gid·i·ties

tur·moil
turn
turn·key
turn-key job
turn·out
turn·over
turn·pike
turn·stile
tur·pis cau·sa
tur·pis con·trac·
  tus
tur·pi·tude
tus·sle
  tus·sled
  tus·sling
tu·te·la
  pl tu·te·lae

tu·tor
tu·tor·age
tu·tor ali·en·us
tu·tor-at-law
tu·tor·hood
tu·tor pro·pri·us
tu·tor·ship
tu·to·ry
tu·trix
  pl tu·tri·ces
  or tu·trix·es

twin
two-par·ty
two-way
tym·pa·ni·tes
  also tym·pa·ni·tis
  swollen abdomen
  (*see* tympanitis)

tym·pa·nit·ic

tym·pa·ni·tis
  ear inflammation
  (*see* tympanites)

tym·pa·num
  pl tym·pa·na
  also tym·pa·nums

tym·pa·ny
  pl tym·pa·nies

ty·phoid
ty·phoi·dal
ty·pho·pneu·mo·nia
ty·phous
ty·phus
tyr·an·nize
  tyr·an·nized
  tyr·ran·niz·ing
tyr·an·niz·er
tyr·an·ny
  pl tyr·an·nies

ty·rant

U

uber·ri·ma fi·des
ubi re ve·ra
ubi su·pra
udal
uit·land·er
ukase
ul·cer
ul·cer·ate
  ul·cer·at·ed
  ul·cer·at·ing
ul·cer·a·tion
ul·cero·gen·ic
ul·cer·ous
ul·lage

ul·laged
ul·na
  pl ul·nae
  or ul·nas

ul·nad
ul·nar
ul·no·car·pal
ul·no·ra·di·al
ul·te·ri·or
ul·te·ri·or·ly
ul·ti·ma·cy
  pl ul·ti·ma·cies

ul·ti·ma ra·tio
ul·ti·mate
ul·ti·mate·ly
ul·ti·mate·ness
ul·ti·ma·tion
ul·ti·ma·tum
  pl ul·ti·ma·tums
  or ul·ti·ma·ta

ul·ti·mo
ul·ti·mo·gen·i·ture
ul·tra
ultra·haz·ard·ous
ul·tra·ism
ul·tra·ist
ul·tra·ma·rine
ul·tra·mon·tane
ul·tra·son·ic
ul·tra·sound
ul·tra·struc·tur·al
ul·tra·struc·tur·al·
  ly
ul·tra·struc·ture
ul·tra·vi·o·let
ul·tra vi·res
ul·tro·ne·ous

um·bil·i·cal
um·bi·li·cus
  pl um·bi·li·ci
  or um·bi·li·cus·es
um·brage
um·bra·geous
um·brel·la
um·pir·age
um·pire
  um·pired
  um·pir·ing
um·pire·ship
un·abat·ed
un·able
un·ac·cept·able
un·ac·cep·tance
un·ac·cept·ed
un·ac·ces·si·ble
un·ac·count·abil·i·ty
un·ac·count·able
un·ac·count·ably
un·ac·count·ed
un·ac·crued
un·ac·cus·able
un·ac·cused
un·ac·knowl·edged
un·ac·knowl·edg·ing
un·ad·just·ed
un·ad·min·is·tered
un·adul·ter·at·ed
  also un·adul·ter·ate
un·ad·ver·tised
un·ad·vis·able
un·ad·vised

un·af·fil·i·at·ed
un·alien·able
un·alien·ably
un·alien·at·ed
un·al·low·able
un·al·lowed
un·al·ter·abil·i·ty
un·al·ter·able
un·al·ter·able·ness
un·al·ter·ably
un·al·tered
un·am·bi·gu·ity
un·am·big·u·ous
un·am·big·u·ous·ly
un·amend·able
un·amend·ed
un·am·or·tized
un·anes·the·tized
una·nim·i·ty
  pl una·nim·i·ties

unan·i·mous
unan·i·mous·ly
un·an·swer·able
un·ap·peal·able
un·ap·pli·ca·ble
un·ap·plied
un·ap·pro·pri·at·ed
un·ap·proved
un·ar·gu·able
un·arm
un·armed
un·ar·rest·ed
un·as·cer·tain·able
un·as·cer·tained
un·as·sail·able
un·as·sent·ed

un·as·sign·able
un·as·signed
un·as·sist·ing
un·at·tached
un·at·tend·ed
un·at·test·ed
un·au·dit·ed
un·au·then·tic
un·au·then·ti·cat·ed
un·au·tho·rized
un·avail·able
una vo·ce
un·avoid·abil·i·ty
un·avoid·able
un·avoid·able·ness
un·avoid·ably
un·avowed
un·awares
un·bail·able
un·be·com·ing
un·be·known
  or un·be·knownst
un·be·queathed
un·be·sought
un·bi·ased
un·bi·ased·ly
un·bind·ing
un·blam·able
un·blam·ably
un·blamed
un·blurred
un·born
un·brand·ed
un·break·able
un·brib·able

un·bribed
un·bro·ken
un·called
un·called-for
un·cap·i·tal·ized
un·cen·sored
un·cen·sured
un·cer·tain
un·cer·tain·ty
  pl un·cer·tain·ties

un·chal·lenge·able
un·chal·lenged
un·change·able
un·charged
un·char·tered
un·chaste
un·chas·ti·ty
  pl un·chas·ti·ties

un·cir·cum·cised
un·cir·cum·stan·
  tial
un·claimed
un·clar·i·ty
  pl un·clar·i·ties

un·clas·si·fied
un·cle
un·clean hands
un·clear
un·cleared
un·cle·hood
un·cle-in-law
  pl un·cles-in-law

un·col·lect·ed
un·col·lect·ible

un·com·mis·sioned
un·com·pelled
un·com·pen·sat·ed
un·com·plet·ed
un·com·pli·cat·ed
un·com·ply·ing
un·com·pro·mis·ing
un·con·cealed
un·con·di·tion·al
un·con·di·tion·al·
  i·ty
un·con·di·tion·al·ly
un·con·doned
un·con·fessed
un·con·firmed
un·con·form·able
un·con·scio·na·bil·
  i·ty
un·con·scio·na·ble
un·con·scio·na·bly
un·con·scious
un·con·scious·ness
un·con·sti·tu·
  tion·al
un·con·sti·tu·tion·
  al·i·ty
un·con·sti·tu·tion·
  al·ly
un·con·strained
un·con·sum·mat·ed
un·con·tam·i·
  nat·ed
un·con·test·able
un·con·test·ed
un·con·tra·dict·ed
un·con·trol·la·ble

un·con·trolled
un·con·tro·vert·ed
un·con·tro·vert·ible
un·con·ven·tion·al
un·co·op·er·a·tive
un·co·or·di·nat·ed
un·cor·rupt·ed
un·cov·e·nant·ed
un·cov·ered
un·cum·bered
un·cus·tomed
un·dam·aged
un·dat·able
un·dat·ed
un·de·bat·able
un·de·cid·able
un·de·clared
un·de·clin·able
un·de·fend·able
un·de·fend·ed
un·de·lib·er·ate
un·de·liv·er·able
un·de·liv·ered
un·de·ni·able
un·de·nied
un·de·priv·able
un·der
un·der·age
un·der·arm
un·der·as·sessed
un·der·as·sess·ment
un·der·bill
un·der·build
un·der·cap·i·tal·ize
un·der·cap·i·tal·
  ized

un·der·cap·i·tal·
  iz·ing
un·der·charge
  un·der·charged
  un·der·charg·ing
un·der·cov·er
un·der·cut
  un·der·cut
  un·der·cut·ting
un·der·de·vel·oped
un·der·de·vel·op·
  ment
un·der·draw
  un·der·drew
  un·der·drawn
  un·der·draw·ing
un·der·em·ployed
un·der·em·ploy·
  ment
un·der·es·ti·mate
  un·der·es·ti·mat·
    ed
  un·der·es·ti·mat·
    ing
un·der·es·ti·mate
  or un·der·es·ti·ma·tion
un·der·fill
un·der·flow
un·der·grade
un·der·ground
un·der·ground·er
un·der·hand
un·der·hand·ed
un·der·hand·ed·ly
un·der·hand·ed·
  ness

un·der·housed
un·der·in·sur·ance
un·der·lease
  un·der·leased
  un·der·leas·ing
un·der·les·see
un·der·let
  un·der·let
  un·der·let·ting
un·der·lie
un·der·lay
un·der·lain
un·der·ly·ing
un·der·li·er
un·der·lip
un·der·load
un·der·look·er
un·der·manned
un·der·mine
  un·der·mined
  un·der·min·ing
un·der·min·er
un·der·not·ed
un·der·nour·ished
un·der pain of
  var of on pain of
un·der·pay
  un·der·paid
  un·der·pay·ing
un·der·pay·ment
un·der·pin·ning
un·der·price
  un·der·priced
  un·der·pric·ing
un·der·re·port
un·der·sell

un·der·sold
un·der·sell·ing
un·der·sexed
un·der·sher·iff
un·der·sign
un·der·signed
  pl un·der·signed
un·der·sign·er
un·der·sized
  also un·der·size
un·der·stand
un·der·stood
un·der·stand·ing
un·der·stand·abil·
  i·ty
un·der·stand·able
un·der·stand·ing
un·der·stand·ing·ly
un·der·state
un·der·stat·ed
un·der·stat·ing
un·der·state·ment
un·der·take
un·der·took
un·der·tak·en
un·der·tak·ing
un·der·tak·er
un·der·ten·an·cy
  pl un·der·ten·an·cies
un·der·ten·ant
un·der-the-
  count·er
un·der-the-ta·ble
un·der·time
un·der·val·u·a·tion
un·der·val·ue

un·der·val·ued
un·der·valu·ing
un·der·wa·ter
un·der·way *adv*
un·der·way *adj*
un·der·weight
un·der·work
un·der·world
un·der·write
un·der·wrote
un·der·writ·ten
also un·der·wrote
un·der·writ·ing
un·der·writ·er
un·de·scend·ed
un·de·signed
un·de·sir·abil·i·ty
un·de·sir·able
un·de·tach·able
un·de·tect·able
un·de·tect·ed
un·de·ter·min·able
un·de·ter·mi·nate
un·de·ter·mined
un·de·vel·op·able
un·de·vel·oped
un·de·vised
un·di·ag·nosed
un·di·gest·ed
un·di·rect·ed
un·dis·bursed
un·dis·charged
un·dis·ci·plin·able
un·dis·ci·pline
un·dis·ci·plined
un·dis·closed

un·dis·posed
un·dis·pu·ta·ble
un·dis·put·ed
un·dis·trib·ut·ed
un·di·vid·ed
un·di·vulged
un·dock
un·doc·u·ment·ed
un·dow·ered
un·du·bi·ta·ble
un·due
un·due in·flu·ence
un·du·ly
un·du·ti·ful
un·earned
un·earth
un·ed·it·ed
un·eman·ci·pat·ed
un·em·bar·rassed
un·emend·able
un·em·ploy·abil·
     i·ty
un·em·ploy·able
un·em·ployed
un·em·ploy·ment
un·en·closed
un·en·cum·bered
un·en·dorsed
un·en·force·able
un·en·forced
un·en·fran·chised
un·en·tailed
un·en·tered
un·en·ti·tled
un·equal
un·equal·ly

un·eq·ui·ta·ble
un·equiv·o·cal
un·equiv·o·cal·ly
un·equiv·o·cal·ness
un·err·ing
un·err·ing·ly
un·es·tranged
un·eth·i·cal
un·eth·i·cal·ly
un·evoked
un·ex·cep·tion·abil·
     i·ty
un·ex·cep·tion·able
un·ex·cused
un·ex·e·cut·ed
un·ex·er·cised
un·ex·pect·ed
un·ex·pend·ed
un·ex·pired
un·ex·plained
un·ex·pressed
un·ex·ten·u·ated
un·fair
un·fair·ly
un·fair·ness
un·faith·ful
un·faith·ful·ly
un·faith·ful·ness
un·fa·vor·able
un·fenced
un·fet·tered
un·feued
un·find·able
un·fin·ished
un·fit
un·fit·ness

un·fo·ren·sic
un·fore·see·able
un·fore·seen
un·for·feit·able
un·for·giv·able
un·found·ed
un·free
un·freeze
  un·froze
  un·fro·zen
  un·freez·ing
un·friend·ly
un·ful·fill
un·ful·fill·able
un·ful·fill·ment
un·fund·ed
un·gov·ern·abil·i·ty
un·gov·ern·able
un·gov·erned
un·grad·ed
un·grant·ed
un·gual
  also un·gui·nal
un·guar·an·teed
un·guard·ed
un·guilt·i·ly
un·guilty
un·guis
  pl un·gues
un·hab·it·able
un·hal·lowed
un·ham·pered
un·harmed
un·harm·ful
un·haz·ard·ous
un·hin·dered

un·iden·ti·fi·able
un·iden·ti·fied
uni·form
uni·for·mi·ty
  pl uni·for·mi·ties
uni·form·ly
uni·form·ness
uni·fy
  uni·fied
  uni·fy·ing
uni·grav·i·da
  pl uni·grav·i·das
  or uni·grav·i·dae
uni·lat·er·al
uni·lat·er·al·ly
uni·lo·bar
un·im·paired
un·im·peach·abil·
  i·ty
un·impeach·able
un·impeached
un·im·proved
un·in·closed
un·in·cor·po·rat·ed
un·in·cum·bered
un·in·dorsed
un·in·hab·it·able
un·in·hab·it·ed
un·in·ju·ri·ous
un·in·spect·ed
un·in·sur·able
un·in·sured
un·in·tend·ed
un·in·ten·tion·al
un·in·ten·tion·al·ly
un·in·ter·rupt·ed

un·in·ter·rupt·ed·ly
un·in·ven·tive
un·in·vest·ed
uni·oc·u·lar
union
union·ist
union·is·tic
union·iza·tion
union·ize
  union·ized
  union·iz·ing
unip·a·ra
  pl unip·a·ras
  or unip·a·rae
uni·pa·ren·tal
unip·a·rous
unique
un·is·sued
unit
uni·tary
unite
  unit·ed
  unit·ing
unit·iza·tion
unit·ize
  unit·ized
  unit·iz·ing
uni·ty
  pl uni·ties
uni·ver·sal
uni·ver·sal·i·ty
uni·ver·sal part·
  ner·ship
uni·ver·si·tas
  pl uni·ver·si·ta·tes
uni·ver·si·tas fac·ti

uni·ver·si·tas ju·ris
uni·ver·si·tas per·
  so·na·rum
uni·ver·si·tas re·
  rum
uni·ver·si·ty
  pl uni·ver·si·ties

univ·o·cal
un·ju·di·cial
un·ju·di·cial·ly
un·ju·di·cious
un·just
un·jus·ti·fi·able
un·jus·ti·fi·ca·tion
un·jus·ti·fied
un·just·ly
un·known
un·lad·en
un·land·ed
un·law
un·law·ful
un·law·ful·ly
un·law·ful·ness
un·leased
un·leash
un·le·gal
un·less lease
un·let
un·let·ta·ble
un·li·a·ble
un·li·censed
un·lim·i·ted
un·lim·i·ted·ness
un·liq·ui·dat·ed
un·list·ed

un·liv·able
un·liv·ery
  pl un·liv·er·ies

un·load
un·lo·cat·ed
un·mail·able
un·main·tain·able
un·man·age·able
un·man·u·fac·tured
un·mar·ket·able
un·mar·ry
  un·mar·ried
  un·mar·ry·ing
un·ma·tured
un·med·i·tat·ed
un·mer·chant·able
un·merge
  un·merged
  un·merg·ing
un·mo·lest·ed
un·mort·gaged
un·nat·u·ral
un·nec·es·sar·i·ly
un·nec·es·sary
un·ob·li·gat·ed
un·ob·li·gat·ing
un·oc·cu·pan·cy
un·oc·cu·pied
un·of·fi·cial
un·of·fi·cious
un·of·fi·cious·ly
uno fla·tu
un·or·ga·nized
un·owned
un·paid

un·pat·ent·able
un·pat·ent·ed
un·pay·able
un·pay·ing
un·peg
  un·pegged
  un·peg·ging
un·per·jured
un·per·mis·sive
un·per·mit·ted
un·plat·ted
un·pos·sessed
un·prec·e·dent·ed
un·prej·u·diced
un·pre·med·i·tat·ed
un·pris·on
un·pro·duc·tive
un·pro·fes·sion·al
un·prof·it·able
un·pro·hib·it·ed
un·pros·e·cut·ed
un·pro·test·ed
un·prov·able
un·proved
un·pro·vid·ed
un·pun·ish·able
un·pun·ished
un·qual·i·fi·able
un·qual·i·fied
un·qual·i·fied·ly
un·ques·tion·able
un·rat·able
un·rat·ed
un·real
un·rea·son·able
un·rea·son·ably

un·re·cord·ed
un·re·cov·er·able
un·re·cov·ered
un·re·deem·able
un·re·deemed
un·re·dressed
un·re·fut·able
un·re·fut·ed
un·reg·is·tered
un·reg·u·lat·ed
un·re·lat·ed
un·re·lin·quished
un·re·mar·ried
un·re·mit·ted
un·re·mu·ner·at·ed
un·re·mu·ner·a·
tive
un·rent·able
un·re·paid
un·re·peal·able
un·re·pealed
un·rep·re·sent·ed
un·re·prieved
un·re·quit·able
un·re·served
un·re·sist·ing
un·re·spon·sive
un·re·strict·ed
un·re·stric·tive
un·re·view·able
un·re·voked
un·right
un·right·ful
un·rul·i·ness
un·ruly
  un·rul·i·er

un·rul·i·est
un·safe
un·sal·abil·i·ty
un·sal·able
un·sal·a·ried
un·san·i·tary
un·sat·is·fac·to·ry
un·sat·is·fied
un·sched·uled
un·seal
un·seat
un·sea·wor·thi·ness
un·sea·wor·thy
un·se·cured
un·seem·ly
un·seg·re·gat·ed
un·sen·tenced
un·served
un·ser·vice·able
un·set·tled
un·sex
un·signed
un·skilled
un·skill·ful
un·skill·ful·ness
un·sold
un·sol·emn
un·so·lic·it·ed
un·sound
un·sound·ness
un·stat·ut·able
un·sub·stan·tial
un·sub·stan·ti·at·
ed
un·suc·cess·ful
un·suit·abil·i·ty

un·suit·able
un·suit·able·ness
un·suit·ably
un·su·per·vised
un·sur·veyed
un·sus·tain·able
un·sus·tained
un·sworn
un·taxed
un·ten·ant
un·ten·ant·abil·i·ty
un·ten·ant·able
un·ten·ant·ed
un·tend·ed
un·time·ly
un·trans·fer·able
un·treat·ed
un·us·able
un·usu·al
un·usu·al·ly
un·usu·al·ness
un·vac·ci·nat·ed
un·val·ued
un·vend·ible
un·ver·i·fi·able
un·ver·i·fied
un·vouched
un·vowed
un·war·rant·able
un·war·rant·ed
un·whole·some
un·whole·some·
ness
un·will·ing
un·wor·thi·ness
un·wor·thy

un·writ·ten
up·hold
  up·held
  up·hold·ing
up·hold·er
up·keep
up·land
up·lift
up·on pain of
  var of on pain of

up·set
  up·set
  up·set·ting
up-to-date
up·zon·ing
ur·ban
ur·ban·iza·tion
ur·ban·ize
  ur·ban·ized
  ur·ban·iz·ing
urea
ure·al
ure·mia
  or urae·mia

ure·mic
  or urae·mic

ure·sis
ure·ter
ure·ter·al
  or ure·ter·ic

ure·ter·itis
ure·thra
  pl ure·thras
  or ure·thrae

ure·thral

ure·thri·tis
ure·thro·cys·ti·tis
ure·thro·pros·tat·ic
ure·thro·rec·tal
ur·gen·cy
  pl ur·gen·cies

ur·gent
uri·nal
uri·nal·y·sis
  pl uri·nal·y·ses

uri·nary
uri·nate
  uri·nat·ed
  uri·nat·ing
uri·na·tion
urine
uri·nif·er·ous
uri·no·gen·i·tal
urin·ous
uro·gen·i·tal
uro·log·ic
  or uro·log·i·cal

urol·o·gist
urol·o·gy
  pl urol·o·gies

uro·tox·ic
uro·tox·ic·i·ty
  pl uro·tox·ic·i·ties

ur·ti·car·ia
ur·ti·car·i·al
ur·ti·car·io·gen·ic
ur·ti·cate
  ur·ti·cat·ed
  ur·ti·cat·ing
ur·ti·ca·tion
uru·shi·ol

us·abil·i·ty
us·able
us·able·ness
us·age
us·ance
use
  used
  us·ing
us·ee
use·ful
use·ful·ness
us·er
ush·er
us·que ad coe·lum
us·que ad fi·lum
  aquae
usu·al
usu·al·ly
usu·ary
  pl us·u·ar·ies

usu·cap·tio
usu·cap·tion
usu·fruct
usu·fruc·tu·ary
  pl usu·fruc·tu·ar·ies

usu·ra
  pl usu·rae

usu·rer
usu·ri·ous
usu·ri·ous·ly
usurp
usur·pa·tion
usur·pa·tive
usur·pa·to·ry
usur·pa·ture
usurp·er

usu·ry
    pl usu·ries

uter·al·gia
uter·ine
uter·i·tis
utero·ab·dom·i·nal
utero·cer·vi·cal
utero·ges·ta·tion
utero-ovar·i·an
utero·sac·ral
uter·ot·o·my
    pl uter·ot·o·mies

utero·tub·al
utero·vag·i·nal
uter·us
    pl uteri
    also uter·us·es

util·i·ty
    pl util·i·ties

uti·li·za·tion
uti·lize
    uti·lized
    uti·liz·ing
uti pos·si·de·tis
ut·most
ut·ter
ut·ter·ance
ut·ter·er
ut·ter·ing
ut·ter·ly
uvea
uve·al
uve·itis
uvu·la
    pl uvu·las
    or uvu·lae

uvu·lar
uvu·lec·to·my
    pl uvu·lec·to·mies

uvu·li·tis
ux·o·ri·al
ux·or·i·cide

V

va·can·cy
    pl va·can·cies

va·cant
va·can·tia
    or va·can·tia bo·na

va·cat·able
va·cate
    va·cat·ed
    va·cat·ing
va·ca·tion
va·ca·tur
vac·ci·na·ble
vac·ci·nate
    vac·ci·nat·ed
    vac·ci·nat·ing
vac·ci·na·tion
vac·ci·na·tor
vac·cine
vac·cin·ee
vac·ua pos·ses·sio
va·cu·ity
    pl va·cu·ities

va·des
    pl of vas

vad·i·mo·nium
    pl vad·i·mo·nia

vad·i·mo·ny
    pl vad·i·mo·nies

va·di·um mor·tu·um
va·di·um vi·vum
vag
    vagged
    vag·ging
vag·a·bond
vag·a·bond·age
vag·a·bond·ism
va·gi·na
    pl va·gi·nae
    or va·gi·nas

vag·i·nal
vag·i·nal·ly
vag·i·ni·tis
vag·i·nos·co·py
    pl vag·i·nos·co·pies

va·gi·tus
va·gi·tus ute·ri·nus
va·got·o·mize
    va·got·o·mized
    va·got·o·miz·ing
va·got·o·my
    pl va·got·o·mies

va·grance
va·gran·cy
va·grant
vague
    vagu·er
    vagu·est
vague·ness
va·gus
    pl va·gi

va·keel
 or va·kil

val·gus
val·id
val·i·date
 val·i·dat·ed
 val·i·dat·ing
val·i·da·tion
val·i·da·to·ry
va·lid·i·ty
val·id·ly
val·id·ness
val·o·ri·za·tion
val·o·rize
 val·o·rized
 val·o·riz·ing
valu·able
valu·able·ness
val·u·ate
 val·u·at·ed
 val·u·at·ing
val·u·a·tion
val·u·a·tion·al
val·u·a·tive
val·u·a·tor
val·ue
 val·ued
 valu·ing
val·ue add·ed *n*
val·ue-add·ed *adj*
val·ue·less
valu·er
valve
van·a·date
va·na·di·um
va·na·di·um·ism

van·co·my·cin
van·dal
van·dal·ic
van·dal·ism
van·dal·is·tic
van·dal·iza·tion
van·dal·ize
 van·dal·ized
 van·dal·iz·ing
va·nil·la
va·nil·lism
va·por
va·por·iza·tion
va·por·ize
 va·por·ized
 va·por·iz·ing
vari·abil·i·ty
vari·able
vari·able·ness
vari·ance
vari·ant
vari·a·tion
vari·a·tion·al
vari·a·tive
var·i·co·cele
var·i·cog·ra·phy
 pl var·i·cog·ra·phies
var·i·coid
var·i·co·phle·bi·tis
var·i·cose
 also var·i·cosed
var·i·co·sis
 pl var·i·co·ses
var·i·cos·i·ty
 pl var·i·cos·i·ties
var·i·cot·o·my
 pl var·i·cot·o·mies

var·ix
 pl var·i·ces

vary
 var·ied
 vary·ing
vas
 pl va·des
 a pledge or surety

vas
 pl va·sa
 bodily duct

va·sa ef·fer·en·tia
va·sal
vas·cu·lar
vas·cu·lar·i·ty
 pl vas·cu·lar·i·ties

vas def·er·ens
 pl va·sa def·er·en·tia
va·sec·to·mize
 va·sec·to·mized
 va·sec·to·miz·ing
va·sec·to·my
 pl va·sec·to·mies

vas·i·tis
va·so·con·stric·tor
va·so·de·pres·sor
va·so·di·la·ta·tion
va·so·di·la·tion
va·so·di·la·tor
va·so·mo·tor
va·so·sec·tion
vas·sal
vas·tum
vec·tor
vec·to·ri·al
veg·an

veg·an·ism
veg·e·ta·ble
veg·e·tar·i·an
veg·e·tar·i·an·ism
ve·hi·cle
ve·hic·u·lar
vein
ve·jours
vel non
ve·loc·i·ty
  pl ve·loc·i·ties
ve·lum
  pl ve·la
ve·na
  pl ve·nae
ve·na ca·va
  pl ve·nae ca·vae
ve·na ca·val
ve·nal
  open to bribery
  (see venial)
ve·nal·i·ty
ve·nal·ly
ve·nal·ness
vend
vend·ee
vend·er
ven·deuse
ven·di
vend·ibil·i·ty
vend·ible
  or vend·able
ven·di·tion
ven·di·tio·ni ex·
  po·nas
ven·dor

ven·due
ve·nec·to·my
  pl ve·nec·to·mies
ven·e·nate
  ven·e·nat·ed
  ven·e·nat·ing
ven·e·na·tion
ve·ne·punc·ture
  var of venipuncture
ve·ne·re·al
ve·ne·re·o·log·i·cal
ve·ne·re·ol·o·gist
ve·ne·re·ol·o·gy
  or ven·er·ol·o·gy
  pl ve·ne·re·ol·o·gies
  or ven·er·ol·o·gies
ven·ery
  pl ven·er·ies
vene·sec·tion
  also veni·sec·tion
ven·geance
ven·geant
venge·ful
venge·ful·ness
ve·nial
  not grave
  (see venal)
ve·ni·punc·ture
  also ve·ne·punc·ture
ve·ni·re
ve·ni·re fa·ci·as
ve·ni·re fa·ci·as de
  no·vo
    also ve·ni·re de
    no·vo
ve·ni·re fa·ci·as
  ju·di·ca·tio·nis

ve·ni·re·man
  pl ve·ni·re·men
veni·sec·tion
  var of venesection
ven·om
ven·om·ous
ve·nous
vent
  or vent brand
ven·te à ré·mé·ré
ven·ter
ven·ti·late
  ven·ti·lat·ed
  ven·ti·lat·ing
ven·ti·la·tion
ven·trad
ven·tral
ven·tral·ly
ven·tri·cle
ven·tro·lat·er·al
ven·tro·lat·er·al·ly
ven·tro·me·di·al
  also ven·tro·me·di·an
ven·tro·me·di·al·ly
ven·ture
  ven·tured
  ven·tur·ing
ven·ue
ven·ville
ve·ra·cious
ve·ra·cious·ly
ve·ra·cious·ness
ve·rac·i·ty
  pl ve·rac·i·ties

ve·ra·trine
ve·ra·trum
ver·bal
ver·bal·ly
ver·ba·tim
ver·biage
ver·big·er·a·tion
ver·bo·ma·nia
ver·bo·ten
ver·der·er
   or ver·der·or

ver·der·er·ship
ver·dict
verge
ver·i·fi·abil·i·ty
ver·i·fi·able
ver·i·fi·able·ness
ver·i·fi·ca·tion
ver·i·fi·ca·to·ry
ver·i·fi·er
ver·i·fy
   ver·i·fied
   ver·i·fy·ing
ver·i·ly
ver·min
ver·min·o·sis
   pl ver·min·o·ses

ver·min·ous
ver·min·ous·ly
ver·ru·ca
   pl ver·ru·cae

ver·ru·cose
ver·ru·co·sis
   pl ver·ru·co·ses

ver·ru·cous

ver·sion
ver·sus
vert
ver·te·bra
   pl ver·te·brae
   or ver·te·bras

ver·te·bral
ver·te·bral·ly
ver·tex
   pl ver·tex·es
   or ver·ti·ces

ver·ti·cal
ver·ti·cal·i·ty
ver·ti·cal·ly
ver·ti·cal·ness
ver·tig·i·nous
ver·ti·go
   pl ver·ti·goes
   or ver·ti·gos
   or ver·tig·i·nes

ves·i·cant
ves·i·cate
   ves·i·cat·ed
   ves·i·cat·ing
ves·i·ca·tion
ves·i·ca·to·ry
   pl ves·i·ca·to·ries

ves·sel
vest
vest·ed
vest·ing
ves·ture
vet·er·an
ve·ti·tum na·mi·
  um
ve·to *n*
   pl ve·toes

ve·to *vb*
  ve·toed
  ve·to·ing
vex·ata quaes·tio
   pl vex·atae quaes·tio·
   nes

vex·a·tion
vex·a·tious
vex·a·tious·ly
via
vi·a·bil·i·ty
   pl vi·a·bil·i·ties

vi·a·ble
via·duct
via or·di·na·ria
via re·gia
vi·at·i·cum
   pl vi·at·i·cums
   or vi·at·i·ca

vi aut clam
vic·ar
vic·ar-gen·er·al
   pl vic·ars-gen·er·al

vi·car·i·al
vi·car·i·ate
vice *n*
vi·ce *prep*
vice-ad·mi·ral·ty
vice-chan·cel·lor
vi·ce mea
vice·roy
vice ver·sa
vic·i·nage
vi·ci·ne·tum
vi·cin·i·ty
vi·cious

vi·con·ti·el
or vi·coun·ti·el

vic·tim
vic·tim·iza·tion
vic·tim·ize
vic·tim·ized
vic·tim·iz·ing
vic·tim·iz·er
vic·tim·less
vict·ual·er
vi·de
vi·de·li·cet
vi·di·mus
vi·du·al
vi·du·ity
pl vi·du·ities

vi et ar·mis
view
view·able
view·er
vif·gage
vig·i·lance
vig·i·lant
vig·i·lan·te
vig·i·lan·tism
vig·o·rish
vi·is et mo·dis
vil·lage
vil·lag·er
vil·lainy
pl vil·lain·ies

vin·cu·lo mat·ri·
mo·nii
vin·cu·lum le·gis
vin·di·ca·ble

vin·di·cate
vin·di·cat·ed
vin·di·cat·ing
vin·di·ca·tion
vin·di·ca·tor
vin·di·ca·to·ry
vin·dic·tive
vi·nous
vi·o·la·bil·i·ty
vi·o·la·ble
vi·o·late
vi·o·lat·ed
vi·o·lat·ing
vi·o·la·tion
vi·o·la·tive
vi·o·la·tor
vi·o·lence
vi·o·lent
vi·o·lent·ly
vi·per
vi·ra·gin·i·ty
vi·rag·i·nous
vi·ra·go
pl vi·ra·goes
or vi·ra·gos

vi·ral
vire·ment
vir·gin
vir·gin·i·ty
pl vir·gin·i·ties
vi·ri·cid·al
vi·ri·cide
vir·ile
vir·il·ism
vi·ril·i·ty
pl vi·ril·i·ties

vir·il·iza·tion
vir·il·ize
vir·il·ized
vir·il·iz·ing
vi·ro·log·i·cal
or vi·ro·log·ic

vi·ro·log·i·cal·ly
vi·rol·o·gist
vi·rol·o·gy
pl vi·rol·o·gies

vi·ro·sis
pl vi·ro·ses

vir·tu·al
vir·tu·al·ly
vir·tue
vir·tu·ous
vir·tu·te of·fi·cii
vir·u·lence
or vir·u·len·cy
pl vir·u·lenc·es
or vir·u·len·cies

vir·u·lent
vi·rus
vi·sa
vi·saed
vi·sa·ing
vis-à-vis
vis·cer·al
vis·cer·al·gia
vis·cus
pl vis·cera

vi·sé
vi·séd
also vi·séed
vi·sé·ing
vis·i·ble

vis·i·bly
vis·it
vis·i·ta·tion
vis·i·ta·to·ri·al
vis·i·tor
   also vis·it·er

vis·i·to·ri·al
vis·i·tress
vis ma·jor
   pl vi·res ma·jo·res

visne
vi·tal
vi·tal·iza·tion
vi·tal·ize
   vi·tal·ized
   vi·tal·iz·ing
vi·ta·min
vi·ti·ate
   vi·ti·at·ed
   vi·ti·at·ing
vi·ti·a·tion
vi·ti·a·tor
vi·va·ry
   pl vi·va·ries

vi·va vo·ce
vi·vum va·di·um
vo·ca·tion
vo·ca·tion·al
vo·cif·er·ous
void
void·able
void·able·ness
void·ance
void·er
void·ness
voir dire

vo·lens
vo·lent
vo·li·tion
vo·li·tion·al
vol·un·tari·ly
vol·un·tary
vol·un·teer
vom·it
vom·i·tus
vot·able
vote
   vot·ed
   vot·ing
vote·less
vot·er
vouch
vouch·ee
vouch·er
vouch·er·able
vow
vow·er
vox sig·na·ta
voy·age
voy·eur
voy·eur·ism
voy·eur·is·tic
vul·gar
vul·ner·a·bil·i·ty
   pl vul·ner·a·bil·i·ties

vul·ner·a·ble
vul·va
   pl vul·vae

vul·val
vul·var
vul·vi·tis
vul·vo·vag·i·ni·tis

W

wad
wad·set
wad·set·ter
wage
wage·less
wa·ger
wa·ger·ing
waif
wain·bote
wait
waive
   waived
   waiv·ing
   to give up voluntarily
   (*see* wave)

waiv·er
   a waiving
   (*see* waver)

walk·ing
   pos·ses·sion
walk out *vb*
walk·out *n*
walk·up
walk·way
wall
wall·eye
wall·eyed
wand
wan·der
want
want·age
want·ing
wan·ton
wan·ton·ly

wan·ton·ness
war
  warred
  war·ring
ward
war·den
war·den·cy
  pl war·den·cies

war·den·ship
ward·er
ward·er·ship
ward·ing
ward·mote
ward·ress
ward·ship
ware
ware·house
  ware·housed
  ware·hous·ing
ware·house·man
  pl ware·house·men

war·fare
war·fa·rin
war·like
warn
warn·ing
warp
warp·age
war·ran·dice
war·rant
war·rant·able
war·ran·tee
war·rant·er
war·rant·less
war·ran·tor

war·ran·ty
  pl war·ran·ties

war·ren
wash out *vb*
wash·out *n*
wash sale
Was·ser·mann
  re·ac·tion
wast·age
waste
  wast·ed
  wast·ing
waste·ful
wast·er
waste·way
wast·rel
wasty
  wast·i·er
  wast·i·est
watch
watch·dog
watch·er
watch·ful
watch·man
  pl watch·men

wa·ter
wa·ter·age
wa·ter·bail·age
wa·ter·course
  channel for water

wa·ter·course
  defective concrete

wa·ter crack
wa·tered
wa·tered-down

wa·ter-gav·el
  or wa·ter-gav·il

wa·ter·log
wa·ter·logged
wa·ter·log·ging
wa·ter·proof
wa·ter·soak
wa·ter ta·ble
wa·ter·tight
wa·ter·way
wa·ter·works
wa·ter·wor·thy
wave
  waved
  wav·ing
  to swing or shake
  (see waive*)*

wa·ver
  wa·vered
  wa·ver·ing
  to be irresolute
  (see waiver*)*

wave·son
way
way·bill
way ex vi ter·mi·ni
way·far·er
way·far·ing
way·go·ing crop
way·lay
  way·laid
  way·lay·ing
way·leave
way·ward
way·ward·ly
way·ward·ness

weal
wealth
wealth·less
weap·on
weap·on·less
wear
  wore
  worn
  wear·ing
wear and tear
wear-out *n*
weath·er
wed
  wed·ded
    also wed
  wed·ding
wed·lock
week·day
week·ly
weigh
weigh·age
weigh·er
weigh·man
  pl weigh·men
weigh·mas·ter
weigh·ment
weight
welch
  var of welsh
wel·fare
well
  bet·ter
  best
well-be·ing
well-con·di·tioned
well-de·fined

well-found·ed
well·head
welsh
  or welch
welsh·er
Welsh mort·gage
west·bound
west·er·ly
west·ern
west·ward
west·ward·ly
wet
wet·back
wet·proof
wharf
  pl wharves
  also wharfs
wharf·age
wharf·in·ger
wharf·mas·ter
Wharn·cliffe
  meet·ing
what·ev·er
what·so·ev·er
wheel·age
wheel·wright
whence
whence·so·ev·er
when·ev·er
when-is·sued
when·so·ev·er
where·abouts
where·af·ter
where·as
where·at
where·by

where·ev·er
where·for
  for which
where·fore
  also where·for
  for that reason
where·from
where·in
where·in·so·ev·er
where·of
where·on
where·so·ev·er
where·through
where·to
where·un·der
where·un·to
where·up·on
where·with
where·with·al
wheth·er
which·ev·er
which·so·ev·er
whilst
whip
  whipped
  whip·ping
whip·lash
whip·saw
  whip·sawed
  whip·sawed
    or whip·sawn
  whip·saw·ing
white
white·cap
  also white·cap·per
white·cap·ping

white damp
white·wash
Whit·ley coun·cil
who·ev·er
whole
whole·sale
  whole·saled
  whole·sal·ing
whole·sal·er
whole·some
whol·ly
whom·ev·er
whom·so·ev·er
whore
  whored
  whor·ing
whore·dom
whore·house
whore·mas·ter
whore·son
whose·so·ev·er
whos·ev·er
who·so·ev·er
wid·get
wid·ow
wid·ow-bench
wid·owed
wid·ow·er
wid·ow·ered
wid·ow·er·hood
wid·ow·hood
wife *n*
  pl wives

wife *vb*
  wifed
  wif·ing

wife·hood
wife·less
wild
wild·cat
  wild·cat·ted
  wild·cat·ting
  wild·cat·ter
will
will·able
will·ful
  or wil·ful
will·ful·ly
  or wil·ful·ly
will·ful·ness
  or wil·ful·ness

will·ing
will·ing·ly
will·ing·ness
will-less
wind
wind·fall
wind·ing up *n*
wind·ing-up *adj*
wind·pipe
wind shake
wind-shak·en
wind·storm
wind up *vb*
  wound up
    also wind·ed up
  wind·ing up
wind-up *n*
win·ner
win·ning
wire·tap
  wire·tapped

wire·tap·ping
wire·tap·per
wish
with
with·draw
  with·drew
  with·drawn
  with·draw·ing
with·draw·able
with·draw·al
with·draw·er
with·er·nam
with·hold
  with·held
  with·hold·ing
with·in
with·out
with re·spect to
wit·ness
wit·ness·able
wit·ness-box
wit·ness·eth
wit·ting
wit·ting·ly
wive
  wived
  wiv·ing
wolfs·bane
wom·an
  pl wom·en

wood·ward
wool-sort·er's dis·
  ease
word
words of
  lim·i·ta·tion

work
work·away
work·day
work·er
work·hand
work·house
work·less
work·man
  pl work·men

work·man·like
work·man·ship
work·mas·ter
work·out
work·shop
work·wom·an
  pl work·wom·en

world·ly
wor·ry *vb*
  wor·ried
  wor·ry·ing
wor·ry *n*
  pl wor·ries

worse·ment
worth
worth·less
wor·thy
  wor·thi·er
  wor·thi·est
wound
wound·ing
wran·gle
  wran·gled
  wran·gling
wreck
wreck·age

wreck·er
wring
  wrung
  wring·ing
wrist·drop
writ
writ·able
writ co·ram no·bis
writ de quar·ran·
  ti·na ha·ben·da
write
  wrote
  writ·ten
  writ·ing
write down *vb*
write-down *n*
write in *vb*
write-in *n*
write off *vb*
write-off *n*
writ·er
write up *vb*
write-up *n*
writ·ing oblig·a·
  to·ry
    pl writ·ings oblig·a·
    to·ry

writ of ca·pi·as
writ of en·try
wrong
wrong·do·er
wrong·do·ing
wrong·er
wrong·ful
wrong·ful·ly
wrong·ly

wrong·ness
wrong·ous
wry·neck

X

x *vb*
  x-ed
  also x'd
  or xed
  x-ing
  or x'ing
  x'es
  or xes

xan·tho·ma
  pl xan·tho·mas
  or xan·tho·ma·ta

xan·tho·ma·to·sis
  pl xan·tho·ma·to·ses

xan·tho·ma·tous
xan·tho·pro·te·ic
xan·tho·pro·tein
xan·tho·sis
  pl xan·tho·ses

xan·thous
X-dis·ease
xe·no·di·ag·no·sis
  pl xe·no·di·ag·no·ses

xe·no·di·ag·nos·tic
xe·no·ge·ne·ic
xe·no·pho·bia
xen·oph·thal·mia
xe·ro·der·ma
xe·roph·thal·mia
xe·roph·thal·mic

xe·ro·sis
  pl xe·ro·ses
xe·rot·ic
xi·phi·ster·nal
xi·phi·ster·num
  pl xi·phi·ster·na
xipho·cos·tal
xi·phoid
  also xi·phoi·dal
X-ir·ra·di·ate
  X-ir·ra·di·at·ed
  X-ir·ra·di·at·ing
X-ir·ra·di·a·tion
X-ra·di·a·tion
x-ray *vb*
X ray *n*

Y

yair
yard·age
yard·man
  pl yard·men
yard·mas·ter
yard·stick
year·book
year·ling
year·ly
yegg
  or yegg·man
  pl yeggs
  or yegg·men
yel·low-dog
yield
yield·ing
yo·him·bine

Z

zeal·ous
zeal·ous·ly
zinc
  zinced
    or zincked
  zinc·ing
    or zinck·ing
zinc·al·ism
zinc·if·er·ous
Z-mark
zo·ac·an·tho·sis
  pl zo·ac·an·tho·ses
zo·na
  pl zo·nae
  or zo·nas
zon·al
zon·al·ly
zo·na·ry
zone
  zoned
  zon·ing
zon·es·the·sia
zoo·eras·tia
zoo·gen·ic
zo·og·e·nous
  also zo·o·ge·ne·ous
zoo·lag·nia
zoo·no·sis
  pl zoo·no·ses
zoo·not·ic
zoo·phil·ia
  also zo·oph·i·lism
zoo·phil·ic
zo·oph·i·list

zo·oph·i·lous
zoo·pho·bia
zos·ter·i·form
zos·ter·oid
Z-plas·ty
zyg·apoph·y·sis
  pl zyg·apoph·y·ses
zy·go·ma
  pl zy·go·ma·ta
  also zy·go·mas
zy·go·mat·ic
zy·mo·sis
  pl zy·mo·ses
zy·mot·ic
zy·mot·i·cal·ly

ABBREVIATIONS

Most of the abbreviations included in this list have been normalized to one form. Variation in the use of periods, in typeface, and in capitalization is frequent and widespread (as *mph,* mph, MPH, m.p.h., Mph).

a   acre, answer

AAA   approved as amended

AACSL   American Association for the Comparative Study of Law

A and M   agricultural and mechanical

ab   about

AB   able-bodied seaman, bachelor of arts

ABA   American Bar Association

abbr   abbreviation

ab init   ab initio (*Latin,* from the beginning)

abp   archbishop

abr   abridged, abridger, abridgment

abs   absolute, absolutely, abstract

abs re   absente reo (*New Latin,* the defendant being absent)

abstr   abstract, abstracted

abt   about

ABTA   American Board of Trial Advocates

ac   account

acad   academic, academy

acc   acceptance, accepted, accompanied, accompaniment, accordant, according, according (to), account, accountant, accusative

accomp   accompaniment

acct   account

ack   acknowledge, acknowledgment

acpt   acceptance

act   action, active, actual

actg   acting

ACTL   American College of Trial Lawyers

ad   administration, administrative, adverb

AD   after date, anno domini (*Latin,* in the year of our Lord)

ADA   assistant district attorney

add   additional, additions

addn   addition

addnl   additional

ad fin   ad finem (*Latin,* at [to] the end)

ad int   ad interim (*Latin,* for the intervening time)

288

adj adjective
ad loc ad locum (*Latin,* to [at] the place)
adm administration, administrative, administrator, admission
Adm admiral, admiralty
admin administration
admix, admrx, admx administratrix
adms, admstr administrator
ads ad sectam (*Latin,* at the suit of), advertisements
ADS autograph document signed
adv adverb, adverbial, adverbially, adversus, advertisement, advice, advocate
ad val ad valorem (*Latin,* according to value)
advg advertising
advt advertisement
aet, aetat aetatis (*Latin,* of age)
aff affairs
afft affidavit
AFLA American Foreign Law Association
Ag August
AG adjutant general, attorney general
agcy agency
AGO adjutant general's office
agst against

agt against, agent, agreement
AI ad interim (*Latin,* for the intervening time)
AINL Association of Immigration and Nationality Lawyers
AJ associate justice
AK Alaska
AKA also known as
AL, Ala Alabama
ALA Automobile Legal Association
Alas Alaska
Alba Alberta
ald alderman
ALI American Law Institute
ALJ administrative law judge
ALS autograph letter signed
ALSA American Law Student Association
alt alter, alternate, alternative
Alta Alberta
alter alteration
am ante meridiem (*Latin,* before noon)
Am America, American
AM master of arts
AMA American Medical Association
amb ambassador
amdt amendment
Amer America, American
amt amount
anal analogy, analysis,

analytic
ann annals, annual, annuity
anon anonymous
ans answer, answered
ANS autograph note signed
ant antonym
a/o account of
ap apud (*Latin,* according to)
AP above proof, accounts payable, additional premium
app apparatus, apparent, apparently, appellate, appended, appendix, appointed, apprentice
appmt appointment
approx approximate, approximately
appt appoint, appointment
Apr April
apt apartment
apx appendix
ar arrival, arrive
AR Arkansas
arb arbitration, arbitrator
arch archaic, architecture
Ariz Arizona
Ark Arkansas
arr arranged
art article, artificial
asm assembly
ass assistant, association
assd assessed, assigned, assured
assn association
assoc associate, associated, association

asst assistant
at attorney
ATL antitrust law
ATLA American Trial Lawyers Association
ats at the suit of
att attached, attention, attorney
Att Gen attorney general
attn attention
atty attorney
aud audit, auditor
Aug August
auth authentic, author, authoress, authorities, authority, authorized
aux auxiliary
av avenue, average, aviation, avoirdupois
AV ad valorem (*Latin,* according to value)
avdp avoirdupois
ave avenue
avg average
AZ Arizona

B bachelor, bancus (*Middle Latin,* bench), bar, baron, bid, bond, born, British thermal unit
BA bachelor of arts
bach bachelor
bal balance
bankr bankruptcy
barr barrister
Bart Baronet

BB bail bond, bankbook, bearer bond
BBA bachelor of business administration
BBB Better Business Bureau
bbl barrel
BC bail court, bankruptcy cases, before Christ
B Can L bachelor of canon law
BCL bachelor of canon law, bachelor of civil law, bachelor of commercial law
BCS bachelor of commercial science
bd board, bond, bound
BD back dividend, bank draft, bills discounted, brought down
BE bill of exchange
bef before
beg begin, beginning
bet between
bf boldface, brief
BF brought forward
BG bonded goods
bibliog bibliographer, bibliography
biog biographical, biography
bk bank, book
bkcy bankruptcy
bkg banking, bookkeeping
bkgd background
bkpt bankrupt
BL bachelor of law, bill of lading

bldg building
bldr builder
BLL bachelor of laws
BM bill of material
BN bank note
BO branch office, broker's order, buyer's option
bor borough
BP bills payable, blood pressure
BPB bank post bill
bpl birthplace
br branch, brand, bridge, brother
BR bank rate, bedroom, bill of rights, bills receivable
brf brief
BS balance sheet, bill of sale, bill of store, British standard
BS,BSc bachelor of science
bsc basic
BSL bachelor of science in law
bt baronet, bought
BT basic training, board of trade
BTA board of tax appeals
BTU British thermal unit
btwn between
bull bulletin
bur bureau, buried
bus business
BV book value
bx box

c cents, century, chancellor,

chapter, college, copyright, court

ca case, circa

CA California, chartered accountant, chief accountant, court of appeal

CAB Citizens' Advice Bureau

CAF cost and freight; cost, assurance, and freight; clerical, administrative, and fiscal

cal calendar, caliber

calc calculating

Calif, Cal California

canc canceled

C and F cost and freight

cap capacity, capital, capitalize, capitalized

caps capitals

carr carriers

cas casualty

cat catalog

CAV curia advisari vult (*Latin*, the court will be advised)

CB cashbook, chief baron, common bench

CBD cash before delivery

CC chief clerk, chief counsel, circuit court, city council, civil cases, civil code, county court, criminal cases, crown cases

CCA circuit court of appeals

CCLS court of claims

CCLSR court of claims reports

CCP court of common pleas

CCPA court of customs and patent appeals

CD congressional district

CE caveat emptor, chemical engineer, civil engineer

cen central

cent central, century

cert certificate, certification, certified, certify

cf confer (*Latin*, compare)

CF carried forward, cost and freight

CFI cost, freight, and insurance

ch chairman, chancellor, chancery, chapter, choice, church

CH clearinghouse, courthouse, customhouse

chap chapter

chem chemical

chg change, charge

chm, chmn chairman

chron chronicle, chronological, chronology

CI cost and insurance

cía compañía (*Spanish,* company)

cie compagnie (*French,* company)

CIF cost, insurance, and freight

cir, circ circa, circle, circuit circular, circulation,

circumference
cit citation, cited, citizen
civ civil, civilian
CJ chief judge, chief justice
ck cask, check
ckd completely knocked
down
cl centiliter, claim, claiming,
class, classification, clause,
clerk, close, closure
CL carload, civil law, civil
liberties, common law
CLB bachelor of civil law
cld called, cleared
CLD doctor of civil law
CLI cost of living index
cm centimeter, cumulative
CM causa mortis (*Latin*, by
reason of death),
courtmartial
CMA court of military
appeals
cml commercial
CMR court of military review
cn canon, consolidated
CN circular note,
consignment note, cover
note, credit note
cnr corner
co company, county
c/o care of
CO carried over, cash order,
certificate of origin,
Colorado, conscientious
objector
cod codex

COD cash on delivery, collect
on delivery
codd codices
COL cost of living
coll college
collat collateral
colloq colloquial
com comment, commerce,
commercial, commissioner,
committee, commoner,
commonwealth,
communication, communist,
community
comd command, commander,
commanding, commissioned
coml commercial
comm commission,
commonwealth
commn commission
commr commissioner
comp companion, company,
comparative, compare,
compensation, compilation,
compiled, compiler,
complement, complete,
composed, composer,
composite, composition,
compositor, compound,
compounded, comprehensive,
comprising, comptroller
compt compartment,
comptroller
comr, coms commissioner
con conjunx (*Latin*, wife),
consul, contra (*Latin*,
against)

conf conference

cong congress, congressional

Conn Connecticut

cons constable, consul

consol consolidated

const constant, constituent, constitution

constr construction

cont containing, contents, continued, continuous, contract, control

contbd contraband

contd continued

contrib contribution, contributor

conv convict

cor coroner

corp corporate, corporation

corr corrected, correction, correspondence, corresponding, corrugated

Corr Fell corresponding fellow

cos companies, consul, consulship, counties

COS cash on shipment

coun council, counsel

cp compare, coupon

CP civil power, civil procedure, clerk of the peace, code of procedure, common pleas, court of probate

CPA certified public accountant, chartered public accountant

cpd compound

CPD common pleas division

CPFF cost plus fixed fee

cr credit, creditor, crown

CR civil rights

crim criminal

crt court

cs case, census, consul

CS civil service, court of sessions

CST Central standard time

ct cent, count, court

CT Central time, Connecticut

CTA cum testamento annexo (*Latin*, with the will annexed)

CTCLS court of claims

ctge cartage

ctn carton

ctr center

cts cents

cum cumulative

cur currency, current

CWO cash with order

cwt hundredweight

CZ Canal Zone

d date, daughter, degree, died

DA days after acceptance, deposit account, district attorney, don't answer

DAD deputy assistant director

db debenture, daybook, Doomsday Book, double biased

d/b/a doing business as

dbl double

dbn de bonis non (*Latin*, of the goods not)

DC defense counsel, district court, District of Columbia, doctor of chiropractic

DCL doctor of canon law, doctor of civil law, doctor of commercial law

D Cn L doctor of canon law

D Comp L doctor of comparative law

DCS deputy clerk of sessions

DD days after date, demand draft, dishonorable discharge, doctor of divinity

DDD direct distance dialing

DDS doctor of dental science, doctor of dental surgery

DE Delaware

deb debenture

dec deceased, decrease

Dec December

decd deceased

def defendant, defense, definite, definition

deft defendant

del delegate, delegation

Del Delaware

dely delivery

Dem democrat, democratic

dep depart, departure, deposit, deputy

depr depreciation

dept department, deponent, deputy

deriv derivation, derivative

des deserted, deserter, desertion

desc descendant

dev developed, developer, development, deviation

DF damage free

dft defendant

DG Dei gratia (*Late Latin*, by the grace of God), director general

dict dictator, dictionary

diff difference

dig digest

dir director

disc discount

Dist Atty district attorney

distr distribute, distribution, distributor

div divided, dividend, division, divorce

DJ district judge, doctor juris (*Latin*, doctor of law)

DJS doctor of juridical science

D Jur doctor of jurisprudence

D Jur Sc doctor of juridical science

dk dark, deck, dock

DL demand loan, doctor of law

DLit, DLitt doctor of letters, doctor of literature

DLO dead letter office

DMD doctor of dental

medicine

dn down

do ditto

DO district officer

DOA dead on arrival

doc document

dol dollar

dom domestic, dominant, dominion

doz dozen

DP data processing, displaced person

DPB deposit passbook

dpt department

dpty deputy

DQ direct question

dr debit, debtor

Dr Doctor

DR deposit receipt, differential rate, district registry, dock receipt

Dr Jur doctor juris (*Latin,* doctor of law)

Dr LL doctor of laws

DS deputy sheriff

DSC doctor of surgical chiropody

dsp decessit sine prole (*Latin,* died without issue)

DST daylight saving time

dup, dupl duplicate

DV Deo volente (*Latin,* God willing)

DVM doctor of veterinary medicine

DWI died without issue

E error, evidence, excellent

E & OE errors & omissions excepted

EC error corrected, exempli causa (*Latin,* for example)

econ economics, economist, economy

ed edited, edition, editor, education

ED election district, ex dividend, extra duty

EDT Eastern daylight time

educ education, educational

EE electrical engineer, errors excepted

EEG electroencephalogram

eff efficiency

e.g. exempli gratia (*Latin,* for example)

EKG electrocardiogram

el eldest, elected, electric, electricity, element, elevated, elevation

eld eldest

elect electric, electrical, electrician, electricity

elem element, elementary

emb embankment, embargo, embark, embarkation, embassy

emer emergency, emeritus

emp emperor, empire, employment, empress

EN exception noted

enc enclosed, enclosure, encyclopedia

encl enclosed, enclosure

end endorsed, endorsement

eng engine, engineer, engineering

engr engineer

enl enlarged, enlisted, enlistment

ent entered, entertainment, entomology, entrance

env envelope, envoy

EO errors and omissions, executive officer, executive order, ex officio

EOM end of month

EP endpoint, en passant (*French,* in passing), estimated position, excess profits, extreme pressure

EPD excess profits duty

EPT excess profits tax

eq equal, equipment, equitable, equity, equivalent

equip equipment

equiv equivalent

ER en route

ERA equal rights amendment

erron erroneous

ES executive secretary

esp especially

Esq, Esqr Esquire

est established, estate, estimate, estimated

EST Eastern standard time

ET Eastern time

ETA estimated time of arrival

et al et alii (*Latin,* and others)

etc et cetera (*Latin,* and so forth)

eth ethical, ethics

et seq et sequens (*Latin,* and the following one), et sequentes *or* et sequentia (*Latin,* and those that follow)

et ux et uxor (*Latin,* and wife)

ex examined, example, exception, exchange, excluding, excursion, executed, executive, exempt, exercise, exhibit, export, express, extra, extract, extremely

exc excellency, excellent, except, excepted, exception, exchange, excuse

exch exchange, exchanged, exchequer

exd examined

ex div without dividend

exec executed, execution, executive, executor

exor executor

exp expansion, ex parte (*Latin,* on behalf), expense, experience, experiment, experimental, expiration, explosive, exponential, export, exported, exposure, express

exper experience, experienced, experiment, experimental

expt experiment, expert, export

exptl experimental

exr executor

ex rel ex relatione (*Latin,* by or on the relation or information of)

exrx executrix

ext extended, extension, exterior, external, extra, extract, extreme, extremely

exx examples, executrix

f fecit (*Latin,* he made), female, fiat (*Latin,* let it be done, let it be made), filius (*Latin,* son), finance, financial, folio, following, frater (*Latin,* brother), from

FA felonious assault, financial advisor, forage acre, free alongside, free astray, free of all average, freight agent

FAA free of all average

fac facsimile, factor, factory, faculty

FAD free air delivered

fam family

FAQ fair average quality, free at quay

FAS free alongside ship, free

alongside steamer

FB freight bill

FBA Federal Bar Association

FBI Federal Bureau of Investigation

FBM foot board measure

FC fidei commissum, follow copy

FC&S free of capture and seizure

fcap foolscap

FCC first-class certificate

fco franco (*Italian,* postage free *or* delivered free)

fcp foolscap

FCS free of capture and seizure

fcty factory

fcy fancy

FD free delivery, free discharge, free dispatch, free dock

FDD franc de droits (*French,* free of charge)

FDIC Federal Deposit Insurance Corporation

fdn foundation

fdry foundry

Feb February

fec fecit (*Latin,* he [she] made it)

fed federal, federation

fedl federal

fedn federation

ff fecerunt (*Latin,* they made), folios, following

FF folded flat, fratres (*Latin,* brothers), freight forwarder

FFA foreign freight agent, for further assignment, free foreign agency, free from alongside, free from average

FFT for further transfer

FGA foreign general agent, foreign general average, free of general average

fgn foreign

fgt freight

fi for instance

FIA full interest admitted

FIB free into barge, free into bunker

FICA Federal Insurance Contributions Act

fi fa fieri facias

FIFO first in, first out

fin finance, financial, finish, finished

fisc fiscal

FIT Federal Income Tax, free of income tax

fl floruit (*Latin,* he flourished)

FL falsa lectio (*Latin,* false reading), Florida, foreign language

Fla Florida

fltg floating, flotage

flx flexible

fm fathom, form

FM field marshal, foreign mission, frequency modulation

fn footnote

fnd found

fndd founded

fndg founding

fndn foundation

fndr founder

fo folio

FO firm offer, foreign office, for orders, free overside

FOB free on board

FOC free of charge

fol folio

FOQ free on quay

for foreign, forensic, forestry

FOR free on rail

FOS free on steamer

FOT free on truck

fp freezing point

FP flash point, floating policy, freight and passenger, fully paid

FPA free of particular average

FPC for private circulation

fprf fireproof

fr father, frater (*Latin,* brother), from

FR fire resistant, fire retardant, freight release

freq frequent, frequently

frl fractional

frm from

FRS Federal Reserve System

frt freight

frwy freeway**

FSLIC Federal Savings and Loan Insurance Corporation
furn furnished, furniture
fut future
fwd forward
FYI for your information

g good, government
GA general agent, general assembly, general average, Georgia
gal gallon
galv galvanized
gar garage
GAT Greenwich apparent time
GAW guaranteed annual wage
GB gold bond
GC general counsel
GCA general claim agent
GCL Guild of Catholic Lawyers
GCM general court-martial
GCT Greenwich civil time
gdn guardian
gds goods
gen, genl general
geog geographic, geographical, geography
geol geologic, geological, geology
GFA general freight agent, good fair average
GG governor-general
GJ grand jury

GL graduate in law
GM general manager, general mortgage, Greenwich meridian
GMT Greenwich mean time
GNP gross national product
GO general office, general officer, general order
gov governor
govt government
gp group
GP general practitioner
GPA general passenger agent
GPO general post office, Government Printing Office
gr grade, gross, group
grad graduate
GRI guaranteed retirement income
gro gross, group
GS general schedule, general secretary, general service
GST Greenwich sidereal time
GT gross ton
GTC good till canceled, good till countermanded
gtd guaranteed
GTM good this month
GTW good this week
gu guarantee, guaranteed
GU Guam
guar guarantee, guaranteed, guarantor, guaranty

h hence, hour, house,

husband
hab corp habeas corpus
HB house bill
HBM Her Britannic Majesty, His Britannic Majesty
HC House of Commons, house of correction
HCL high cost of living
hcp handicap
HD heavy-duty
hdbk handbook
hdg heading
hdqs headquarters
hdwe, hdwre hardware
HE Her Excellency, high explosive, His Eminence, His Excellency
hf half
HH Her Highness, His Highness, His Holiness
HHG household goods
HI Hawaii
HJR House joint resolution
hl hoc loco (*Latin,* in this place), hujus loci (*Latin,* of this place)
HL House of Lords
HM Her Majesty, Her Majesty's, His Majesty, His Majesty's
HMG Her Majesty's Government, His Majesty's Government
HMS Her Majesty's ship, His Majesty's ship
HO head office, home office

hon honor, honorable, honorary, honored
honble honorable
hosp hospital
hp horsepower
HP hire purchase, House of Parliament
HQ headquarters
hr hour
HR home rule, House of Representatives
HRH Her Royal Highness, His Royal Highness
HS high school, house surgeon
hse house
hsg housing
HSH Her Serene Highness, His Serene Highness
HSM Her Serene Majesty, His Serene Majesty
hwy highway
hyp, hypoth hypothesis, hypothetical

i id (*Latin,* that), incendiary, incomplete, independent, indicated, indicative, industrial, inspector, instantaneous, institute, institution, instrumental, international
Ia Iowa
IA incorporated accountant, inter alia (*Latin,* among other things), Iowa

IAC industry advisory committee

IALS International Association of Legal Science

I and E information and education

I and P indexed and paged

I and R initiative and referendum

I and S inspection and security, inspection and survey

ib ibidem (*Latin,* in the same place)

IB in bond, inbound, incendiary bomb, invoice book

IBA Independent Bar Association, International Bar Association

IBI invoice book, inwards

ibid ibidem (*Latin,* in the same place)

IC in charge, information center, information circular, inspected and condemned

ICJ International Commission of Jurists, International Court of Justice

id idem (*Latin,* the same), island

ID Idaho, identification, inside diameter, inside dimensions, internal diameter

IDC industrial development certificate

i.e. id est (*Latin,* that is)

IE industrial engineer, initial equipment

IF in full, ipse fecit (*Latin,* he did it himself)

IG inspector general, intendant-general

ign ignition, ignotus (*Latin,* unknown)

II indorsement irregular, inventory and inspection

IL Illinois, including loading

ILA International Law Association

ILAA International Legal Aid Association

ill illustrated, illustration, illustrator

Ill Illinois

illus, illust illustrated, illustration

imp imperfect, imperial, import, imported

imperf imperfect

impv imperative

in inch

IN Indiana

inbd inboard

inc inclosure, included, including, inclusive, income, incoming, incorporated, incorporation, increase, incumbent

incl including, inclusive

incog incognito
incr increase
ind independent, index, industrial, industry
Ind Indiana
indemy indemnity
indre indenture
indus industrial, industry
inf information
infl influenced
ins, insce insurance
insp inspector
inst instant, institute, institution
instl installation
instn institution, instruction
int interest, interim, interior, intermediate, internal, international, interval, interview
int al inter alia (*Latin,* among other things), inter alios (*Latin,* among other persons)
intg interrogate, interrogator
intl international
intn intention
introd introduction
inv inventory, investment, invoice
invt inventory
IOU I owe you
IP installment paid
i. q. idem quod (*Latin,* the same as)
IQ intelligence quotient

IRA individual retirement account
IRO inland revenue officer, internal revenue officer
IRS Internal Revenue Service
IS interstate
ISC interstate commerce
IT immediate transportation, income tax, in transitu (*Latin,* in transit)
ital italic, italicized
IV increased value, intravenous, in verbo *or* in voce (*Latin,* under the word), invoice value

J journal, judge, justice
JA joint account, joint agent, judge advocate
JAG judge advocate general
Jan January
JB jurum baccalaureus (*Latin,* bachelor of laws)
JC jurisconsultus (*Latin,* jurisconsult), justice clerk, juvenile court
J Can B juris canna baccalaureus (*Latin,* bachelor of canon law)
J Can D juris canna doctor (*Latin,* doctor of canon law)
JCB juris canonici baccalaureus (*Latin,* bachelor of canon law), juris civilis baccalaureus (*Latin,*

bachelor of civil law)

JCD juris canonici doctor (*Latin,* doctor of canon law), juris civilis doctor (*Latin,* doctor of civil law)

JCL juris canonici licentiatus (*Latin,* licentiate in canon law)

JCM juris civilis magister (*Latin,* master of civil law)

JD juris doctor (*Latin,* doctor of law), jurum doctor (*Latin,* doctor of laws), jury duty, justice department, juvenile delinquent

Je June

JEA joint export agent

JJ judges, justices

JM juris magister (*Latin,* master of laws)

jnr junior

jnt joint

jour journal, journey

JP justice of the peace

jr junior, jurist

JSC joint-stock company

JSD jurum scientiae doctor (*Latin,* doctor of the science of the law)

jt joint

jud judge, judgment, judicature, judicial, judiciary

Jul July

jun junior

Jun June

jur juridical, jurist

juris, jurisp jurisprudence

Jur M juris magister (*Latin,* master of jurisprudence)

jus, just justice

juv juvenile

Kans Kansas

KB King's Bench

KC King's Counsel

KD kiln-dried, knocked down

KS Kansas

Ky, KY Kentucky

l lady, lake, land, large, law, legitimate, lex (*Latin,* law), libra (*Latin,* pound), licentiate, line, liter, loco (*Latin,* in the place), locus (*Latin,* place)

La Louisiana

LA law agent, legislative assembly, local agent, local authority, Louisiana

lab labor

Lat Latin

lb libra (*Latin,* pound)

LB local board

lc loco citato (*Latin,* in the place cited), lower case

LC label clause, law courts, letter of credit, Library of Congress

LCJ lord chief justice

LCL less-than-carload

LCM legis comparativae magister (*New Latin,* master

of comparative law)

ld land, load, lord

LD lethal dose

ldg landing, loading

le lease

LE labor exchange

lect lecture, lecturer

led ledger

leg legal, legislation, legislative, legislature

legis legislation, legislative, legislature

lf leaf, lightface

lg large, long

LI Long Island

lib liberal, librarian, library

LIFO last in, first out

lit liter, literature

Lit D, Litt D doctor of letters, doctor of literature

LJ lord justice

LJJ lords justices

ll leges (*Latin,* laws), lines

LL limited liability

LLB legum baccalaureus (*Latin,* bachelor of laws)

LLD legum doctor (*Latin,* doctor of laws)

LLJJ lords justices

LLM legum magister (*Latin,* master of laws)

ln lane, lien, loan

loc local, location, loco (*Latin,* in the place)

loc cit loco citato (*Latin,* in the place cited)

log logic, logistic

loq loquitur (*Latin,* he [she] speaks)

LP lord provost

LS letter signed, listed securities, locus sigilli (*Latin,* place of the seal)

LT legal tender, long ton

ltd limited

LTL less than truckload

ltr letter

lv leave

m male, married, meridian, meridies (*Latin,* noon)

M master, medium, mille (*Latin,* thousand), Monday, monsieur

MA Massachusetts, master of arts, mental age

mach machine, machinery, machinist

MALD master of arts in law and diplomacy

man manual

manuf manufacture, manufacturing

mar maritime

Mar March

masc masculine

Mass Massachusetts

max maximum

MC master of ceremonies, member of congress

MCJ master of comparative jurisprudence

MCL master of civil law, master of comparative law

M Comp L master of comparative law

Md Maryland

MD doctor of medicine, Maryland, months after date

mdse merchandise

Me Maine

ME Maine, mechanical engineer, mining engineer

meas measure

mech mechanical, mechanics

med mediator, medical, medicine

mem member, memoir, memorial

mer meridian

Messrs messieurs

met metropolitan

MFBM mille (*Latin,* thousand) feet board measure

mfd manufactured

mfg manufacturing

mfr manufacture, manufacturer

mgr manager, monseigneur, monsignor

mgt management

MI Michigan, military intelligence

MIA missing in action

Mich Michigan

mil military

min mineral, minimum, mining, minister, minor, minute

Minn Minnesota

misc miscellaneous

Miss Mississippi

mixt mixture

MJ military judge

mk mark

mkt market

ML magister legum (*Latin,* master of laws)

M Laws master of laws

MLD minimum lethal dose

Mlle mademoiselle

MLT master of law and taxation

MM messieurs

Mme madame

MN Minnesota

mo month

Mo Missouri

MO mail order, medical officer, Missouri, modus operandi, money order

mod modern

modif modification

MOM middle of month

Mon Monday

Mont Montana

mos months

MP member of parliament, metropolitan police, military police, military policeman, mounted police, municipal police

mpg miles per gallon

mph miles per hour
MPL master of patent law
MR master of the rolls
MS manuscript, master of science, Mississippi, motor ship
MSCJ master of science in criminal justice
msg message
msgr monseigneur, monsignor
msp mortuus sine prole (*Latin*, dead without issue)
MSS manuscripts
MST Mountain standard time
MT metric ton, Montana, Mountain time
mtg, mtge mortgage
mun, munic municipal
mut mutual
MV market value, merchant vessel, motor vessel

n name, net, neuter, noon, north, note, number
Na no account, not applicable
nat national, nationalist, native, natural, naturalized
natl national
nav naval, navigable, navigation
NB Nebraska, no bid, note bene (*Latin*, note well)
NBS National Bureau of Standards
NC no charge, noncollectible, North Carolina
ND national debt, no date, North Dakota, northern district
N Dak North Dakota
NE national emergency, Nebraska, New England, northeast, not exceeding, not to exceed
Neb, Nebr Nebraska
neg negative, negotiable
nei non est inventus (*Latin*, he was not found)
NEI not elsewhere included, not elsewhere indicated
NEM not elsewhere mentioned
nem con nemine contradicente (*Latin*, no one contradicting)
nem diss nemine dissentiente (*Latin*, no one dissenting)
NES not elsewhere specified
Nev Nevada
NF no funds, nonfundable
NG national guard, no good, not good
NH New Hampshire
ni pr *or* **ni pri** nisi prius (*Latin*, unless before)
NJ New Jersey
NK not known
nl non licet (*Latin*, it is not permitted), non liquet

(*Latin,* it is not clear)

NL, NLT   night letter

NM   nautical mile, New Mexico, night message, no mark, not marked

N Mex   New Mexico

NN   names, notes

no   north, number

NO   name of, no orders

NOIBN   not otherwise indexed by name

nol pros   nolle prosequi (*Latin,* to be unwilling to prosecute)

non obst   non obstante (*Latin,* notwithstanding)

non pros   non prosequitur (*Late Latin,* he does not prosecute)

non seq   non sequitur

NOS   not otherwise specified

nov   non obstante veredicto (*Latin,* notwithstanding the verdict)

Nov   November

np   new paragraph, nisi prius (*Latin,* unless before)

NP   no protest, notary public

NPL   nonpersonal liability

NPV   no par value

nr   near, number

NR   net register, no risk

NS   not specified

NSF   not sufficient funds

NT   new terms

NU   name unknown

NV   Nevada, nonvoting

NY   New York

NYC   New York City

o/a   on account, on or about, open account, our account

O and R   ocean and rail

ob   obiit (*Latin,* he [she] died)

OB   opening of books, ordered back

OBL   order bill of lading

obs   obscure, observation, obsolete, obstacle, obstruction

oc   ocean, ope consilio *or* ope et consilio (*Latin,* by aid and counsel), opere citato (*Latin,* in the work cited)

OC   office copy, officer in charge, official classification, old charter, old crop, open charter, order canceled, overcharge

oct   octavo

Oct   October

OD   officer of the day, on demand, on duty, ordinary seaman, outside diameter, outside dimensions, overdose, overdraft, overdrawn

OE   omissions excepted

ofc   office

ofcl   official

off   offered, office, officer, official, officinal

OH   Ohio

OK, Okla Oklahoma

OL occupational level, overflow level, overload

OM old measurement, outer marker

ON order notify

op operation, operative, operator, opposite, opus

OP old prices, open policy, out of print, overprint, overproof

op cit opere citato (*Latin,* in the work cited)

opn operation, opinion

opp opportunity, opposed, opposite

OPP out of print at present

OR official receiver, on request, ordered recorded, Oregon, owner's risk, own recognizance

ORB owner's risk of breakage

ORC owner's risk of chafing

ord ordained, order, orderly, ordinance, ordinary, ordnance

ORD owner's risk of damage

Oreg, Ore Oregon

ORF owner's risk of fire, owner's risk of freezing

org organization, organized

orig original, originally

ORL owner's risk of leakage

ORS owner's risk of shifting

orse otherwise

ORW owner's risk of becoming wet

OS only son, on sale, on sample, on schedule, ordinary seaman, out of stock

OS and D over, short, and damaged

OSC order to show cause

OT oiltight, on time, on track, on truck, overtime

p page, past, per, point, population, populus (*Latin,* people), port, post, postage, present

pa per annum

Pa Pennsylvania

PA passenger agent, Pennsylvania, post adjutant, power of attorney, press association, private account, prothonotary apostolic, public administration, public assistance, purchasing agent

Pac Pacific

PAL prisoner at large

pam pamphlet

P and I protection and indemnity

P and L profit and loss

par paragraph, parish

parl parliament, parliamentary

part participating, particular, partner

pass passage, passenger,

passim
pat patent, patented, patrol, pattern
payt payment
PB passbook, patrol boat, privately bonded
PBA permanent budget account
pc percent, percentage, piece, postcard
PC parliamentary cases, patent cases, penal code, petty cash, pleas of the crown, police constable, political code, practice cases, price current, privy council, privy councillor
PCB petty cashbook
pchs purchase
pcl parcel
PCS principal clerk of session
pct percentage
pd paid, passed, pound
PD per diem (*Latin,* by the day), police department, port dues, port of debarkation, postal district, postdated, property damage, public domain
PE port of embarkation, probable error
PEG prior endorsement guaranteed
Penn, Penna Pennsylvania
per period
perf perfect, perforated

perm permanent
per proc per procuration, per procurationem (*Latin,* by proxy *or* by the agency of)
pers person, personal
pert pertaining
pf, pfd preferred
PF procurator fiscal, pro forma
pg page
pgt per gross ton
PH public health
pharm pharmaceutical, pharmacist, pharmacy
PhD doctor of philosophy
PHP packing-house products, pump horsepower
phr phrase, phraseology
PHV pro hace vice (*Latin,* for this turn, for this purpose or occasion)
PIO public information office, public information officer
PJ police justice, presiding judge, probate judge
pkg, pkge package
pkr packer
pkt packet, pocket
pkwy parkway
PL partial loss, private line, profit and loss, public law, public liability
plf, plff, pltf plaintiff
pm post meridiem (*Latin,* afternoon), premium

PM paymaster, per month, police magistrate, postmortem, prime minister, prize money, pro mille (*Latin,* per thousand), provost marshal, purchase money

PMG paymaster general, postmaster general, provost marshal general

PMH production per man-hour

pmk postmark

pmt payment

PN promissory note

PNG persona non grata

PO personnel officer, postal order, post office, probation officer

POC port of call

POD pay on delivery

POE port of embarkation, port of entry

pol political, politician, politics

pop popular, population

POR pay on return

pos position, positive, possession

POW prisoner of war

pp pages

PP parcel post, per procurationem (*Latin,* by proxy *or* by the agency of), personal property, postpaid, prepaid, propria persona

(*Latin,* in his [her] proper person, in his [her] own person)

PPA per power of attorney

PPC pour prendre congé (*French,* to take leave)

ppd postpaid, prepaid

PPI policy proof of interest

PPS post postscriptum (*Latin,* an additional postscript)

PR Puerto Rico

prac practical, practice, practitioners

prec preceding

prelim preliminary

prem premium

prep preparatory

pres presidency, president, presidential, presumptive

prev previous

prf proof

prin principal

PRN pro re nata (*Latin,* for an occasion that has arisen, as occasion arises)

prob probable, probably, probate, problem

proc procedures, proceedings

prod production

prof professor

prop propeller, property, proposed, proposition, proprietary, proprietor

pro quer pro querente (*Latin,* for the plaintiff)

pro tem pro tempore (*Latin,* for the time being)

prov province, provincial, provisional

ps pseudo

PS passenger steamer, permanent secretary, police sergeant, postscriptum (*Latin,* postscript), privy seal, public sale, public school, public stenographer

pseud pseudonym

PSS postscripta (*Latin,* postscripts)

PST Pacific standard time

psych psychology

pt part, payment, port

PT Pacific time, physical therapy, physical training, post town, private terms, pro tempore

PTA Parent-Teacher Association

ptd printed

pte private

PTO Parent-Teacher Organization, please turn over

pub public, publication, published, publisher, publishing

publ publication, published

PV par value, post village

pvt private

PW packed weight, prisoner of war, public works

PX please exchange, private exchange

q quarto, query, question

Q quarter, quarterly, queen

QB Queen's Bench

QC Queen's Counsel

QDA quantity discount agreement

qe quod est (*Latin,* which is)

QED quod erat demonstrandum (*Latin,* which was to be demonstrated)

QEF quod erat faciendum (*Latin,* which was to be done)

QEI quod erat inveniendum (*Latin,* which was to be found out)

qlty quality

qn question

qqv quae vide (*Latin,* which see)

qr quarter

qrly quarterly

qrtly quarterly

QS quarter sessions

qt quantity, quart

qtly, qtr quarterly

qty quantity

qu quarterly, quasi, query, question

ques question

quot quotation

quotid quotidie (*Latin,*

every day)

qv quod vide (*Latin,* which see)

qy query

r railroad, railway, range, registered, right, road, route, rule

R regina (*Latin,* queen), rex (*Latin,* king)

RA refer to acceptor

R and D research and development

RC release clause, relief claim, Roman Catholic

rcd received, record

RCL ruling case law

rcpt, rct receipt

rcvr receiver

rd road, rod, round

RD refer to drawer, regional director, rural delivery, rural district

RDC running-down clause, rural district council

RDY royal dockyard

re reference, regarding

RE rate of exchange, real estate, repayable to either

reaptd reappointed

rec receipt, receive, receiver, reclamation, recommended, record, recorded, recorder, recording

recd received

recip reciprocal, reciprocity

rec sec recording secretary

rect receipt, rectified

ref referee, reference, referred, refinery, refining, reform, reformed, refunding

reg register, registered, regular, regulation

reg gen regula generalis (*Latin,* a general rule)

rel relating, relative

rep report, reporter, representative, republic

Rep Republican

repl replace, replacement

rept receipt, report

res reserve, residence, residency, resident, residential, resistance, resolution

resp respective, respectively

retd retained, retired, returned

retnr retainer

rev revenue, review, reviewed, revised, revision

Rev St, Rev Stat Revised Statutes

RFD rural free delivery

rg regulae generales (*Latin,* general rules)

RI Rhode Island

riv river

rls release

rly railway

rm ream, room

RM resident magistrate

rnd round

ROG receipt of goods

ROW right of way

RPO railway post office

rpt repeat, report

rqn requisition

RR railroad, rural route

RS recording secretary, revised statutes

RSVP répondez s'il vous plaît (*French,* please reply)

RTN registered trade name

RW right of way

rwy, ry railway

s second, section, series, son, statute

S Saturday, senate, Sunday

Sa Saturday

SA sine anno (*Latin,* without date), subject to approval

S and C shipper and carrier

S and FA shipper and forwarding agent

S and T supply and transport

sanit sanitary, sanitation

SANR subject to approval no risk

Sat Saturday

savs savings

SB bachelor of science, savings bank, senate bill, small bonds, statement of billing

sc scilicet (*Latin,* that is to

say), small capitals

SC salvage charges, same case, select cases, South Carolina, summary court, supreme court

scd schedule

ScD doctor of science

sch school

sci science

scil scilicet (*Latin,* that is to say)

SCL student of the civil law

SCM summary court-martial

sd sine dato (*Latin,* without date), sine die (*Latin,* without day)

SD same day, sea damage, several dates, short delivery, sight draft, South Dakota, special delivery, supply department, supply depot

S Dak South Dakota

SDBL sight draft, bill of lading attached

SDD store door delivery

SE stock exchange

sec second, secretariat, secretary, section, secundum (*Latin,* according to), security

sec leg secundum legem (*Latin,* according to law)

sec reg secundum regulam (*Latin,* according to rule)

sect section

secy secretary

Sept, Sep September

seq sequens (*Latin,* the following [singular]), sequitur (*Latin,* it follows)

seqq sequentia (*Latin,* the following [plural])

ser serial, series

serv service

sess session

SG solicitor general, surgeon general

sgd signed

sh share, shipping

shg shipping

shipt, shpt shipment

shr share

shtg shortage

si short interest

sig signal, signature

sigill sigillum (*Latin,* seal)

SIT stopping in transit, storage in transit

sj sub judice (*Latin,* under consideration)

SJC Supreme Judicial Court

SJD scientiae juridicae doctor (*Latin,* doctor of juridical science)

sl secundum legem (*Latin,* according to law)

SL seditious libeler, sergeant-at-law, session laws, solicitor-at-law, statute law

slan sine loco, anno, vel nomine (*Latin,* without place, year, or name)

SL and C shipper's load and count

SL and T shipper's load and tally

sld sailed, sealed

slp sine legitima prole (*Latin,* without lawful issue)

SM master of science, senior magistrate, stipendiary magistrate

smp sine mascula prole (*Latin,* without male issue)

sn sine nomine (*Latin,* without name

snr senior

SO seller's option, sex offender, shipping order, ship's option, shop order, special order, standing order

soc social, socialist, society, sociology

socy society

SOD seller's option to double

sol soldier, solicitor, solution

SOL shipowner's liability

solr solicitor

SOP standard operating procedure, standing operating procedure

sp sine prole (*Latin,* without issue), spell, spelled, spelling

SP shore patrol, starting price, stop payment

SPCA Society for the Prevention of Cruelty to Animals

SPCC Society for the Prevention of Cruelty to Children

spec special, specialist

specif specific, specifically

spl sine prole legitima (*Latin*, without legitimate issue)

spm sine prole mascula (*Latin*, without male issue)

SPM smaller profit margin

sps sine prole superstite (*Latin*, without surviving issue)

sr senior

SR shipping receipt

SR and O statutory rules and orders

srch search

SRO standing room only, statutory rules and orders

SS shipside, social security, special session, sworn statement

SSC solicitor before the supreme court

st state, statute, street

ST short ton, standard time

sta station

stat statute

std standard

STD doctor of sacred theology

ster, stg sterling

stk stock

subs subscription, subsidiary, substitute

Sun Sunday

sup superior, superlative, superseded, supplement, supplementary, supply, support, supra (*Latin*, above), supreme

supt superintendent, support

surg surgeon, surgery, surgical

surr surrogate

surv survey, surveying, surveyor, surviving

sv sub verbo *or* sub voce (*Latin*, under the word)

sw shipper's weight

syst system

T tempore (*Latin*, in the time of), term, Thursday, title, Tuesday

TA tax agent

T and O taken and offered

TB trial balance, tuberculosis

TBL through bill of lading

TBW to be withheld

TC tariff circular, tariff commission, tax court, temporary constable, till countermanded, top of column, town clerk, town councillor, traffic commissioner, traffic consultant, training center, training circular

TCP traffic control post

TD temporary disability,

temporary duty, time
deposit, tons per day, traffic
director, treasury decision,
treasury department

TDY temporary duty

tec technical, technician,
technology

tech, techn technical,
technically, technician,
technological, technology

tel telegram, telegraph,
telephone

teleg telegraphy

temp temperature,
temporary, tempore (*Latin,*
in the time of)

Tenn Tennessee

ter, terr territory

Tex Texas

Th Thursday

ThD doctor of theology

thou thousand

Thu, Thur, Thurs Thursday

tk tank, truck

TL time loan, total loss,
truckload

TLO total loss only

TM tons per minute,
trademark, traffic manager,
training manual, trainmaster

TMG track made good

TMH tons per man-hour

TML three mile limit

TMO telegraph money order

tn ton, town

TN tariff number, Tennessee,

thermonuclear, true north

tnge tonnage

tnpk turnpike

TO table of organization,
technical order, telegraph
office, transport officer, turn
over

top topographic,
topographical

TOP temporarily out of print

topog topography

tp title page, township

tpk turnpike

TPO traveling post office

tr tare, transaction,
translated, translation,
translator, treasurer, trustee

TR tariff reform, technical
regulation, technical report,
technical representative,
tons registered, trust receipt

trans transaction, transfer,
transferred, transitional,
translated, translation,
translator, transport,
transportation

treas treasurer, treasury

trf tariff, transfer

trfd transferred

trfr transfer

trib tribunal, tribune,
tributary

TS transport and supply

Tu, Tue, Tues Tuesday

TV television

tx tax

TX Texas
txn taxation

UA underwriting account
U and O use and occupancy
UC under charge, utility cargo
UD urban district
UDC urban district council
UDT underdeck tonnage
UI unemployment insurance
ult ultimate, ultimately, ultimo
um unmarried
UMS universal military service
UMT universal military training
univ universal, universally, universe, university
unk, unkn unknown
unl unlimited
unm unmarried
unsgd unsigned
UP underproof
UR uniform regulations, unsatisfactory report
us ubi supra (*Latin,* where above mentioned), ut supra (*Latin,* as above)
US undersecretary, united service, United States, unserviceable
USA United States of America
USC under separate cover,

United States Code
USES United States Employment Service
USP United States Pharmacopeia
USPO United States Patent Office
USS United States ship, United States standard
usu usual, usually
UT Utah
UW underwriter
ux uxor (*Latin,* wife)

v vagabond, value, variable, variation, velocity, versus, vice, vide (*Latin,* see), village, viscount, volume
va variance
Va Virginia
VA Veterans Administration, Virginia, vixit annas (*Latin,* he [she] lived . . . years)
vac vacant
val valuation, value
valn valuation
var variable, variant, variation, various
VAT value-added tax
vb, vbl verbal
VC valuation clause, vice-chairman, vice-chancellor
VD various dates, venereal disease
vel vellum, velocity

ven venerable
vet veterinarian, veterinary
vg verbi gratia (*Latin,* for example)
VG very good
vi vide infra (*Latin,* see below)
VI Virgin Islands
vic vicinity
vid vide (*Latin,* see), vidua (*Latin,* widow)
vil village
VIP very important person
viz videlicet (*Latin,* namely)
vl varia lectio (*Latin,* variant reading)
VLOL violating local option law
VO verbal order
vol volume, volunteer
VOP valued as in original policy
vou voucher
VP vice-president
vs verse, versus, vide supra (*Latin,* see above)
vss versions
Vt, VT Vermont
VTC voting trust certificate
vv vice versa

w wanting, warden, warehouse, warehousing, week, weight, widow, wife, with
W Wednesday

WA Washington
WAE when actually employed
W and I weighing and inspection
war warrant
Wash Washington
wb warehouse book, water ballast, waybill, weather bureau
WBS without benefit of salvage
WC will call, without charge, working capital
WD war department, when distributed, works department
Wed Wednesday
wf wrong font
WG weight guaranteed
wh which
whol wholesale
whs, whse warehouse
whsle wholesale
WI when issued, Wisconsin
wid widow, widower
Wis, Wisc Wisconsin
wmk watermark
w/o without
WOC without compensation
WOG with other goods
WOL wharf owner's liability
WP without prejudice
wpm words per minute
WR with rights
wrnt, wt warrant

WV, W Va West Virginia
WW warehouse warrant,
  with warrants
WWA with the will annexed
WY, Wyo Wyoming

X experimental
XD, x div ex dividend
XI, x in, x int ex interest
XQ cross-question
XW without warrants

y year
YB yearbook
yld yield
YO year-old
YP yard patrol, yellow pine,
  yield point
yr year, your
yrs yours
yst youngest

ZIP Zone Improvement Plan
ZT zone time

PUNCTUATION MARKS

,	apostrophe	-	hyphen
*	asterisk	( )	parentheses
[ ]	brackets	.	period
:	colon	?	question mark
,	comma	" "	quotation marks, double
—	dash	' '	quotation marks, single
. . . *or*	ellipsis	;	semicolon
!	exclamation point	/	virgule

Apostrophe

An apostrophe indicates possession:
> the attorney's client, the attorneys' clients; anyone's guess, everyone's questions; the witness's [*or* witness'] testimony, the witnesses' testimonies; Appleton and Delayney's client, Appleton and Delayney's clients, Appleton's and Delayney's respective clients.

An apostrophe also indicates implied or understood possession:
> The book is at your local bookseller's.

An apostrophe sometimes occurs in expressions of time and money:
> a year's probation, two years' probation; a dollar's worth, two dollars' worth.

An apostrophe may be used to indicate omission of letters or numbers:
> you're; isn't; ass'n; sec'y; '78.

An apostrophe + *s* often pluralizes letters, figures, or words, especially when they are referred to as such:
> dotting one's *i*'s and crossing one's *t*'s; *1*'s and *7*'s looking similar; can't pronounce her *the*'s.

NOTE: Such plurals may also be shown without punctuation:
> can't pronounce her *the*s.

Asterisk
Three spaced and centered asterisks indicate omission of one or
more paragraphs of text:

                                  *   *   *

Brackets
Brackets serve as parentheses within parentheses:
   Local regulation (City Ordinance 46 [§ 5]) prohibits it.

Brackets are used within quoted matter to enclose the word *sic*
which indicates that a recognized error has not been changed in
the quotation:
   . . . said that "two [sic] witnesses are prepared to testify;
   namely, Jonathan D. Simpson, Marietta A. Lyons, and Kenneth
   Richardson."

Brackets are also used within quoted matter to enclose cor-
rections or explanations made by someone other than the person
being quoted:
   The correspondence states that "this amount [$2,000,000.00]
   together with costs and expenses related to the litigation had
   been provided in 19– as a charge to corporate operations for
   the years involved [19– through 19–]."

Colon
A colon introduces a phrase or a clause that explains, restates,
illustrates, or amplifies what has gone before:
   . . . Harrison T. Brown shall be awarded the complete custody
   and control of the infant children of the parties: John Thomas
   Brown and Ann Marie Brown shall be in the custody of the
   plaintiff, subject to reasonable rights of visitation by the
   defendant to see the children once a week.

   He has had trial experience on three judicial levels: county,
   state, and federal.

A colon introduces an extended quotation comprising more than three typewritten or printed lines:

> I quote from page 1 of Mr. Montcalm's May 24, 19—, letter addressed to me:
>
>> Mr. Samuelson and I are now attempting to arrive at a hearing date acceptable to him, to the Special Commissioner in Chancery, and to me. I surmise that a Final Decree can be entered just before the end of January, 19—.

A colon may separate a publication title from a subtitle:

> *Business of the Supreme Court: A Study in the Federal Judicial System*

A colon can serve as a divider in set formulas such as those expressing ratios, time, volume and page references, biblical citations, and place and publisher:

> a ratio of 3:5; 2:30 p.m.; is found in *Words and Phrases* 12:261; see Luke 2:12; Springfield, MA: G. & C. Merriam Company.

A colon is often used after business-letter salutations, in some subject lines in business correspondence, and in memorandum headings:

Gentlemen:	SUBJECT:	TO:
Dear Ms. Lee:	In Re:	VIA:

A colon punctuates writer/typist identification initials and carbon-copy notations in business correspondence:

MWK:hg	cc:	MWK	cc:	Ms. Leeds
		FCM		Mr. Manson
				Ms. Sherry
				Mr. Watson

Comma

A comma punctuates a closed series joined by *and* or *or:*

> The Will stipulates that his estate is to be divided equally among his wife, his sons, and his daughters.

We expect you to greet clients, take dictation, transcribe dictated material, and do research.

Ms. Smith, Mr. Inge, or Mrs. Williams will advise you.

A comma separates independent clauses joined by coordinating conjunctions (*and, or, but, nor,* and sometimes *so* and *yet*) and very short clauses not so joined:

The Supreme Court of the United States is scheduled to hear oral arguments on this matter on March 1, 19–, and a decision is expected in the late spring.

The defendant needed legal representation, so he asked for an attorney.

The witness knew, she was there, she saw it happen.

NOTE: Two brief and tightly connected clauses joined by a coordinating conjunction are sometimes unpunctuated. Two predicates governed by a single subject and joined by a coordinating conjunction are usually unpunctuated:

We have denied the charges and we have prepared our defense.

The Court will take the matter under advisement and will announce its decision at a later date.

A comma sets off adverbial clauses from main clauses:

Although that evidence would be very helpful, it is still inadmissable by law.

A comma often sets off participial, infinitive, or prepositional phrases preceding main clauses:

Having adjourned the court, the judge returned to chambers.

To understand the importance of this ruling, you have to be familiar with the precedents.

On the following Monday, ten indictments were handed down.

The comma sets off from the rest of the sentence interrupting transitional elements (as the phrase *on the other hand*), conjunctive adverbs (as *however, nevertheless, still, yet,* and so forth)

when they do not introduce a clause, and expressions introducing
explanations or examples (as *i.e., e.g., namely, that is,* and so on):

> The second charge against you is, on the other hand, much more
> serious.

> In view of the broad and largely undefined relief sought, how-
> ever, an adverse decision could have a significant effect on this
> Corporation's operations.

> The Board of Directors have been advised by the general
> counsel that, although the legal responsibility in respect to
> such suits and other similar litigation cannot be ascertained, it
> is her opinion that any ultimate liability will not be materially
> important in relation to the consolidated financial position of
> the corporation.

> I believe in ethics, i.e., professional ethics.

A comma often separates coordinate adjectives (i.e., adjectives
that share an equal relationship to the noun they modify):

> Thorough, careful pretrial preparation is necessary.
> *but*
> We have filed a civil antitrust complaint.

NOTE: The test to use before inserting commas is to insert *and*
between questionable adjectives, and then to decide whether
the sentence still makes sense. Compare the two examples above to
discern the difference. In the second example, *and* could not be
inserted between *civil* and *antitrust*.

A comma sets off from the rest of the sentences parenthetic elements (as nonrestrictive modifiers and appositives) whose inclusion
or omission is not critical to the meaning of the entire sentence:

> **nonrestrictive**
> This man, who is now being represented by a public defender,
> will appear in court tomorrow.

> Mr. Ogden, one of my associates, delivered the opening argu-
> ments.

restrictive
The defendant who was convicted of conspiracy yesterday will be sentenced next week.

My associate Mr. Ogden will have to approve your request.

A comma introduces a run-in direct quotation, ends a run-in direct quotation, and punctuates segments of a split quotation:
In a letter dated March 30, 19–, his attorney said, "We have filed a petition for a Writ of Certiorari with the Supreme Court of the United States, seeking review of that decision."

"We have filed a petition for a Writ of Certiorari with the Supreme Court of the United States, seeking review of that decision," his attorney said in a letter dated March 30, 19–.

"We have filed a petition for a Writ of Certiorari with the Supreme Court of the United States," his attorney said in a letter dated March 30, 19–, "and we are seeking review of that decision."

A comma sets off words in direct address:
Your Honor, the Defense rests.

We would like to discuss the matter with you in person, Mr. Johnson.

A comma sets off contrastive words and phrases from the rest of a sentence:
The fee is $2,500.00, not $2,300.00.
The procedure, not the law, has changed.

A comma sets off a tag question from the rest of a sentence:
This matter is still in litigation, is it not?

A comma indicates the omission of a word or words—especially those used earlier in a sentence:
Common stocks are favored by some investors; bonds, by others.
Some attorneys hold LLBs; others, JDs.

A comma is conveniently used to group numerals into units of three in separating thousands, millions, and so on:

The fee for my services will be Two Thousand Dollars ($2,000.00), payable . . . .

NOTE: Set units such as measurements of horsepower, street numbers, suite and room numbers, and page numbers are typically unpunctuated:
    3600 rpm; 4560 South Main Street; Suite 3000; Room 1800; pp. 1234–1235.

A comma often punctuates business-letter date lines and sets off dates within running texts:
    January 1, 19– (business-letter date line)
    On December 1, 19–, the Court issued its opinion that there had been no violations of state or federal law.
    In June, 19–, [*or* In June 19–,] corporate counsel met several times with them.
    . . . on or about the 21st day of June, 19–, the defendant, Martha A. Flood, willfully deserted your complainant . . . .

A comma often punctuates the complimentary close of a business letter:
    Very truly yours,   Best regards,

A comma may separate a name from a professional title if the title appears on the same line as the name (as in an inside address):
    Mr. I. L. Lee, General Counsel
    XYZ Corporation
    1234 Smith Boulevard
    Smithville, ST 56789

A comma separates a name from a following academic degree abbreviation or an honorific:
    John M. Jones, JD   John M. Jones, Esq.
    Mary A. Jones, LLB   Mary A. Jones, Esq.

Commas set off geographic names and locations from the rest of a running text. Also, a comma is placed between the name of a city

or a town and the name or abbreviation of a state in an inside
address:

running text
Washington, DC, is the seat of the United States Supreme Court.

Mail your check to Appleton and Delayney, Law Offices,
345 Johnson Square, Suite 12, Smithville, ST 56789

inside address
Appleton and Delayney
Law Offices
345 Johnson Square   Suite 12
Smithville, ST 56789

A comma may separate elements within some corporate names:
Leedy Manufacturing Co., Inc.

A comma ought to be used whenever its inclusion will avoid
ambiguity:
In 1978, 79 new clients were seen.

Dash

A dash marks an abrupt interruption of the continuity of a
sentence:
The Grand Jury testimony—it is very sensitive testimony—has
not yet been made public.

A dash often introduces a summary statement that follows a
series of words or phrases:
Self-destruction, suicide, and *death by his own hand*—these are
synonyms defined in *Words and Phrases* as "the voluntary
destruction of one's self."

A dash is often used to make parenthetic or explanatory matter
stand out emphatically:
Our arguments—and especially the one presented by our partner
John Smith—impressed the jury.

Ellipsis
Ellipsis indicates by three spaced periods the omission of one or
more words within a quoted passage; and by four spaced periods,
the omission of one or more sentences within a quoted passage
or the omission of a word or words at the end of a quoted passage:

> The Court also found that the terms of the proposed merger
> were fair to both parties and their respective stockholders, and
> stated that "plaintiffs did not produce . . . evidence that im-
> proper motivations or divided loyalties were responsible for
> what the Court regards as a sound negotiating stratagem which
> ultimately resulted in a discount higher than any previously
> approved by the SEC . . . ."
>
> *—DuPont Annual Report 1976*

> An extra allowance, in New York practice, is not included
> within the term "costs" . . . . Code Civ. Proc. § 3253 describes
> it as "further sum."
>
> *—Words and Phrases*

Exclamation Point
An exclamation point terminates an exclamatory phrase or
sentence:

> We expect that you will conform to our expectations—now!

> Oh, no! Not that!

Hyphen
A hyphen marks the division of a word at the end of a line:

> We expect to meet the XYZ Co.'s former general coun-
> sel on Friday, May 30, 19–, at 9:45 a.m.

> I think that the matter will first be presented to a three-
> judge panel.

A hyphen suspends the first part of a hyphenated compound when
used with another hyphenated compound in attributive position:

> five- and ten-year prison sentences

A hyphen or hyphens may link two or more words used as unit modifiers:

a small-business man; a larger-than-life
situation; a four-judge panel.

Hyphens punctuate written-out numbers between 21 and 99:

forty-two; thirty-five;
one hundred twenty-eight.

NOTE: In some documents and proclamations, *and* is used after *hundred* in dates:

In the year one thousand nine hundred and sixty . . . .

A hyphen is used between the numerator and the denominator in a written-out fraction that functions as an adjective:

a two-thirds majority *but* a majority of two thirds.

Hyphens are used between some prefix + root combinations, as

prefix + proper name	pro-Supreme Court
some prefixes ending in a vowel + a root word beginning with another vowel	re-ink *but* reissue
some prefixes ending in a vowel + a root word beginning with the same vowel	co-opted *but* cooperated
stressed prefix + root word, especially when this combination is similar to a different word	re-treat a patient *but* retreat from an argument

A hyphen serves as an arbitrary equivalent of the phrase "(up) to and including" when used between numbers and inclusive dates:

pages 45–55; the years 1970–1980.

A hyphen may be used to compound two or more capitalized names:
  a New York-Chicago flight; a New York-London-Paris
  trip; U.S.-U.S.S.R. trade relations.

Parentheses
Parentheses set off parenthetic, supplementary, or explanatory
material which is not part of the main statement and the inclusion
of which is not essential to the meaning of the sentence:
  He is hoping (as we all are) that the economy will take an
  upswing.

  The chart (see Fig. 4) explains the situation.

  The personal property of both parties (there being no real
  property) can be divided satisfactorily between them.

Parentheses enclose numbers introducing individual elements of a
run-in enumeration:
  We must set forth (1) our long-term goals, (2) our immediate
  objectives, and (3) the means at our disposal.

Parentheses enclose Arabic numerals confirming written-out
numbers:
  The fee for my services is Two Thousand Dollars ($2,000.00),
  payable . . . .

  Delivery will be made in thirty (30) days.

  . . . both parties being over the age of twenty-one (21)
  years . . . .

Parentheses enclose abbreviations synonymous with and following
written-out forms:
  . . . a ruling by the Federal Communications Commission (FCC).

Period
A period terminates a sentence that is neither exclamatory nor
interrogative.
  Take dictation. She took dictation. She asked whether dictation
  was necessary.

A period terminates polite requests, especially those in business letters:
> Will you please sign the enclosed releases and return them to this office as soon as possible.

A period may punctuate an abbreviation; since styling often varies, consult the Abbreviations section of this book or a dictionary before typewriting the material:
> ABA *or* A.B.A.; LLB *or* L.L.B.; Esq.; Dal. C.P.; Wis. 2d; *A.B.A. Jour.; Sulloway* v. *Rolfe,* 47 A. 2d 109, 110, 94 N.H. 85.

A period punctuates personal-name abbreviations:
> John R. Smith   John R. W. Smith   J. Robert Smith
> J. R. W. Smith

A period punctuates monetary units and decimal amounts:
> $5,000.00; $5,000.50; 0.567; 16.6 feet.

Question Mark

A question mark terminates a direct question:
> Who witnessed the Will?
> "Who witnessed the Will?" he asked.

A question mark terminates each element of an interrogative series:
> Can you give us a reasonable forecast? back up your figures? compare them with fourth-quarter earnings?

A question mark, usually enclosed in parentheses, can be used to indicate a writer's uncertainty:
> Jonathan D. Smythe, President (?) of that organization, said . . . .

Quotation Marks, Double

Quotation marks enclose direct quotations:
> The witness said, "I saw the accident."

"I saw the accident," the witness said.

"I saw the accident," the witness said, "and I heard the impact."

Quotation marks enclose fragments of quoted matter when they are reproduced exactly as originally stated:

The agreement makes it quite clear that she "will be paid only upon our receipt of an acceptable manuscript."

Judge Brown has ruled that "the retrial of this case will occur without a jury." We are appealing this ruling at the present time.

Quotation marks are sometimes used to emphasize a particular word or to set off a highly unusual word:

We will indeed cross-examine their "expert" witness.

He was arrested for smuggling "smack."

Quotation marks enclose the titles of legal documents introduced by the word *entitled,* titles of reports, titles of catalogs, titles of short publications, titles of lectures, and chapter titles:

the document entitled "Indenture of Trust"; the report "Paralegal Education in the Seventies"; the catalog "Office Copying Equipment"; an article headlined "Malpractice Claims Mount in Plastic Surgery"; the pamphlet "Office Etiquette for the Legal Secretary"; his lecture "Legal and Ethical Aspects of Human Organ Transplantation"; the chapter entitled "Torts."

NOTE: The period and the comma fall *within* the quotation marks:

The witness said, "I heard a loud scream."

"I heard a loud scream," the witness said.

A street term for heroin is "horse."

"Horse," "smack," "speed," and "coke" are common street terms for drugs.

The semicolon falls *outside* the quotation marks:

He spoke of his "honesty"; however, he was later charged with perjury.

The dash, the question mark, and the exclamation point fall *within* the quotation marks when they refer to the quoted matter only; they fall *outside* the quotation marks when they refer to the entire sentence:

The prosecutor asked, "What did you see?"

"I just can't—" and then he stopped talking abruptly.

The police officer shouted, "Halt!"

but

What is the meaning of the term "addict"?

The chapter entitled "Malpractice Claims in the High-risk Specialties"—written by a noted attorney—is indeed informative.

I simply *cannot* understand why you insist on "fighting this thing out in the courts to the bitter end"!

NOTE: Quotation marks are *not* used with quoted matter comprising more than three typewritten or printed lines and only one paragraph. Such material is indented and blocked to set it off from the running text:

The corporate counsel advises us of the following in her letter dated August 1, 19—:

Damage claims asserted in the pending cases previously discussed are substantial. The Company has, at my suggestion, denied the charge. We are vigorously contesting the actions as well as the damage claims involved.

In view of the above comments, we now feel that . . . .

NOTE: Quotation marks *are* used with long quotations comprising more than three typewritten or printed lines and more than one paragraph. Double quotation marks are typed at the beginning of each paragraph and at the end of the last paragraph. The entire quotation is indented. Individual paragraphs are further indented. Example:

We received the following comments from our attorney on Friday, August 4, 19—:

"The cases that you inquired about in your July 16 letter seek treble but unquantified damages and allege conspiracy among practically all domestic producers to fix and stabilize prices and freight charges for this product.

"In October, 19–, an administrative law judge of the Federal Trade Commission handed down an initial decision adverse to our Corporation and four other domestic producers in an FTC administrative proceeding initiated in 19–."

This background information, as well as other data, leads us to believe that . . . .

Quotation Marks, Single
Single quotation marks enclose a quotation within another quotation:

The witness said, "I distinctly heard him say, 'Don't be late,' and then I heard the door close."

Semicolon
A semicolon links main clauses not joined by the coordinating conjunctions *and, or, but,* and *nor:*

Make no terms; insist upon full restitution.

We have a copy of the document; you may keep the original.

The jury was unable to reach a verdict; the judge declared a mistrial.

A semicolon links main clauses joined by conjunctive adverbs (as *furthermore, however, nevertheless,* and others):

We are involved in various litigation; however, we believe that our position is sound.

A semicolon separates phrases which themselves contain commas:

The assets in question include land, buildings, machinery, and office equipment; $250 million in cash and long-term investments; $340 million in accounts receivable; and $409 million in inventories.

A semicolon is sometimes used before expressions introducing expansions or illustrations:

We discussed an important matter with Judge Smith; namely, the settlement of the Stanley T. Williams estate.

Virgule

A virgule separates alternatives:

My wife and/or my attorney are authorized to sign the papers.

Our client seeks to patent the following device designed for high-speed and/or high-temperature molding operations: . . . .

A virgule may separate successive divisions of an extended time period:

the years 1978/79

A virgule can be used with figures and units of measure to indicate *per:*

traveling at a speed of 31 km/hr. . . . .

ITALICS

Italics are used in legal citations, in both their full and their shortened forms, except when the party or parties involved rather than the cases themselves are being discussed, in which instance the reference is typed in Roman:

Massachusetts v. *Jones; Jones*
Jones v. *Dawson et al; Utah* v. *XYZ Corporation*

but

the Jones trial and conviction; the Dawson litigation; the XYZ antitrust suit

NOTE: The abbreviation *v.* for *versus* is typed in Roman.

Italics are sometimes used in legal documents to set off foreign words or phrases; however, current American usage shows a trend toward typewriting such words and phrases in Roman, especially in running texts of correspondence and similar material:

legal instrument
IT IS, THEREFORE, ADJUDGED, ORDERED, and DE-CREED that the complainant, John T. Keys, Jr., be and hereby is divorced *a vinculo matrimonii* from the defendant, Alice Royce Keys.

correspondence
I am pleased to send you a certified copy of the Decree A Vinculo Matrimonii entered in your husband's divorce suit on June 3, 19–, by the Honorable William A. Lyons, Jr.

Italics are used to set off the titles of books, magazines, and newspapers:

Words and Phrases; the *A.B.A. Journal;* the [Helena, MT] *Independent-Record;* the Helena *Independent-Record; The Wall Street Journal.*

337

NOTE: The geographic location of a newspaper is italicized only if the location is part of the actual masthead title.

Italics set off words, letters, and figures when they are referred to as such:

The word *responsibility* can have several different meanings in the law.

The *a* in that signature is illegible.

The *1* in the ZIP Code is smudged.

Italics are used with New Latin names of genera, species, subspecies, and varieties (but not groups of higher rank such as phyla, classes, or orders, or derivatives of these, or vernaculars derived from any taxon) in botany and zoology:

a wild tobacco (*Nicotiana glauca*); the bacterium *Clostridium botulinum* causing botulism; the rhesus monkey (*Macaca mulatta*); the spirochete *Treponema pallidum*

but

The lion (*Felis leo*) belongs to the order Carnivora of the class Mammalia.

and

nematodes; felid; a streptococcus; an amoeba.

CAPITALIZATION

The following guidelines are intended to assist secretaries in type-writing legal material. For complete general capitalization rules, see *Webster's Secretarial Handbook* where 81 of them are discussed and illustrated. See also *A Uniform System of Citation* published by the Harvard Law Review Association for the capitalization and styling of the components of legal citations. The current edition of the U. S. Government Printing Office *Style Manual* also contains detailed guidance in capitalization.

Capitalize *act* and *code* when they are part of full titles of documents:
   Robinson-Patman Act
   The Labor Management Relations Act
   Napoleonic Code
   The United States Internal Revenue Code
   but
   a number of recently passed acts; various codes of law.

Capitalize *bill* in *Bill of Rights*; lowercase *bill* in other contexts:
   several bills before the Congress; Senate bill 416; House bill 61.

NOTE: Lowercase the term *statute*:
   statute of limitations.

Capitalize *constitution* when naming in full any constitution or when referring to the U. S. Constitution but lowercase *amendment*, *article*, and *part* in this context:
   the United States Constitution; the [U.S.] Constitution
   but
   the fifth (*or* 5th) amendment, article III; the Tobey amendment; the proposed Equal Rights amendment; part 2, part A, part II.

Capitalize *whereas* and *resolved* in minutes and in legislation; capitalize *that* or an alternative expression immediately following either

or both of the above in such contexts:
> Resolved, That . . . .
> Whereas, Substantial damages . . . .
> Whereas, The American Bar Association . . . .
> Resolved by the Judicial Council, the membership concurring, that . . . .

Capitalize *court* when naming any court in full or when referring to the Supreme Court of the United States:
> the United States Court of Appeals for the Second Circuit; the Michigan Court of Appeals; the Court of Queen's Bench
> *and*
> the Supreme Court of the United States; the United States Supreme Court [when referring to the above]
> *but*
> the federal court in Montgomery, Alabama; the state court of appeals; the state supreme court, the federal court, the county court; the court; the supreme court in Virginia.

Capitalize the full name of international courts:
> International Court of Arbitration; International Court of Justice; Court of Justice of the European Communities.

Capitalize *court* when it is personified:
> The Court has found Mr. ——— in contempt.

Capitalize *Your Honor* and *Bench* in these and similar contexts:
> Your Honor, the defense rests.
> Will the two defense attorneys please approach the Bench.

Capitalize *circuit* only when used as part of a full title:
> a Supreme Court Justice sitting alone in the capacity of Circuit Justice; the United States Court of Appeals for the Second Circuit
> *but*
> circuit courts; circuit court judges.

Capitalize *federal* and *national* only when they are part of full
proper names and full specific titles:

federal judge John M. Doe; John M. Doe, a federal judge; federal
prosecutors, federal agents, federal troops; federal courts, the federal court in Montgomery, Alabama; a federal form of government; the party's national convention, national security, national
anthem
but
the Federal Government, the Federal Reserve Board (*also*
System), the Federal Bureau of Investigation, the Federal Building (in Washington, DC); the National Security Agency, Arling-
ton National Cemetery; National Archives, National Socialist
Party.

Capitalize words designating global, national, regional, or political
divisions when they are essential elements of specific names:

Common Market, Common Market countries; the Commonwealth of Virginia; Oregon State; Bedford County; Ward 1
but
several states designated as commonwealths, the state of Virginia,
the county of Bedford, fires in two wards.

Capitalize written-out monetary units (as in contracts):

The fee for my services is Five Thousand Dollars ($5,000.00),
payable upon receipt of . . . .

Capitalize the full names of accords, pacts, plans, policies, treaties,
and similar documents:

the Geneva Accords, the Helsinki Accords; Kellogg-Briand Pact,
Warsaw Pact countries; the first Five Year Plan; New Economic
Policy; Treaty of Versailles, North Atlantic Treaty; Panama Canal Treaty
but
signed an accord; various pacts among nations; several anti-
pollution policies; oil and gas rationing plans; signed a treaty in
Paris.

The full names (and sometimes partial titles) of legal documents are often capitalized especially in correspondence; consult your employer for his or her preference:

> Enclosed is a certified copy of the Decree A Vinculo Matrimonii entered on May 2, 19–.

> We have filed a petition for a Writ of Certiorari with the Supreme Court of the United States.

> The Will was witnessed and signed.

FORMS OF ADDRESS: THE FEDERAL JUDICIARY

The following are the traditionally acceptable forms of address used in envelope address blocks and in inside addresses (left column) and in salutations (right column) in correspondence directed to members of the federal judiciary. When more than one form is shown, it is understood that the first is the more formal styling. Similar forms of address for state and local judiciaries and for attorneys follow the first section.

federal judge
The Honorable (*full name*)
Judge of the United States
District Court for the _____
District of _____

Sir: Madam:
My dear Judge (*surname*):
Dear Judge (*surname*):

**Supreme Court,
associate justice**
Mr. Justice (*surname*)
The Supreme Court
of the United States

Sir: *or* Mr. Justice:
My dear Mr. Justice:
Dear Mr. Justice:
Dear Mr. Justice (*surname*):

**Supreme Court,
chief justice**
The Chief Justice
of the United States
The Supreme Court
of the United States
or

Sir:
My dear Mr. Chief Justice:
Dear Mr. Chief Justice:

The Chief Justice
The Supreme Court

Sir:
My dear Mr. Chief Justice:
Dear Mr. Chief Justice:

**Supreme Court,
retired justice**
The Honorable (*full name*)   Sir:
(*local address*)   Dear Justice (*surname*):

STATE AND LOCAL JUDICIARIES

judge
The Honorable (*full name*)   Dear Judge (*surname*):
Judge of the _____
Court of _____

**supreme court, state
associate justice**
The Honorable (*full name*)   Sir: Madam:
Associate Justice of the   Dear Justice (*surname*):
Supreme Court of _____

**supreme court, state
chief justice**
The Honorable (*full name*)   Sir: Madam:
Chief Justice of the   Dear Mr. (*or* Madam *or* Mme.)
Supreme Court of_____   Chief Justice:

**supreme court, state
presiding justice**
The Honorable (*full name*)   Sir: Madam:
Presiding Justice   Dear Mr. (*or* Madam *or* Mme.)
_____Division   Justice:
Supreme Court of _____

ATTORNEYS

**attorney general
(of the United States)**
The Honorable (*full name*)   Sir:
The Attorney General   Dear Mr. Attorney General:

**attorney general
(state)**
The Honorable (*full name*)   Sir: Madam:
Attorney General   Dear Mr. (*or* Madam *or* Mme.)
of the State of _____   Attorney General:

**attorney, state's
or commonwealth's**
The Honorable (*full name*)   Dear Mr. /Ms./Miss/
(*full state title*)   Mrs. (*surname*):

**city attorney
(includes city counsel,
corporation counsel)**
The Honorable (*full name*)   Dear Mr./Ms./Miss/
(*full local title*)   Mrs. (*surname*):

district attorney
The Honorable (*full name*)   Dear Mr./Ms./Miss/
District Attorney   Mrs. (*surname*):

ATTORNEYS IN PRIVATE PRACTICE

(*full name*), Esq.   Dear Mr./Ms./Miss/
(*office address*)   Mrs. (*surname*):

NOTE: The honorific *Esq.* may be used after the names of male and
female attorneys; however, *Esq.* is not used if the name is preceded
by a courtesy title (as *Mr., Ms., Miss,* or *Mrs.*):

   Mr./Ms./Miss/Mrs. (*full name*)
   Attorney-at-Law

COURT OFFICER

clerk of a court
(*full name*), Esq.   Dear Mr./Ms./Miss/
Clerk of the Court   Mrs. (*surname*):
of _____

WEIGHTS AND MEASURES

Unit	Equivalents in Other Units of Same System	Metric Equivalent
length		
mile	5280 feet 320 rods 1760 yards	1.609 kilometers
rod	5.50 yards 16.5 feet	5.029 meters
yard	3 feet 36 inches	0.914 meters
foot	12 inches 0.333 yards	30.480 centimeters
inch	0.083 feet 0.027 yards	2.540 centimeters
area		
square mile	640 acres 102,400 square rods	2.590 square kilometers
acre	4840 square yards 43,560 square feet	0.405 hectares 4047 square meters
square rod	30.25 square yards 0.006 acres	25.293 square meters
square yard	1296 square inches 9 square feet	0.836 square meters
square foot	144 square inches 0.111 square yards	0.093 square meters
square inch	0.007 square feet 0.00077 square yards	6.451 square centimeters
volume		
cubic yard	27 cubic feet 46,656 cubic inches	0.765 cubic meters
cubic foot	1728 cubic inches 0.0370 cubic yards	0.028 cubic meters
cubic inch	0.00058 cubic feet 0.000021 cubic yards	16.387 cubic centimeters
weight *avoirdupois*		
ton short ton	20 short hundredweight 2000 pounds	0.907 metric tons
long ton	20 long hundredweight 2240 pounds	1.016 metric tons

346

hundredweight		
short hundredweight	100 pounds	45.359 kilograms
	0.05 short tons	
long hundredweight	112 pounds	50.802 kilograms
	0.05 long tons	
pound	16 ounces	0.453 kilograms
	7000 grains	
ounce	16 drams	28.349 grams
	437.5 grains	
dram	27.343 grains	1.771 grams
	0.0625 ounces	
grain	0.036 drams	0.0648 grams
	0.002285 ounces	

troy

pound	12 ounces	0.373 kilograms
	240 pennyweight	
	5760 grains	
ounce	20 pennyweight	31.103 grams
	480 grains	
pennyweight	24 grains	1.555 grams
	0.05 ounces	
grain	0.042 pennyweight	0.0648 grams
	0.002083 ounces	

apothecaries'

pound	12 ounces	0.373 kilograms
	5760 grains	
ounce	8 drams	31.103 grams
	480 grains	
dram	3 scruples	3.887 grams
	60 grains	
scruple	20 grains	1.295 grams
	0.333 drams	
grain	0.05 scruples	0.0648 grams
	0.002083 ounces	
	0.0166 drams	

capacity
(U.S. liquid measure)

gallon	4 quarts	3.785 liters
	(231 cubic inches)	
quart	2 pints	0.946 liters
	(57.75 cubic inches)	
pint	4 gills	0.473 liters
	(28.875 cubic inches)	
gill	4 fluidounces	118.291 milliliters
	(7.218 cubic inches)	
fluidounce	8 fluidrams	29.573 milliliters
	(1.804 cubic inches)	

fluidram	60 minims (0.225 cubic inches)	3.696 milliliters
minim	1/60 fluidram (0.003759 cubic inch)	0.061610 milliliters

(U.S. dry measure)

bushel	4 pecks (2150.42 cubic inches)	35.238 liters
peck	8 quarts (537.605 cubic inches)	8.809 liters
quart	2 pints (67.200 cubic inches)	1.101 liters
pint	1/2 quart (33.600 cubic inches)	0.550 liters

**British imperial
liquid and
dry measure**

bushel	4 pecks (2219.36 cubic inches)	0.036 cubic meters
peck	2 gallons (554.84 cubic inches)	0.009 cubic meters
gallon	4 quarts (277.420 cubic inches)	4.545 liters
quart	2 pints (69.355 cubic inches)	1.136 liters
pint	4 gills (34.678 cubic inches)	568.26 cubic centimeters
gill	5 fluidounces (8,669 cubic inches)	142.066 cubic centimeters
fluidounce	8 fluidrams (1,7339 cubic inches)	28.416 cubic centimeters
fluidram	60 minims (0.216734 cubic inches)	3.5516 cubic centimeters
minim	1/60 fluidram (0.003612 cubic inches)	0.059194 cubic centimeters

tution

1